Torn

TORN FAMILIES

*Death and Kinship at the
Battle of Gettysburg*

Michael A. Dreese

McFarland & Company, Inc., Publishers
Jefferson, North Carolina, and London

The present work is a reprint of the illustrated case bound edition of Torn Families: Death and Kinship at the Battle of Gettysburg, *first published in 2007 by McFarland.*

LIBRARY OF CONGRESS CATALOGUING-IN-PUBLICATION DATA

Dreese, Michael A., 1963–
Torn families : death and kinship at the Battle
of Gettysburg / Michael A. Dreese.
1. Gettysburg, Battle of, Gettysburg, Pa., 1863.
2. Gettysburg (Pa.)—Social conditions—19th century.
3. Death—Social aspects—Pennsylvania—Gettysburg—History—19th century.
4. Family—Pennsylvania—Gettysburg—History—19th century.
5. Kinship—Pennsylvania—Gettysburg—History—19th century.
6. Pennsylvania—History—Civil War, 1861–1865—Social aspects.
7. United States—History—Civil War, 1861–1865—Social aspects.
I. Title.
p. cm.
Includes bibliographical references and index.

ISBN 978-0-7864-6913-0
softcover : acid free paper ∞

E475.53.D765   2012   973.7'349—dc22   2006033337

BRITISH LIBRARY CATALOGUING DATA ARE AVAILABLE

On the cover: *The Battle of Gettysburg, Pa.,*
July 3, 1863 (Library of Congress)

Manufactured in the United States of America

*McFarland & Company, Inc., Publishers
Box 611, Jefferson, North Carolina 28640
www.mcfarlandpub.com*

To the brave men and women of the Armed Forces
serving our country far from home and their loved ones,
and in memory of PFC Justin W. Dreese, 82nd Airborne Division,
killed in action September 2, 2006.

Contents

Acknowledgments

Given the fact that the subjects of this book hailed from Maine to Florida, I am deeply indebted to the numerous organizations and individuals that assisted me over the long months of research and writing. Without their kindness and expertise this project would have never reached fruition.

I especially wish to acknowledge those persons who graciously provided me with copies of material from their personal collections. Without them, a rich texture would be absent from these pages. I am deeply indebted to Debby Neves, Black Mountain, North Carolina; Charlie Clark, Bruce, Mississippi; Steve Roberts, Northville, Michigan; John DeVinney, Collierville, Tennessee; Thomas Gentry, Mountain City, Tennessee; Will Conyngham and Arthur Kuschke, Dallas, Pennsylvania; Dr. John P. Hobson, Jr., Cambridge Springs, Pennsylvania; and Curvin Krout, Gettysburg, Pennsylvania.

A wide array of public and private repositories offered me invaluable assistance during my research visits, or, when travel proved prohibitive, sent copies of material to my home. Many thanks to the following: Richard Sommers, Randy Hackenburg, and Clifton Hyat, United States Army Military History Institute, Carlisle Barracks, Pennsylvania; Wayne Motts, Russell Swody, Timothy Smith, and Elwood Christ, Adams County Historical Society, Gettysburg, Pennsylvania; Kathy Harrison, Senior Historian, John Heiser, Ranger/Historian, and Dean Knudsen, Curator, Gettysburg National Military Park, Gettysburg, Pennsylvania; Dr. Lenore Barbian, Assistant Curator, Anatomical Collections, and Alan Hawk, Collections Manager, Historical Collections, National Museum of Health and Medicine, Washington, D.C.; Richard Sorensen, Smithsonian American Art Museum, Washington, D.C.; Mrs. Bonnie Weatherly, Assistant to the Archivist, Daughters of Charity Archives, St. Joseph's Provincial House, Emmitsburg, Maryland; Steve Massengill, North Carolina Department of Archives, Raleigh, North Carolina; Martha Bennett, Fort Delaware Society; Barbara J. Dix, County Historian, and Justin White, Records Clerk, Oswego County, New York; Lisa McCown, Special Collections Assistant, Leyburn Library, Washington and Lee University, Lexington, Virginia; Dr. James Cusick, University of Florida, Gainesville, Florida; Theresa Costa, Administrative Assistant, Jefferson County (Pennsylvania) Historical and Genealogical Society; Leigh McWhite and Jennifer Aronson, J. D. Williams Library, University of Mississippi, Oxford, Mississippi; Kerry Chartkoff, Historian, Michigan State Capitol, Lansing, Michigan; Dr. Robert Himmer, Associate Professor of History, Penn State York, York, Pennsylvania; Mark Schumacher, Reference Department, Jackson Library, University of North Carolina: Greensboro, Greensboro, North Carolina; Ian Graham, Special Collections & Archives Assistant, Bowdoin College Library, Brunswick, Maine; Roxanne M. Rogers, Multimedia Coordinator, and Joyce M. Geaghan, Archivist, Maine Medical Center Archives, Portland, Maine; Betsy Caldwell, Collections Assistant, Reference Services, Indiana Historical Society; Douglas Macneal, Centre County Historical Society, State College, Pennsylvania; Hazel Monahan, Curator, Hudson Museum, Hudson, Michigan; and the staffs of the Selinsgrove Community Library, Selinsgrove, Pennsylvania; the New Orleans Public Library; the Free Library of Philadelphia; the Portland Public Library, Portland, Maine; and the Sharlot Hall Museum Archives, Prescott, Arizona.

Fellow historians Jeff Kowalis, Sue Boardman, Gregory Coco, Keith Snipes, Robert Kelly, David Richards, and George Wilkinson kindly took time from their own projects to offer their expertise. Pete Wilson proofread the entire manuscript, offering valuable suggestions and pointing out some obvious errors and typos that I had somehow overlooked.

And, I hope that Heather, Brooke, and Shane will forgive me for breaking our family ties on numerous occasions so that I could resurrect the long forgotten stories of other families who witnessed one of the darkest chapters in our nation's history.

Preface

With few exceptions, Civil War soldiers displayed remarkable courage and resilience. How did these civilian volunteers perform so admirably in the face of extreme adversity? How did they push forward through a hail of bullets? What bonds cemented a collection of individuals into a cohesive fighting unit? I believe that in large part these answers can be found in the unique composition of Civil War regiments: community-based companies comprising friends, neighbors, cousins, brothers, and even fathers and their sons.

I'll never forget the powerful analogy employed by a licensed battlefield guide at the Gettysburg National Military Park to explain how these relationships influenced an individual's reaction to an intense combat situation. After having his audience conjure up a hypothetical traffic accident, he asked: If they had been safely thrown from the burning vehicle, would they save themselves or rush back into the flames and attempt to rescue their loved ones? For most of us, it is a rhetorical question.

Having researched the Battle of Gettysburg for over a decade, I became increasingly curious about the family connections of the men who fought there. What was it like to look into the eyes of your brother just before stepping off to attack an enemy position? How did it feel to cradle a dying son in your arms?

Given Gettysburg's distinction as the bloodiest battle of the war, I had little difficulty in finding examples of traumatic incidents in letters, diaries, and regimental histories. In several cases, I was able to focus on two families that opposed one another during the course of the battle, each time with tragic consequences. As a husband and father, I could not help but be deeply affected by these accounts.

However, as I began to compile the stories for the respective chapters on fathers and sons, Union brothers, and Confederate brothers, it became increasingly apparent to me that something was missing. What do we know about soldiers' connections beyond the battlefield? Did a soldier, dying alone and far from home, take comfort in a vision of his mother, father, or wife in his final moments? What about family members on the home front and in the aftermath of the battle—how did they go on?

For some, the dreaded news of a loved one's death initiated an arduous journey to the battlefield for the closure offered by a proper burial at home. Other visitors overcame the indescribable horrors of a field hospital to offer the tender care that only a mother could provide.

In addition to parental and sibling influences, the bonds of love between a soldier and his wife or sweetheart could have a tremendous impact. An encouraging word or reassurance

1

of devotion could steel his resolve, while words to the contrary could take away his will to live. Romance can be sparked under even the most adverse of circumstances, and there are examples of these uplifting scenes at Gettysburg as well.

The inclusion of these additional themes provided a layered depth to the experiences of both Union and Confederate soldiers. I round out the book with a selection of improbable sibling reunions and homecomings that would be considered far too contrived for even a Hollywood script.

I hope that by presenting these human interest stories that focus on the family relationships of those who struggled at Gettysburg in July 1863 a more personal and meaningful aspect of the battle will be revealed, one that cannot be understood through casualty figures and innocuous tactical descriptions like "the regiment sustained heavy losses when its left flank was enfiladed by an overlapping line of the enemy." Not only are these stories endlessly fascinating, but they constantly remind us of what is truly important.

Introduction

Well, whether I ever march home again
To offer my love and a stainless name,
Or whether I die at the head of my men,
I'll be true to the end all the same.
William Gordon McCabe, 1864

Following the great battle at Gettysburg, company and regimental officers on both sides faced the sad task of sending letters of condolence to the next of kin of those killed in action. The immediate superior of 39-year-old Private Wesley Raikes, a member of the 75th Ohio who fell victim to a Rebel bayonet on the evening of July 2, 1863, assured the deceased soldier's brother-in-law that "to talk of his home, his wife and children was his greatest pleasure. Not a day passed that he did not talk to me of his family."[1]

Later that month, the Reverend Franklin J. F. Schantz visited the Gettysburg area field hospitals to distribute donated goods and to provide spiritual guidance for the wounded. His circuit included a stop at his alma mater, the Lutheran Theological Seminary, which at the time housed hundreds of wounded Confederate and Union soldiers. Deeply touched by the heartrending scenes he witnessed, the Lutheran minister later wrote that he was "by the bedside of dying men who departed this life away from their homes and friends, thus no mother, no father, no sister or brother, no wife or children near to hear the last word of their beloved."[2]

Indeed, Schantz's lament told the tragic tale of many of the 7,000 men in blue and gray, such as Private Raikes, who were killed outright during the three-day battle, and of the hundreds of others who would later succumb to their wounds. But due to the unique composition of Civil War combat units, a surprising number of soldiers met their fate with a loved one at their side.

Consisting of about 100 men, a company was the fundamental building block of both Northern and Southern armies. These recruits usually resided in the same county, small town, or neighborhood within a metropolitan area. In most cases they had known one another for years. Throughout the patriotic fervor of 1861 and 1862, fathers and sons, brothers, cousins, and other relatives often enlisted together. Ten companies, often raised from the same region of a state, were then fused together to form a regiment. Thus the army became a large extended family.[3]

For instance, of the 91 men in Company F, 26th North Carolina that marched into Pennsylvania in the summer of 1863, 50 shared a surname with someone else in the regiment, and there were three sets of twins in the Caldwell County unit. Also part of this company was the Coffey clan which hailed from the hollows of the Globe, an isolated farming community situated in the picturesque Blue Ridge Mountains. At one time or another 17 members of this family served in the Confederate outfit.[4]

This phenomenon was by no means limited to regiments organized in the Appalachian region. Among the 88 men from Snyder County in Company G of the 147th Pennsylvania were nine sets of brothers, four first cousins, one father and son, and one uncle with two nephews. These men departed from the river town of Selinsgrove in the fall of 1862. Before they returned to the Susquehanna Valley at the end of the war, they had participated in 20 battles and skirmishes, traveled through 12 states, and logged over 5,000 miles.[5]

This kinship produced highly efficient military units by providing a built-in deterrent against cowardice and desertion. However, if a regiment found itself in a tight spot during a fight, the losses from a particular locality could be extremely high, and the constant worry over the welfare of a loved one could extract a severe emotional toll. While lying in a Brooklyn hospital in September 1864, Private Willard Beeman of the 83rd Pennsylvania told Walt Whitman that he had not heard from his younger brother John since the last battle. He was greatly concerned since his sibling was in the habit of writing him twice a week.

Whitman described the pair as "affectionate brothers, always together, always loving, always true." Beeman confessed to the poet-turned-nurse, "If it were to do over again, I think I should rather enlist alone—the feeling about my brother when going in a battle and anxiety about him at other times, is more than I can stand." Fortunately, this story has a happy ending. Both brothers survived the war.[6]

However, for some soldiers the fear of witnessing the death of a family member became a painful reality. During my tenure as program chairman of the Susquehanna Civil War Round Table, I had the privilege of entertaining a number of interesting and knowledgeable speakers. One evening, my son Shane and I met Don Ernsberger and his son Mike for dinner prior to their presentation for the group. Afterwards, the pair delivered a dramatic first person portrayal of a real life father and son who served together in the Union army. After witnessing the mortal wounding of his boy at Gettysburg, the father turned to the bottle to mask the pain. He was later found dead on the streets of Washington, D.C. Following the shocking conclusion of the program, I couldn't help but think that had my son and I or the Ernsbergers lived 140 years ago, perhaps we could have met a similar fate instead of enjoying a meal together.

Lydia Ziegler, a teenager residing with her family at the Lutheran Seminary at Gettysburg, recalled in her memoirs another family tragedy. About a week after the battle she remembered meeting an elderly couple who had walked nearly 30 miles from Chambersburg in search of their son Charlie. They told her that he was their last living son as four others had already perished fighting for the Union. Charlie was soon found in a dying condition in an upper floor of the Seminary. "The cries of that mother as she bent over the body of her boy were heartbreaking," recalled Lydia. "For a short time consciousness returned to Charlie, and he knew his parents, who shortly after had at least some measure of comfort in taking his dead body home for burial."[7]

This was not the only instance in which a family was shattered as a result of the battle. During the second day of fighting, Corporal William C. Shultz, a 21-year-old member of the 71st Pennsylvania, suffered wounds to both of his thighs. Nurse Anna Holstein marveled that for weeks the young man calmly bore the untold agony from his mortal injuries. She learned that her patient's oldest brother had died at Antietam the previous September, leaving William as the only surviving child of his widowed mother back in Norristown, Pennsylvania.

William Shultz lost his battle for survival at Camp Letterman Hospital on September 29, 1863. According to Nurse Holstein, he constantly expressed one anxious thought: "Mother, do not grieve; it is best, and right; bury me with my comrades on the field." His wish was granted, and he was interred in the newly established Soldiers' National Cemetery at Gettysburg.[8]

Through his famous address at the cemetery dedication that November, President Abraham Lincoln consecrated the grave of Corporal Shultz and the 3,511 other Union dead (a few of whom were actually Confederates) who would eventually be buried there. He used the solemn occasion to beseech his fellow countrymen "to be here dedicated to the great task remaining before us ... that this nation shall, under God, have a new birth of freedom, and that government of the people, by the people, for the people, shall not perish from the earth."

Faith in God and democratic ideals resonated deeply with Civil War soldiers on both sides. Supported by the twin pillars of family and community, these values bolstered the resolve of a fighting man and supplied him with the courage to face death or serious injury.

The longing for home also provided a needed distraction. According to Reid Mitchell, author of *The Vacant Chair*, "Remembering home, dreaming of it, planning for an eventual return to it allowed men to focus on something other than the army and the war and thus to a certain extent retain their prewar identities. In most cases the lure of home was sufficient to prevent the civilian from being permanently submerged in the soldier."[9]

At times, however, these ties created a confusing crosscurrent. During the grueling series of marches that characterized the Gettysburg campaign, Lt. Colonel George F. McFarland, the commander of the 151st Pennsylvania, struggled to control his emotions as he and his men entered their home state with a month remaining in their enlistment term. "My anxiety to see home and the dear ones there is growing with the flying moments," he wrote. "I resist the feeling all I can, for I know it can do no good, while it will make me more uncomfortable and more likely not to encourage the men as I should. Reason and feeling are in direct conflict."[10] As news of the Confederate invasion reached the army one of McFarland's men asked, "What is the use of coming home as long as our home is in danger?" He answered himself, "The war must be ended and then we will fly to our love[d] ones at home, never to part till parted by death."[11]

These sentiments were vividly expressed in the music and prose of the era. Just as popular as patriotic war songs were ballads such as the classic *Home Sweet Home* and the mournful *Weeping, Sad and Lonely*, better known as *When This Cruel War Is Over*. The latter tune became so destructive to morale that officers often forbade its playing. With lyric sheet sales nearing one million copies, it could easily be considered the signature song of the 1860s.[12]

On Christmas night 1862, less than two weeks following the bloody battle of Fredericksburg, Confederate soldier William Gordon McCabe penned these lines:

> There's not a comrade here to-night
> But knows that loved ones far away
> On bended knees this night will pray:
> "God bring our darling from the fight."[13]

The act of a father sending a son off to war, perhaps to shed his blood for his country, has an almost ritualistic quality about it. Colonel Isaac Avery fell with a mortal wound while leading a brigade of North Carolinians during the evening assault upon Cemetery Hill on July 2, 1863. Taking a pencil and a piece of paper from his pocket, Avery scrawled a last message to his friend, Major Samuel Tate: "Major, Tell my father I died with my face to the enemy."[14]

Matrilineal ties often struck the deepest chord, however. George Frederick Root's *Just Before the Battle, Mother* tells us that before combat a soldier is "filled with thoughts of home and God," but Mother, "I am thinking most of you."[15] It has been recorded that a wounded soldier in the 86th New York sung the plaintive lyrics of *Mother Kissed Me in My Dream* to his comrades as they rested near the Wheatfield at Gettysburg on the morning of July 3. No doubt tears were shed by more than a few of the hardened veterans as they heard the opening stanza:

> Lying on my dying bed
>   Thro' the dark and silent night,
> Praying for the coming day,
>   Came a vision to my sight.
> Near me stood the forms I loved,
>   In the sunlight's mellow gleam:
> Folding me unto her breast,
>   Mother kissed me in my dream.[16]

Indeed, the final thoughts of many dying young soldiers were of their mothers and their faith. Just before leading his troops into Pickett's Charge, a Confederate major penned in his diary: "In line of battle, expecting to move forward every minute. With our trust in God, we fear not an earthly enemy. God be with us!" Mortally wounded during the assault, the officer died later that day. The regimental chaplain recorded his last words: "Tell my mother I died a true soldier, and I hope a good Christian."[17]

For others the bonds of love felt for a wife or a sweetheart were just as strong. The greatest sentimental song of the South was *Lorena* followed closely by *One I Left There*. Northerners took solace in *The Girl I Left Behind Me*.

Certainly no one who watched Ken Burns' epic PBS series *The Civil War* will ever forget the haunting words of Major Sullivan Ballou's letter to "my very dear Sarah" back home in Smithfield, Rhode Island, one week before meeting his fate at the First Battle of Bull Run. "But, O Sarah! If the dead can come back to this earth and flit unseen around those they loved, I shall always be near you; in the gladdest days and in the darkest nights ... *always, always*, and if there be a soft breeze upon your cheek, it shall be my breath, as the cool air fans your throbbing temple, it shall be my spirit passing by. Sarah do not mourn me dead; think I am gone and wait for thee, for we shall meet again."[18]

A good number of Americans, particularly those living in border states, were forced to deal with dissension within their own families. Both President Lincoln and General George G. Meade had relatives fighting for the Confederacy. Melvin Dwinnell, a native Vermonter, moved to Rome, Georgia, in 1851 to teach school. When war broke out he cast his lot with the South, serving as a lieutenant in the 8th Georgia Infantry. Shortly after First Bull Run he wrote to his parents in New England: "If I should meet any of my relatives on the field in Lincoln's army they will be considered as my enemies and treated as such. My whole heart is with the South. Several brothers have already met in the opposing armies. The scenes are affecting but the Southerners have never to my knowledge flinched from their patriotic duty."[19] These bittersweet reunions would take place throughout the war, giving literal meaning to the phrase "The Brothers' War."

Even more bizarre were instances at Gettysburg where a native son returned to his boyhood haunts wearing the uniform of the invading army. On the other hand, a company of Yankee soldiers recruited from the town and surrounding countryside found themselves in the surreal situation of defending their nearby homes and family against the intruders. These individuals literally fought on their home soil.

In the weeks following the battle, hundreds of visitors descended upon the Adams County community, many of them seeking to locate the grave of a loved one, while the more fortunate hoped to nurse a wounded family member back to health. The Reverend William Fee and John Fee arrived at Gettysburg from Ohio to bring home the body of their brother-in-law, assistant surgeon William Moore, 61st Ohio Infantry, who had been mortally wounded by a shell during the final day of the action.

While successfully carrying out this melancholy task, Reverend Fee made an unusual observation: "We spent nearly two days in passing over the battle-ground.... I passed by many places where near relatives, fathers, mothers, brothers, sisters were disinterring their friends. So fearful was the spectacle, it was too much for tears. I never saw a tear shed by any person on that historical battle-field."[20]

In his published recollections of the war, Charles A. Fuller, a former officer in the 61st New York, described his critical wounding at Gettysburg and the loving care provided by several close relatives who traveled there to be with him. After apologizing to his readers for the personal nature of this account, he explained:

> There is this to be said of it: It shows what was going on in thousands of families the land over—North and South—and it is the kind of matter that does not get into books on war subjects. The reality of war is largely obscured by descriptions that tell of movements and maneuvers of armies, of the attack and repulse, of the victory and defeat, and then pass on to new operations. All of this leaves out of sight the fellows stretched out with holes through them, or with legs and arms off.[21]

Over the years there have been hundreds of books and articles devoted to the strategy, tactics, leaders, and controversies of the Gettysburg Campaign, and, considering the magnitude of these events, it is certain that these issues will be discussed and debated well into the future. However, the following pages will not add to this growing genre. Rather, the reader will be immersed in the human drama and emotion of the three-day conflict for I believe, like Charles Fuller, that these experiences provide us with a raw and unvarnished view of the Civil War. Indeed, no matter what their ages, background, or political affiliation, all of the roughly 160,000 soldiers who fought at Gettysburg were deeply affected by the loving ties that bound them to their family members whether they fought beside them or found themselves separated by hundreds of miles.

I approached this task with great humility. Speaking of the countless personal tragedies he witnessed at Gettysburg, a delegate of the U.S. Christian Commission cautioned, "No pen can write out those histories—no heart can enter into and be made fully to partake of those varied and unmingled sorrows, which identify so many thousand hearts, with the hills and fields, the rocky places, the swamps, the houses and barns around the lines of that terrible battle. Like the roll of the prophet, it must be written within and without, with lamentations and mourning and woe."[22]

1

Fathers and Sons

Father, I have done my duty in the camp and 'mid the strife;
Soon I'll seal my deep devotion to my country with my life.
But it soothes my dying moments when I know that you are by,
Put your loving arms around me; kiss me, father, ere I die.

T. R. Walker

Samuel and Bayard Wilkeson, USA

A sense of anxiety pervaded the headquarters of the Army of the Potomac throughout the morning of July 3, 1863. At the Widow Lydia Leister's farm, just behind Cemetery Ridge, General George G. Meade and staff listened intently to the continuous roar of musketry that echoed for hours from nearby Culp's Hill. With the approach of noon the firing finally sputtered away. The right flank of the Union line was secure. With the exception of some desultory shots between the opposing pickets, a peaceful lull settled over the battlefield.

Seeking solace from the oppressive heat, *New York Times* correspondent Samuel Wilkeson joined a group of fellow journalists and staff officers gathered on the shady side of the widow's whitewashed two-room cottage. Harnessed to a nearby fence, the horses belonging to the officers and their aides munched contentedly on bags of oats while periodically flicking their tails to ward off the menacing swarms of flies. A nesting songbird warbled away from a nearby peach tree, further enhancing the bucolic scene.

It was a welcome respite for Wilkeson. After an arduous journey via Frederick, Maryland, the 46-year-old reporter had reached the battlefield during the previous morning with his good friend Whitelaw Reed of the *Cincinnati Gazette*. The pair had enjoyed precious little food and rest for several days. Although he was a veteran 12-year correspondent who had covered the Army of the Potomac since the beginning of the war, nothing could have prepared Wilkeson for the ordeal he would soon face at Gettysburg.

In the midst of one of the war's most decisive battles, his thoughts were undoubtedly focused on the family that had blossomed from his marriage to Catherine Cady, a sister of Elizabeth Cady Stanton. Soon after reaching the field, he had received some distressing news concerning one of his sons.

The peaceful interlude abruptly ended at about 1:00 p.m. when about 150 Confederate artillery pieces roared to life on Seminary Ridge. Within seconds, shells of all types

Samuel Wilkeson, photographed by Alexander Gardner, Studio of Mathew B. Brady, in 1859 (Smithsonian American Art Museum, Museum purchase from the Charles Isaacs Collection made possible in part by the Luisita L. and Frank H. Denghamsen Endowment).

"shrieked, whirled, moaned, whistled, and wrathfully fluttered" across the valley, landing upon the center of the Union lines on Cemetery Ridge. According to Wilkeson, this "tempest of orchestral death" lasted for nearly two hours as measured by watches that "ran, O, so languidly!" Many of the projectiles intended for the blue infantrymen and artillerymen deployed near the ridge crest overshot their marks and landed in rear echelon areas along the Taneytown Road.

The area surrounding Meade's headquarters was particularly hard hit. Wilkeson recalled as many as six shells bursting overhead every second. Projectiles perforated the Widow Leister's house and barn. Unable to escape the deadly storm, the tethered horses reared and plunged in terror. By the end of the bombardment, sixteen of the poor creatures lay dead and mangled in the yard. Wilkeson never forgot the agonizing final moments of several Yankee soldiers who "were torn to pieces in the road and died with the peculiar yells that blend the extorted cry of pain with horror and despair."

Wilkeson survived the inferno and witnessed the grand charge of Pickett's, Pettigrew's, and Trimble's columns. "They rushed in perfect order across the open field up to the very muzzles of the guns, which tore lanes through them as they came," he marveled. "But they met men who were their equals in spirit, and their superiors in tenacity."

On the following evening Wilkeson filed his dispatch of the battle. With vivid prose and imagery, he brought the awful conflict into the parlors and living rooms of his readers. But this was not the finest achievement of the piece. Through his own personal tragedy,

The Lydia Leister property after the battle (Library of Congress).

the reporter conveyed the human price of war, something that numbers and casualty lists failed to do.

He opened his article with a heartrending question: "How can I write the history of a battle when my eyes are immovably fastened upon a central figure of transcendingly absorbing interest—the dead body of my oldest born son, caused by a shell in a position where the battery he commanded should never have been sent, and abandoned to die in a building where surgeons dared not to stay?"

At age 19, Lieutenant Bayard Wilkeson, Battery G, 4th United States Artillery, was among the youngest artillery commanders serving in the Army of the Potomac. On the opening day at Gettysburg, he displayed courage and leadership that belied his tender years.

Reaching the field at about 11:00 a.m., Lieutenant Wilkeson received an order to report to Brigadier General Francis Barlow, the commander of the First Division of the Eleventh Corps, which was engaged about three quarters of a mile north of the town. Barlow directed his subordinate to deploy his guns on an open knoll, later dubbed "Barlow's Knoll," near the Harrisburg Road. Eleventh Corps Artillery Chief Major Thomas W. Osborn did not approve of this placement, noting that it was too close to the enemy's infantry line and outmatched by Confederate cannon on nearby Oak Hill. Osborn asserted that no battery could possibly withstand this concentrated fire.

After dutifully unlimbering his pieces on the knoll, Wilkeson sat calmly on his horse directing the fire of his Napoleon guns in the midst of the deadly storm. Moments later, a shell tore into the lieutenant's lower right leg, nearly severing it at the knee joint. Placed upon the ground, the wounded officer fashioned a tourniquet from his sash and sword and then severed the mangled limb with his pocketknife. He retained command of his battery until he grew faint from shock and loss of blood. Four of his men carried him to the rear and placed him inside the county almshouse.

When Union forces retreated through the town to Cemetery Hill during the late afternoon of July 1, Wilkeson was left behind. Just before he died that evening the youthful lieutenant asked for a drink of water. As a canteen was being passed to him a wounded soldier lying nearby begged, "For God's sake, give me some!" Reportedly, the officer handed the canteen untouched to the man, who drank every drop. Wilkeson smiled, turned over slightly, and passed away.

Upon reaching Meade's headquarters the next day Samuel Wilkeson learned that his son had suffered a severe wound and had fallen into the hands of the enemy. Any lingering hopes of his survival were dashed on July 4 when the Confederates withdrew from the town and the body of Lieutenant Bayard Wilkeson was recovered. Like his son had done three days earlier, Samuel performed his duty under the most adverse of circumstances. In the conclusion of the news article, the reporter memorialized his son and the hundreds of others who had been slain at Gettysburg with a powerful allegorical image:

> Oh, you dead, who at Gettysburg have baptized with your blood the second birth of freedom in America, how you are to be envied! I rise from a grave whose wet clay I have passionately kissed, and I look up to see Christ spanning this battlefield with His feet and reaching fraternally and lovingly up to heaven. His right hand opens the gates of paradise; with his left he beckons to these mutilated, bloody, swollen forms to ascend.

Wilkeson accompanied his son's remains back home to Buffalo, New York, where they were laid to rest in the Forest Lawn Cemetery. Bayard's posthumous promotion to lieutenant colonel did little to comfort the grieving family. The distraught father grew increasingly bitter over the circumstances surrounding his beloved child's death. Shortly after the battle, he sent a recriminating letter to Major General Oliver O. Howard, the commander of the Eleventh Corps, in which he alleged that the general had displayed no interest in his boy and failed to care for him in his time of need.

Initially, the accusations angered Howard. As the commander of 9,000 men he was responsible only for the general disposition of the troops. He could not possibly look out for the welfare of every man. Upon deeper reflection, however, the general realized that "these words were but the expression of a sore heart, a father's wounded spirit."

Well-known throughout the army as a refined gentleman and a devout Christian, Howard responded according to the teachings of his faith. "Immediately I wrote as kind and Christian an epistle as I could, explaining the circumstances and sympathizing with the suffering," he wrote. "It was not long before my patience was rewarded, for I received from the stricken father a reply worthy of a great heart. It called upon me for forgiveness."

Howard never forgot the experience and years later he used it to illustrate the war's lasting significance:

> I have thought that the death of Wilkeson in the very bloom and freshness of his youth, with its echoing sorrow, had its counterpart in many thousands of precious, loving households in the land. If, then, liberty and Union have been purchased at the cost of blooming youth, and bleeding, broken hearts behind them, the sacrifice is very sacred.... Let not our children or children's children forget it.

One can only imagine Samuel Wilkeson's mortification when his 16-year-old son ran away from home to join the army in the spring of 1864. Enlisting in the 11th New York Artillery, Frank Wilkeson participated in some of the bloodiest campaigns of the war. By the end of his service, he received a commission as second lieutenant and an honorary brevet to captain.

After the war Samuel Wilkeson continued to work as a journalist, but his restless spirit eventually led him westward. In 1869, he helped survey the Pacific Northwest for the Northern Pacific Railroad. He and his son Frank were among the first white men to explore the Cascade Mountains. Samuel's resulting report, "Notes on Puget Sound," became one of the most famous pieces of Western promotional literature. But perhaps his greatest literary effort was penned as he knelt by his son's fresh grave at Gettysburg, where, in the depths of sorrow, he struggled to display the power of faith and shared his pain with a broken nation.

Isaac and William J. Fisher, USA

Among the "many thousands of precious, loving households" touched by sorrow after the Battle of Gettysburg was the family of Isaac and Sarah Fisher. In many respects their story mirrored that of the Wilkesons. Prior to the war, the Fishers raised their nine children on a 100-acre farm near Seaford, Delaware, known as the Fisher Fancy Farm or the Nanticoke Farm. The Lord Baron of Baltimore had granted the property to Isaac's grandfather in 1732.

When the Fishers' oldest son, 18-year-old William James Fisher, went off to war in the summer of 1861, he brought along a black servant named George. This was not an unusual event since nearly 2,000 slaves resided in the small border state of Delaware in 1860. Reflecting the complex political climate of the times, the Fisher family remained loyal to the Union despite their ties to the institution of slavery. Isaac Fisher exerted his influence to help his son obtain a commission as a second lieutenant in the United States Regular Infantry.

Participating in nearly all of the early campaigns in the Eastern Theater, Lieutenant Fisher had ample opportunity to test his leadership ability. The well-bred youngster soon earned the respect and admiration of the professional soldiers who served with him. Lieutenant George Lauman declared simply, "I do not think there is a braver or more honest officer in the U.S.A." A veteran of the prewar army, Lieutenant George Hamilton, stated, "a more brave young man I do not know and as to being honest and upright his superior does not live, and he had the respect of all that knew him from the highest to the lowest in the army."

The enlisted personnel who served under Fisher in Company G of the 10th U.S. agreed. First Sergeant Terance McCabe described him as "an officer who was regarded with the utmost esteem, affection, and respect by his inferiors as well as by his superiors for his fine soldierly qualities, his gentlemanly deportment and his extreme kindness and unassuming manners towards those under him.... He behaved with a coolness, intrepidity—and personal bravery almost unequaled during my long time of service. While in the Army, he was always of a sedate, contemplative character and never did I hear a profane word come from his lips."

William Fisher, ca. 1861 (Gettysburg National Military Park).

Private John A. Buchan, who first served under Fisher's command at the bloody Battle of Fredericksburg on December 13, 1862, noted that the lieutenant was "as cool in the battle as he was out of it and as brave a man as there is in the regiment. There was not one man in the regiment but what thought a great deal of him and when on duty with him he wasn't cross like some of them, he was kind and genteel to all of us."

Considering this universal praise, it is unlikely anyone grumbled upon Fisher's promotion to first lieutenant during the campaign that culminated in the Battle of Gettysburg. The grueling marches from Falmouth, Virginia, to Pennsylvania tested the endurance of even the most hardened veterans. Several days before the battle, Fisher complained to Lieutenant Hamilton that he felt ill and that his foot had become very sore. Hamilton advised him to report to the ambulance, but the young officer refused, stating he feared a battle was imminent and that he would rather suffer than not be with his company.

As part of Major General George Sykes's Fifth Corps, the U.S. Regulars arrived at Gettysburg early on the morning of July 2 after a fatiguing night march. Consisting of about 2,500 soldiers, the Regulars were organized into two brigades of five regiments each. The 10th U.S. was part of Colonel Sidney Burbank's Second Brigade. While most volunteer regiments carried a full complement of ten companies, only three companies of the 10th were present at Gettysburg, the remainder being on detached assignments. With a mere 93 officers and men, it was among the smallest Union regiments on the field.

After all of its divisions had arrived on the scene, the Fifth Corps was posted in a reserve position along the Baltimore Pike behind the center of the Union line. Late in the day, as furious Confederate assaults threatened to break through the left of the Federal line, Sykes's men were rushed in as reinforcements.

The Regulars were initially deployed along the northern shoulder of Little Round Top facing west towards the deep ravine cut by the sluggish waters of Plum Run. On the opposite side of the valley, nearly surrounded by woods, stood farmer George Rose's 20-acre wheat field. As the men prepared for action, Fisher and Lieutenant Robert G. Welles talked and joked with one another as they contemplated when they would enter the fight.

They did not have long to ponder the question. Orders soon arrived for the two brigades to advance into the Wheatfield in support of Brigadier General John C. Caldwell's Second Corps division. For the past hour, Northern and Southern troops had charged and countercharged across the ripening grain field, littering the ground with the dead and the dying.

With Burbank's brigade in the lead, the Regulars scrambled down the rocky slope at the double-quick. At the base of the hill the troops struggled through the swampy mire bordering the run before panting up a wooded knoll that bordered the eastern edge of the Wheatfield. As Burbank's troops crossed over a stone fence and entered the edge of the field, Caldwell's men began falling back on their right. The two brigades were soon caught in a deadly vise as swarming Confederates fired upon them from the front and both flanks.

Positioned at the center of the brigade line, the diminutive 10th U.S. began to incur heavy losses. Less than ten minutes after the start of the engagement, a bullet slammed into the chest of Lieutenant Fisher. Standing within two feet of him at the time, Lieutenant Hamilton remembered Fisher raising his left arm to drape around his neck as he secured his sagging body by the waist. Lieutenant Welles, Sergeant McCabe, and a private from Company H responded to Hamilton's call for assistance.

As the men gathered around him, Fisher looked at one and then another in a manner "more appealing than any words he could have uttered." Sergeant McCabe later wrote that "he rolled his eyes full of gratitude towards us but already he was speechless.... It moves me to tears now to recall this gloomy scene to my memory."

Near the same time that the small detail began to carry their wounded comrade to safety, the Regulars were ordered to conduct a fighting withdrawal back to their starting point. One observer marveled as they "marched off the field in admirable style, with well-aligned ranks, facing about at times to deliver their fire and check pursuit." Captain Richard Robbins, 11th U.S., never forgot the fearful price of this discipline and steadiness under fire. "The few hundred yards to the foot of Little Round Top, already strewn with our disabled comrades, became a very charnel house, and every step was marked by ghastly lines of dead and wounded," he wrote.

Less than 200 yards from the spot of Fisher's wounding, Sergeant McCabe was hit in the back by a bullet. Somehow, he avoided capture and survived the injury. Reduced to three men, the party approached the boggy meadow near Plum Run. At this time Lieutenant Welles felt his friend's body turning rigid and recalled that he "died like one going to sleep." In those final moments, a smile appeared upon his face. According to all of the eyewitnesses, the young officer did not say anything in the short interval, perhaps five minutes, between his wounding and his death.

Near the run a projectile clipped Welles in the leg and sent him sprawling into the muck. After going a short distance farther, Lieutenant Hamilton glanced back and spotted enemy soldiers rapidly closing in on himself and the private from H Company. They had no other recourse but to lay Fisher down and make good on their escapes. They placed the body in a conspicuous location by a lone tree and two large rocks in hopes of recovering it at a later time.

Near twilight a Union counterattack drove back the Southerners and secured the area. It had been a costly day for the Regulars. Nearly half of the men in Burbank's brigade were killed, wounded, or missing, with the 10th U.S. losing 51 of its members.

The next morning a burial detail retrieved Fisher's body and moved it to a site along a crop fence about 125 yards northwest of the Jacob Weikert farmhouse. Private John Buchan, a member of the detail, related that the corpse was wrapped in a clean blanket and then carefully laid in the grave they had prepared. The entire group agreed that their comrade looked very natural and was "the prettiest corpse they ever saw."

Buchan became concerned that the rain might wash off the identifying information written upon a slip of paper attached to the temporary headboard. Determined to create a more indelible marker, he walked to a nearby wagon where he found a portion of an empty cigar box. With his pocketknife the private painstakingly carved in the dead officer's name and unit, later tracing over it in ink, because he "thought as much of him as if he had been my own brother." Fisher's comrades also secured his personal effects as mementos for the family.

In the days following the battle the Fishers learned that their son was among those killed at Gettysburg, but this information could not be officially verified. Any lingering hopes were dashed on July 13 when Isaac Fisher spoke with a wounded officer from the 10th U.S. who was recuperating at his home in Wilmington. The officer confirmed that William had been killed on July 2 and that he had personally observed his corpse. Later that evening a grief-stricken Isaac retired to a room in the city and wrote his wife Sarah:

Our worst fears are realized and I know that William is no more.... My heart sinks, as I contemplate this sad information, we have made the most costly sacrifice on the altar of our country, and if it is not sufficient we must perish. How my heart bleeds as I call up past reminiscences of our poor boy. I well remember the first sound I ever heard issue from his mouth, poor innocent little babe. If I have ever done wrong by him in anything I trust I may be forgiven. I leave at 5 o'clock in the morning for Baltimore and thence by the nearest route to the battlefield from whence I will write again if I can.

After arriving in Baltimore the next day, Mr. Fisher spoke to a surgeon at a government hospital who presented him with a note to deliver to a fellow doctor serving with the Fifth Corps, asking for his assistance in the recovery of William's body. At 10 o'clock that night the determined father arrived in Gettysburg by train. Due to overcrowded conditions he spent the last 18 miles of the journey on top of one of the cars during a rainstorm.

Obtaining directions from a wounded U.S. Regulars officer lying in an area field hospital, Isaac located his son's grave the following day. The body was exhumed and then embalmed. After securing a coffin, the elder Fisher accompanied the remains back home to Delaware on July 17. Because of the great care shown by William's comrades, the Fisher family obtained a degree of comfort and closure. Hundreds of other families, particularly those from the South, would never know this peace.

Like his compatriot, Bayard Wilkeson, Lieutenant William Fisher received a posthumous promotion for "gallant and meritorious service at the Battle of Gettysburg." Both men had been ordered into combat zones that proved to be untenable and neither lived to see his twentieth birthday.

James and Albion Mills, USA

While breaking the news to his wife of their son's death at Gettysburg, Isaac Fisher borrowed a phrase used by countless Americans during the course of the war: "We have made the most costly sacrifice that we could possibly offer on the altar of our country...." A year later, in his famous letter to Mrs. Bixby, President Lincoln drew upon the same imagery: "...and the solemn pride that must be yours, to have laid so costly a sacrifice upon the altar of Freedom." Similarly, while mourning the loss of his own son, reporter Samuel Wilkeson poured out, "Oh, you dead, who at Gettysburg have baptized with your blood the second birth of freedom in America, how you are to be envied!"

These statements, which on the surface appear to elicit martyrdom, are more than a little disturbing to the modern ear. However, during the Civil War, soldiers and civilians, North and South, fervently believed that they were fighting for a righteous cause and that victory or defeat had been preordained. To believe that the bloody trial could have somehow been averted would have been an admission that thousands of men had died in vain. Awash in death and suffering, the nation soaked its pain in a salve of fatalism.

The string of personal calamities that befell the Reverend James Evelyn Mills during the war calls to mind the epic sufferings of Job in the Old Testament. His wife Dorcas died in 1856 just five weeks after giving birth to the couple's daughter, Emma. Afterwards, the Baptist minister moved his five children from Madison, New Hampshire to Vassalboro, Maine. Soon after the relocation, he remarried and was blessed with a baby boy named Eddie. Three of the reverend's five sons were in their teens when war broke out and all three eventually fought for the Union.

Allen Winslow Mills was the first to depart. Joining the 3rd Maine Infantry in 1861 while only 16 years of age, he fought in the war's first major clash at Bull Run on July 21. The oldest son, 18-year-old Horace, left the family farm in late September to sign up with the 11th Maine. Following in the footsteps of his older siblings, Albion ran off in August 1862 and enlisted with Company E of the 16th Maine. As Allen had done a year earlier, he lied about his age to the mustering officer. According to the Mills family Bible, Albion's birth date of December 4, 1846, made him only 15 at the time of his enlistment.

Soon afterwards, with three of their boys in the army, the Reverend and Mrs. Mills suffered the trauma of losing two young children. On August 26 their infant son, Eddie, died, and then a month later, six-year-old Emma fell victim to diphtheria. On the heels of these painful losses, Reverend Mills learned that Allen had been hospitalized with a severe illness following the Seven Days' Battles near Richmond. The ailing soldier was sent to Hammond Military Hospital at Point Lookout, Maryland, where his father reached him on December 12. James obtained his son's discharge and arrived back home with him near Christmas.

The New Year ushered in more despair for the Mills family. On January 9, 1863, Allen Winslow Mills passed away and was laid to rest near his young siblings in the Union Cemetery in East Vassalboro. That summer, following the great battle in Pennsylvania, more melancholy news reached the New England family.

On the opening day of the battle, the 16th Maine, with less than 300 men, was sent to an advanced position on Oak Ridge, their forlorn mission being to hold back a mass of Confederate forces to facilitate the escape of other Union troops. The greater portion of the small band was sacrificed during this Herculean task. By nightfall, only 43 officers and men answered to roll call.

Private Albion Mills suffered a gunshot wound to his right leg, necessitating its amputation above the knee. Generally, the closer a limb was removed in relation to the body trunk, the lesser the odds were of survival. In the weeks following the battle hundreds of patients were transported by rail to permanent hospitals located in the larger cities. The more severe cases were collected at Camp Letterman, a tent hospital established just east of the town.

Nurse Anna Morris Holstein recorded her most memorable experiences at this site in her published memoirs. She devoted considerable space to the youthful private from Maine who died there on October 7.

> In the "Union tent," as it was called, standing alone in a rebel row, I found a boy of seventeen, wounded and "sick unto death," whose wan, emaciated face, and cheerful endurance of suffering, at once enlisted my sympathy. He was the son of a clergyman in Maine; and in answer to inquiries about his wound, told me ... that the stump was doing badly; he had enlisted simply because it was his *duty* to do so; now he had no regret or fear, let the result be as it might. I wrote immediately to his home, to tell them he was sinking rapidly; my next briefly stated how very near his end was; there was but a few days more of gentle endurance, and the presentiment of the child we had so tenderly cared for proved true—when, with murmured words of "home and heaven," his young life ebbed away—another added to the many thousands given for the life of the nation.

A week later, Reverend Mills reached the battlefield, where he met the nurse who had so tenderly cared for his son. The New Englander's strength as well as his humility struck Mrs. Holstein. Referring to the two sons he had now lost as a result of the war, she wrote, "They were his treasures, but he gave them freely for his country." Apparently, the lack of financial resources prevented the shipment of Albion's remains back home.

Camp Letterman around August 1863 (Gettysburg National Military Park).

By this time a national cemetery was being established on Cemetery Hill adjacent to the Citizens' Evergreen Cemetery. During the middle of October, with the arrival of cooler weather, a notice appeared in local newspapers stating that the scattered bodies of the Union dead would systematically be removed to this central location. The friends and relatives of deceased soldiers who wished to take the remains home for burial were urged to give proper notice. Albion Mills now rests under plot G-1 in the Maine section of the Soldiers' National Cemetery.

Despite the deaths of his two younger brothers, Corporal Horace Mills reenlisted after the expiration of his original term. He survived a wound in July 1864 and endured a short stint as a prisoner near the end of the war before returning home safely. Deborah Dyer Neves related that her father, William Mills Dyer, Sr., remembered that his grandfather customarily led the Fourth of July parade in North Berwick, Maine, in his old uniform, but that, right up

Horace Mills, ca. 1862 (Debby Neves).

until his death in 1923, he would never talk about the war. For the Mills family, those turbulent years were a source of an immense pride but also ones of great pain.

Because of the considerable distance, it is possible that Reverend Mills never returned to Gettysburg to visit his son's final resting place before his death in 1887 at age 72. In the family Bible he recorded Albion's dying message: "Tell them I have given my life for my country and do not regret the sacrifice if it can help forward the cause." During his final days perhaps the young man often thought of Christ's declaration in Matthew 15:13: "Greater love has no one than this, than to lay down one's life for his friends."

James Bullock Woodard and Sons, CSA

The blighting hand of war made no distinction between politics and geography. Far away from the rugged coasts of Maine, the Woodard family of eastern North Carolina was nearly decimated by the conflict. When the Tar Heel State seceded from the Union in May of 1861, 69-year-old James Bullock Woodard owned seventeen slaves and more than 700 acres of land in Wilson County. Straddling the coastal plain and the piedmont, the gently rolling topography of the region was ideal for growing tobacco and cotton. Bullock had five children, including three sons, through his first wife. He had remarried following her death. A veteran of the War of 1812 and a deacon in the White Oak Primitive Baptist Church, the advanced stages of cancer had sapped his vitality by the summer of 1863.

Determined to defend their native land, all three of Woodard's sons, ranging in age from 26 to 35, left the plantation to fight for the Confederacy. His second son, John Bunyan Woodard, nicknamed "Bun," enlisted in the "Wilson Light Infantry," which became Company F of the 4th North Carolina, on June 28, 1861. Eleven months later, Gray Woodard and his younger brother, George W., who stood just under five feet, four inches, enlisted together as privates in Company A of the 55th North Carolina. On May 3, 1863, Bun Woodard was wounded in the left hip at Chancellorsville and would not return to active duty until the following spring.

The next month brought more severe hardships to the family. On June 3, James Woodard wrote to sons Gray and George: "I am not well but keep up and about. Your mother continues down yet and gets no better.... It seems that she can't stand her afflictions much longer, but how long I don't know." Six days later, Sarah King Woodard, the boys' stepmother, passed away. "A cultivated and estimable woman," her death would come as a hard blow to the entire family.

A week later, the gray legions of Major General A. P. Hill's newly formed Third Corps hustled out of Fredericksburg, Virginia, for the Shenandoah Valley to join in the invasion of southern Pennsylvania. The 55th North Carolina, a relatively inexperienced unit, had never before fought with the Army of Northern Virginia.

Ironically, as the advance elements of the two armies clashed west of Gettysburg early on the morning of July 1, the 55th fired one of the initial Southern volleys. During the confused fighting near the unfinished railroad, Private Gray Woodard fell dead. In a cruel twist of fate, his father died the next day far away in Wilson County. George Woodard survived the battle but chronic diarrhea claimed his life on March 23, 1864, at a Gordonsville, Virginia, hospital.

Following the death of her twin brother, George, Mary Jane Woodard lost her husband of six years when he was decapitated by a cannon ball during the defense of Petersburg on June 15. After losing his stepmother, his father, and two brothers within a year, the news of his brother-in-law's death nearly devastated John "Bun" Woodard. In a letter to Mary, he poured out his emotions: "Oh, sister, I can't tell, neither can I write, my awful and miserable feelings. I can ... see poor Henry's very features and form.... Oh, can it be possible that poor Henry is no more! ... I hope the good Lord will provide for you and protect you and your little ones and enable us all to meet again and pass off the balance of our days in peace and tranquillity."

Then, on September 19, 1864, Bun was captured at Cedar Creek, Virginia, and imprisoned at Point Lookout, Maryland, until near the end of the war. Following his release, he returned home to farm, but the debilitating effects of his military service contributed to his death on October 27, 1866, at age 34, completing the circle of tragedy and loss for one Southern family.

Dr. George Kirkman and Sons, CSA

In one sense, James Woodard was quite fortunate. His death prevented him from ever knowing the fate of his three sons. Many others, including Dr. George Kirkman of St. Lawrence, Chatham County, North Carolina, could not escape the grief and heartache that the war spread indiscriminately throughout the land. During the war's opening months, the prominent physician and father of fourteen watched three of his boys depart home to serve with other Chatham men in the 26th North Carolina, a unit destined for unparalleled glory and sacrifice at Gettysburg. Henry, Wiley, and schoolteacher William Kirkman, ages 18, 20, and 23, respectively, entered the Confederate service on June 10, 1861, and were assigned to Company G.

The 26th fought its maiden battle at New Bern, North Carolina, on March 14, 1862, against a Federal amphibious force under the command of General Ambrose E. Burnside. The regiment fought well in this Southern defeat and suffered relatively minor losses. Private Wiley Kirkman was captured during the engagement but returned to his unit five months later following an exchange of prisoners. Not long afterwards, the trio was joined by younger brother George, who had just been drafted.

Following a tour of duty in southeastern Virginia and eastern North Carolina, the 26th joined the Army of Northern Virginia just before the invasion of Pennsylvania. The Tar Heels marched out of Fredericksburg on the afternoon of June 15, 1863, to the strains of their very own Moravian brass band. Their "splendid grey uniforms" provided a stark contrast to many of Lee's tattered veterans, many of whom had no shoes. However, any doubts about the dapper regiment's fighting ability were forever dispelled on the bloody fields west of Gettysburg on the opening day of the battle.

During the late afternoon of July 1, Brigadier General James J. Pettigrew's brigade, the 11th, 26th, 47th, and 52nd North Carolina, assailed the Union stronghold on McPherson's Ridge. Over 800 strong, the 26th, led by their youthful colonel, Henry King Burgwyn, Jr., stepped off from Herr Ridge with parade ground precision. A mile away, the waiting Union troops could not help but admire the steadiness and discipline of their foe. Company G and the Kirkman brothers marched near the colors at the center of the regiment.

The 26th's perfect alignment began to slowly unravel from the effects of incoming artillery fire. After struggling through the thick underbrush skirting the banks of Willoughby Run, the regiment clambered up the hillside and entered Herbst's Woods. The bullets flew "as thick as hail stones in a storm" as the North Carolinians ran head-long into the 24th Michigan and other elements of the hard-fighting "Iron Brigade." After a fierce struggle, the Tar Heels pushed the tough Midwesterners out of the woods.

By this time a heavy sulfurous smoke obscured the afternoon sun. Suddenly, a new Federal line emerged ghost-like from the fog of battle in the southeastern corner of the wood lot. It was the 467 officers and men of the 151st Pennsylvania, the "Schoolteachers' Regiment." The opposing forces closed to within twenty paces and exchanged a series of devastating volleys. After both sides incurred heavy losses, the Keystoners gradually gave way. McPherson's Ridge finally belonged to the Southerners.

The staggering casualties incurred by the units involved reveals the severity of the fighting in this locale. The 24th Michigan's loss of 363 men and the 151st Pennsylvania's tally of 337 ranked as the two highest total casualty figures (killed, wounded, and miss-ing) within the Union army during the entire battle.

The 26th North Carolina lost nearly 600 men during this action, including fourteen soldiers with the regimental flag. Losses were particularly high in the companies nearest to the colors. Private George Kirkman was killed in action, while Sergeant William Kirk-man was mortally wounded and died on July 2 or 3. The possibility exists that a fellow teacher from Pennsylvania shot him down.

On July 3 the battered 26th once again found itself in the heat of the action during "Pickett's Charge." With slightly over 200 remaining soldiers, the regiment crossed nearly a mile of open ground to strike the Union line north of the Angle. The lethal combina-tion of canister fire and musketry volleys decimated the ranks. After losing over 100 more men, the survivors staggered back to Seminary Ridge. No other unit at Gettysburg on either side suffered a higher total loss than did the 26th North Carolina.

Private Henry Kirkman was severely wounded in the foot and was among those rounded up by the victorious Yankees. However, his prospects for recovery seemed very favorable. A month later, he wrote his father back in North Carolina: "I write you a few lines to let you know how I am and where I am. I am in the General Hospital [Camp Letterman] at Gettysburg, Pa., wounded very bad in the left foot by a minie ball. My wound is improving slowly. I am in very good health...."

Henry mistakenly reported that both George and William had survived their wounds. "I suppose you have heard from them before," he casually noted. Of course, his father had not. In early December a letter arrived for Dr. Kirkman from W. Burton Owen, the chap-lain of the 17th Mississippi. The envelope had been mailed from Richmond with postage due of ten cents. It read:

> Dear Sir, Your son H.C. Kirkman Co. "G" 26th NC Regt. was wounded in the foot at Gettysburg. He was attacked with pneumonia and died with a good home in heaven, Sept. 1st, 5 o'clock p.m. at the General Hospital, Gettysburg. All the soldiers' graves are plainly marked, may the Lord give you and all his relatives sustaining and sanctifying grace under so sad a bereavement. Let me know from you that I may know you have seen this."

Meanwhile, Private Wiley Kirkman was captured during the Confederate retreat from Gettysburg. By this point the prisoner exchange system that had been formally established a year earlier had ground to a halt due to conflicts on a number of legal and political issues. With the resultant overcrowding at prison facilities, thousands of captives from both sides died from disease as a result of poor nutrition, exposure, and the lack of proper sanitation measures. Sadly, with better medical care and resources readily available in the North, the deaths of many Confederate captives could have been prevented.

Following the Gettysburg Campaign, Federal authorities created a new prison depot at Point Lookout, Maryland, about eighty miles south of Washington, D.C., to help accommodate the large influx of Confederate POWs. Formed at the confluence of the Potomac River and the Chesapeake Bay, the thin, low-lying peninsula was plagued by swarms of insects, floods, extreme heat, and biting winds and storms in the winter. As the prison population swelled to over 20,000 at various times, double the intended capacity, diarrhea, malaria, typhoid, and scurvy ravaged the inmates. The latter ailment was related to the lack of fresh fruit and vegetables in the diet.

In less than two years of operation, between 3,500 and 4,000 Confederates perished at Point Lookout. Tragically, many of these deaths occurred near the end of the war when the mortality rate climbed to 60 to 65 per day. Among these victims was Wiley Kirkman, who died of scurvy on March 10, 1865. The cause of his death must have enraged his physician father.

Directly or indirectly, the Battle of Gettysburg had cost Dr. Kirkman four of his sons. With no victory to celebrate and their way of life quickly evaporating, the postwar years ushered in difficult times for many Southerners, who must have wondered for what purpose their loved ones had been taken from them. During the fiftieth anniversary of Gettysburg, the following editorial appeared in a Charleston, South Carolina, newspaper:

> It is not the battle itself which is being celebrated, but the heroism of the men who took part in it. The battle itself was an abominable thing ... in all its crimson horror ... not a thing to celebrate.... At Gettysburg thousands died in utmost agony ... good and gentle women were widowed and the happiness of homes was destroyed.... We are not celebrating the battle ... but the valor of the men who faced without flinching a thing that was infernal.

William P. Yearger and Father, CSA

Not every mortally wounded soldier faced death with quiet resignation. Indeed, the last thoughts of many of these individuals did not center upon a country, a cause or a flag. Rather, they struggled to comprehend the irreversible finality facing them: the unfulfilled dreams of their shattered futures, and the sobering realization that they would never again experience the tender touch of a wife or sweetheart, nor watch a precious child take his or her first awkward steps, nor enjoy a holiday meal with parents and siblings. Suddenly, the war seemed inconsequential, even trivial.

Private William P. Yearger, a youthful soldier in the 22nd Georgia of Brigadier General Ambrose R. Wright's Brigade, certainly fits in this group. Late in the day on July 2, Wright's forces attacked Cemetery Ridge. Although initially successful, the Georgians were repulsed with heavy losses. Crippled with a leg wound, Private Yearger was left behind and eventually carried to the Union Second Corps hospital located on the Jacob Schwartz farm. John Y. Foster, a civilian nurse from Philadelphia who volunteered at this site from July 10 to July 14, took considerable interest in the young soldier. He later wrote of his special patient:

> A soldier from Georgia was brought to our hospital greatly prostrated from the loss of his left leg. We at once saw that his case was hopeless, and bestowed upon him the closest care

possible under the circumstances. From the first his mind seemed full of images of home, and he talked of little else besides his relatives. "I have an old father at home," he would say, "and brothers and sisters; oh, if I could only go to them and sit in their midst once more!" Then his thoughts would seem to go back to the beginning of the war, and he would bemoan his folly in having entered the army, declaring, with despairing voice, that his heart had never been in the contest—that he would give years of his life if he could only go back again and be as he was before he took up arms.

Upon being informed that he had but a short time to live, Yearger sobbed, "I am not prepared to go." After regaining his composure, he dictated a final letter to his loved ones. As Foster copied down the words "all the love in his heart poured forth." He described his wounding and suffering along with the tender care he received from strangers. He implored his father to never permit his younger brothers to join the army and thereby avoid his cruel fate. Punctuated by frequent sobs, he struggled to convey his final message: "Father, brothers, sisters, I hope to meet you in heaven."

The following day Foster recorded the final moments of his dear friend:

> Half erect, leaning on my arms, he stretched out his own, spreading his palms heavenward, lifted his eyes with an inexpressible longing upward, as if he would appease, in one last absolute surrender, divine justice; and so, without a word, he died, his head falling on his breast, his hands dropping limp and prone, life going out as softly as a summer dream flits its wings over the sleep of a babe.... I clipped a lock of hair, as he had requested, from his pallid temples, wrote upon it the day and hour of his decease, and sent it with his small effects, by an officer of his regiment, to the friends he was never again to see.

Another source states that William Yearger died at the U.S. General Hospital at Chester, Pennsylvania, on August 11, 1863, and that his remains were later removed to the Philadelphia National Cemetery in 1891. In either case, the Georgia private died far from home and the ones he loved so dearly.

Richard Price, Sr., and Richard Price, Jr., USA

During the early morning of July 2, 1886, the father of a New Jersey veteran accompanied a group of his son's former comrades and their wives to the Soldiers' National Cemetery. As the group stood near the grave of Private Richard S. Price, the veterans recalled his "pleasant ways, genial, kindly disposition, and brave deeds." After quietly listening to the respectful tributes, Richard Price, Sr., cried aloud, "My boy, my boy, O God, why did you take my boy? He was all I had."

Twenty-three years earlier, Captain Adoniram Judson Clark's 1st New Jersey Artillery, Battery B, was part of the growing array of cannon lined up along the Wheatfield Road to support the center of the Federal Third Corps infantry line near the Peach Orchard. Major General Daniel E. Sickles admonished Captain Clark to "Hold this position while you have a shot in your limbers or a man to work your guns." This order would be an extremely hazardous one to carry out.

When Southern infantrymen pressed towards the line of Union artillery, the gun crews switched to rounds of canister, tightly packed charges of iron balls designed to wreak havoc upon troop formations at close range. Drenched with sweat and coated with the dirty grime of powder smoke, the artillerists worked at a furious pace throughout the sweltering afternoon. According to official returns, Clark's six 10-pound Parrott guns fired over 1,300 rounds of ammunition on July 2.

However, when Brigadier General William Barksdale's Mississippians smashed through the Federal line at the Peach Orchard, the Jersey gunners and adjacent units had no option but to limber up their pieces and dash back for the main line on Cemetery Ridge. As the various sections of Battery B started off, a single Confederate gun rolled into position near the Emmitsburg Road and hurled a round at their fleeing counterparts. The deadly blast killed ten horses and wounded four men, including Private

Richard Price's grave in the Soldiers' National Cemetery, Gettysburg, Pennsylvania.

Richard Price, who had joined the battery two years earlier at age 25.

Two comrades stopped to assist Price, but both were taken prisoner. One of the men, Henry C. Buffum, died at Andersonville a year later. The Confederates no doubt thought that Price would not live long as he had been struck in both legs and in one arm. Sometime after the battle, a stretcher crew found the mangled artilleryman and transported him to the Third Corps hospital set up south of Gettysburg near the confluence of White Run and Rock Creek. Two days later, a surgeon amputated Price's right arm near the elbow and removed the damaged portion of his lower right leg.

The heavy rains that fell in the area following the battle triggered flash flooding and a number of helpless wounded soldiers lying near the banks of the creeks drowned before attendants could rescue them. By propping his elbows on a nearby dogwood tree, Private Price managed to keep his head above the rising water. Glancing over to a nearby patient, he called out, "Billy, they talk about Napoleon climbing the Alps, why isn't there a marker to Dick Price climbing the dogwood?" Although he survived the flood, Price would later die of exhaustion at Camp Letterman on August 23 after contracting a severe case of diarrhea. It was said that his singing cheered his comrades to the last.

Following the elder Price's emotional breakdown at his son's grave in 1882, the wives of the assembled veterans attempted to comfort him. These efforts were in vain until Mrs. Ogden Woodruff embraced the anguished father and directed his attention to a flag floating high on a pole above the cemetery. "Uncle Richard, look at that flag," she demanded. "Your boy died for that flag, and while this nation endures his deeds will never be forgotten. When you and I are dead, patriots, standing where we are now, will remember his name and fame." After partaking of breakfast at a local hotel, Richard Price left for home, perhaps finally reconciled to the fate of his boy.

Nelson Reaser's Last Letter to His Father, USA

Shortly after his arrival upon the field, a U.S. Army medical inspector filed a report to his superiors in which he declared, "The period of ten days following the battle of Gettysburg was the occasion of the greatest amount of human suffering known to this nation since its birth." Indeed, the town and surrounding countryside seemed like one vast hospital as 21,000 wounded soldiers, including 6,000 to 7,000 Confederates, could be found lying in churches, schools, and other public buildings as well as private homes, barns, and stables.

Equipped to handle about 10,000 patients, the medical department of the Army of the Potomac faced a logistical nightmare. The surplus numbers of men requiring care was exacerbated by a severe shortage of food, medicine, and other supplies due to the rapid march of the Union army into the area. Most of the army's supply trains and medical wagons had been parked at Westminster, Maryland, nearly 30 miles from the battlefield. In addition, only a few over 100 surgeons remained behind as the army took up the pursuit of Lee's forces. It was believed that another major conflict would erupt before the Southerners reached the Potomac River.

Located on High Street in the southwestern section of the town, St. Francis Xavier Roman Catholic Church provided refuge for many wounded soldiers of the Third Division of the Union First Corps. "All night long I heard from downstairs moans, groans, shrieks, and yells from the wounded and suffering soldiers," wrote a wounded officer lying in the gallery of the church during the evening of July 1, 1863. A nurse from the Catholic Sisters of Charity described the horrible conditions she encountered at the hospital on the following Sunday:

> The soldiers lay on the pew seats, under them and in every aisle. They were also in the sanctuary and in the gallery, so close together that there was scarcely room to move about. Many of them lay in their own blood and the water used for bathing their wounds, but no word of complaint escaped from their lips. Others were dying with lockjaw, making it very difficult to administer drinks and nourishment.

The overworked doctors and volunteer nurses at St. Francis must have admired the dignity and courage displayed by Private Nelson Reaser, a member of the 151st Pennsylvania. The teenager from Pike County waited patiently for his turn at the amputation table. After his mangled right leg was severed above the knee joint, the youthful private remained optimistic about his prospects for recovery. When Reaser wrote his father on July 18, it is apparent that he longed for a familiar face. Despite his poor grammar, his deep pride and love for his family shines through the ages:

> I now set down to rite you a few more lines for to see if you will answer these. I thought it very strange in you for not answern my other. I suppose that you know where I am wounded. I will tell you anyhow. My right leg is amputated, but the doctor says it is a getting along the best of any of them. It is a shame for to see how some of the boys worie themselves to death. The doctor says he never saw a man keep up such good spirits as I do. I do my own riting. I am gaining very much. I can get out on a chair without any help, but I have wished for to see some of you so bad. I have not seen any botty that I knowed yet.... Well I will bring my letter to a close for I am very week now. So no more at present.

Five days later, Nelson Reaser died inside the church hospital. His remains were later removed to the National Cemetery (A-39, Pennsylvania plot). One hopes that the young soldier heard from his father or another family member before his untimely death.

Stephen and Azor Nickerson, USA

In contrast to Nelson Reaser, who expected to make a full recovery from his injuries, Captain Azor Howett Nickerson believed that he had just a few days to live. The July 8, 1863, issue of the *Elyria* [Ohio] *Independent Democrat* conveyed this sad news: "We have just learned by telegraph that brave Capt. Nickerson of Company I, 8th Regiment, was mortally wounded at the great battle of Gettysburg." A week later, however, the *Democrat* offered some hope concerning the hometown officer:

> A letter was received here from Gettysburg, Monday [July 13], that strengthens our hopes somewhat, respecting the condition of Capt. Nickerson. It is impossible to tell, however, at present, what will be the result in his case. It appears that he was shot through the left arm below the elbow, the ball then penetrated the chest and passed through the right lung, coming out under the right arm. He has suffered already considerably from spitting blood and difficulty of breathing. The question of recovery depends upon the extent and severity of inflammation. The solicitude felt in this community over the fate of this brave and gallant officer is convincing proof of its high estimation of his many virtues and exalted worth.

This grim news had an even deeper impact in nearby Medina, Ohio, where the officer had entered the world in 1837 as the firstborn of Elizabeth and Stephen Nickerson. Elizabeth's untimely death left her schoolteacher husband alone with four young children. This traumatic event must have strengthened the bond between the father and his eldest child in a family that would have been considered large even by nineteenth century standards. Following his father's remarriage, the maturing Azor Nickerson could count no less than 11 siblings and half siblings, plus an adopted sister. In an effort to make his own mark upon the world, or perhaps simply to obtain some peace and quiet, the young man struck off on his own when he reached adulthood. The outbreak of the war found him in Elyria working as a law clerk.

Commissioned a second lieutenant in the summer of 1861, Nickerson sustained a wound to his right shoulder during the assault on the Sunken Road at Antietam. Returning to duty in time to take part in the Battle of Chancellorsville, he received official praise for being "particularly conspicuous and attentive." At Gettysburg, the 8th Ohio could muster just something over 200 officers and men. Nevertheless, the small band of Buckeyes would play a dramatic role in the repulse of Pickett's Charge by helping to dissipate the left wing of the Confederate assault column.

Captain Nickerson would not witness this pivotal event. His Gettysburg odyssey began hours earlier during one of the largely forgotten skirmish actions that preceded the climax of the battle. As the desultory firing heated up along the Emmitsburg Road throughout the morning of July 3, Rebel bullets marred opposite sides of Nickerson's body. One ball passed through the left forearm and a more damaging hunk of lead entered three inches to the right of his left nipple. Corporal Edgar Irish and Sergeant Ransom Braman carried their bleeding captain to the rear, and after a stretcher was procured laid him down upon the east slope of Cemetery Hill to die, it was thought.

Incoming Confederate artillery rounds made this location extremely precarious. In desperation, Nickerson first crawled and then struggled to his feet, but after taking a few awkward steps, blood gushed from his mouth, causing him to faint. He regained consciousness when an ambulance attendant bathed his blood-streaked face. As the attendant and driver placed the officer upon the conveyance beside another wounded soldier a shell crashed through one of the wheels. Undeterred, the driver sped away.

During the jostling ride to a nearby aid station, the two patients repeatedly thudded into one another until both lost consciousness. After being revived with a drink of brandy, Nickerson was examined by an old acquaintance, Henry McAbee, the surgeon of the 4th Ohio, who quickly discovered the gaping exit wound. Knowing that he would receive an honest answer, the captain inquired if there was any hope for his recovery. "No," replied the doctor as he patted his patient gently on the forehead. Then, looking away he repeated, "No, my boy, none whatever."

Despite this grim prognosis, Nickerson later experienced a stroke of good fortune when he was reunited with his youthful Negro servant, Jerry, at the Second Corps hospital several miles south of Gettysburg. Jerry's duties consisted of blacking Nickerson's shoes when in camp and carrying his haversack and rubber coat while on the march. He must also have been a source of amusement for the Ohioan, who described him as "a mite of a fellow whom it would be base slander to mention as a 'colored boy,' for he was the blackest Negro I ever saw ... and about as broad as he was tall."

Since nearly all of the wounded were still lying in the open, the rubber coat in Jerry's possession provided some degree of protection from the torrential rains that pelted the area one evening. Sometime before morning, however, a saturated Nickerson awoke to find the garment gone. As it turned out Jerry had checked in on his master during the night, thought him to be dead, and thereby appropriated the coat for his own use.

The detailing of Corporal Irish as his personal nurse paid even greater dividends. As the banks of Rock Creek began to overflow, the devoted corporal hastily fashioned an elevated platform from wood stakes, several poles, and staves from an old barrel. Afterwards, he hoisted his commander upon the makeshift cot, saving him from the rising waters.

Having endured everything that the enemy and Mother Nature hurled at him, Nickerson's flagging spirits received a much-needed boost from the daily visits of the Reverend Jonathan E. Adams of New Sharon, Maine. The New England clergyman provided much more than food for the soul. After learning that his invalid friend yearned for a helping of roasted potatoes, Rev. Adams hiked over ten miles to procure them. This level of caring left an enduring impression upon the soldier. "I felt as though I had really been with one who walked arm in arm with the Master, and knew when and how to work as well as when and how to pray," he remarked.

All of this kindness prepared the dying man for the inevitable. Writing on July 13, hospital steward Charles H. Merrick informed his wife that he had eight soldiers under his care, three of them, including Captain Nickerson, he considered past hope, as did all the doctors. Merrick also noted the presence of both Stephen Nickerson and George C. Washburn, editor of the *Elyria Independent Democrat*, at the hospital.

In a correspondence titled, "Among the Wounded," Washburn informed his readers that "On entering the field where the wounded of the 8th lay, I proceeded to the tent occupied by Capt. Nickerson, who was so overjoyed at seeing me so unexpectedly, that for some time he could not be composed." Later, he wrote by the side of the officer's couch, "He is sleeping under the effects of opiates I have administered and fear will soon fight his last great battle. He says he is ready to die, and has every attention he needs."

The sight of his father must have caused even more excitement, but within a short time the elder Nickerson's behavior proved a bit perplexing to the son. "He became very much interested in the Confederate soldier who was lying in my tent," recalled the captain, "and was careful to divide any luxury he got for me with him. The man, though apparently grateful, said little, and I think half suspected that my father was not aware that he belonged to the Confederate army."

One day Mr. Nickerson asked the man to what regiment he belonged. The patient hesitated for a moment, and then answered: "The—th Mississippi." As tears welled up in his eyes the shocked Good Samaritan exclaimed that he might have been the very man that shot his boy. But after regaining his composure, he took the Confederate by the hand

and said, "Never mind, my boy, pardon me for having such an unwelcome thought. I am sure you believed you were doing your duty, whatever you did." Although perhaps a little jealous, Nickerson noted with a touch of pride that his father afterwards showed more attention to the Southerner than he did to him.

Nickerson's father also played an indirect role in another unusual incident. Through Reverend Adams, Captain Nickerson learned that an acquaintance, Captain John J. P. Blinn, was lying in another section of the same hospital with a wound similar to his own. Blinn, a widower from Terre Haute, Indiana, hoped to live long enough to see his mother, who having received the news by telegraph was en route to Gettysburg. This discovery led to the initiation of a daily ritual described by Nickerson:

> I then sent a message to Blinn, that if I was alive at ten the next morning, I would join him in a glass of wine, at least, we could each take one at the same moment. We continued this long distance greeting for several mornings, until one day, just before the time for my glass with Blinn, a message came to my father. Instead of opening the bottle of wine for me as had been his custom, he came over by my bunk, laid his hand gently on my forehead, and looking sadly across the green fields toward the hospital of the Second Division, he said: "Poor Captain Blinn can't drink with you this morning; he is dead."

Fortunately, Dorthea Blinn reached her son before the time of his passing. It is often difficult to determine how one patient pulls through a critical period while another in a similar condition does not. After the death of his friend, Nickerson defied his doctors by improving so much that they consented to let him travel home near the end of July.

As a group of attendants carried the officer down Baltimore Street towards the railroad depot, Stephen Nickerson held an umbrella over his son's head to shield him from the summer sun. When the group paused to rest along the sidewalk in front of the large brick home of Samuel Witherow, one of the daughters immediately offered to prepare a lunch banquet. The parlor doors soon swung open and the men enjoyed a "delicious repast." At the end of the feast, the ladies presented Captain Nickerson with a miniature national flag, an item destined to become one of his most cherished mementos.

Having arrived back in Elyria about a week earlier, editor Washburn reported the details of the captain's memorable homecoming in his paper:

> Captain Nickerson arrived from Gettysburg on Friday last [July 31], having so far recovered as to be able to be brought home on a stretcher. He is stopping with Mr. J. L. Cole where he is receiving the kindest attention, and we trust in a few days he will be able to leave his room. His faithful nurse and fellow soldier E. H. Irish, is still with him. Not one man in a hundred would survive the wound he received.... His temperate habits, and well conditioned vital system, has measurably overcome the effect of the wound, and we hope he will long live to serve the country he has so nobly defended.

This wish was granted. That November at the intercession of Ohio governor David Tod, Nickerson enjoyed a front row seat at the dedication ceremony of the Soldiers' National Cemetery at Gettysburg. Lincoln's remarks transfixed the convalescent officer, who later declared: "I thought then, and still think, it was the shortest, grandest speech, oration, sermon, or what you please to call it, to which I ever listened. It was the whole matter in a nutshell, delivered distinctly and impressively.... My own emotions may perhaps be imagined when it is remembered that he was facing the spot where only a short time before we had our death-grapple with Pickett's men, and he stood almost immediately over the place where I had lain and seen my comrades torn in fragments by the enemy's cannon-balls."

Azor Nickerson (standing) with General George Crook (seated on right). The other man is unidentified. This photograph was taken in 1875 (Sharlot Hall Museum Photography, Prescott, Arizona).

Nickerson took Lincoln's words to heart. Although his Gettysburg wounds never completely healed, he devoted much of his remaining life to the military. After serving a dozen years as General George Crook's adjutant and aide-de-camp, Nickerson was appointed to the post of assistant adjutant general of the U.S. Army in 1878.

Two years earlier, at the Battle of the Rosebud, the prelude to Little Big Horn, an Indian warrior nearly finished what the Rebs had started by inflicting a chest wound that displaced the bones originally fractured at Gettysburg. The indefatigable soldier finally fell victim to lung disease on April 1, 1910, thus closing the curtain on one of the rare father/son Gettysburg sagas with a happy ending.

William D. W. and Albert Mitchell, USA; John A. Redd, CSA

Children are often thought of as helpless, innocent creatures, but history has often proved otherwise. Thirsting for adventure, thousands of American boys ran off to enlist in the military from 1861 to 1865, with or without the blessing of their parents. According to one estimate, anywhere from 250,000 to 420,000 Civil War soldiers illegally signed up for duty while under the age of 18. Many others served legitimately as drummer boys as well as in other noncombat roles. For these youngsters the hardships of army life would forge in them a level of maturity well beyond the norm for their age group.

It was also fairly common for the sons of Union and Confederate officers to accompany their fathers during active campaigns. Although well intentioned, this practice could have unforeseen consequences. Fred Grant traveled with his father, General Ulysses S. Grant, during the Vicksburg Campaign, which culminated on July 4, 1863, with the capitulation of the city. "The horrors of a battlefield were brought vividly before me," recalled Fred. "I joined a detachment which was collecting the dead for burial. Sickening at the sights, I made my way with another detachment, which was gathering the wounded, to a log house which had been appropriated for a hospital. Here the scenes were so terrible that I became faint, and making my way to a tree, sat down, the most woebegone twelve-year-old in America."

He was mistaken. Hundreds of miles away two young noncombatants at Gettysburg were impacted even more deeply by the war. Nurse Emily Souder could never forget one of these incidents. It transpired near the end of July within the Baltimore Street home of Henry and Marie Comfort: "A captain in an Ohio regiment died yesterday directly opposite to the house where we are staying ... the captain's wife in spasms all day. It was pitiful to witness the efforts at consolation made by her son, a little fellow in uniform, who had been with his father in the army, although a mere child."

Although not identified by Mrs. Souder, the available evidence strongly supports the deceased officer as being Captain William D. W. Mitchell, Company H, 82nd Ohio, who died on July 22 after being wounded in the right arm and right leg on the opening day of the battle. Mitchell was 40 years old at the time of his enlistment on August 15, 1862. The week prior to his death marked the fifteenth anniversary of his marriage to Sarah Jane Maynard. Their union resulted in seven children, ranging in age from eleven months to fourteen years at the time of the battle. More than likely, it was his oldest child, 14-year-old Albert, who witnessed his death at Gettysburg, since the only other son was under the age of six. Sarah Mitchell remarried in 1865 and resided in Springfield, Ohio. (Captain John Costin, another officer in the 82nd Ohio, was also mortally wounded on July 1, but he died on July 11 and was single with no children).

A young Virginia boy experienced a similar loss. Although not yet a teenager, John A. Redd came to the army to be with his father, perhaps after the death of his mother. Separated from his father during the battle, young Redd was inadvertently rounded up with a group of 700 Confederate prisoners and shuffled off to the prison camp at Fort Delaware on Pea Patch Island. Despite these terrifying circumstances, the boy quickly adapted to his new surroundings. In his prison diary, James L. McCown of the 5th Virginia devoted his entire entry for August 3, 1864, to Redd:

> John A. Redd—You must have a place in my diary: his father was either killed or captured at the Battle of Gettysburg. He ... was brought to this island as a Rebel prisoner of war. His age now seems to be nine or ten years. The boy is a general pet amongst all the men on the island and seems perfectly contented and happy. He has learned to play all sorts of games with cards, swears and feels as much a man as anyone. He is one of the stubborn Rebs, young as he is, he being the only one who can abuse the Yanks and they rather seem to enjoy it and to their credit would do a good part for him. They all seem to like the boy.

A sketch of Fort Delaware in 1863 by a Union guard (*Harper's Weekly*).

> He will not stay with them, says he must be with my own men. He never suffers for anything to eat, helps himself and is free to do as he pleases.

When prison authorities learned of Redd's plight they immediately made arrangements to release him from their custody, but the lad told them that he had no place to go and that his fellow inmates were his only "family."

Ashton and William Tourison, USA

For most fathers, the thought of watching helplessly as one of their children suffers or dies is incomprehensible. Yet, in several instances, these dreadful scenes unfolded at Gettysburg on the final day of the battle. One such occurrence took place during the fierce struggle for Culp's Hill on the morning of July 3, 1863.

The incessant roar of musketry echoed from the woodlands for seven hours as waves of Southern infantrymen assailed the steep, boulder-strewn slopes in an effort to dislodge the Union defenders. Fighting from behind prepared breastworks and by skillfully utilizing the terrain, the Northern troops successfully repelled the assaults. Shortly after daylight, Colonel Charles Candy's brigade took cover in a narrow ravine near the southern base of the hill opposite an open meadow afterwards known as Pardee Field. A soldier in the 147th Pennsylvania described the ensuing action:

> The enemy with their famous Rebel yell made repeated charges upon our lines, but were as often swept back with fearful slaughter, our men holding their fire until the enemy was at close range and finally, broken and dispirited, the Rebels were driven from the field. Owing to the nature of the ground where our regiment stood, the enemy's fire passed, for

the most part, harmless over our heads and, consequently, the loss was small compared with that which we inflicted.

In fact, the 147th suffered just seven fatalities, but as the news slowly rippled to the affected families and communities, each one was deeply felt. One of the deaths, recorded in great detail by drummer boy William T. Simpson, 28th Pennsylvania, had a more immediate impact. As was often the case during combat, Simpson and his fellow musicians served as stretcher-bearers once the fighting commenced on Culp's Hill. After helping to load one of the first casualties into an ambulance, the drummer witnessed a scene that he could never erase from his memory:

> I saw Capt. Tourance (sic) of Co. E, of the 147th following four boys with a man in a blanket, who, I thought was wounded. Capt. Tourance formerly belonged to our regiment, and he was good to us drummer boys. We loved him. He was an old Mexican War fighter ... and was a drummer boy himself in earlier years. I went up to him with a laugh, for I was glad to see him and expected a happy greeting in return. But he just looked at me, and said: "My poor boy is dead." I was thunderstruck. It took all the ginger out of me. It was Will Tourance, who was the second lieutenant in his father's company. We boys were so accustomed to see the men about us killed and wounded that it hardly fazed us, but I did feel sorry for Capt. Tourance. I felt as though I had met with a personal loss and I stood and watched him following the body of his boy until he was out of sight. It was the last I saw of the dear old man.

In the fall of 1861, Ashton S. and William H. Tourison enrolled in a company of volunteers from Philadelphia that would become Company P of the 28th Pennsylvania. Not only had Ashton Tourison served in the Mexican War, he also bore a scar from a bullet that pierced his leg. In the antebellum period he derived his living as a shoemaker and as a messenger for the U.S. Customs House. His men remembered him being a temperate and excellent officer.

At the time of his enlistment the younger Tourison was cohabiting with his childhood sweetheart, 22-year-old Emma S. Hughes. Several months after his enlistment, William learned that Emma was pregnant. The couple was joined in marriage on May 14, 1862, and just two days later, a son named Stephen Geary Tourison entered the world.

Despite the scandalous nature of the wedding, the new father gushed with pride over his baby son. Shortly after returning to the front, he wrote home to Emma, "I don't want you to talk too much about that little boy of mine. If you continue you will have me running home to see him." Later in the year he penned lovingly, "How is my dear little Geary, I do miss him so much. I cannot help thinking of little Stephen. How I would like to see him, but never mind when I get home his mamma will have taken such good care of him, that he will be such a good little boy that I will never leave him again."

That fall five companies of the 28th Pennsylvania were consolidated into the newly formed 147th Pennsylvania. Ashton and William Tourison served respectively as captain and first lieutenant of Company E.

Lieutenant Tourison returned to his German Street home on a ten-day furlough in March of 1863. Afterwards, he passed safely through the Battle of Chancellorsville, where his unit was heavily engaged. The bullet that extinguished his life at Gettysburg spared him the reality of his beloved son's condition. Stephen suffered from a series of mental and physical maladies, including epilepsy, asthma, "feeble mindedness," and partial paralysis. By 1891, a court declared him to be "a perfect imbecile" totally dependent on others for his care.

Because of the unusual circumstances surrounding her marriage to William, Emma

Left: William Tourison, ca. 1861 (Jeff Kowalis). *Right:* Ashton Tourison, ca. 1861 (Jeff Kowalis).

Tourison endured a lengthy battle with red tape to secure a government pension. As her husband had predicted years earlier, Emma proved to be a loving and devoted mother, raising her handicapped child almost single-handedly to the day of her death on June 9, 1919. On that same day Stephen was admitted to the "Nervous Ward" of the Department of Public Health and Charities on 24th and Pine Streets in Philadelphia.

The boy would never know his father nor of the sacrifice he had made for his country. For Ashton Tourison there was no escape. A week after his son's death he received a pass to accompany William's body home for burial. Wracked by malaria and heart trouble, he tendered his resignation that August. The veteran of two wars died at his home of heart disease just three years later.

Michael and Hezekiah Spessard, CSA

As a stunned William Simpson watched Captain Tourison until he disappeared from view, Pickett's Division filed into position at the foot of Seminary Ridge near Spangler's Woods. After playing a prominent role in the spring and summer campaigns of 1862, the division had seen little action during the past ten months. The Virginians were in good condition and spoiling for a fight. Nonetheless, they were far too experienced to harbor any naïve notions of bloodless glory.

Pickett's Charge from the Union lines. The Angle and the Copse of Trees are depicted in the center of the illustration (U.S. Army Military History Institute).

Perhaps the 8th Virginia's Colonel Eppa Hunton best expressed these sentiments when he wrote, "All appreciated the danger and felt it was probably the last charge to most of them. All seemed willing to die to achieve a victory there, which it was believed would be the crowning victory and the end of the war."

Although Hunton's final prediction did not come true, his assessment of the human toll of the afternoon's action proved hauntingly accurate. During the course of the two-hour artillery duel and the ensuing infantry assault that spanned about an hour from start to finish, Pickett's Division was cut in half. Many soldiers in gray fell in the lethal zone between the Emmitsburg Road and the crest of Cemetery Ridge. Within these several hundred yards of precious real estate occurred numerous scenes too horrible to contemplate for the participants.

As one of sixteen of Pickett's officers on horseback during the charge, Colonel Hunton enjoyed an excellent view of the field. Out of all the images that filled his senses in those eventful sixty minutes, one particular incident stood out in his memory. Riding close behind the advancing troops, Hunton discovered 41-year-old Captain Michael Peters Spessard sitting on the ground cradling the head of a young man in his lap. As Hunton rode towards him, Captain Spessard, his eyes transfixed with shock and grief, wailed out, "Look at my poor boy, colonel." The wounded soldier was Hezekiah Spessard, who served as a private in his father's company of the 28th Virginia. A short time earlier, Michael's wife and other children had died of disease back in Virginia.

Resigned to the fact that his last remaining family member would not live, he left him his canteen of water, kissed him, and then carefully laid his head down. Instead of being numbed with shock, the Virginian seemed hell bent on avenging his son's suffering and probable death. Rising to his feet, he swung his sword up to his shoulder and barked out "Forward, boys!" In his haste to engage the enemy, Spessard's Craig Mountain Boys began to outdistance the other companies in the regiment, forcing Colonel Robert Allen to send an order to slow up the pace.

Moments later, the two forces collided and furious hand-to-hand combat broke out. Leaping over the stone fence, Spessard slashed wildly at the despised Yankees with his sword. It took three of them to wrestle the weapon from his grasp. Still, the enraged officer refused to surrender. He scooped up a handful of loose rocks and hurled them at his opponents. Stunned by the furious counterattack, the trio took flight, providing Spessard the opportunity to escape.

The distraught father later found his boy at a field hospital and did all he could to comfort him. Hezekiah died in Pennsylvania on July 19, two weeks after the Southern army retired from the field. Michael Spessard's bravery did not go unnoticed. He would soon be promoted to major in recognition of his gallant conduct at Gettysburg. Spessard was among the 75 survivors of the 28th who surrendered at Appomattox. Following the war, he returned alone to his farm in New Castle and died in 1889.

John Harvey, Sr., and John Harvey, Jr., USA

As Pickett's legions swept across the valley toward Cemetery Ridge like an incoming tide, a lone Union regiment braced itself to receive the initial blow of the assault. Positioned behind a low stone fence directly in front of the Copse of Trees, the 250 men of the 69th Pennsylvania held the most advanced position on the Union battle line. The regiment carried a distinctive green flag that reflected its state and ethnic pride: the state coat of arms appeared on one side and the Maid of Erin Harp wreathed in shamrocks on the other.

The majority of the men who made up the 69th hailed from Philadelphia and they were among the over one million recent Irish immigrants who had flocked to the New World during the four decades preceding the American Civil War. The nucleus of the regiment contained several prewar militia companies such as the Irish Volunteers, the Hibernian Greens, the Meagher Guards, and the Patterson Light Guards.

As part of the Philadelphia Brigade, which also included the 71st, the 72nd and the 106th Pennsylvania, the 69th had fought in nearly all of the major engagements of the Army of the Potomac from the debacle at Balls Bluff, Virginia, in October 1861 through the recent setback at Chancellorsville. On the evening of July 2, they had helped to repel an attack by Ambrose Wright's Georgia Brigade against the Union center on Cemetery Ridge.

But it was on the final day of the battle, as Pickett's three brigades converged on the clump of trees, that the men of the 69th would face their biggest challenge to date. If the Pennsylvanians gave way it was likely that other regiments would also break to the rear, perhaps setting off an irreversible chain reaction.

It is ironic that so much was riding on the performance of these particular soldiers. Ever since arriving in the New World the Irish, as well as the Germans, had battled discrimination at the hands of the growing Nativist movement that swept over the country and this prejudice had followed them into the army.

Fully aware that the eyes of the entire army and of the nation would be upon the 69th, Colonel Dennis O'Kane told his men "that we would render an account of ourselves this day that would bring upon us the plaudits of our country." The remainder of his address was more pragmatic. He issued orders not to fire until the enemy appeared within close range and that should any man flinch in his duty, the nearest comrade was expected to kill him on the spot. The band of Irishmen had prepared well for the task at hand. Each had at least six loaded guns at his disposal. This handy arsenal was collected following the fight of the previous evening.

They would need all of this available firepower as the Virginians struck their position like an angry wave crashing onto the shore at the Outer Banks. Hand-to-hand fighting broke out and the enemy lapped around both ends of the regiment's isolated battle line, threatening to surround them, but the Irish soldiers stood firm. Near the climax of the attack, Brigadier General Lewis Armistead led a squad of about 100 men over the stone fence just to the north of the Copse of Trees. Two companies of the 69th managed to shift position to meet this threat. Loading and firing as they went, this movement required a great degree of discipline to execute properly.

The grave of John Harvey, Jr., Soldiers' National Cemetery.

For one soldier in Company A, it required an even greater measure of commitment and personal courage. Earlier in the day, Private John Harvey, Sr., a prewar lawyer and native of Tyrone County, Ireland, watched in horror as a shell fragment struck his son, John, Jr., in the head, inflicting a mortal injury. The Harveys enlisted together in August of 1861 and had survived a long series of battles before that horrific July afternoon. Leaving his dying son behind, Private Harvey dutifully joined his comrades and fought on until Union reinforcements arrived and turned the tide of the battle. Among his adversaries was Captain Michael Spessard, who had left the side of his mortally wounded son to lead his company in the final stage of the attack.

Following the Battle of Gettysburg, the middle-aged soldier from Philadelphia would face an opponent that he could not see and that would not retreat. Consumed by grief, Harvey deserted his unit two weeks after the battle. He hit the bottle to mask his pain. A list of deserters described him as being 46 years of age, five feet, eleven inches tall, with a sallow complexion, blue eyes, and gray hair. He was eventually found lying on a Washington street without a weapon or his equipment. On November 11, 1863, an examining surgeon diagnosed the private as being severely ill with scurvy and diarrhea. He noted grimly that his recovery seemed doubtful.

This prognosis proved accurate. Four days later, chronic alcoholism accomplished what enemy bullets had failed to do and Harvey's misery came to an end in an Alexandria, Virginia, hospital. His wife and two grown children survived him. John Harvey, Sr., is not counted as one of the 40 men of the 69th Pennsylvania who offered their lives at Gettysburg to preserve the Union, but he, too, was certainly a casualty of the battle.

Thomas, Jonathan, and Albert Clark, CSA

The majority of the soldiers in blue and gray who tramped along the roads that bisected the rolling farmlands of southern Pennsylvania during the final days of June 1863 were combat veterans. These men "saw the elephant" at Malvern Hill, Second Manassas, Antietam, Fredericksburg, and Chancellorsville. In addition to these seasoned campaigners both armies included a few units that could boast of little or no experience under fire. For these neophyte organizations, a jolting introduction to warfare awaited them.

Early on the morning of July 1, Major General Henry Heth's Confederate division marched eastward at a leisurely pace along the Chambersburg Pike. The 2,900-man division was on its way to Gettysburg as part of a reconnaissance force. A day earlier, a smaller expedition uncovered an enemy force approaching the town and had turned back to avoid an engagement.

Despite this intelligence, Heth and his command felt little apprehension. They expected to encounter only light resistance from raw militia or home guard troops, certainly not any elements of the Army of the Potomac. Recent showers had settled the dust on the pike and as heavy drops of moisture glistened from the ocean of ripening grain heads surrounding them, the Southerners puffed on pipes and engaged in good-natured bantering. Shortly after 7:00 a.m., the column reached the low ground along Marsh Creek about three miles from the town. Suddenly, the sharp crack of a carbine broke the early morning stillness.

Among Heth's force was a brigade commanded by Brigadier General Joseph R. Davis, the nephew of President Jefferson Davis. Apparently, nepotism contributed in part to Davis's rapid ascension from captain to general. His background was primarily law and politics and much of his Civil War service consisted of staff work. One of his regiments, the 42nd Mississippi, shared his combat inexperience.

Organized in Richmond the previous summer, the 42nd spent the winter of 1862-63 performing guard duty in Goldsboro, North Carolina, and then participated in the siege of Suffolk, Virginia, in the spring. The regiment had marched hard and had skirmished with the enemy but had not yet painted a major battle honor upon its colors.

During the first week of January 1863, 47-year-old Captain Thomas Goode Clark told his wife Margery, "I think that if we ever have a chance that Co. F ... will do their selves honor by doing some good fighting, but I hope that this cruel war may come to a close before long and let the soldiers come home.... I want to see you and the children the worst I ever did in my life but I am tied up here and must reconcile it to myself the best I can putting my trust in God for the future and I hope you will not forget to pray for me and the boys and for yourself and the children."

The boys referred to by Thomas were his oldest sons, Jonathan, age 20, and 18-year-old Albert Henry, who served as privates in their father's company. Six younger children remained at home with Margery B. Rogers Clark on the family farm near Sarepta, situated in the gentle hill country of north central Mississippi.

Through two years of political turmoil and war, Thomas Clark found himself constantly torn between duty to his country and his abiding love and devotion for his family. Although inextricably linked, these concerns were often in direct competition. In order to reconcile these conflicting emotions, the husband and father relied heavily upon his Christian faith.

Thomas Goode Clark, ca. 1861 (Charlie Clark).

In the fall of 1861, Thomas, his two sons, and Marcellus Church, Thomas's half brother, helped form a company of Mississippi State troops for a sixty-day enlistment period. In one of his earliest letters after departing home, Thomas instructed Margery: "If I should not get to come home I want you to try and take the best care you can of yourself and the children.... Teach the children to love and fear God and if I should never see you more I want you to try and train the children up in the best manner you can.... The

Jonathan (left) and Albert Clark, 1861 (Charlie Clark).

Lord only knows what is our lot." Reflecting his heritage as the grandson of a Revolutionary War patriot, he declared a short time later, "I came out for the purpose of doing my country all the service that was in my power and I am determined to do my duty as far as I can."

When the two months passed without incident, Margery Clark might have privately prayed that the patriotic fires of her husband had been extinguished by the rigors of army life and that he and the boys would return home to stay. If so, she received disappointing news when Thomas wrote her in mid–January of his intention to raise a new company upon the expiration of his present term. The Clark family would be reunited for several months, but Thomas and the boys departed once again after being mustered into service on April 29, 1862.

Just days before leaving home, Albert Clark penned a letter to a friend who was away in the army. Almost apologetically, he explained, "Bill you must not think that it is my fault that I am staying at home now for we are and have been trying to get our company off ever since Pa got well." He also revealed his reasons for wanting to be a soldier: "The time is come when we will have to fight or be conquered and I believe that it is the firm resolution of every true Southerner to never be whipped.... It is the duty of every one to encourage each other and I tell you Bill I am for southern rights, right or wrong let me go."

The teenager also discussed the universal concerns of all boys coming of age—socializing and fitting in with his peers, and of course, girls. After providing the details of a recent party, including his dancing partners, Albert promised his friend that when they both got home again, he would have "a frolic fixed up and we will have a grand time." He closed by fondly reminiscing about his school days, which were "our happiest days, but silly foolish boys did not know it and consequently we did not enjoy life at all." More revelations lay ahead.

Perhaps due to his standing in the community or his prior military experience, Thomas Clark won the election for captain of what would soon become Company F, 42nd Mississippi. Stationed near Richmond, the early days of the regiment were fairly routine and carefree. As the summer of 1862 drew to a close, Thomas told Margery that Jonathan weighed over 140 pounds and that Albert Henry is "fat as you ever saw him."

Optimism abounded throughout much of the South, as developments in both theaters of the war seemed to favor the Confederacy. "We are whipping them so bad that they are bound to give up the ghost," declared Jonathan. Near the same time, however, Albert Henry was overcome with a deep sense of foreboding. "I am afraid this war will turn out to be the most barbarous war that history could ever tell." With amazing clarity he foresaw the great sacrifice that lay ahead for his countrymen; he urged his 14-year-old brother Isaac to form a company of 10 to 15-year-old boys and "drill them and have them ready if they are needed in a year or two." The youngster also appeared to be homesick. He could picture his mother knitting by the fireplace with the children gathered around her.

As the New Year unfolded, the thoughts of many Mississippi soldiers serving in the east turned to home when they learned of a series of Union raids into the northern part of their state. "I never wanted to see you all as bad in my life," wrote Thomas to Margery, "but when I think of home I only resolve to fight on through the war with more firmness than ever." He advised her to try and hide as much as possible but if the Yankees came to the house not to insult them and worsen the situation. A party of foragers did make off with Jonathan's horse, but the family escaped major damage to their property.

At the same time, the troubled husband voiced concern over the recent behavior of Isaac after he learned that the boy was running with a bad crowd in the nearby town of Sarepta. Near the middle of January he heard a rumor that Isaac planned to join a cavalry company. This news caused Thomas much consternation, as he had expected his oldest son left at home to look after the household and to run the farm and mill.

Ike's older brothers agreed with their father. "Tell him that I know he can't stand it and besides that it would be more honor to him to stay at home and take care of his mother than to go to the army," wrote Albert to his mother on January 18. He was feeling melancholy at this time as a comrade of his had recently died of illness, leaving behind a dependent wife and elderly mother. "There is not honor attached to them that die in the army," he despaired. "They are forgotten forever among those that were well." The experience forced him to face his own mortality. He told his mother that if they should never again meet on earth that they would be reunited in Heaven.

Jonathan, who would soon turn 21, stated, "I would be glad if I was but fourteen, then I would stay at home." He mailed his mother an ambrotype of himself but was embarrassed by it and told her not to show it to anyone. Fighting a bout of homesickness, he fantasized about the once mundane chores of feeding livestock and plowing fields.

An exasperated Thomas Clark eventually instructed Margery to send Isaac to him and the troubled youth arrived in Goldsboro on February 13. For a time Thomas contemplated mustering him into the company, much to the displeasure of Jonathan, but Ike's frequent bouts with illness prevented him from doing so. After the failure of numerous previous attempts, Captain Clark was granted a furlough to return home briefly in the spring of 1863. He returned to the army by the middle of May.

In the absence of their father, the boys participated in the unsuccessful siege of Suffolk. From a camp near Ivory, Virginia, Jonathan updated his mother on the affair: "We had a very merry time of shooting at the Yankees, I shot at them until I got tired of it and I think that I killed some of them.... I have [never] seen so many men broke down in my life, thousands lying along the roadside, then I felt like I had to be at home doing anything that may be termed work ... but never mind that ... I'm willing to do all I can to save our country and I think we will save it."

With U.S. Grant tightening his grip on Vicksburg, Mississippi, Robert E. Lee convinced his superiors that the only way to relieve the pressure on the vital river city was to launch an offensive of his own. Just before A. P. Hill's Corps swung west and then north to begin the long march that would lead them into Pennsylvania, Captain Clark contemplated his future. He closed his letter of June 13 with a promise that must have delighted his wife: "In justice to myself and family at home it is my duty to quit the army at least for awhile." Accordingly, after the present campaign he planned to resign, citing his poor health and the fact that his men were now experienced enough to get along without him.

On the same day, Albert wrote, "Ma, I cannot tell you when I will get home, if ever, but I can stay and do my duty as long as the Lord will permit me to have my health." He reported that seven men from Company F had recently deserted, perhaps due to the unfolding crisis in their own state. Meanwhile, Thomas sent Isaac on his way home.

On July 1, as the opening shots of the battle echoed along the ridges west of the town, General Heth continued his inexorable advance towards Gettysburg. When the resistance began to stiffen, the general shifted his troops from a marching formation into a line of battle. Davis's Brigade deployed north of the pike, with the 42nd Mississippi holding the right flank of the line.

Wading through the undulating grain fields, the Confederates pushed back a screen of dismounted Federal cavalry and began to ascend the gentle western slope of McPherson's Ridge. As they reached the crest an unexpected sight greeted them—the blue-clad infantrymen of Brigadier General Lysander Cutler's brigade, the vanguard of the Federal First Corps. The two forces met with crashing volleys of musketry. For the next hour intense fighting rolled across the fields adjacent to the Edward McPherson farm and along the bed of an unfinished railroad that ran parallel to the road.

In its first stand-up battle the 42nd sustained a substantial number of casualties. Numbered among the dead were Captain Thomas Clark and Private Albert Henry Clark. After Southern troops emerged victorious later in the day, a soldier, most likely Jonathan Clark, returned to the site and prepared a burial trench for the two Clarks and for another officer, Captain James Gaston of Company G. The names of the deceased were carefully etched upon a crude wooden headboard.

What unbearable anguish Jonathan Clark must have endured! Perhaps mercifully, his sorrow lasted but a brief time. Two days later, he was killed during Pickett's Charge. Ironically, on that very day Ike Clark arrived safely back home completely oblivious to the terrible events that had just transpired in Pennsylvania.

According to a later account by one of her granddaughters, when Margery Clark received the news of the triple tragedy, "she cried and shouted all night long. The greatest sorrow that came into the life of Grandmother Clark was that of giving up her husband and two sons in the cause of freedom."

Her despair was deepened by the fact that she could never visit the graves of her beloved. With a fair degree of accuracy it can be assumed that Union burial parties working after the battle tossed Jonathan's body unceremoniously into a shallow trench near Cemetery Ridge with hundreds of other corpses. A decade later these unidentified Southerners were exhumed and shipped to Hollywood Cemetery in Richmond.

The final disposition of the bodies of Thomas and Albert Clark remains a perplexing mystery to this day. Nearly 25 years after the battle, the following news brief appeared in the *Gettysburg Compiler*:

Relic—Mrs. Clayton Hoke, some time ago, found, near the Chambersburg turnpike, a piece of white pine board, about nine inches square, marked as follows:

Capt. J. M. Gaston.
Capt. T. G. Clark and son.
42nd Miss. Vols.
Killed July 1st, 1863.

The marking is very distinct; looks as if the letters had been cut with a sharp-bladed knife, and the lines afterwards followed by a pointed piece of iron or course wire heated. This notice of the relic is made with the hope that it may meet the eye of someone directly interested.

Considering the care taken to preserve the burial site of these three men it is indeed tragic that no record exits of their removal. For several years after the battle, Dr. John W. C. O'Neal, a prominent Gettysburg physician, took great pains to record the locations of identified Confederate burials that he observed during his travels. For some reason, he failed to make note of the Clark/Gaston site.

In the early 1870s Dr. Rufus Weaver was contracted by several Southern Ladies Memorial Societies to remove the Confederate dead from the area and ship them to various cities in the south for proper burial. Weaver laboriously recorded and tagged the locations and names, if known, of the nearly 3,000 bodies he exhumed in 1872–73. Unfortunately, the three men do not appear on this list, either.

Historian Gregory A. Coco, a leading authority on Confederate burial sites at Gettysburg, surmises that the bodies of these soldiers could have accidentally been mixed in with the many unknowns removed by Weaver's work crew from the vicinity or that they might have long since moldered into the earth at the original burial location. Interestingly, the wooden headboard that once marked their resting place briefly surfaced in Chicago as part of a museum of Civil War memorabilia near the end of the nineteenth century before vanishing away like the bodies it had once mournfully stood over.

Isaac Clark carried on the family tradition of service to the Confederacy when he left home to join a cavalry unit, an act his father had earlier forbidden. Not only did Isaac survive the war but he also lived seven decades afterwards, dying in 1936 at the age of 89. Wounded and captured on the opening day at Gettysburg, Marcellus Church, Thomas Clark's half brother, later died in the prison camp at Point Lookout, Maryland.

The postwar years were extremely difficult ones for Margery Clark. Although doing the best she could to raise the remaining children and to keep the farm up and running, she was eventually forced to sell much of the property to pay off mounting debts. Her final years were spent living in the home of one of her sons until she passed away in 1918.

Today, no vestige of the Clark farm and mill remains, though the bittersweet memories of its former occupants hang thickly, like a hot summer day in Mississippi. Less than ten miles from the old homestead resides Mr. Charlie Clark, the great grandson of Captain Thomas Goode Clark. As a young boy Charlie fondly recalls reading the Civil War letters of his ancestors while visiting his grandmother. Over the years he has carefully preserved the history of his family and their great sacrifice at Gettysburg.

In a detailed article authored by Mr. Clark in 2000, he concludes with a poignant comment on the now sacred headboard: "The family continues the search for this little marker, which is so representative of the tragic loss sustained by families on both sides of the conflict."

Elias and DeGrasse Hanness, USA

When the Union war effort took a decided turn for the worse during the summer of 1862, President Lincoln issued calls for 600,000 new troops. Ironically, a little over a year earlier, following the firing on Fort Sumter, patriotic fervor ran so high throughout the north that thousands of would-be volunteers were turned away. But predictions of a quick victory had long since dissipated and the glory and adventure so eagerly sought by the patriots of 1861 remained elusive. Thus, for the men who answered Lincoln's call in 1862, the prospect of military service was a sobering thought indeed.

To put some teeth into the president's proclamation, a quota of troops was assigned to each loyal state. These state quotas were divided into county quotas, and then subdivided into borough and township quotas. In order to satisfy these requirements, state and local governments commonly offered cash bounties to the new recruits. The legislation also authorized drafts as a final measure of compliance.

In New York State, Oswego County responded to the call by raising the 147th New York for a three-year enlistment term. Situated upon the shores of Lake Ontario about 135 miles from the state capital of Albany, Oswego County stretched for over 1,000 square miles in the rural western part of the state. Agricultural enterprises and small manufacturing establishments constituted the bulk of the economy. The numerous tributaries that flowed into the lake provided ample power for a variety of mills. In fact, by 1860, the county led the state in flour production.

Not surprisingly, the majority of the men who formed the 147th New York worked in some farm-related occupation, hence the nickname, "The Plowboys." The regiment also had a distinct ethnic flavor, with entire companies being of either German or Irish descent. Most of the recruits of Company C resided near the small village of Richland. This locale could boast of 19 sawmills, 8 shingle mills, 6 flour and gristmills, and 2 paper mills, many of them operating along the banks of the aptly named Grindstone Creek.

In April 1855, 36-year-old Elias Hanness settled in the Richland area with his wife Ann, age 32, and their four children. It is likely that Elias derived his living as a farmer and miller. On September 27, 1862, Ann Hanness paid a tearful farewell to her husband and her 19-year-old son Degrasse when they departed for Elmira, New York with the newly formed 147th New York.

Over 800 strong, the New Yorkers arrived in Washington two days later and became part of the city's extensive network of defenses. Later that fall, the regiment shipped out for duty at Aquia Creek, the location of a major Union supply base near Fredericksburg, Virginia, where it served as part of the provost guard. Finally, in March of 1863, the 147th received orders to join the four veteran regiments of General Lysander Cutler's brigade, officially known as the Second Brigade, First Division, First Corps, Army of the Potomac. Having played only a limited role at the Battle of Chancellorsville, the 147th New York was still considered an untried unit as the Federal army pushed relentlessly northward in mid–June in pursuit of Lee's forces.

Throughout their nine months of service it is almost certain that Elias and DeGrasse Hanness sent and received a steady stream of letters from home. Unfortunately, none of them have survived through the intervening years so we can only speculate as to their contents. In all likelihood they were similar to those mailed by Thomas Clark and his sons, expressing a longing for home and love and concern for those that remained there.

What is known is that the members of the 147th faced terror and carnage in the fields west of Gettysburg on the morning of July 1 as they encountered General Davis's Confederates, including the 42nd Mississippi. The regiment's baptism by fire took place under desperate circumstances. An officer from the 147th recalled, "While we were advancing in the wheatfield the battle opened on our right, and the bullets from the enemy were flying thick and fast as we marched rapidly towards our opponents. The wheat heads fell with rapid noddings, as the bullets from the Confederate line commenced their harvest of death."

Purely by chance, Davis's battle line extended a considerable distance beyond the right flank of Cutler's men. The opportunistic Southerners took advantage of the situation and poured in a hot fire along the entire length of the exposed Union formation. In response, Cutler sent orders directing his troops to fall back to a more sheltered location.

Unfortunately for the 147th, their commander sustained a wound to his throat before he could convey the order, and due to their advanced position and the topography, the men failed to observe the withdrawal of their sister regiments. Unaware of their fate, the now isolated New Yorkers gamely slugged it out with elements of three Confederate units. The rapidly shrinking line gradually evolved into an inverted v-shape to fend off the converging enemy forces.

Finally, after nearly a half-hour of this unequal contest, a courier rode into the maelstrom and delivered the retreat order. The survivors dashed eastward through the railroad cut and along the adjacent fields. The regiment's magnificent stand had come at a horrific price. Out of 380 officers and men that entered the fray, 207 were struck by enemy bullets, including 44 killed and 163 wounded.

Degrasse Hanness was killed instantly during this action and his father received a mortal wound. Elias would linger for two more weeks before he died at the Spangler's Warehouse Hospital, which was located across from the railroad depot on Carlisle Street. He was initially buried in the Presbyterian graveyard in Gettysburg but was later removed to the Soldiers' National Cemetery (A-142, New York plot). Evidently DeGrasse was placed in an unmarked grave and the present location of his remains is not known. It is likely that he now rests in an "unknown" plot near his father.

When news of the 147th New York's demise reached Richland, it triggered a long and painful odyssey for Ann Hanness. Historian J. Howard Wert, a teenager at the time of the battle, wrote the following account of Mrs. Hanness in a 1907 newspaper article:

> Amongst the earliest arrivals on that field of death was the stricken mother. With difficulty she obtained from the Harrisburg provost marshal a permit to continue her journey. She walked ten miles through the mud from New Oxford to Gettysburg and found a home in the house of that noble man, David Warren, of Carlisle Street, whose latch string was ever out, through this whole period of calamity, to those who searched for their loved ones.
>
> Her husband mortally wounded had been carried into a private house and had already breathed his last. Her son could nowhere be found. She searched over miles and miles of hospitals, in fields and barns, in churches and warehouses. She enlisted hundreds in the quest.
>
> Then, with a lifelong grief in that gentle heart, she turned to the suffering crowd around her and went to the Second Corps field hospital where thousands moaned as they hovered between life and death. Daily as a volunteer nurse she passed from cot to cot, prayed with the dying, soothed the anguish of the living; yet all the time hoping against hope that, in some mysterious way, she would find that lost son.

Following her daily work at the hospital, Mrs. Hanness often visited the farmhouse of Adam and Catherine Wert near the Baltimore Pike. She made a lasting impression upon their son, the aforementioned J. Howard Wert, who described her as "a woman with a pleasant face, auburn hair, and clear blue eyes, who, despite the sadness she carried, always had a cheerful word and a subdued smile for all."

Ann Hanness is listed in the 1865 census of Oswego County as a resident of Richland living with two of her children and a nine-year-old female border. Son Oscar, about 13 when his father and older brother died, matured into a successful businessman, first as a miller and later as the proprietor of the Lewis House in the nearby city of Fulton. In 1867, Ann Hanness married Elijah Fairchild, a widower with five children. The following year she gave birth to a son.

Charlie Clark's comment that the wooden headboard that once marked the grave of his ancestors represented "the tragic loss sustained by families on both sides of the conflict" is remarkably poignant given the many similarities that existed between the Clark family of Mississippi and the Hannesses of New York. Therein lies the tragedy.

2

Mothers and Sons

God could not be everywhere, and therefore he made mothers.
Jewish Proverb

All that I am, or hope to be, I owe to my angel mother.
Abraham Lincoln

Margery and Andrew Tucker, USA

The scene described by the *Union County Star and Lewisburg Chronicle* on August 29, 1862, was repeated often in many Northern communities throughout the war:

> The greatest crowd ever assembled at the Lewisburg Depot, was on Tuesday morning last, when the companies raised principally by Messrs. Crotzer and Merrill took the cars for Harrisburg.... We observed very many spectators in tears—mothers and children, in some cases, of those who were going to danger, and possibly to death—and also strong men, "all unused to the melting mood."

In the midst of this crowd of anxious onlookers stood a middle-aged widow by the name of Margery Gregg Tucker. Mrs. Tucker was undoubtedly one of the many spectators affected by the "melting mood" of the moment as she watched her only son, Andrew Gregg Tucker, go off to war.

Less than a month earlier, the slender, handsome seventeen-year-old had marched with nine classmates to Commencement Hall of the University at Lewisburg (modern-day Bucknell University), where he received his bachelor of arts diploma and graduated with the class of 1862. It was noted that this class comprised "several most promising characters, and the best wishes of very many go with them all as they now enter upon the more public and responsible duties of life."

For young Tucker, the most paramount of duties entailed service to his imperiled country, and immediately following his graduation, he helped to recruit a company of volunteers from Union County in response to President Lincoln's call for additional troops. It is doubtful, however, that the young man needed any stimulus to offer his services for the Union cause. His family tree was filled with notable examples of civic and military service. Andrew was named in honor of his distinguished grandfather, U.S. Senator Andrew Gregg, of Bellefonte, Pennsylvania. His first cousin was Pennsylvania governor Andrew Gregg Curtin, and two other cousins, David McMurtrie Gregg and John Irvin Gregg, served as generals in the Army of the Potomac's Cavalry Corps.

Andrew's father, the Reverend Charles Tucker, pastor of the First Tabernacle Baptist Church in Philadelphia, had died in 1850. After his death, the Tucker family relocated to Lewisburg, a small central Pennsylvania community of about 3,000 residents, where Andrew and his two older sisters were educated at the university.

Tucker and his comrades were mustered into Federal service as Company E of the 142nd Pennsylvania Volunteers at Camp Curtin in Harrisburg, Pennsylvania. During this organizational phase, the popular and intelligent teenager was elected second lieutenant. The green recruits fought their maiden battle at Fredericksburg on December 13, where the 142nd lost 250 men in the morning's battle south of the town.

Following the Union defeat at Chancellorsville the following spring Tucker authored a resolution that appeared in the May 22 edition of the *Chronicle*. The statement affirmed that Tucker and his comrades

Andrew Gregg Tucker, University at Lewisburg, Class of 1862 (courtesy Special Collections/University Archives, Ellen Clarke Bertrand Library, Bucknell University).

in Company E would not "shirk from dangers and death in defence of our principles." This devotion would be tested two months later on the bloody fields of Gettysburg.

By the time the Union army pushed north to head off Lee's invasion of Pennsylvania, Tucker had been promoted to first lieutenant and acting regimental adjutant. Captain Charles Evans, his immediate superior and former classmate, remarked that he "was the most brilliant one I ever saw and was fast developing into a man."

Arriving at Gettysburg during the late morning of July 1, the 142nd lined up with other units to form a defensive position along McPherson's Ridge west of the town. Later in the day, the onrushing North Carolinians of General James J. Pettigrew's Brigade overwhelmed the Union defenders. As the line began to crumble from the increasing pressure, the 142nd launched a desperate counterattack, but enemy fire "mowed down" the Pennsylvanians and "shot the whole to pieces."

Mounted on horseback, Tucker presented a conspicuous mark. During the initial volley, he was shot in the right forearm and his horse severely disabled. Captain Evans begged, then ordered him to go to the rear. Instead, the young adjutant remained with the regiment, "cheering and urging the men by going into the thickest of the fight himself."

Nearby, Lieutenant Jeremiah Hoffman was incapacitated when a shell fragment cut through his pelvis and lodged near his spine. Tucker pushed Hoffman onto his wounded mount and sent him off to the nearby Lutheran Theological Seminary, where Union surgeons operated a primary aid station. He and the rest of the 142nd Pennsylvania began to fall back toward the Seminary as well, making a final stand there before retreating through the town to Cemetery Hill.

During the brief battle on Seminary Ridge, a ball struck Tucker in the middle of the upper back. While being assisted toward the Seminary for treatment, another round penetrated his lower back and entered his bowels. The severely wounded officer finally reached the four-story brick sanctuary, which was rapidly filling with the bodies of torn and bleeding soldiers. A surgeon examined his wounds and pronounced them to be mortal. "I am a very young man, but I am willing to die for my country," replied Tucker.

He clung to life long enough to learn of the Union triumph. On Sunday morning, July 5, at 3:00 a.m., Andrew Tucker's struggle for life ended. His last thoughts were with his family: "I would like to see my mother and sisters, but I never will."

Tucker was deeply mourned by his comrades. "Andrew was brave, very brave, and acted well the part of a soldier," lamented Evans. Another member of the regiment remembered him as "a friend I prized so highly ... a hero and a Christian, who suffered and died for his country without a murmur."

Captain Evans remained by Andrew's side until his death and then attended to his burial in the garden outside the Seminary. Lieutenant Hoffman, who may have owed his life to Tucker's selflessness, vividly recalled this melancholy event:

Lieutenant Andrew Gregg Tucker, 1862 (courtesy Special Collections/University Archives, Ellen Clarke Bertrand Library, Bucknell University).

They roughly lined his grave with fence palings and buried him beside the Colonel. I was then lying on the bunk, and by lifting my head could see into the garden.... They were holding the body over the grave when the head slipped over the edge of the blanket and the lieutenant's beautiful, jet black hair dragged over the ground. The thought of his mother and sisters was called up, and surely it cannot be called unmanly that a few tears stole down my cheeks.

After learning of her son's wounding, Margery Tucker, in company with the Reverend Stephen Mirick, professor George Bliss, and university president Justin Loomis, started for the battlefield to care for the Union County soldiers. After an arduous journey, the party finally reached Gettysburg. They beheld a shocking scene. The debris of battle was strewn everywhere, marking the lines of the vicious struggle. Piles of amputated limbs were massed around the buildings used as field hospitals and the stench of decaying flesh blanketed the area.

Bucknell faculty of 1874. Sitting, left to right: Professor George Bliss and University President Justin Loomis; standing, left to right: Professor Francis W. Tustin, Professor Robert Lowry, and Professor Charles S. James (courtesy Special Collections/University Archives, Ellen Clarke Bertrand Library, Bucknell University).

The grave of Andrew G. Tucker in the Lewisburg Cemetery, Lewisburg, Pennsylvania.

One can only imagine Mrs. Tucker's shock and grief upon discovering her son's freshly made grave and its wooden headboard upon which his name and regiment were carefully etched. Andrew's remains arrived back in Lewisburg by the same route he had taken to the seat of war less than a year earlier. The body was laid to rest on the peaceful slope of the Lewisburg Cemetery adjacent to the university in the presence of a large and mourning congregation. The university alumni immediately passed a series of resolutions that displayed their esteem for the young hero while expressing their sorrow that one so young had been cut down in the very opening of his manhood.

Grief revisited Margery Tucker again just a year later when daughter Martha died at the age of 22. The legacy of her only son lived on. When Lewisburg Civil War veterans formed a Grand Army of the Republic Post in 1867, they named it in honor of Andrew Gregg Tucker. On August 20, 1873, Dr. Loomis, who had accompanied Mrs. Tucker to Gettysburg, married her oldest daughter, Augusta. The couple named their first born Andrew Gregg Loomis.

Caroline and Henry Chancellor, USA

Throughout the summer and fall of 1862, recruiting officers throughout the North pulled out all of the stops to attract potential soldiers. The citizens of Philadelphia witnessed one of the more creative schemes in mid–August as the companies that would later be formed into the 150th Pennsylvania scrambled to fill up their rosters. The regimental historian described this colorful incident:

> To further the work of obtaining men an expedient was adopted ... which resulted most satisfactorily. A huge furniture car of the platform variety was hired for the purpose, tastefully decorated with the national colors, and showily placarded with appeals to "Enlist in the Bucktail Brigade!" From poles planted in the body of the van hung a seductive array of bucktails to be bestowed upon the expected recruits. With ample provision of horses and martial music, this gigantic vehicle ... began its journey through the principal streets, attracting attention wherever it appeared.... Its progress was a triumph, bringing resolution to many who had been balancing between the desire to serve their country and indisposition to leave their homes and families. The car rolled on to the music of the drums and fifes, which grew in intensity at every moment, catching the spirit of the recruiting officers, whose appeals could have scarcely have been more impassioned if they had been preaching a new religion. By nightfall many men had been gathered in, to whom the record of the original

bucktails was familiar, and who were proud to decorate their hats with an emblem so favorably known in our own army and so highly respected—if not feared—by the enemy.

The original "Bucktails," known variously as the 1st Pennsylvania Rifles, the 13th Pennsylvania Reserves, and the 42nd Pennsylvania Infantry, had already earned a reputation as an elite fighting force after experiencing severe combat during the Peninsula Campaign and in the Shenandoah Valley. Composed mainly of backwoodsmen and lumbermen from the northern tier of the Keystone State, these rugged individuals often served as skirmishers and in other front line duties that utilized their superb marksmanship abilities. These soldiers wore a distinctive badge on their kepis—a deer tail—making them instantly recognizable by both friend and foe.

Hoping to build upon this success, Governor Andrew Curtin heartily approved a proposal by Major Roy Stone to recruit an entire brigade of Bucktails. This effort yielded two regiments, the 149th Pennsylvania (Second Bucktails) and the 150th Pennsylvania (Third Bucktails). Not surprisingly, these newcomers drew the disdain of their predecessors, who derisively dubbed them the "bogus bucktails."

In some respects, this unflattering sobriquet accurately described some of the members of the 150th Pennsylvania. Four full companies of this regiment hailed from the streets of Philadelphia, far from the state's mountain region. Nevertheless, many of these city slickers became excellent soldiers. In August 1863 one city newspaper observed: "It has been proved, to the surprise of many, that the young men in our counting-houses, stores, offices, etc., frequently short in stature and slight in proportions ... all unused to muscular labor, make among the best soldiers in the field! They stand the marches as well, submit without complaining to the hardest and scantiest fare of the soldier, and fight as bravely and unflinchingly as the best. We should not have believed this, had it not been repeated to us over and over again by eyewitnesses."

The primary example cited by the writer was that of Henry Chancellor, Jr. Born in the City of Brotherly Love on June 23, 1842, he was the youngest son of Caroline and Henry Chancellor, Sr., "a wealthy and estimable citizen." Reared in the luxury of a spacious home in the Germantown section of the city, the young man received a fine education at a classical school in Lawrenceville, New Jersey, where his kind and gentle ways endeared him to his teachers and schoolmates.

But the slender boy was of delicate health, having suffered from asthma since his birth. Perhaps for this reason he was something of a "momma's boy." Caroline Chancellor recalled that he was never separated from her until the time he boarded at his school. Therefore, his parents must have looked on suspiciously when their 20-year-old son entered the army as second lieutenant of Company B, 150th Pennsylvania, in August of 1862. Within three months, however, Chancellor's intelligence and perseverance earned him a promotion to first lieutenant.

Due to poor health Lieutenant Chancellor was granted a ten-day furlough just before the Army of the Potomac took up the pursuit of Lee's army in mid–June 1863. The young officer refused it, however, and in the midst of the grueling marches that would lead through Maryland and into his native state, he proclaimed, "My country first, if God spares me I will go home in July."

On the opening day at Gettysburg, Stone's brigade, consisting of the 150th as well as the 143rd and 149th Pennsylvania, occupied an advanced position near the center of the Union First Corps line near the farm of Edward McPherson. The untried Bucktails fought tenaciously throughout the early afternoon as they fended off attacks from two different directions. Near the climax of the battle Lieutenant Chancellor remained in an exposed position, encouraging his men amid a shower of bullets until one of the missiles thudded into his leg, badly fracturing the limb.

In the face of overwhelming numbers Stone's troops slowly retired eastward along the Chambersburg Pike. The orchards and fields surrounding the farm were thickly strewn with the dead, while many of the wounded, including Lieutenant Chancellor, fell into enemy hands. At some point before the end of the battle the wounded officer was picked up by an ambulance detail and transported to the Lutheran Theological Seminary.

The 300 wounded Union POWs left behind at this facility received precious little food, water, or medical attention during the Confederate occupation of Seminary Ridge from July 1 to the evening of July 4. Five sultry days elapsed before Chancellor's mangled leg was finally removed. During this trying ordeal the Philadelphia native suffered patiently without uttering a complaint.

His courageous conduct earned him the respect of his roommate, Lieutenant Colonel George F. McFarland, 151st Pennsylvania, who had also lost a leg as a result of the battle. Naturally, a close bond developed between the two men. McFarland recalled later:

> It was my fortune to lay in the same room, eat the same food, and receive the same attendance with this brave boy for several weeks after the battle. While there with him I learned to admire his fortitude under sufferings and privations that would have crushed the spirit of men of sterner mold and stronger frame.... The patient, cheerful, hopeful manner in which he conducted himself would have done credit to the strongest and bravest veteran, and could not fail to elicit the admiration and win the sympathies of those around him.

George's wife, Addie, arrived at Gettysburg a week after the battle with the couple's two young children, and Henry Chancellor quickly became a member of the family. Thanks in part to Addie's tender ministrations, the lieutenant's stump healed rapidly throughout the month of July and he appeared lively and hopeful. When a friend paid him a visit at the hospital, he remarked, "Harry, your fighting days are over now," to which the gritty officer responded, "Yes, I'm afraid they are, but I should like to have one crack at the Rebels yet."

Then, suddenly, near the beginning of August, Chancellor began to sink rapidly and on the sixth of that month he died, probably of tetanus, gangrene, or some other postoperative infection. His loss came as a severe blow to his aged parents and his large circle of friends, who had felt assured of his recovery. "Among the noble youth who were mortally wounded at Gettysburg, there were none whose death affected me more deeply," lamented George McFarland. A veteran officer in the 150th memorialized Chancellor in his regimental history: "He had hardly passed the limits of boyhood, but in intelligence, courtesy, courage and all the traits which constitute a useful and efficient officer, he had few superiors."

Five days after his death, Henry Chancellor, Jr., finally came home. His remains were embalmed and interred with military honors in the family vault at St. Peter's Church, located on Third and Pine streets in Philadelphia. Among those present on the mournful occasion was Colonel Langhorn Wister, the commander of the 150th Pennsylvania, and Captain George W. Jones, Chancellor's immediate superior.

After his wife and children returned home at the end of August, Lieutenant Colonel McFarland beseeched Addie to write Mrs. Chancellor "while your feelings are yet warm." This proved to be timely advice. Following on the heels of their son's unexpected death at Gettysburg, the family endured two additional back to back tragedies. Mr. Chancellor's only sister passed away on October 19. At the same time, his niece caught a severe illness while traveling to reach her side, the effects from which she would not recover.

On Thanksgiving morning Caroline Chancellor opened an envelope which contained two very welcome letters from Mr. and Mrs. McFarland. She wrote back to Addie, "Your kindness to my beloved precious boy I can never be thankful enough to you for. You knew my brave child and formed a lasting attachment to him.... I shall always look upon you & welcome you as a relative."

Her deep anguish poured out onto the pages: "My precious child was taken from me, the silver cord is loosed that bound him to me, the bright flower has been plucked from the garden of my affection only to bloom again, transplanted in the garden of paradise."

She despaired that she could never recover from this loss. Almost everything reminded her of Henry, evoking a flood of memories that rushed over her in angry waves and nearly swept away her sanity. When the ladies of Germantown prepared a bountiful Thanksgiving dinner for the sick and convalescent soldiers at a nearby hospital, Caroline confessed, "I could not go there, my heart bleeds whenever I see any of the poor soldiers and the [sound of] the drum almost drives me crazy. I am sick and miserable."

But there was a ray of hope that pierced through her melancholy. On October 31 her daughter gave birth to a healthy baby boy, whom she named Henry. A friend of the family wrote, "I hope he may inherit the noble brave heart of the dear boy who distinguished the name he left as his earthly inheritance." Thus the names of two young Pennsylvania officers, both of whom died at the Seminary, Andrew Tucker and Henry Chancellor, lived on.

Elizabeth and Joseph Kinnier, USA

During the late afternoon of July 2, 1863, the orderly, well-groomed peach orchard opposite the farm house of Joseph Sherfy erupted into a fiery inferno as the Union gunners posted there dueled with their Confederate counterparts at close range. The deafening roar of the guns shattered the usual stillness of a lazy Pennsylvania summer day. After a few discharges, ghostly white smoke enshrouded the orchard. Shells exploded overhead, showering the area with sprays of deadly iron. Other missiles caromed through the rows of trees, splintering the stocky trunks and severing the fruit-laden branches.

Instinctively, the soldiers of Brigadier General Charles K. Graham's brigade flattened themselves upon the grass. As the concussions of the belching iron monsters vibrated through their prostrate bodies, the infantrymen frantically scooped up the rich earth with their bayonets and piled it in front of them.

Graham's six Pennsylvania regiments occupied the midpoint of Major General Daniel E. Sickles' battle line after the impetuous commander had repositioned his Third Corps troops to seize the high ground that rose near the Peach Orchard along the Emmitsburg Road. This bold move isolated his command from the remainder of the army and created a salient near the orchard that would be vulnerable to attack from several directions.

Colonel Calvin A. Craig's 105th Pennsylvania, known as the "Wildcat Regiment," formed a short distance northeast of the Sherfy house with its right flank resting on a farm lane. Recruited from the western Pennsylvania region in the fall of 1861, the Wildcats were no strangers to combat. During the Peninsula Campaign in the spring of 1862 the regiment served under the hard-fighting General Phil Kearny. The 105th was heavily engaged at Fair Oaks and throughout the Seven Days' Battles and then saw action at Second Bull Run, Fredericksburg, and Chancellorsville.

Shortly after 6:00 p.m. on July 2, Brigadier General William Barksdale's 1,600 Mississippians emerged from the cover of Pitzer's Woods on Seminary Ridge and rushed towards the Peach Orchard with a shrill Rebel yell. Graham's troops rose up to meet them and the opposing lines crashed together. Perhaps unnerved by the artillery barrage, the Pennsylvanians could do little to stop the momentum of the Confederate onslaught, and the resistance evaporated.

Positioned on the far right of the brigade line, the 105th Pennsylvania was the last of Graham's regiments to retreat. Colonel Craig formed his 274 officers and men across the road in an effort to halt Barksdale's drive, but the Southerners quickly lapped around the regiment's left flank and poured in a murderous fire. According to Craig, his men rallied eight or ten times as they were slowly driven back.

This unflinching discipline came at a steep price, as the regiment lost nearly half of its strength that fateful afternoon. During the fighting withdrawal, Sergeant Joseph Kinnier, a member of Company I and a recipient of the Kearny Cross for his bravery at Chancellorsville, was shot in the left thigh. The ball passed upward and lodged deep inside his abdomen.

As the decimated units of the Third Corps regrouped on Cemetery Ridge, reinforcements arrived just in time to drive back the victorious Confederates. When darkness settled in, ambulance details scoured the bloody fields in search of the wounded, and surgeons labored tirelessly by the light of overhanging lanterns in makeshift hospitals established in barns and farmhouses along the Taneytown Road.

Private James Hawthorne found his cousin, Sergeant Kinnier, lying wounded on the wet ground near the division hospital. He procured some straw, erected a shelter tent, and placed Joseph and another wounded comrade inside. The sergeant exclaimed, "I am willing to suffer all my pain if the Rebels are defeated." His comrades purchased bread and milk for him from an old farmer who resided nearby.

Realizing the mortal nature of his wounds, Kinnier cried out, "This will be a hard blow on my mother and sisters at home." During a severe paroxysm of pain he moaned, "Oh, that my mother or my dear sisters were here to pour water on my wound!" As tears streamed down his face, he closed his eyes in prayer. Later that evening, he uttered his final words to his cousin, "Well, Jim, I think I have done my duty, in this war, to my country."

Sergeant Isaiah Davis wrote Elizabeth Kinnier, the deceased soldier's mother: "He has fallen in defence of the God-given rights of man, and not only is his name enrolled as one among the bravest of his country's defenders, but it is also written in the Lamb's book of life. I, who lay with him upon the tented field ... heard his prayers, like incense, ascend to his heavenly Father for you, for his country, as well as himself."

Captain James Hamilton, who was not with his company at Gettysburg due to a wound he received at Fredericksburg, also sent a letter of condolence upon learning the news. "It was with a deep pang of regret that I heard of his fall, while nobly defending the soil of his native state," he wrote. "Joseph was always my favorite. At Fredericksburg it was all I could do to keep him from going ahead, and when I fell, he was the first to offer me assistance."

Both Davis and Hamilton would be killed in action by the following summer. During its four years of service, 202 men, 59 of which were drafted men and substitutes, enrolled in Company I. From this total, 47 were killed or mortally wounded, the largest number sustained by any company in the regiment.

The remains of Joseph Kinnier were brought home to Jefferson County and buried at the Beaver Run Church near Stanton, Pennsylvania, where he loved to worship before the call to arms led him away from his boyhood haunts. He was 21 at the time of his death. His mother, who had been widowed over 11 years earlier, died in 1884 at the age of 73.

Patience and Jeremiah Sanders Gage, CSA

During the Civil War, institutions of higher learning throughout the land contributed their fair share of soldiers to both the Union and the Confederacy. Comprised mainly of students or recent graduates of the University of Mississippi in Oxford, the University Greys were among the most famous of these scholarly outfits. The young men from "Ole Miss" became Company A of the 11th Mississippi Infantry, a regiment that would go on to earn a distinguished place in the annals of American military history. On the final day at Gettysburg, this unit suffered more casualties than any other regiment in the Army of Northern Virginia.

This potential had not been foreseeable during its formation back in May of 1861. "No more disorderly mob of men were ever got together to make an army," confessed a member of the University Greys. Another soldier was more flattering, boasting that the ranks were "made up in large measure from the choicest spirits of the state—intelligent, honorable, and brave."

Perhaps no man in the regiment displayed these attributes more fully than Jeremiah Sanders Gage. The son of a prosperous planter and slaveholder, he grew up with his seven sisters and four brothers in Holmes County, Mississippi. Matthew Gage, Jr., died prior to the Civil War, but he left ample provision for his family and his slaves. Jeremiah's mother, Patience Williams Sanders Gage, was described as "an artist with brush and needle."

After graduating from the literary department of the University of Mississippi, Jeremiah Gage entered law school there at Oxford in the fall of 1860. But the following spring he placed his aspirations on hold and signed on with many of his fellow scholars as a member of the University Greys.

There can be no doubt that "Jere" Gage was a big man on campus. A sunburned blond with a strong and ruddy countenance framed by the muscular physique of an athlete, he possessed a singular self-confidence. A deferential politeness and his steadfast, gray-blue eyes tempered these striking physical attributes.

Jeremiah Sanders Gage, 1861 (University of Mississippi, Archives and Special Collections).

Private Gage immediately displayed a reckless courage on the battlefield. Comrade Richard Lipsey related: "J. S. Gage was in First Manassas, Williamsburg and at Seven Pines where we were under a furious fusillade of canister and grape shot.... The order given to lie down was quickly obeyed, except by Colonel Frank Liddell and Jere Gage, who had seventeen bullet holes through his clothes. He did not know what fear was." Gage suffered a severe hip wound a short time later during the battle at Gaines' Mill on June 27, 1862. From that point forward he walked with a noticeable limp.

At the outset of the Gettysburg campaign it appeared as though Gage's military career was near its end. In a letter written to his sister from Fredericksburg on June 10, 1863, Gage expressed delight in the fact that his bother-in-law had nearly completed a negotiation for a hired substitute to take his place and that the colonel of the 11th Mississippi had consented to the arrangement. Either the deal fell through or the army moved off before the transaction took place because Gage was still in the ranks when the Southern army marched into Pennsylvania.

When Heth's Division marched towards Gettysburg on the early morning of July 1, the 11th Mississippi remained behind to guard the division's wagon train at Cashtown. By this stroke of good fortune the regiment avoided the fate of the remainder of Davis's Brigade at the Railroad Cut. Rejoining their comrades on July 2, the nearly 600 members of the 11th would more than compensate for their absence by the end of the next day.

As eight battered brigades of A. P. Hill's Corps assembled to the left of Pickett's Virginians, the Mississippi regiment suffered its first casualties at Gettysburg during the heavy cannonade preceding the July 3 charge. To Hugh Q. Bridges of the University Greys the very ground seemed "to shake from the plunge of solid shot and the detonations of bursting, shrieking shells, which appeared to rake and search out every square yard of the ground we occupied." Bridges noted that most of the men were in a lying position with the notable exception of the officers and Private Gage.

Suddenly, a shell exploded in front of the 11th Mississippi. One of the fragments ripped through Gage's left arm while another pierced his abdomen. Private James Dailey and three other litter bearers gathered up the wounded soldier and dashed off to the nearest aid station. About 200 yards to the south, at a large stone barn, they found assistant surgeons Dr. Joseph Holt and Dr. LeGrand Wilson, along with a Dr. Shields, waiting for the inevitable onslaught of mangled bodies.

As the first rescue party of the day neared the barn, the young soldier on the litter raised his head and exclaimed loudly, "Doctor, they have got Jere Gage at last. I thought I would go through safely, but they have got me." After being placed upon a makeshift examining table, Gage asked that the doctors be truthful concerning his condition.

Discovering that his patient's left arm had been nearly severed between the elbow and the shoulder, Holt offered an encouraging remark. In response, Gage smiled and said, "Why, Doctor that is nothing; here is where I am really hurt," as he peeled back a blanket from his lower abdomen to reveal a hideous sight. Another piece of shell had struck his left side near the stomach, tearing away a rib, the entire bladder, much of the intestine, and part of the pelvis, leaving only a twisted mass of tissue and bone.

Despite the ghastly nature of his wounds, Holt was awestruck by the attractiveness and manliness of the soldier as well as the tender devotion displayed by his litter bearers. "No word or detail of this scene has faded from my memory," recalled Holt. "There was no thought of the dramatic; it was dreadfully genuine and naturally spontaneous, in the unconscious creating and acting of a grander tragedy than we might ever hope to play."

"Doctor, how long have I to live?" asked Gage in a calm voice.

"A very few hours."

"Doctor, I am in great agony; let me die easy, dear Doctor; I would do the same for you."

It appeared to Holt that the very soul of the dying soldier peered out from the depths of his eyes in an appeal of anguish that cut him to the heart.

"You dear, noble fellow, I will see to it that you shall die easy."

The doctor called to one of his assistants to bring him a concentrated solution of opium, which he mixed with some water in a tin cup. Just before offering the drug to his patient, a thought flashed into Holt's mind. "Have you no message to leave?" he asked.

For the first time, Gage's composure left him. "My mother, O, my darling mother, how could I have forgotten you? Quick! I want to write," he cried out in a low wail. A pencil and a sheet of paper were secured and the smooth lid of a hospital knapsack improvised as a desk. As Dr. Holt supported him and the small group of onlookers wept silently, Gage hastily scrawled his final message:

> This is the last time you may ever hear from me. I have time to tell you that I died like a man. Bear my loss the best you can. Remember that I am true to my country and my greatest regret at dying is that she is not free and that you and my sisters are robbed of my worth, whatever that may be. I hope this will reach you and you must not regret that my body cannot be obtained. It is a mere matter of form anyhow.... This letter is stained with my blood.

He softly repeated the last line and pressed the back of the letter upon his oozing wound before handing it over to Holt. After being handed the cup of opium, Gage feebly waved it as he called out, "Come around, boys, and let us have a toast. I do not invite you to drink with me, but I drink the toast to you, and to the Southern Confederacy, and to victory!" Gage then requested Jim Dailey to bury him in his old shawl. It was the fashion of the boys at the University to wear shawls in lieu of topcoats, and it was this garment that would become his winding sheet.

As he slowly drifted in and out of consciousness from the effects of chloroform and liquid sedatives, Gage gurgled, "How dark it grows. Come nearer, boys. I can't see you, but take my hand, each one of you, so I can feel that you are all near me." Next he made his friends promise to bury him deep "so the beasts won't get me."

As the shattered columns of Southern soldiers drifted back to Seminary Ridge, Holt laid aside the cover from the face of the 23-year-old soldier and discovered that his spirit had departed. "His death surpassed in tenderness of love, in philosophical resignation, in courage and willing sacrifice of self, if it were possible, even that of Socrates, as revealed to us in the Phaedo," proclaimed Holt. Although the team of doctors witnessed numerous personal tragedies throughout the day and well into the evening, Dr. Wilson later admitted that the loss of Gage "wrung our hearts with anguish and blinded our eyes from weeping for many days."

Upon reaching Virginia, Holt mailed the letter entrusted to him to Mrs. Gage in Richland, Mississippi. She would not be the only one receiving a sad missive. The 11th Mississippi had the distinction of suffering more casualties on July 3 than any other regiment in the Army of Northern Virginia. The unit lost 103 killed, 166 wounded, and 41 captured, nearly all of these losses incurred in the space of one hour during the assault. Of the 31 members of the University Greys present at Gettysburg, 14 were killed and 17 wounded.

Jeremiah Gage could have easily been just another faceless statistic, the courage and humility of his final moments lost forever, had it not been for the reminiscences of Dr. Holt that appeared in the *New Orleans Times-Democrat* near the fiftieth anniversary of the Battle of Gettysburg. Following the war, Holt served as the professor of obstetrics at his alma mater, the New Orleans School of Medicine, and was later named president of the Louisiana state board of health. Despite these accomplishments and the passage of time, he could never forget the heroic death of one Mississippi soldier on that historic July afternoon in 1863, and much of his account was devoted to this subject.

Holt's vivid description stirred the interest of many readers, particularly Virgie Gage Armistead, a resident of 2616 Royal Street and the youngest sibling of Jeremiah Gage. Recalling many details of the story, Mrs. Armistead immediately wrote to the doctor and asked him to confirm that it was indeed her brother that he wrote of in his piece. "I was such a small child when he enlisted that I do not remember him at all, but I know the story of his life and death from others," she related.

A special messenger personally delivered Holt's reply across town. It read in part:

> That you, his sister, have announced his name, from this time hence the story of his departure will live in cherished memories of the Southern people, and as part of the common heritage of the magnanimity and valor of American manhood in even balance. He needs no tablature in marble, brass or bronze. That you are his sister, I profoundly congratulate you, madam, and myself in being the medium of information.

A follow-up article appeared in the June 29, 1913, issue of the *Times-Democrat* accompanied by a photo of Gage during his college days and a reproduction of the hastily scrawled letter to his mother. The gracious, refined, and soft-spoken Mrs. Armistead told a reporter, "It is such a wonderful thing to have read ... the story of how our brother died. It brought all the recollections back—how our mother tried to find his grave, and the stories of his bravery that I treasured as a little girl."

James L. Goodloe, a Memphis attorney, was also profoundly moved by the tribute to his old schoolmate and Delta Psi fraternity brother. Although reading about him had reopened old wounds in Goodloe, he also confided to Mrs. Armistead, "I have all my life felt that my loved friends who have preceded me to the Great Beyond are still with me in spirit, and that I can almost commune with them. This always affords me intense pleasure.... My love for Jerrie was, & is, unbounded by time."

William E. Hutchinson and Mother, CSA

Many young Southern soldiers who died at Gettysburg spent their final moments in great agony, without the comfort of a loving mother. Corporal John Day Smith, a member of the 19th Maine, recorded one of these pathetic incidents following the fighting of July 2:

> The boys of the Nineteenth lay down upon the ground to rest for the night at nearly the point from which we charged in the late afternoon. There was not much sleep that night. The cries of the wounded men, lying between the lines, suffering with pain and burning with fever were most pitiful. The writer vividly remembers responding to a cry for water a few rods in advance of where the regiment was lying. It was yet hardly dark and the moon was shining. The poor fellow calling for help was a Confederate soldier. He was a fine looking boy, of some seventeen years, and stated that he belonged to one of the Georgia regi-

ments of [Brigadier General Ambrose R.] Wright's Brigade. He was shot through one of his lungs and was bleeding internally. The boy stated that he was the only child of a widowed mother and that he had run away from home, to enlist in the Southern army. His pallid face, blue eyes and quivering lips appealed for sympathy and encouragement. He said that his mother was a Christian woman, but that he was not a Christian. Kneeling by his side, and at the earnest request of this young soldier, the writer, poorly prepared for the sacred duty, tried to pray with and comfort this dying boy. At the first dawn of day upon the following morning this Confederate boy was found in just the position the writer had placed him the evening before,—his eyes glazed in death, looking up into the morning sky, yet not seeing nor caring then. The poor mother waiting at the lonely hearthstone never knew what had become of her only child. She no doubt lived in the belief, as well she might, that her prayers had followed and influenced the life and character of her boy. Other mothers, heartbroken, all over the country waited in vain for the coming of the boy who never returned. Such is war.

The identity of this teenager from Georgia will forever remain a mystery. The final thoughts of Private William E. Hutchinson, who enlisted in the 52nd North Carolina from Wilkes County at age 19 on September 22, 1862, also focused on his mother. A relief party from New York State that arrived in Gettysburg following the battle encountered this Tar Heel soldier and later mentioned him in a report of their activities:

> As soon as possible, after our arrival, we devoted our time to the hospitals of the Union soldiers; on our way to one of them, a young boy who was trying to follow some Confederate troops came towards us and laid down at our feet fainting in his exhaustion; when revived by wine, Mr. Barclay's kind manners won his confidence, and he begged to be "taken home to his mother," who lived near Raleigh, North Carolina. In his pocket was a letter from her saying she should become crazy if she did not hear from him; the little fellow was fed and taken into a house and placed in a comfortable bed and well nursed, but at the end of three days, without having a wound, he died from exhaustion. His name was Wm. Hutchinson. His letters and a statement of his death and place of burial were sent to his mother.

Mrs. A. T. Mercer and Oliver E. Mercer, CSA

With few exceptions, the citizens of Gettysburg freely shared their limited resources with the wounded of both sides following the town's occupation by upwards of 160,000 men. None of them considered these acts to be heroic at the time. They were ordinary citizens who for the past several days had been caught up in a hellish nightmare. They merely did what the residents of any other community in the country would have done under similar circumstances.

However, the extraordinary efforts of a few townspeople, such as Dr. John W. C. O'Neal, garnered the praise of both Union and Confederate soldiers. "With a heart filled with the milk of human kindness and the spirit of brotherly love, he ministered, without thought of reward, to the severely wounded of both sides," one Union veteran wrote of the 42-year-old physician.

A native of Fairfax County, Virginia, Dr. O'Neal attended Pennsylvania College in Gettysburg before receiving his medical training from the Maryland Medical School in Baltimore. He operated practices in Baltimore and then in Hanover, Pennsylvania, before permanently establishing his office on the northeast corner of Baltimore and High Streets in Gettysburg in early 1863.

On the opening day of the fighting O'Neal cared for a Louisiana soldier suffering from exhaustion. Despite his best efforts, the soldier died in a barn along the Mummasburg Road. The Confederates would not permit the doctor to return home until the evening of July 1. Throughout the final two days of the battle, O'Neal treated the wounded quartered at the County Almshouse, and he later cared for soldiers in his home.

Ironically, the good doctor is better known today for his attention to the Southern dead. During his daily house calls throughout the countryside, he meticulously recorded the names and burial locations of Confederate soldiers with the thought that this information would later aid the relatives seeking to bring home the remains.

Mrs. A. T. Mercer of Brunswick County, North Carolina, expressed the feelings of many Southern mothers in a letter to O'Neal dated August 16, 1866:

> Our Wilmington papers bring the welcome intelligence to many bereaved Southern hearts that you have cared for the graves of many of our Confederate dead at Gettysburg, replaced headboards and prepared a list of their names. May the Lord bless you is the prayer of many Southern hearts—Oh! We have lost so much. There are but few families that do not mourn the loss of one or more loved ones, and only a mother who has lost a son in that awful battle can and does appreciate fully such goodness as you have shown. I, too, lost a son at Gettysburg, a brave, noble boy in the full bloom of youth, and my heart yearns to have his remains ... brought home to rest in the soil of the land he loved so well. I need your assistance and I am confident you will aid me. No sorrow-stricken mother could ask and be refused by such a heart as yours.

In the spring of 1861, Oliver Evans Mercer had left the family farm to defend the newly formed Confederate States of America. At the age of 20 he was elected as second lieutenant of the "Brunswick Guards," Company G, 20th North Carolina. Less than a month prior to Gettysburg, he advanced in rank to captain. Unfortunately, he would not have long to enjoy the promotion.

On the early afternoon of July 1, Mercer and his company marched blindly with the remainder of Brigadier General Alfred Iverson's ill-fated brigade into the jaws of a deadly ambuscade on Oak Ridge. The young captain and hundreds of other Tar Heels fell to the ground in neat rows as if a giant scythe had reaped a ghastly harvest of flesh and blood.

Mercer's name does not appear on the burial rosters for either Oakwood Cemetery in Raleigh, North Carolina, or Hollywood Cemetery in Richmond. Perhaps Mrs. Mercer had her son buried in a private plot or in a church graveyard. Dr. O'Neal, the object of her lavish praise, continued to practice medicine in Gettysburg until his death on April 24, 1913, at age 92.

John Mosely and Mother, CSA

The troops of Brigadier General Evander Law's Alabama Brigade found themselves far to the rear performing picket duty several miles from Chambersburg, Pennsylvania, as the advance elements of the opposing armies clashed at Gettysburg on July 1. At about 3:00 o'clock on the next morning, the men were roused from their slumbers and by daylight began the steep ascent of South Mountain over the Chambersburg Pike. Without halting, the winding column inched its way up the crest and stumbled down the eastern slope, emerging into the valley below at the tiny village of Cashtown. Finally, after a grueling march of almost thirty miles, the weary infantrymen reached the vicinity of Marsh

Dr. John W. C. O'Neal. This photograph was taken sometime after the war (U.S. Army Military History Institute).

Creek by early afternoon. "The day was hot, and we were thirsty and had not stopped to rest or drink," remembered Private William C. Ward, 4th Alabama Infantry.

Ward and his fellow Alabamians groaned and cursed when they were once again ordered to their feet following an all too short respite. The exhausted and grimy infantrymen logged several more miles in the building heat and humidity as they marched and countermarched with their fellow veterans in Longstreet's Division to get into position for an attack upon the left flank of the Army of the Potomac.

A short time later, Law's veterans stepped off from Seminary Ridge and hustled on towards the looming heights of the Round Tops less than a half mile to the east. After splashing across Plum Run, the 4th Alabama struggled up the heavily timbered northwest slope of Big Round Top, marking the second mountain climb of the day. The pesky fire of Union sharpshooters and skirmishers further retarded the advance on this occasion as the attacking formation picked its way over fallen snags and around the large boulders on the steep mountainside.

Emerging in front of a rocky shelf at the foot of the smaller elevation, the now broken formation received a concentrated blast of musket fire from the hidden Federal defenders up ahead. A long line of butternut soldiers collapsed to the ground, including Private Ward. As the rear ranks passed over him to continue the assault on Little Round Top, the private dragged himself along the stony ground until he reached the protection of a man-sized boulder. Several stragglers joined him behind the natural breastwork before passing to the front.

Ward recognized the last of these men as Sergeant John Mosely, one of his messmates. An unmarried 24-year-old merchant at the beginning of the war, Mosely had been excused from duty on account of illness this day. Somehow, he persevered and caught up with his comrades in Company G. The sickly and exhausted sergeant must have been stunned by the cold reception that ensued.

"What are you doing here, John?" demanded Ward.

Seeing the blood oozing from under his friend's prostrate body, Mosely countered, "What can I do for you?"

The response must have surprised him even more: "You can do nothing. Your place is with our company. Do you not hear that they have joined battle with the enemy?"

His pride injured by the acerbic comments of an enlisted man, Mosely rushed off to participate in the final stages of the doomed attack until a Yankee bullet thudded into his body. Private Ward lived to see the next century; Mosely had just a few days to live.

Not long after the last shots had echoed from the hills and fields, the vanguard of a small army of relief workers began to arrive. "The first volunteer attendant I saw on the field of Gettysburg was a woman," recalled a convalescing Union officer. "She carried writing materials, envelopes, and postage stamps, and wrote letters to the friends of those who were too desperately wounded to do so themselves. She took down just what each wanted to say, without abridgment, and in this manner many a mother, sister, and sweetheart received their first, last, and only message from their loved ones, whose lives ebbed out on this fatal field."

Sergeant Mosely dictated one such letter. Dated July 4, 1863, from the "Battlefield, Gettysburg," it appeared later in the July 26 issue of the Montgomery *Advertiser* and read as follows:

> Dear Mother:
> I am here a prisoner of war, and mortally wounded. I can live but a few hours, at farthest. I was shot fifty yards from the enemy's line. They have been exceedingly kind to me. I have no doubt as to the final result of this battle, and I hope I may live long enough to hear the shouts of victory before I die. I am very weak. Do not mourn my loss. I had hoped to have been spared; but a righteous God has ordered it otherwise, and I feel prepared to trust my ease in his hands. Farewell to you all! Pray that God may receive my soul. Your unfortunate son, John.

Accepting his fate with quiet resignation, Private Mosely entered eternal rest the next morning without hearing the accustomed shouts of victory from the ranks of the Army of Northern Virginia.

Elisa and James Weida/James Ashworth and Mother, USA

The presence of a mother was an immeasurable comfort to a wounded or dying soldier. Georgeanna Woolsey, a volunteer at the United States Sanitary Commission Lodge east of Gettysburg, warmly remembered "a nice old German mother" who traveled all the way from Wisconsin to be with her dear boy. Among the items she brought with her was a patchwork bed quilt. "[T]here he lay, all covered up in his quilt, looking so home-like, and feeling so, too, no doubt, with his good old mother close at his side," wrote Woolsey.

The benefits provided by mothers, wives, and other relatives as they cared for their loved ones extended far beyond the psychological. In fact, for several weeks after the conflict, when the resources of the Union medical department were spread dangerously thin, it could spell the difference between life and death. For instance, the recoveries of two critically wounded Pennsylvania captains had much to do with their respective mothers.

Before the war, Captain James W. Weida of Berks County, Pennsylvania, worked as a stonemason, a literary agent, and a music instructor. In the late summer of 1862, he left his wife of two years and his toddler son to lead a company of men in the newly formed 151st Pennsylvania Infantry. During the fighting west of Gettysburg on July 1, a bullet slammed into the side of the 28-year-old captain, breaking a rib and punching through his liver before passing through the base of his right lung.

Weida was carried inside the hospital at the Lutheran Theological Seminary, where he received little care until after the battle ended. Dr. Amos Blakeslee, the regimental surgeon, probed into the officer's chest and removed what foreign material he could reach, but there was little else that he could do.

The prospects for a full recovery were slim indeed. During the Civil War there was a 62 percent mortality rate associated with injuries to the chest area. Lying near Weida in the hospital, Private Aaron Smith testified that his captain "was very low and often complained to me of great pain in the region of his heart [and] also [of] pain in his arms and legs. He was short in his breath and could not speak above a whisper."

Fortunately, Weida received plenty of personal attention. Soon after the battle, his mother, Elisa, arrived at the Seminary hospital, and along with a Mrs. Findlay of New York, did all she could for his well being. Miraculously, the captain was convalescing at his home by the beginning of August.

Although plagued by his injuries for the rest of his life, Weida fathered four additional children and lived another 44 years after his near fatal wounding before succumbing to intestinal cancer. His mother preceded him in death in 1874.

If, like many veterans, Weida chose not to discuss his war days, then perhaps his post–Gettysburg children may not have known how close they had come to never being born. If the bullet that struck their father had taken a slightly different course, it could well have proved fatal. It is also entirely possible that without the love and devotion of his mother, he would never have persevered through those dark days in July 1863.

Captain James Ashworth had every right not to be involved in the combat at Gettysburg. Suffering from a pulmonary disorder, he was heading home on sick leave when he learned that the army had broken camp to begin a major movement. At once the ailing officer decided it would be "better to die in the line of duty & defending our flag than to survive its disgrace, for I felt that the crisis had come." He rejoined his regiment at Centreville and accompanied it north into Pennsylvania. This type of devotion did not bode well for Robert E. Lee and the Army of Northern Virginia.

Born in Bury, Lancashire, England, on September 11, 1836, Ashworth immigrated to the United States with his parents two years later. The family eventually settled in Frankford near Philadelphia. When the war began, Ashworth was employed at a local shipping house. Not wishing to miss the action, the 24-year-old civilian accompanied General Robert Patterson's command to Hagerstown and took part in a skirmish near Williamsport, Maryland. Afterward, he was mistakenly arrested as a Confederate spy, but his comrades cleared him by their testimony. A year later, Ashworth helped to raise Company I of the 121st Pennsylvania and was elected as its captain.

He paid a dear price for his patriotism at Gettysburg, where he served as acting major. The 121st occupied the extreme left of the Union infantry line on the afternoon of July 1. When Brigadier General James Pettigrew unleashed his attack on McPherson's Ridge, the Southerners worked their way around the flank of the regiment's vulnerable position, delivering a crushing volley. After a confused attempt to change front under fire, a large number of the Pennsylvanians broke for the rear. As Captain Ashworth attempted in vain to rally the crumbling regiment, he was hit successively below the breast, twice in the right arm, as well as in the right knee.

He fell into enemy hands but was later taken to the home of Peter and Hannah Myers on West High Street, a sanctuary for wounded soldiers of the First Army Corps. The couple's oldest daughter, Salome "Sallie" Myers, a 21-year-old Gettysburg schoolteacher, kept a daily diary throughout the war years. Her 1863 entries detail her tireless efforts and compassion for the soldiers under her family's care.

The badly wounded Ashworth arrived at the Myers home on the evening of July 7. The captain's brother arrived two days later and on the 11th Sallie recorded, "Capt. Ashworth's mother is here with us, taking care of her son." Her subsequent entries reveal the patient's up and down condition. Although she noted an improvement by the fourteenth, a setback took place later in the week when Ashworth was described as being very ill. Her growing despair was reflected in her remarks for July 20: "Capt. Ashworth is better but I suppose it will not amount to much. Our family physician is attending him."

Ashworth and his mother stayed at the Myers home for six weeks during his protracted recovery. Ashworth later wrote to a fellow officer that his leg "was saved by the careful nursing of my mother & another but is perfectly stiff." Indeed, his injuries left him permanently lame.

Despite this handicap he returned to active duty that fall, receiving a promotion to lieutenant colonel. Much to his displeasure he was discharged on disability the following February and finished his service as a captain in the Veteran Reserve Corps. Ashworth later took charge of the Freedmen's Bureau in Louisa Courthouse, Virginia. He finished his career as a revenue assessor in southeastern Pennsylvania, a position to which President Grant appointed him. He resigned in February 1882 and died one month later in Gainesville, Florida. The quality of his post-war years had much to do with the tireless efforts of his mother and the generosity of the Myers family.

John C., Lucie, John C. L., and Thomas J. Mounger, CSA

"I know not how to write you in this hour of affliction." Lucie Mounger's heart sank as she collapsed into a chair in her Quitman, Georgia, home to finish reading the letter that opened with this ominous line. Written in the hand of her husband, Lieutenant Colonel John C. Mounger, it had been sent from the headquarters of the 9th Georgia Infantry on May 23, 1863. The missive conveyed the sad news that, during the recent battle at Chancellorsville, Captain Terrell Mounger, the couple's eldest son, fell with a mortal wound while leading a charge. Terrell had commanded a company in the 14th Georgia while his father and two brothers served together in the 9th Georgia.

Captain Mounger had lingered for nine days after being wounded. Word was sent to his father, but it arrived a week too late. After receiving confirmation of his son's death, Colonel Mounger immediately traveled to the nearly deserted battlefield. Following a desperate and unsuccessful search for the remains, he rode off to General A. P. Hill's headquarters at Guinea Station, where he learned that his son had died at the Lacy House. A surgeon stationed at this hospital site then directed him to the temporary grave he had been seeking. Someone had lovingly inscribed the name of the deceased soldier on a rough-hewn headboard with the following inscription: "Peace be to thy ashes, thy work is done."

Physically and mentally scarred, the colonel told his wife that out of duty to his family he felt compelled to resign his commission. The long-time lawyer had left a lucrative practice and a comfortable home to fight for the Confederacy. Now he was a man filled with conflicting emotions. "Bear your affliction with Christian patience and fortitude," he counseled Lucie. "It is the fate of thousands—even the immortal Jackson fell in this great struggle. I am prepared to meet the will of heaven.... I have no ambition to serve, no malice to gratify; I go forth, I trust with the approval of God, to stay and destroy the cruel enemies of my beloved country."

In many cases these words could be written off as patriotic bluster, not so with Mounger. A soldier in the 9th Georgia later wrote of his leader:

> Veterans were never led into the jaws of death by a more gallant officer than Lt. Colonel Mounger; and a more generous heart than his never beat in a human breast. Though far advanced in years, and, with a constitution not naturally robust, greatly impaired by disease, his whole-souled devotion to his country, and her cause, still kept him in the field. He received a painful wound in the head at Manassas No. 2, and despite the earnest remonstrance of all his friends, remained in action. He commanded the Regiment in the first Maryland campaign; was wounded severely in the arm, in the early morning of the Sharpsburg fight; kept the field all day, was again wounded, still would not leave, and finally having his arm broken by a shell was taken from the field.

Although the fire of combat still burned in his soul, Mounger kept his promise to his wife by drafting a letter of resignation. But the invasion of Pennsylvania intervened and he decided to stay on until the end of the campaign.

The 9th Georgia formed on the left flank of George "Tige" Anderson's Brigade on July 2 as it marched towards the Stony Hill that jutted above the famous Wheatfield. The Georgians soon passed through a deadly gauntlet. "A full half mile of wheat fields, ready for the harvest, enclosed with stone fences intervene between our line and the rocky rampart where the enemy's bayonets glisten and cannons send forth their screaming, hustling and bursting shells," described one veteran.

As the battle line approached within three hundred yards of the Union position, an iron projectile tore through the bowels of Colonel Mounger as another punched through his breast. "Boys, they've killed me, now," he moaned and moments later he died in the arms of Thomas. Afterwards, the grieving son clipped off a lock of his father's hair and cut the stars from his coat before the body was placed inside a wooden coffin.

Absent on a foraging expedition, Lieutenant John Mounger was not with his father and brother during the bloodiest day of the battle. It was he who informed his mother of the tragic event at Gettysburg, and that, due to the close pursuit of the Union army, the body was buried in a family graveyard about a half mile outside of the town. In the midst of their grief, the boys encountered more pragmatic concerns. They anguished over what to do with their father's horse. With no authorization to draw forage they would soon be forced to sell the animal at a low price.

Near the middle of the same letter are these moving lines: "Dear Mother, let us all try to meet him in Heaven. Tom and myself will try and be better boys." These simple words strike a chord. What American boy has not felt a twinge of guilt over a mischievous past? In light of what was to follow, John's simple but heartfelt promise underscores the unremitting sorrow of one Southern mother.

The next spring at the Battle of the Wilderness, Lieutenant John Mounger knelt down to instruct some of his men prior to an assault when a bullet thudded into his head, killing him instantly. His brother Tom pressed forward to the enemy breastworks only to be fatally shot in the neck. In less than a year, Lucie Mounger endured three separate bereavements, "thus destroying the whole of this family, and leaving an aged lady to mourn over the death of all her hopes."

3

Husbands, Wives, and Sweethearts

When this dreadful war is ended,
I will come again to you,
Tell me, dearest, ere we sever,
Tell me, tell me, you'll be true.
Though to other scenes I wander,
Still your mem'ry pure and bright
In my heart will ever linger,
Shining with undying light;
Do not weep, love, sit beside me,
Whisper gentle words of cheer,
Be not mournful now, my darling,
Let me kiss away each tear.

"When This Dreadful War Is Ended,"
written by George Cooper,
music by Stephen Collins Foster

Joel and Laura Blake, CSA

Screened by the Blue Ridge Mountains to the east, the long and narrow Shenandoah Valley provided the Army of Northern Virginia with a natural invasion corridor for a thrust into Pennsylvania. Although more than a few soldiers from the Deep South commented on the natural beauty and bountifulness of the area, a Florida officer serving in A. P. Hill's Corps was awestruck. After breaking camp near Berryville, Virginia, on June 22, 1863, Lieutenant Joel C. Blake described the "Eden on Earth" to his wife:

> I have thought a hundred times as I passed along, how happy I could be if I had you all with me, and was peaceably settled upon one of these farms here in Western Virginia. I am attached much you know to Florida and our dear home there, but in all candor I must think this surpassed it or any other country I have ever seen for beauty, fertility & fine living. The cattle are almost as large as elephants, some of the cows look as though they would give a half bushel of milk & not half try—the udders of some are as large around as my wrist.

Since his family operated a 2,600-acre plantation near Lake Miccosukee east of the state capital of Tallahassee, the 32-year-old Floridian possessed more than a passing interest in the agricultural aspects of the region. The Blakes owned 118 slaves to help tend the cotton, sugar cane, and livestock. Like many large plantation owners, they appeared to be land rich but were cash poor. In the spring of 1863, Joel Blake confided to his wife Laura, "I hope we may be able to feed and clothe our Negroes & pay our taxes, we will do well to do it."

Given the endless demands of running such a large enterprise, Blake was forced to make a difficult decision after Florida seceded from the Union on January 10, 1861. A little over a year later, Joel and his older brother Walter signed up with the Dixie Yeoman (Company K, 5th Florida Infantry). Isham Blake, another sibling and the plantation overseer, joined the same unit later that spring.

After reaching Richmond on August 10, 1862, the 5th Florida first saw combat at Second Manassas and Antietam. Private Isham Blake was slightly wounded during the later engagement and furloughed a short time later. Apparently, Joel Blake missed this action, for on September 18 he informed his wife that he was still recuperating from a case of diarrhea in a private residence in Winchester, Virginia.

Two days earlier, a letter from Laura cured him of the more serious ailment of homesickness. "I eagerly broke open the envelop and commenced to devour its contents," he told her. "I was at times completely overcome, and could not read for the tears which fell thick and fast down my cheeks, I was overcome with gratitude to God for his goodness to me. Once more he had permitted me to hear from home and to hear, too, that all were well.... I would cry a little, laugh a little, and then read a little. I never felt so completely childish in my life."

Indeed, home was always paramount in the thoughts of Lieutenant Blake. Although he was much amused by the antics of ice skaters in Richmond that winter, a care package that contained some sugar cane triggered a nostalgic reaction. "How time lags when we are thus separated from all that is dear to us on earth," he wrote to his sister Annie. Near the close of the letter, Blake declared, "I had rather be a private in the ranks in Florida fighting for the defense of my own State, for the protection of my family & home than to be a Major General in Virginia."

During the spring of 1863, Blake endured a scary period when an epidemic of scarlet fever ravaged northern Florida. After not hearing from his wife for several days, he naturally assumed the worst. When a welcome letter finally arrived, Blake confessed, "My uneasiness for the last three or four days has rendered me almost entirely unfit for duty.... My imagination has troubled me no little."

By this time, Joel Blake no longer had the company of his brothers to help speed the time. On March 17, Walter resigned his lieutenancy due to health problems, and after recovering from his Antietam wound Isham had transferred into the 1st Florida Cavalry. He would spend the remainder of the war fighting in the West. "Camp is getting to be quite a bore to me & were it not for the cheerfulness of our men, I should sometimes have the blues badly," Joel confided to Laura.

Clearly the long separation from her was weighing heavily upon his thoughts. "I know you have much to trouble and annoy you, but I hope everything will go well with you. I am daily praying for the time to come when I shall be returned to you, and become an equal participant in all your sorrows & joys, trials & troubles, God speed that time.... The picnics upon the lake must be very pleasant now, the fishing no doubt is fine. I often wonder if I shall ever live to see and enjoy such times again on that old lake."

He then related a story that must have melted his wife's heart. A body servant named

Simon had recently discovered one of Laura's cuff pins in the pocket of his master's carpetbag. "I am now wearing the pin, and highly appreciate it as a souvenir of brighter days," shared Blake. "The little hand now rests on my breast near the heart and there I intend it shall remain until I take it to look for its mate."

Although there is no doubt that Joel Blake loved and adored his marriage partner, the male-dominated society of the 1860s demanded that he attempt to control business and family affairs from a distance. On April 10, 1863, he instructed Laura, "If you can get anything like 25 cents sell one load of cotton and pay off all indebtedness ... then hold on to the rest.... Be certain & have the bales patched up before sending them off, and caution Vaughn to see that they are not so exposed."

In the same letter, Blake also offered detailed advice on the rearing of his two young boys, Willie and Cliff, who had been misbehaving recently. Upon learning that Willie was indulging in vulgar language, he advised his wife to "teach him to fear God as well as the rod.... Whip him seldom, but give him a good one when you have it to do and never punish him in an angry moment. Much depends upon the spirit in which punishment is inflicted, and none are more quick than children themselves to perceive whether it is done from principle or from anger." His tone continued to soften when he discussed Cliff. "I scarcely know how I should have felt if I had seen you switching the little chap. I don't think I could have stood by and witnessed it, however great the necessity.... How I should like to hear some of his prattle about now."

It has often been stated that the life of a Civil War soldier was characterized by long periods of monotony interrupted by brief moments of sheer terror. For Lieutenant Joel Blake and the Dixie Yeoman, the tedium of camp life ended abruptly with the start of the Chancellorsville Campaign. After a week of constant marching and fighting, the fatigued officer penned a lengthy letter from a camp near Fredericksburg on May 8, 1863. "I tell you there has been many a heart made sad, and many an eye to weep over the scenes which we have been compelled to witness," he wrote.

While en route to head off Union General Joseph Hooker's powerful flanking force, the soldiers of the 5th Florida passed a small dwelling where an elderly lady had been beheaded by an artillery shell. A younger woman, apparently her daughter, ran off in fright and lost track of her two young children. Her frantic cries anguished the men and firmed their resolve for the impending combat.

On Sunday, May 3, the decisive day of the battle, Brigadier General Edward Perry's Florida Brigade participated in the overwhelming assault that dislodged the Federals from their entrenched position near the Chancellor house. Lieutenant Blake expressed deep pride in his company's performance, but after surveying the scene afterwards, his exuberance gave way to compassion. "The cries of the wounded—the groans of the dying on every side fill the air, & the dead, mangled & bruised and torn to pieces in every conceivable way, are scattered over the whole field.... Touched with sympathy for my race, I could feel for our wounded enemies, and though a fallen foe, I administered unto them as friends." At the end of the campaign he felt relieved that "We are once more quietly encamped again and have been permitted to resume our drills and usual camp duties."

The respite did not last long. A month later, the gray columns were on the move again. The breathtaking scenery of the Shenandoah region, along with the ample food and provisions, more than offset the series of long marches. When the 5th Florida passed through Charlestown on the morning of June 23, the ragged troops received a hearty reception from the locals. Confederate flags waved from nearly every window as the ladies passed out food, drinks, and bouquets of flowers to the men. One of the women reminded Lieutenant Blake of his beloved sister.

The next day the Floridians crossed the Potomac River near Shepherdstown. Six days later from a camp near Fayetteville, Pennsylvania, Blake took the opportunity to update his wife on recent events as the scattered elements of the Army of Northern Virginia converged towards Cashtown along a pass in South Mountain. "Old General Lee rode by about an hour ago," he reported. "His presence thrilled our whole army with a spirit of enthusiasm. All are in the best of spirits and look for nothing but victory, though we may have bloody work ahead of us."

Not surprisingly, the news of the recent burning of Thaddeus Stevens' ironworks at Caledonia delighted him and he hoped that the "abolition scoundrel" could be captured. The hopeful but anxious husband closed his letter with the following: "Good-bye. May God bless you and my dear boys. I hope, if not on earth again, to meet you in Heaven."

Laura Blake would never read these tender thoughts. Just two days later, her husband was killed in action during a failed assault against Cemetery Ridge. Reportedly, his body was so completely mutilated that it could not be identified. According to family tradition, on the day of Blake's death his mother, Susan Parrish Blake, was eating dinner at the plantation when she suddenly screamed out, "Oh my God, my Joel is dead!"

Following the battle local resident J. Howard Wert combed the area for relics and souvenirs. Among the many interesting items that he collected was a letter discovered in the pocket of a dead Confederate officer. In a 1907 newspaper article that featured transcribed sections of the letter, Wert identified the author as a member of Company K, 5th Florida Infantry. From various clues, including a reference to his brother Walter, it is obvious that the letter came from the body of Lieutenant Joel Blake.

Wert's comments on the cherished artifact drew a powerful lesson for his readers and illustrate the fact that the true cost of any war is impossible to determine:

> It is sad to think of the faithful wife long waiting for the missive that never came, whilst the one of whom she fondly dreamed was a festering corpse, thrown with fifty others into a shallow trench of a Northern battlefield. In those four sad years there was many a letter written which never reached its destination. In those four sad years there was many a wife and mother that never knew aught of their loved except that they were war's victim on distant slaughter fields.

Alexander and Elmira Seiders, USA

As Confederate troops marched down the Shenandoah Valley, the Army of the Potomac streamed northward on a parallel course to the east. In the midst of a severe heat wave the Yankee infantrymen endured a torturous series of forced marches in order to keep between the unseen enemy and Washington City. The First Corps logged roughly 100 miles in a five-day period before striking the Loudoun and Hampshire Railroad near Guilford Station, Virginia, 20 miles northwest of the capital. The troops encamped for a week in this area while the high command deciphered incoming intelligence data and pondered strategy for the next phase of the campaign.

Although on a constant state of high alert as the contending cavalry forces clashed in the nearby Loudoun Valley, the weary foot soldiers took full advantage of the respite. The first priority of many involved a welcome dip in the cool waters of Broad Run to wash off a week's accumulation of sweat and dust. Letter writing began in earnest. After bringing his sister up to date on the recent movements and detailing the rich diet he and his comrades had been enjoying at the expense of the local farmers, Private James Norris, Company F, 151st Pennsylvania, related some sad news.

"We have lost another of our dear brother soldiers of our Co., by the name of Dodd, a resident of Spring Creek if I recollect right. He died last week at the hospital. He was just as fine a man as you would wish to see. He left a wife and two little children. He had their miniatures with him and two smart good-looking little children they are, now fatherless, and their mother husbandless. May God be with them and see that they are cared for."

Following the Chancellorsville Campaign, the ranks of the 151st had been ravaged by severe outbreaks of smallpox, typhoid fever, and dysentery. Near the end of May 1863, Sergeant Alexander Seiders, a semi-literate 23-year-old factory worker from Reading, wrote to his wife, Elmira, "We hav a great many sick.... The dockter has excuseed 2 hundred forty some. They hav all got the diarea."

Seiders himself was just then recuperating from this ailment, losing nearly sixty pounds as a result. After taking two days worth of medicine prescribed by the regimental surgeon, the sergeant switched to a homemade concoction of teas prepared by a fellow soldier. He reported that the brew, dubbed "chicken guts tea," soon cured him!

Nearly a month later, on June 21, during the temporary halt in the march that would soon lead into his home state, Seiders warned Elmira that she might not recognize him when he returned home at the end of next month. He eagerly anticipated holding his one-year-old daughter, Annie, and partaking of the simple pleasure of biting into a juicy Pennsylvania peach.

Left: Alexander Seiders, ca. 1862 (Sally Smith). *Right:* Elmira Seiders, ca. 1862 (Sally Smith).

These pleasures dreamed of longingly, so close to becoming reality, would be cruelly whisked away. Less than a month from the end of their enlistment terms, the 151st Pennsylvania engaged in one of the fiercest small unit actions that took place at Gettysburg. Standing toe to toe with the 26th North Carolina on the afternoon of July 1, the regiment endured staggering losses. Out of the 467 officers and men that entered the fight on McPherson's Ridge, just over 100 men answered roll call the next morning.

Sergeant Alexander Seiders was among the majority who did not respond when his name was called out. With half of the regiment comprised of men from Berks County, a lengthy list of casualties soon appeared in area newspapers. Refusing to give up hope until she received official confirmation of her husband's death, Elmira Seiders wrote to Sergeant Major Simon Arnold, the regimental adjutant, who was recovering from a wound in a York, Pennsylvania, hospital.

<blockquote>
July 20th /63

Mrs. Seiders,

    Madame, yours of the 14th came to hand and I now hasten to reply. In regard to the death of Sergt. Alex Seiders, I am sorry to say it is too true. He was shot on the first day of July and from what I can learn of those who saw him fall, he died on the field. I think it would be a hard matter to recover his body as the Rebels had possession of the field for two days and they buried nearly all of our dead that were killed on the first day. The graves were not marked for they were buried while the battle was going on. I expect to get home in a few weeks and any information that I can give you will be cheerfully given.

        I am, very respectfully, your obedient servant,

        Simon J. Arnold

        Sergt. Major, 151st Regt. P.V.
</blockquote>

The body of Alexander Seiders was never identified. It is probable that his remains are buried under an "unknown" marker in the Soldiers' National Cemetery.

Hugh and Susan Miller, CSA

High-ranking Civil War officers enjoyed a privilege not usually available to junior officers and enlisted men. While stationed in semi-permanent camps they could send for their wives and other family members until the resumption of the active campaign season. During the winter of 1862-63, Susan Miller stayed near the capital of Richmond to be close to her husband, Colonel Hugh R. Miller, and the couple's two sons, Edwin and George, all of whom served in the 42nd Mississippi.

The comfortable arrangement ended in early June, when the regiment was stripped from the city's defenses to bolster Lee's army for the invasion of Pennsylvania. Mrs. Miller moved in with her uncle at Sunny Side, Virginia, forty miles to the west. Upon arriving in Fredericksburg, Sergeant Edwin Miller advised his mother: "It would be useless for you to come up here as in probability [we] would be far away before you could get here.... The summer campaign with us has begun in earnest, we will not be able to remain in one locality longer than a few days at a time."

Hugh Miller, a prominent lawyer and judge, had entered the army as a captain in 1861. The following spring he won election as the colonel of the newly formed 42nd Mississippi. Although lauded for his "courteous, dignified and polite bearing as a gentleman and his warm-hearted kindness & unselfish generosity as a neighbor," not everyone was so enamored with the middle-aged officer, as at least a few of Miller's subalterns harbored resentment towards his elite social standing and the authority of his rank.

In mid–January 1863 a captain serving in the 42nd wrote to his wife after being denied a furlough: "Col. Miller thinks that every body must stay in the army until just such a time as suits him. He is a hard master and if I ever get from under him it will do me good to tell him what I think of him for he is the most perfect tyrant that ever lived."

Obviously, Edwin and George Miller, aged 18 and 20 respectively when they entered the Confederate service in May 1862, felt differently. The brothers transferred from the 2nd Mississippi in July of that year in order to serve under their father.

The military and political developments of 1863 would usher in a period of dramatic change and adjustment for all Americans—North and South, rich and poor, slave and free, general and private. It was a time characterized by high anxiety and soul searching. Referring to the stalemate at Antietam the previous autumn, Sergeant Major George Miller told his mother, "I can't help believe if the men went with the same spirit that inspired them last year it would do, but they were dreadfully disheartened by that terrible campaign and look upon this maneuver with a feeling of perfect horror."

This observation runs counter to the almost universal expressions of confidence and high morale that prevailed in the Army of Northern Virginia in mid–June of 1863. Perhaps Miller's inner thoughts clouded his perception. "I have often wished I was better prepared to die, and at no time have I ever felt so awfully the want of that preparation than now," he confessed. Nonetheless, he provided his mother with a detailed set of instructions to carry out if he should not survive the coming battle.

> This will be the last letter you will receive from me—perhaps ever—and certainly until we return, and now is the time for last requests and last words, and one of these is a natural one ... of most exceeding solicitude with me—that I might be taken home and laid close by my own home among those old haunts I loved so well and which have been hallowed by many a happy sunny day—by the old Spanish oak in the grove or on the mound—if I should fall in this inhospitable land.... And as last words, when you write to those at home I love, tell them that my last earthly aspiration was to do something to free them from the oppression of the vandals and avenge their wrongs, and that my only regret in yielding up life for them will be that I and all of us could not fall around our homes and loved ones instead of being sacrificed for the ambition of petty military humbugs.

Susan Miller was experiencing many of the same emotions as her son. After receiving a letter from her husband on June 29, she sat down to respond on July 3, totally oblivious to the fact that the greatest battle of the war was building towards its furious climax. "Your last letter is confirmatory of my fears ever since you were ordered up to Fredericksburg & a feeling of perfect helpless despair is the natural consequence," she wrote. "I know it is useless to fret over what cannot be helped & I am sometimes tempted to pray for perfect oblivion.... I find it hard, hard indeed to be resigned to the suffering & loss of all that makes life endurable."

Her feelings of despondency were exacerbated by the isolation from family and friends back home in Mississippi and the lack of recent news from them. Surrounded by strangers and subjected to a constant stream of unreliable rumors regarding the army's movements, she struggled against a raging current of melancholy:

> Our papers speak hopefully—but oh the anguish individually felt by those whose every hope hangs suspended thus. It is easy for those who have no personal ties involved to speak encouragingly, but to the poor wife & mother there is no relief.... If to be patriotic, we

> must be stoically indifferent in sympathy & expression, I am no patriot. Although you are all in the path of duty, & just where I think my men should be, I cannot but grieve to think of your sufferings and dangers, cannot but dread that one nation's independence will possibly be bought with the sacrifice of those priceless lives. My dear husband although I hope & pray & sometimes feel great confidence that God in his infinite mercy will spare you & my precious children, yet I cannot be insensible to the possibility that one or all may be taken from me.... Oh how glad I should be to know how & where you are today.

Perfect oblivion would have been preferable in this instance. Two days earlier, George Miller sustained a near fatal gunshot wound to his thigh during the initial clash outside of a Pennsylvania town that most Southerners had never heard of prior to that summer. And now as Susan Miller penned her thoughts, her husband led his command across rolling farm fields to attack the enemy lines on Cemetery Ridge. In less than an hour, roughly half of the assault force, including Colonel Miller, was gunned down.

On July 8, the Reverend Andrew B. Cross, a delegate with the U.S. Christian Commission, visited the Southern officer at the Union Second Corps Hospital.

> In a fence corner ... among our men, lay Colonel Hugh R. Miller, of Pontotoc, Mississippi ... an eminent lawyer and judge of that State, shot through the left breast and right knee. We gave him a little wine and a cracker, which he took with great modesty, saying he was not dangerously wounded, but was thankful for our offer to write to his wife, Mrs. Susan G. Miller, at Sunnyside, Cumberland Co., Virginia. The surgeon told us his case was dangerous. Calling again after a short time to see if he would have anything, he modestly said: "I am very much obliged to you, but give it to those around, who are worse, and need it more."

On July 18 the chaplain of the 42nd Mississippi, the Reverend Thomas D. Witherspoon, reached the bedside of Colonel Miller "just in time to receive his dying expression of his faith in Christ and his readiness to depart." Through the generosity of Mary Myers, an embalmer was secured and the body enclosed in a metallic case.

The next day Private Edwin Miller walked into the office of Colonel Henry C. Alleman, the post commander, seeking permission to take the body home. Arrangements were made for a lieutenant from Alleman's staff to escort Edwin Miller and the chaplain to Baltimore with the remains. Witherspoon praised the Union commander as "a true gentleman as well as [a] true soldier." The group carried a letter from Alleman directed to Major General Robert C. Schenck requesting permission for the Southerners to accompany the remains by flag of truce to Richmond.

Schenck served as the commander of the Middle Department and had his headquarters in the city. Unbeknownst to the travelers, they were entering into a decidedly hostile environment, as the political general from Ohio had adopted some harsh measures to subjugate the predominately pro–Southern populace. "Baltimore is literally crushed and broken by high-handed tyranny; the petty, ill-bred plebeians with the shoulder straps on, actually lord it over those unfortunate people, with all the mean oppression which characterized men of low estates who have been suddenly elevated to power," noted one Confederate prisoner with disgust. Witherspoon related the despotic sequence of events that took place in the city:

> The scene on the arrival at General Schenck's headquarters in Baltimore was one that beggars description. The polite and gentlemanly lieutenant who had accompanied us presented the letter from his superior officer, and it was handed to Colonel Fish, General Schenck's adjutant. He read it, and asked, "Where is the body?" The lieutenant produced the receipt of the Adams Express Company, who had it in charge, and the colonel, receiving it, handed

it to one of his subordinates, and said, "Go and get that body and have it buried." "Where shall I bury it?" asked the surprised official—to which the answer was in substance that he did not care where, so as the body was put out of the way, adding that he had stood all that he was going to stand of this paying honors to Rebel dead.

Edwin Miller, overwhelmed with the thought of the dishonor about to be done to his father's remains, pled most earnestly to be permitted to accompany the officer and see the remains interred, and it was only after a long interval, and through the intercession of friends of Colonel Fish, who were the witnesses of the boy's agony, that he was permitted to accompany the remains to their sepulture, and have them placed in a vault instead of being buried in the ground.

Eventually, Private Miller prevailed over Schenck's regime and successfully transported his father's remains to Richmond. President Jefferson Davis attended the colonel's funeral at the First Presbyterian Church on July 29.

A short time later, a committee of officers from the 42nd Mississippi passed a series of resolutions following the death of their commander. One of these declared "that by his thorough and undivided consecration of himself and his talents to his country from the commencement of her persecutions to his death on the memorable and bloody field of Gettysburg, he made the unblemished record of a patriot, that will constitute a rich legacy to his children and canonize his name with departed heroes."

Granted a lengthy furlough, George Miller recuperated with his mother at Sunny Side. The anguish of Gettysburg exacted a severe toll upon Susan Miller. She died on January 10, 1864, and now rests peacefully by her husband's side. Reflecting the sentiments expressed in her son's war-time letter, the couple was reinterred in Aberdeen, Mississippi.

Isaac and Mary Stamps, CSA

During times of national crisis we often assume that our president's heavy burden of responsibility precludes him from the everyday cares and concerns of the populace. But during the Civil War, neither Abraham Lincoln nor his adversary, Jefferson Davis, was immune to personal tragedy. Both men suffered the heartbreaking loss of a child while in office. Davis's young son, Joseph, plummeted to his death after falling from an upper story of the Confederate White House in Richmond on April 30, 1864. Davis had little time to grieve, for his attention would soon be diverted by a series of coordinated offensives under the overall leadership of Lieutenant General U. S. Grant.

In fact, there appeared to be no time during the war that family concerns did not press in upon the over stressed mind of the Confederacy's chief executive. After approving Lee's risky invasion of Pennsylvania the previous spring, he closely monitored the army's movements as it swung northward in early June of 1863. Not only did perhaps the fate of the upstart Confederate nation hang in the balance, but two of his nephews also served as officers under Lee.

One of these kinsmen is well known to students of the battle. Leading his men into combat for the first time, Brigadier General Joseph R. Davis's brigade suffered staggering losses during the opening infantry engagement on McPherson's Ridge. Two days later, his bloodied troops lined up as part of the Southern assault force for Pickett's Charge. Although the general emerged safely from this contest, his questionable leadership of the brigade contributed to its sad distinction of losing more men than any other brigade in the Army of Northern Virginia at Gettysburg.

Interestingly, the Confederate Senate had initially rejected Joseph Davis's nomination for promotion to brigadier general, but it was eventually approved. There is no doubt that President Davis interceded on his behalf. The charges of nepotism would ring loud, particularly after the bloody debacle at Gettysburg, forcing another burden of care upon the president.

On the other hand, Captain Isaac Davis Stamps had been largely forgotten; but thanks to the research of Terrence Winschel, historian at the Vicksburg National Military Park, he has now been rescued from obscurity. Born on April 23, 1828, at Rosemont Plantation, the Davis family estate, Isaac Stamps had always enjoyed a close relationship with his famous uncle. Part of this was due to the special bond between Isaac's mother, Lucinda Davis Stamps, and her younger brother Jefferson.

Growing up in Woodville, Mississippi, one of the oldest towns in the state, young Isaac's neighbors included a number of prominent state and national politicians. But he certainly did not have to look far for inspiration. Before assuming his most famous role, Jefferson Davis served in both houses of the U.S. Congress, fought in the Mexican War as colonel of the First Mississippi Rifles, and was appointed Secretary of War during the administration of Franklin Pierce.

In the spring of 1854, Stamps wed Mary McLaughlin Humphreys. The bride was a natural beauty with an intellectual mind and a charming spirit. After Isaac completed his law studies, the couple set up housekeeping in Woodville, and the proud husband soon established a lucrative practice. Four children, all girls, followed during the next several years. The death of infant Mildred interrupted this period of marital bliss, as did the outbreak of war in 1861.

Isaac Stamps was among the thousands of Mississippians who answered the call to arms. As became customary in both sections of the country, those individuals who held prominent posts in civilian life often landed commissions as officers. Stamps won election as captain of the Hurricane Rifles, one of the companies that would make up the 21st Mississippi Infantry. However, the former lawyer had the unenviable task of serving under his father-in-law, Colonel Benjamin Grubb Humphreys. Before Captain Stamps left for the front, Uncle Jefferson presented him with the sword he had carried into battle at Buena Vista during the Mexican War.

The 21st Mississippi was melded into an entire brigade of Magnolia State regiments soon to be commanded by the fiery ex–Congressman, William Barksdale. The transformation of these neophyte soldiers into a formidable combat unit began in the spring of 1862 during the fighting near Richmond.

While Isaac Stamps and his men defended the capital city, Mary and the children journeyed north to Vicksburg for a visit. Tragedy struck when little Sallie Stamps died from the effects of a sudden illness. Undeterred by the movement of a Federal flotilla up the Mississippi River from New Orleans, Mary secured passage on a southbound steamboat so that she could bury her daughter at Rosemont. The trip nearly ended in disaster when the reckless captain hit a snag. Fortuitously, another steamer arrived upon the accident scene and the relieved passengers quickly transferred from the sinking boat. However, Mary adamantly refused to board the new vessel until she secured the small coffin that held her daughter. The remainder of the trip was completed without incident.

Hundreds of miles apart, Isaac and Mary Stamps waged separate battles against the unrelenting grief. For Captain Stamps the horror of watching friends and neighbors die around him only added to his sorrow. The night of September 17, 1862, was particularly horrific. When the bloodiest day in American history finally drew to a close along the banks of Antietam Creek and the once tranquil farming community of Sharpsburg, Maryland, the plaintive cries of the wounded filled the darkness. Deeply disturbed by these pleas, Stamps crawled out between the hostile lines and provided water to friend and foe alike.

In December of that same year, Barksdale's Brigade took up defensive positions in Fredericksburg overlooking the Rappahannock River as the rest of the army dug in on the heights above the city. The gray infantrymen harassed and delayed the Federal crossing of the river, helping to set the stage for one of the most decisive Confederate victories of the war.

The following spring Mary and her two surviving daughters traveled east to Richmond to spend some time with President Davis and his wife, Varina. Soon afterwards, Isaac Stamps received a furlough and a train ticket so that he could enjoy a brief visit with his family. During the joyful reunion, Isaac confided to his wife his fear that he would not survive the next battle and requested that he be buried at his beloved Rosemont.

The accuracy of this premonition would be tested on the late afternoon of July 2, 1863, as Barksdale's men formed up on Seminary Ridge opposite Joseph Sherfy's peach orchard. For nearly two hours the Mississippi veterans watched and waited as intense firing swelled to the south around Devil's Den, Little Round Top, and the Wheatfield. The suspense must have been galling, particularly for one captain in the 21st Mississippi. Finally, at about 6:00 o'clock, Barksdale's regiments entered the growing fray with a hair-raising Rebel yell.

The charging Southerners engulfed the advanced outpost of Union soldiers near the Sherfy house and barn, then surged across the Emmitsburg Road and into the orchard on the opposite side. The defenders unleashed several well-aimed volleys into the oncoming mass of troops, but they could not prevent the inexorable advance. With an exuberant General Barksdale leading the way, the triumphant band dashed towards Cemetery Ridge and perhaps even greater laurels.

Captain Stamps was not among them. Just as the 21st Mississippi entered the Peach Orchard, a Yankee bullet cut into his bowels and sent him crashing to the ground. Near the close of the day, a Union counterattack thwarted any further gains by the Mississippians. The mortal wounding of Barksdale is certainly the most well known of the brigade's 747 casualties, but as darkness settled over the area a favorite nephew of the Confederate president also lay dying several hundred yards away.

That evening Colonel Humphreys spent several hours with his grievously wounded son-in-law, who frequently spoke of Mary and the girls. The colonel promised to look after them and following a warm embrace he reluctantly parted to rejoin his command.

The following morning an ambulance carried Stamps to the John Crawford farm along Marsh Creek, the brigade hospital for Barksdale's Brigade. Upon examination, Dr. George Peets determined that the patient had sustained mortal injuries. When told that the South was on the verge of a great victory, the fading captain told his comrades that he could die content. But as the roar of cannon that preceded Pickett's Charge filled the humid summer air, the last thoughts of Isaac Stamps focused on the woman he loved. His strength waning, he cried aloud, "My poor wife! God help her bear it!"

Meanwhile, upon learning that a battle had been fought in Pennsylvania, Mary Stamps paced nervously through the parlors of the Confederate White House. After sharing her concerns with the president, he prayed that Isaac would be spared. When her husband's death was validated by reliable sources, Mary fainted and lay ill for several days. Varina Davis attended to her during this critical period.

Upon regaining her strength, Mary began to visit local military hospitals in search of additional information. She soon met Dr. Peets, who delivered the sword that Isaac had carried throughout the war. More importantly, he provided the location of the grave, for she had every intention of honoring her husband's final request.

In his official capacity, President Davis did everything he could to arrange for his niece to travel through the lines. Despite his best efforts, the negotiations quickly bogged down due to red tape and political posturing. At one point, Mary finally seemed to lose hope. Writing to President Davis from Fincastle, Virginia, she poured out, "As day after day passes with no more to do for him and no more to hear, I find myself bowing before the reality of my lonely lot.... Dear Uncle, you will forgive me for leaning, along with my country ... upon your great heart.... Yours can lean only upon its God."

Finally, later in the year, the diplomatic logjam ended and Mrs. Stamps commenced her sad mission. A flag-of-truce boat carried her to Baltimore, where she boarded a train for Gettysburg. On a cold, bleak winter day Dr. John W. C. O'Neal escorted the Southern lady to the Crawford farm, where numerous mounds of disturbed earth were clearly discernible. After finding the crude headboard that marked her husband's grave under a medium-sized oak tree, she fell to the ground crying. For the fee of $133.70 an undertaker exhumed the body and prepared it for shipment to Richmond in a metal coffin.

The final leg of the journey would prove far more difficult. Late in December, the train conveying the 26-year-old widow and the remains of her husband screeched to a halt near Montgomery, Alabama, due to a stretch of destroyed tracks. Once again, however, Mary Stamps displayed her iron will and courage. Purchasing a wagon and a team of horses, she pressed onward in company with a driver and a guard. During the course of the 400-mile journey Mary often slept upon the ground wrapped in her husband's army cloak. Several weeks later, she finally arrived in Woodville. A proper service was held as Isaac Stamps was laid to rest near his precious Sallie.

Many years afterwards, a Union veteran called upon Mary Stamps at her residence in New Orleans. He informed her that Captain Isaac Stamps had answered his calls for water, as he lay badly wounded at Antietam. Having never forgotten this selfless act he traced his benefactor to Woodville, Mississippi, only to find his grave there. Traveling on to New Orleans, he did the next best thing by thanking the deceased officer's widow. There can be no doubt that this emotional meeting did much to assuage the accumulated grief borne through the years by Mary Stamps and rekindled the warm memories she carried of her husband.

George and Adeline McFarland, USA

By the summer of 1862 the impact of the American Civil War had been felt in even the most secluded sections of the country. In the rural village of McAlisterville in south-central Pennsylvania enrollment at the local academy plummeted due to a late harvest on the local farms and the prevailing "war excitement." Reluctantly, principal George Fisher McFarland released part of the faculty, forcing him and the remainder of his staff to double up on classroom work as well as tend the fields and livestock.

Throughout the summer McFarland became increasingly uneasy as he read newspaper accounts of Union reverses near Richmond and at the Battle of Second Bull Run. Adamantly opposed to secession, he supported local recruitment efforts by delivering patriotic war speeches at various war rallies. By early September, following President Lincoln's call for additional troops, McFarland began to consider a more active roll in the growing conflict. It was an agonizing decision, but on September 8 the 28-year-old educator recorded the following passage in his diary:

> Have at last determined to go to war, if a good company is raised.... This determination has not been made lightly or without much serious thought and anxious prayer. I believe my country needs my services, and it is my duty to yield to her wants and go to her relief in this her extremity. It is hard, very hard to leave my home, my school, my Sabbath school; but above all my dear, now doubly dear wife, son, and daughter, and my earnest prayer is that God may spare me and return me to my home on their account. No soldier ever left dearer ties at home than I will; no one a more faithful wife or loving and beloved children.

Family life, teaching, and religion comprised the central interests in McFarland's life. Six years earlier, he had married 23-year-old Adeline Dellicher Griesemer, a Berks County woman "of great vigor." George and "Addie" established strong and enduring bonds of love, which would help sustain them through the many trials they would encounter during their long marriage. The couple's first child, a daughter born in 1857, died before reaching her third birthday. A son named John Horace McFarland arrived in 1859 and daughter, Emma, followed in 1862. A devoted husband and father, George

George McFarland, ca. 1862 (U.S. Army Military History Institute).

McFarland actively supported the Temperance Movement and on Sundays he supervised the local Sabbath school. The storm clouds of war shattered this peaceful existence.

After making the decision to join the army, McFarland devoted nearly all of his time and energy into recruiting a company of men. His persistence paid off six weeks later when his 92 men were mustered into service as Company D of the 151st Pennsylvania Volunteer Infantry. During the regiment's organization at Camp Curtin in Harrisburg, Captain McFarland was unexpectedly elected as lieutenant colonel by his fellow captains.

Before the regiment departed Camp Curtin in late November, McFarland returned home to procure a horse and attend to other last minute details. Walking into his house after a two-month absence evoked strange emotions. Just as the famous scene from *It's a*

Wonderful Life, where George Bailey kisses the perpetually loose staircase knob, every familiar object was suddenly transfigured into a sacred image.

Farewells were exchanged two short days later and the newly minted officer hiked out the boardwalk and into the street. Suddenly, young Horace recalled that he had his father's knife in his pocket and scrambled out to catch him. After another hug, father and son reluctantly parted. The scene deeply moved the elder McFarland. His prayer that evening mirrored the thoughts of citizen soldiers throughout the ages:

> God grant him and his sister and mother protection and guidance, take care of them during my absence, and if I never return, be a husband and father to them! For their sakes, I desire to return. For their sakes I will fight even more bravely than for my country's. For their sakes I will guard my conduct and watch my own self more carefully than ever. May God strengthen my purposes, purify my thoughts, and preserve my affections, and return me, if at all, a better man than when I left.

The early portion of the 151st's service consisted of tedious picket duty along the banks of Bull Run, twenty-two miles west of Washington, where the men battled sickness, mud, and the bitter winter weather more often than the enemy. Time seemed to move at a glacial pace and the first pangs of homesickness set in during the holiday season. "Christmas in camp was dry and lonesome," complained McFarland.

The letters he exchanged with his wife on an almost daily basis staved off the aching emptiness that threatened to consume him. After reading a letter from Addie on New Year's Eve, he scribbled his final diary entry for 1862: "My wife wrote in such a confiding, affectionate manner that I felt unworthy of her. Her anxiety for me and my safety seems so great that it almost makes me sorry I did not remain at home with her, though I have always struggled against such thoughts. Heartily do I wish the contest was over.... I will finish the year by writing home to my dear wife."

With the active campaign season still several months away, the lonely officer arranged for his wife and children to spend several weeks with him in camp. However, an order transferring the 151st Pennsylvania to the front to join the Army of the Potomac disrupted these carefully orchestrated plans. McFarland later wrote of this disappointment: "The regiment had provided comfortable winter quarters, and secured many comforts and conveniences in its present camp, and though on severe duty was quite well satisfied to remain. The order was especially unpleasant to several officers who expected their wives to visit them and to share for a time the comforts of their log cabins."

The McFarlands made the best of the situation and enjoyed a day of sightseeing together in Washington. Since the family had never been apart for more than a few days, it was a joyous occasion. The growing bond between father and son was particularly noticeable as 3-year-old Horace hung upon his father's neck and would rarely leave him for more than a moment. The proud father also noticed that little Emma had grown larger and prettier during the three-month separation. On the evening of February 14 Colonel McFarland boarded the steamboat that would carry him into Virginia.

A month later, as a late season snow piled up outside of his tent, George reflected upon the anniversary of his wedding: "Seven long but pleasant years have passed away in domestic peace and happiness.... I have tried to thank God for his merciful kindness to me and mine thus long but still fear I am too ungrateful.... Wrote to my wife early this morning. How I would love to spend the evening with her and my dear children!"

As winter begrudgingly gave way to spring the slumbering army camps along the Rappahannock River stirred to life and the increased activity invigorated the men. But

McFarland fell into a temporary despondency when the stream of letters from home suddenly halted. At the same time, Addie McFarland received no news from her husband. Soon both fired off recriminating letters accusing one another of not communicating. Finally, after several weeks of agony, the gremlins in the mail system retreated and on April 17 George received five letters and Addie was delighted to find 10 missives from her husband waiting for her at the post office during a two-day period.

In one of her letters Mrs. McFarland apologized to her husband before serving up a cleverly worded admonishment.

> I do not blame you for complaining. And if I said anything in my letters to hurt your feelings I hope you will forgive me. Let us blame Uncle Sam and forgive each other. I want to tell you here that I will write to you for every mail if I keep my health. And I will not blame you anymore if I do not hear from you as often as I want to. I know you are too good and kind to neglect me.... You say in one of your letters that every married man gets more letters than you. That may be so. But I do say that there is not a man in this world that is more beloved by his wife than you are. And has two dearer children than you have. Sometimes I think you must see us here, the children love each other so much and play together so nice. And there is no pleasure we have but you are with us, if not in body, certainly in spirit.

With his marital relations set straight McFarland prepared himself and his men for the inevitable clash against the Confederates on the opposite side of the river. Although the 151st Pennsylvania played only a minor role in the bitter defeat at Chancellorsville, the campaign sapped McFarland's mental and physical reservoirs. "The past 11 days have been severe and eventful," he posted to his diary on May 8. "Hardships and fatigues have been endured by all, and many officers and men are extremely low spirited." The broken down officer noted that he enjoyed no food or drink for 48 hours while getting some eight hours of sleep during the course of four days and nights. Consequently, he admitted to feeling depressed and homesick.

He would have little time to lick his wounds because on June 11 orders passed down from headquarters to prepare his command for an immediate move requiring great mobility. Marches of twenty plus miles were commonplace as the great blue columns trudged northward under a blistering sun and through clouds of suffocating dust. Afflicted with a severe case of diarrhea, Lieutenant Colonel McFarland resolutely stuck to his post.

Soon after the First Corps crossed the Potomac River on June 25, the former schoolteacher observed a sight dear to his heart near Poolsville, Maryland, "a large common school house ... well filled with well dressed, laughing, lovely, innocent-looking girls ... all out to see us pass by." It was the first school he had seen in many months. The morale of the weary troops continued to climb as the loyal citizens of western Maryland turned out in large numbers to greet them and to hand out homemade delicacies with cups of fresh milk and cold water.

By the evening of June 29th the men of the 151st Pennsylvania bivouacked just two miles from the border of their native state after a fatiguing march through the rain. Collapsing on the wet earth McFarland hastily scrawled a letter home that he completed the following morning. He described the surreal feeling of returning home "not to enjoy peace and comfort there, but to drive out an invading foe." He assured his wife that the Rebels "will pay for their temerity" and "will not long pollute the soil of Pennsylvania with impunity."

Meanwhile, widespread panic and unrest erupted throughout southern Pennsylvania as Lee's forces occupied York and Carlisle while threatening to capture the state capital of Harrisburg. Wide ranging Confederate foraging parties only heightened the growing agitation. Addie McFarland reported to George on June 28 that "Persons are bringing droves of horses from the lower counties through this place on further for safekeeping." She also shared her sense of helplessness as the invasion neared its high-water mark:

> Suppose they were to come here. I all alone, and not a soul to care for me. What would I do? I know I should not write this to you. You have hardships and trouble enough to try you without my complaints. But indeed you do not know how bad I do feel. These are truly times to try men's souls and women's too. I for one have endured more trouble these nine months since you are away than I did all my lifetime before. But let us hope for the best and trust in the Lord.

As news trickled into McAlisterville that the much-maligned Army of the Potomac had defeated the Confederates at the crossroads town of Gettysburg, Addie McFarland and her neighbors in Juniata County breathed a collective sigh of relief. This joy was soon tempered when published casualty lists revealed the steep cost of the victory. Of the 33 men of Company D of the 151st Pennsylvania who had been engaged in the fighting, twelve had been killed outright or suffered mortal injuries, while at least eleven more lay wounded. The regiment as a whole was virtually annihilated.

By July 6, Addie McFarland knew that her husband was among the casualties. Imagine her shock upon receiving this brief letter dated July 1, 1863, from Gettysburg:

> My Dear Wife Addie D. McFarland
> I am wounded in both legs and a prisoner. But I am in good spirits and will no doubt recover. Do not worry yourself about me. It will go all right with me. I will be taken care of and no doubt sent where you can come to see me.
> I did my duty and was wounded by my flag. My horse was first hit and will die. After fighting quite a time I was hit by a cross fire, the same ball hitting both legs, about 4 o'clock.
> Your true husband,
> Geo. F. McFarland, Lt. Col. 151 Pa.

On July 5, as the Southern army retired to Virginia, McFarland fired off another letter explaining that following his wounding a nearby private carried him into the Lutheran Seminary building, where he lay on the bare floor in pools of his own blood for two days. Near the end of the correspondence George mentioned the fact that the regimental surgeon amputated his right leg just below the knee on the evening of July 3. "I suppose you can come and see me," he casually told his wife. "There will be work enough for others to do in attending to the wounded too.... You will find me in good spirits and condition. I am doing well. God has been merciful to me for your sakes."

The patient's relaxed tone is surprising considering the ordeal through which he had just passed, including a narrow escape from friendly fire. Prior to his operation a stray Union artillery shell crashed through one of the Seminary's lower windows and passed directly over the recumbent officer's body before lodging in a nearby partition. McFarland had been sitting up in his bed just a moment earlier and the shift in position undoubtedly saved his life. Perhaps by underplaying his true condition he hoped to spare his wife from needless worry.

The day after receiving news of her husband's wounding Addie McFarland was on her way to Gettysburg with the two children and a local doctor. The party traveled nine miles to Mifflin by carriage and then took the train for Harrisburg. Beyond this point, all transportation was in a state of confusion. A determined Mrs. McFarland appealed to Governor Andrew Curtin for assistance and received a special pass to board a construction train. Since the bridge spanning the Susquehanna River between Columbia and Wrightsville had been destroyed during the invasion, the group crossed the waterway in a rowboat.

Finally, on July 10 or 11, the McFarlands enjoyed a reunion inside the Seminary. Sensing his wife's anxiety, the gritty colonel informed his wife, "I am sound of mind and of stomach and I do not intend to die." Although Addie and the children slept at a local boardinghouse during their stay, they spent much of their time in the hospital. According to one witness, Addie not only nursed her wounded husband, "but found time to contribute many acts of kindness to the hundreds of wounded and dying soldiers of both armies, which lay in the Seminary."

Restless and energetic, McFarland could not have always been a cooperative patient. His halting recovery frustrated him immensely as his stump healed ever so slowly and his badly shattered left ankle caused him considerable discomfort. The presence of his family helped pull him through this bleak period.

Therefore, it was with great reluctance that George permitted his wife to return home to attend to a number of business concerns. "As she was with me, and unremitting in her labors for my comfort and welfare, every day for seven weeks it is quite natural that I regret her absence," he recorded in his diary entry for August 1. Although he planned to follow in several days, over two weeks would elapse before his condition improved enough so that he could withstand the train ride home.

Back home in McAlisterville, McFarland would be confined to his bed for over seven months, but he still managed to conduct a daily schedule of classes, the academy students gathering by his bedside for recitals. The following April he walked for the first time since his wounding. Faced with lifelong handicaps, George's strength and perseverance shines through the ages. As a family friend recalled:

> The shattered leg was for many years an open running sore, which was dressed daily by his faithful wife. Over fifty pieces of splintered bone worked themselves out, or were extracted by the surgeon. He was a man of wonderful energy and will power, and worked to maintain his family, hobbling about on crutches and his wooden leg and pushed his business affairs against all obstacles when many a well man would have been disheartened.

McFarland went on to head the Pennsylvania Soldiers' Orphans' School System, an institution created to care for and educate the children of soldiers who had given their lives for the Union cause. Later, he operated a large plant nursery and greenhouse operation in Harrisburg, published a weekly newspaper, and traveled to England as a delegate to a world prohibition convention.

Throughout the postwar period McFarland made several trips to Gettysburg, highlighted by the dedication of the 151st Pennsylvania's regimental monument on July 1, 1888. The old colonel delivered the main address during the ceremony after Emma McFarland, who was just an infant during the battle, unveiled the monument amid the hearty "huzzas" of the crowd.

After years of stubbornly resisting the ill effects of his wound, George's health began to deteriorate rapidly following the Gettysburg ceremonies. Addie recalled his growing weak and emaciated and being so thin that she could carry him herself. In 1891 the couple moved to Tallapoosa in northwestern Georgia with hopes that the warmer climate would help alleviate George's pain.

Veterans of the 151st Pennsylvania during the dedication of their monument on July 1, 1888. George McFarland and his wife, Addie, are standing to the right of the group (U.S. Army Military History Institute).

But after a period of improvement, McFarland was once again prostrated by illness. As usual, Addie maintained her brave composure and attempted to cheer him. This time, however, she knew the end was approaching. On the morning of December 18, 1891, George McFarland passed away peacefully at the age of 57 from pneumonia. His remains were shipped back to Pennsylvania and interred in the Harrisburg Cemetery. Addie McFarland lived until 1904 before joining her dearest friend and companion.

John and Martha Callis, USA

As a volunteer nurse stationed at the refreshment lodge set up the U.S. Sanitary Commission along the Gettysburg & Hanover Railroad, Maryanne Woolsey assisted hundreds of wounded men as they waited to board the cars that would transport them to the government hospitals in the larger cities. A few of them left an indelible impression. Among the most memorable was one described as "an elderly man, sick, wounded, and crazy, singing and talking about home." Woolsey and her companions greatly pleased the eccentric patient by providing him with a red flannel shirt, drawers, and a red calico dressing gown. After dressing in the new attire, he composed a letter to his wife, which he adorned with gingham covers and then entrusted to an attendant to mail for him. The next morning he shipped out with a large company of other convalescent soldiers.

His wife and sister arrived at the lodge that evening. "Fortunately, we had the queer little gingham book to identify him by," stated Woolsey, "and when some one said, 'It is the man, you know, who screamed so,' the poor wife was certain about him. He had been crazy before the war, but not for two years, now, she said. He had been fretting for home since he was hurt, and when the doctor told him there was no chance of being sent there, he lost heart, and wrote to his wife to come and carry him away. It seemed almost hopeless for two lone women, who had never been out of their own little town, to succeed in finding a soldier among so many, sent in so many different directions; but we helped them as we could, and started them on their journey the next morning...."

A week later the ladies wrote a letter of gratitude to the nurses who had assisted them at Gettysburg. They had found their beloved soldier and were headed for home.

Following the battle, Lieutenant Colonel John Callis of the 7th Wisconsin also traveled home with the help of his wife, but his journey was nothing short of an odyssey. Born in Fayetteville, North Carolina, on January 3, 1828, Callis's family moved to Tennessee, his mother's birthplace, when he was ten years old before settling in Lancaster, Wisconsin, two years later. When Confederate forces fired upon Fort Sumter in April 1861, Callis, who earned a living as a merchant, closed his store and together with his clerk signed on to defend the Union.

"I then conceived it to be not only my privilege, but my patriotic duty to abandon my business, my home and my family for a time and go to battle for the Nation's safety," he explained. "My father ... advised otherwise, saying that I was going to war with my own flesh and blood, as all of our relatives lived in the South, but I followed the dictates of my own convictions and went, and ever since have been proud of having done my duty." On the opening day of battle at Gettysburg, Callis paid a steep price for his convictions, and ironically, an enemy officer from his birthplace would come to his aid.

During the early morning rout of Brigadier General James Archer's Brigade along the banks of Willoughby Run, Callis had his horse shot from under him and he himself sustained two slight wounds during the brief encounter. Afterwards, the Iron Brigade reformed on the crest of McPherson's Ridge overlooking the run. Lieutenant Colonel Callis and the 7th Wisconsin held a position near the right of the brigade line along the northern boundary of Herbst's Woods.

John B. Callis (seated at front, center) with officers and staff of the 7th Regiment. Veteran Reserve Corps, in 1864. The other men in the photograph aren't identified (U.S. Army Military History Institute).

In the early afternoon General Henry Heth mounted an attack against the line on McPherson's Ridge as converging Southern forces exerted pressure along the entire length of the Union defensive perimeter that stretched in an arc to the west and north of the town. After a brutal, close-quarters slugfest in the woods, the veteran Iron Brigade soldiers fell back slowly towards Seminary Ridge, contesting every inch of ground.

"We moved by the right of companies to the rear, making the Seminary ... our objective point," recalled Callis. "Being closely pursued by the Confederates," he continued, "we faced, wheeled into line and fired; then again by the right of companies to the rear, loading on the march, and, as before, wheeled into line and fired. We executed the same movement with terrible effect. Many a brave North Carolinian bit the dust in that movement before we reached the Seminary. At this juncture I was shot in the right breast, the ball entering my lung...."

The projectile struck the colonel midway between the sternum and spinal column, fracturing a rib, before lodging deep inside his body. A detail of men started to carry him off the field, but he was abandoned in a small field bordering the Chambersburg Pike after the pursuing Confederates captured the entire party. Soon several Southerners descended upon the helpless Federal officer, removing a portfolio from his coat pocket that contained $220 in greenbacks and gold, an express receipt, and personal papers. The marauders also yanked off one of Callis's boots without unbuckling the spur, inflicting additional pain upon him. Chagrined that the footwear did not fit any of them, they tossed it aside and commenced dividing up the remainder of the loot.

About this time, Callis, wincing with pain, drew the attention of a compassionate Confederate. It turned out that this individual, Lieutenant Henry E. Shepherd of the 43rd North Carolina Infantry, hailed from Callis's hometown of Fayetteville, as did his commanding officer, Colonel Thomas Kenan. After providing the wounded man with a gulp of whiskey, Shepherd reported the discovery to his colonel.

Upon arriving on the scene, Kenan announced, "You are now my prisoner, and I'll treat you well; I may be yours later on." He kept his promise. After Callis pointed out the soldiers who had robbed him, Kenan ordered the culprits to return the items. Fearing that the same men might return once the colonel departed, Callis requested that the money be sent to his family back in Wisconsin. The North Carolinian promised to do so. He also detailed slightly injured men and a Negro servant to look after him. As a token of appreciation Callis presented his adversary with his pair of fancy silver boot spurs.

For nearly two days, the Wisconsin colonel lay on the ground near the Seminary. In one aspect he was more fortunate than the 300 Union patients tightly crammed into the rooms and halls of the brick building. While these men could obtain little relief from the stifling heat, the light rain that fell the first evening relieved Callis's burning fever. Still, he battled a number of other symptoms, including blood loss, intense pain and partial paralysis in the right side of his body, and the development of jaundice. "But oh! Suffering is no name for what I felt during those 43 long hours," declared Callis. As the battle raged farther south, a Confederate surgeon examined the wound and pronounced that the victim could not live longer than six hours.

Somehow, Callis persevered. Following the repulse of Pickett's Charge, Lee's army dug in along Seminary Ridge in preparation of a Union counterattack. Fearing that he might be crushed under a cannon wheel or sliced by the hoof of a horse, the immobile officer begged his small guard to carry him to a small house across the pike near the railroad cut. The owner, "a kind-hearted old Pennsylvania German," placed Callis on a straw bed inside. The following day a Union cavalry patrol rescued the badly wounded colonel and arranged to have him transported by ambulance to the home of Dr. John W. C. O'Neal at the southeast corner of Baltimore and High streets. He remained there for about a month as his condition improved slightly.

Near the beginning of August, Mrs. Martha Callis arrived in town to help care for her husband. At about the same time, the colonel was moved a short distance down Baltimore Street to the home of David Buehler, a lawyer and newspaper editor, who also served as the town's postmaster. Prior to the battle, Francis "Fannie" Buehler had persuaded her husband to leave Gettysburg since she feared that the Confederates would arrest even minor government officials.

Remaining behind with the couple's six children, Mrs. Buehler became fully absorbed in nursing the wounded soldiers that arrived at her home following the first day's battle. When she heard the "cries and groans of suffering humanity" from the county courthouse across the street, she swung into action by delivering food and clothing that had been sent to her from friends living outside the area. After Mr. Buehler returned, he assisted his wife in distributing additional supplies to more distant hospitals. The Buehlers' humanitarian efforts did not end there. They placed their dining room table on the front porch and regularly stocked it with refreshments for hungry visitors and relief workers. Later, Fannie Buehler helped to cook meals for Union and Confederate patients at the Seminary.

Given his serious condition, it is probable that Callis's relocation was necessitated by the need for additional space to accommodate himself, his wife, and the former store clerk that now functioned as his nurse. The Buehler home was among the first three-story residences in the town and the entire third floor was allocated for the care of the Union officer. "We gave his wife the freedom of the house, and did all we could to make her and her husband comfortable, free of expense," noted Mrs. Buehler. Medical officials had told her that the case would undoubtedly prove fatal.

However, Callis continued to show signs of improvement. The entrance wound healed up and both his appetite and general health were on the upswing. Unfortunately, the minie ball remained deep inside of him and it could not be safely removed. The liver hardened and became slightly enlarged, and when the doctors tapped on his chest, they detected a dull percussion at the base of the right lung. The prescribed treatment consisted of the administration of tonics, painkillers, stimulants, and a full diet. In addition, a poultice was applied to the skin over the liver and lungs.

Near the end of the month, Mrs. Callis received word from Wisconsin that her children had contracted the measles, a life-threatening disease at the time. At once she announced her intention to go home and, if necessary, she would return to Gettysburg later. However, after sharing these plans with her husband, he immediately declared that he would accompany her. Although attending doctors strongly objected, stating that the slightest movement would cause the bullet to shift and likely cause a fatal hemorrhage, Callis could not be dissuaded. "We urged his remaining; but he took his life in his own hand, he determined to go home, and all we could do was to give him as comfortable a send off as possible, which we did," recalled Fannie Buehler. "Amid tears of gratitude mingled with pain and anxiety the Col. and his family left us."

Late on the evening of his departure, a telegram arrived from nearby Hanover Junction. Mrs. Callis conveyed the sad news that the motion of the cars had dislodged the bullet just as the doctors had warned and that her husband was now bleeding to death. The

Buehlers could do little but wire back their sympathy and await further news. Five days later, they endured a tragedy of their own when their youngest son died suddenly.

Although consumed by her own grief, Mrs. Buehler "thought often of our friends at the Junction, of the sad death of the colonel and the long, lonely ride of Mrs. Callis ... and her arrival home. We waited day after day for news, but heard nothing." Then near Christmas, a gentleman from the West walked into the office of David Buehler and handed him a recent letter from Colonel Callis! Not only was the officer alive, but he planned a trip to Gettysburg to visit the couple that he referred to as "two of the best living mortals on earth." He made good on this promise and also returned two years later during a laying of the cornerstone for the Soldiers' National Monument in the National Cemetery.

There can be little doubt that Callis also called upon Dr. and Mrs. O'Neal. In a letter mailed from his home on September 28, 1863, he wrote to them: "The kind manner in which I was treated under your roof merits every grateful acknowledgment from me and is not nor will it ever be forgotten.... I am improving slowly. Had an abscess break in my liver and the contents pass off through my lungs on my journey home; came very near going over the dam.... Give my love to little Mary and the rest of the children."

The above incident took place at Altoona, Pennsylvania, following the nearly fatal crisis at Hanover Junction. Callis coughed up poisonous bile all the way to Chicago. At Boscobel, Wisconsin, he remained immobile for nearly two weeks, hacking up about a quart of yellowish green fluid tinged with blood. Finally, Callis reached home, and on October 5 he walked for the first time without assistance.

Inconceivably, Callis attempted to return to his regiment later in the year. After reaching Washington, intense pain compelled him to seek treatment at an officer's hospital in Annapolis. There, on November 16, during a severe "paroxysm of coughing," he ejected two small pieces of blue flannel that had been carried into his body at the time of his wounding. Over Callis's protests he was discharged from the military on December 28, 1863, and pensioned for total and permanent disability.

The following summer, Callis joined the Veteran Reserve Corps with the rank of major. On February 11, 1865, he received a promotion to lieutenant colonel, and a month later he was awarded a brevet to brigadier general of volunteers for meritorious conduct during the war. Following his discharge on May 4, 1868, Callis was returned to the pension rolls.

The pain from his injury would never dissipate. He continued to suffer from partial paralysis of the lower extremities, acute soreness in the right side of the body, and with nearly every breath, "a heavy tearing pain" sliced through the right lung region, where the bullet had permanently lodged.

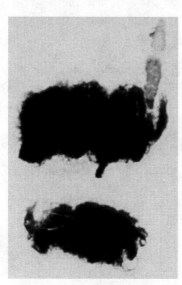

Two pieces of woolen cloth ejected from the lungs of John B. Callis (Historical Collections, National Museum of Health and Medicine, Armed Forces Institute of Pathology).

During the Reconstruction Era, Callis moved to Huntsville, Alabama, perhaps for the health benefits offered by a warmer climate. He subsequently won election to the 40th U.S. Congress, serving from 1868 to 69. Upon his return to

Wisconsin, Callis served briefly in the state assembly before his old wounds finally brought him down. A series of attacks that brought on vomiting, a hacking cough, and the expectoration of bloody pus confined him to bed for months at a time, requiring Martha to dress him and feed him like a child. Callis's suffering mercifully came to an end on September 24, 1898.

Five years before his death, the aging veteran communicated with Thomas Kenan, the North Carolinian who had shown him mercy and compassion years earlier. "I have told the story of the spurs and your kindness until it has become a 'campfire story' all over the State," wrote Callis. "I wish there were more frequently such interchange of friendly greetings between ex–Confederate and Union soldiers as this between you and me."

Amos and Atlannta Sweet, USA

Despite the lengthy ordeals endured by women such as Mrs. McFarland and Mrs. Callis, they could consider themselves blessed. Just as often, the arduous trip to Gettysburg undertaken by a soldier's wife ended in heartbreak. These scenes, all too commonplace throughout the summer of 1863, left permanent scars upon all those who witnessed them.

Of the dozen or so men that Sallie Myers cared for in her father's house, only two died. Sergeant Alexander Stewart expired in her arms on Monday, July 6, and a little over a week later, she witnessed the final moments of Private Amos Sweet, a member of Company H, 150th Pennsylvania. Private Sweet arrived at the Myers house following the amputation of his right leg at the nearby Catholic church. He seemed to be doing well after the operation and wrote his wife, the former Atlannta Fanner, to come to him. Both had been in their early twenties on their wedding day in the spring of 1860. A daughter named Amy entered the world on August 20, 1862. Days later her father had left home in Troy Center, Crawford County, to serve his country.

Traveling from the remote northwestern corner of the state, it took Mrs. Sweet several days to complete the trip to Adams County. Meanwhile, her husband's situation took a dramatic turn for the worse when he suffered a secondary hemorrhage around the stump of his twice amputated limb. According to Miss Myers:

> He had been with us several days and had become very fond of my little sisters. Very frequently they sang for him. His favorite was "There is No Name So Sweet on Earth," at that time a popular Sunday School hymn. He suffered from indigestion, and one night in his restlessness, the bandages became loose. It was after midnight; the nurse, tired out, had fallen asleep, and before we could find a surgeon he was so weakened by loss of blood that he died the next morning. A few days later his wife came. She was young and had never been away from home.... She did not know of his death until she came to us, and her grief was heartrending.

In an earlier account, Myers recorded Private Sweet's final words: "Tell—my wife—I'm—going—home." She also included another detail that forever linked the two personal tragedies that she had witnessed in her home: "Myself & Alexander Stewart's father (who had arrived in the meantime) stood by his bed, the old man with tears in his eyes, exclaimed, 'Oh! Had it been God's will that I could have stood by my own son's death-bed.'"

Atlannta Sweet returned home alone at the approach of daughter Amy's first birthday. Her husband was buried in the Soldiers' National Cemetery. In 1866, Atlannta remar-

ried. A year later, the legal guardian-
ship of Amy Sweet passed to another
individual.

The grave of Amos Sweet in the Soldiers' National Cemetery.

John and Harriet Fly, USA

As sectional strife and political
turmoil gripped the nation, a wedding ceremony took place in West-
borough, Massachusetts, in the
spring of 1860. Bathed in the eupho-
ria of the moment, Harriet Copeland
Fly, the 23-year-old bride, could not have envisioned that a brutal war would soon shat-
ter her happiness and unlock a dark secret about the man she had pledged to love forever.

A year afterwards, John Fly left Harriet and his blacksmith trade to defend the Union
as a private in the 13th Massachusetts Infantry. His strange saga began to unravel on the
afternoon of July 1, 1863, as beleaguered Union troops retreated through the streets of
Gettysburg. This rather ordinary soldier seemed to have a knack for the unusual. Private
Austin Stearns, a comrade of Fly's, had taken refuge in Christ Lutheran Church on Chambersburg Street by posing as a medical assistant. This circumstance led to a fortuitous discovery:

> On going back towards the church I saw a rebel ambulance standing before the door with
> several of our Surgeons standing beside it earnestly talking. On getting near I heard they
> were talking about some one in the ambulance. On looking in I saw there, dressed in a
> rebel uniform and very weak from the loss of blood, John Flye, the first man of our com-
> pany hit. I told the surgeons that I knew that man, that we were of the same company, and
> they immediately ordered him to be taken in. Flye was left on the field, and the rebs find-
> ing him, and seeing his clothes covered and growing stiff with blood, had exchanged his
> pants for one of their own, and brought him in. The surgeons, seeing him in gray, could
> not believe he was a Union soldier. Flye died in a few days.

Thanks to the timely arrival and testimony of Private Stearns, Harriet Fly received
word of her husband's wounding and was at his side when he died on July 27. The story
took an even more bizarre twist when the grieving widow filed an application for a pension with the War Department the following February. Imagine her shock several weeks
later when notified that another Mrs. Fly had already been approved for the claim!

As it turned out, John Fly had married one Rachael Jane Bragg on January 7, 1849,
in Augusta, Maine. The couple had a son together the following spring and named him
John Fly, Jr. The marriage failed, however, and a divorce was granted in 1857. For reasons known only to him, John never disclosed this fact to his new bride.

Stunned and humiliated, Harriet Fly responded with a vitriolic legal suit, presenting
circumstantial evidence that her husband's first wife had committed bigamy and engaged
in prostitution. It was all for naught. The Pension Bureau ruled that she had no rights to
the pension since it had been awarded on behalf of 14-year-old John Fly, Jr., Rachael's
minor son. Harriet Fly's memories of her husband and the war that claimed his life would
be forever tainted.

Charles and Ellen Billings, USA

Near the fiftieth anniversary of the Battle of Gettysburg, Joshua Lawrence Chamberlain, the former commander of the 20th Maine Infantry, returned to the rugged slopes of Little Round Top. On the second day of the battle his men had fought courageously there to help preserve the left flank of the Army of the Potomac. As he sat alone on the storied crest, the veteran underwent a transcendental experience. Once again, he could hear the shouted orders mingled with savage screams, periodically muffled by the ripping volleys of musketry that echoed through the hardwoods. The projecting shelves of diabase became altars for the gallant commanders who fell there in the heat of combat—Vincent and O'Rorke, Weed and Hazlett. On the rocky spur below the main elevation, he could see pools of blood filling the crevices of the ancient boulders, followed by the forms of his own young heroes, "whose remembered faces in every home should be cherished symbols of the true."

One of the faces that reappeared to Chamberlain belonged to Captain Charles W. Billings of Company C, "the valor of whose onward-looking eyes not death itself could quench." In September 1862, the 37-year-old lumberman from Clinton, Maine, left his wife, Ellen, and two daughters for the life of a soldier. As the contest for the spur ebbed and flowed across the inhospitable terrain, a bullet thudded into the captain's left knee, forcing him to relinquish command of his company.

Orderlies from the Ambulance Corps placed Billings inside an old barn on the Michael Fiscel farm along with the most serious hospital cases of the Fifth Corps. The Reverend R. J. Parvin, a delegate with the United States Christian Commission, later spoke of the last days of Captain Billings:

> The brave fellow had some of his own men lying on the floor not far from him. He loved them with a father's love. As one after another died before his eyes, it worked so upon his mind that he became delirious, until it took four or five men to hold him. With great difficulty we got him away from his men into a room by himself, where he rallied and became a little better.

Later, Billings asked the reverend what the surgeon had said concerning his prospects, and he received a candid reply informing him that he would soon die. The captain prepared a final message for his wife and then instructed Parvin, "Don't stay any longer with me, Chaplain; go and help the boys." Afterwards, he requested that his body be embalmed and sent back to Maine.

At about 11 o'clock on the morning of July 15, Captain Charles Billings "passed away in triumph." Late that night, as Reverend Parvin sat in his tent writing letters, there was a knock at the door and in stepped a man asking for Captain Billings.

"Who are you?" asked Parvin.

"I am his brother; I have his wife with me! I have kept her up all the way with the hope that we would find the Captain in good condition. Where is he, sir?"

"You have not brought the Captain's wife out here tonight?"

"No I left her in town until the morning."

"That was well. The body of your brother was sent to the embalmers this afternoon."

Broken with grief, Billings' brother cried that he could not bring himself to break the news to his sister-in-law. "And so our duty was to see the bereaved wife, and deliver to her the messages and tokens of the dying love of her husband, and to speak the words of comfort in the name of the Lord," remembered Parvin. The wife and brother of the deceased captain took the body home to Clinton, Maine, where it was buried in the family plot in River View Cemetery. Ellen Billings had many years to reflect upon her loss, as she lived until 1924.

Hardy and Julia Graves, CSA

Guided by conscience, or perhaps by the natural tenderness of the female gender, the Northern women who labored as nurses at Gettysburg nearly always provided wounded enemy soldiers with the same quality of care that they gave to their own men. Southern women typically expressed heartfelt gratitude when they learned of these acts.

Responding to the urgent request of a Union surgeon, the youthful Sallie Myers paid regular visits to St. Francis Xavier Catholic Church, located just six doors east of her father's home on West High Street. Like the others in the borough, this house of worship had been converted into a hospital and quickly filled to capacity with torn and bleeding soldiers. In a postwar newspaper article, Myers wrote:

> As I entered the Church the first men I saw lying on the floor, to the right of the entrance, were three Southern soldiers. To the best of my knowledge they were the only ones there who were not Union soldiers. I did what I could for them, and had some conversation with them. One of them particularly attracted my attention. He was, or seemed to be, a large man, though he was lying down and I could not tell very well. His complexion was dark, and he had the blackest eyes and hair that I have ever seen. That was fifty years ago, but I can see him as distinctly as then, lying there helpless and the appealing look in his great black eyes.

Several weeks later, while visiting Camp Letterman Hospital, Sallie Myers made a shocking discovery:

> We went into the "dead tent," and there lay the man who had attracted my attention in the Catholic church, but the great black eyes were forever closed. On his breast was pinned his name—Hardy Graves and below it was his wife's name, Julia Graves, Brundidge, Pike Co., Alabama. I cut off a lock of his hair, and told her what I knew of her husband. She replied and asked if I could find his grave.... He had been buried with many others in a plot of ground near Camp Letterman. I gathered some wild flowers and enclosed them to her, telling her how her husband's grave was situated and that it was marked.

Private Hardy Graves, Company C, 6th Alabama, was buried in row 1, plot 18, in the Confederate section of the hospital cemetery following his death on July 25. But Julia Graves could not be convinced of this fact, and she gradually visualized a more sinister role in the selfless actions of Miss Myers. Perhaps to assuage her overwhelming grief, the distraught widow found it less painful to believe that her husband had become romantically involved with another woman. In December of 1868, Mrs. Graves enlisted the help of a local attorney, who subsequently wrote to the Gettysburg postmaster on her behalf:

> [T]he question is why did she put her self to so much trouble concerning this one Mr. Graves, it looks rather suspicious.... this woman wrote in her last letter to Mrs. Graves that she had just returned from a trip to the western part of your state & had that day wedded herself to one Mr. Stuart, a Presbyterian minister, and his wife seems to think that Mr. Graves was the Mr. Stuart that she married on that day & had changed his name. She requested me to write to you & request of you if it is not too much to visit the grave yard & hunt for his grave.... if this supposition of hers is not true & you ever chance to meet this Mrs. Stuart do not divulge to her this for it would insult her after her kindness to her.

There is no record of a response to this inquiry. Sallie Myers had indeed fallen in love as a direct result of the battle but in no way did it involve Hardy Graves, though she obviously noted his striking physical attributes. During the summer of 1864 the family of Sergeant Alexander Stewart traveled to Gettysburg to meet Myers, who had so tenderly cared for their loved one after his mortal wounding. In the course of this visit a romance blossomed between Sallie and Henry F. Stewart, Alexander's younger brother, and on October 17, 1867, the couple exchanged wedding vows in Gettysburg. The two brothers had served in the army together until a camp accident disabled Henry and led to his discharge in February 1863.

The newlyweds set up housekeeping in Mercer County, Pennsylvania, after Reverend Henry Stewart accepted his first pastorate at the United Presbyterian Church in Jamestown. Tragically, less than a year after the wedding, Sallie Myers became a widow when her husband died from the effects of a lingering illness.

The letter written on behalf of Julia Graves eventually reached Sallie Myers Stewart and she preserved it with her personal papers. It is unlikely that she harbored any bitterness towards the Southern widow.

George Cooper, CSA, and Maurice Buckingham, USA

Throughout the ages much of a young man's self worth has been tied to his physical attractiveness and to his ability to provide a decent standard of living for his family. These influences certainly influenced behavioral patterns in the Victorian dominated culture of the 1860s. Accordingly, Civil War soldiers often feared a disfiguring or disabling injury as much as death itself.

While leading the 43rd North Carolina into combat on July 1, Colonel Thomas Kenan observed one such incident involving Private George Cooper, who at age 26 had enlisted in Company A from New Hanover County the previous summer. "He was shot in the face, which caused an almost instantaneous swelling thereof, and a proportionate disfiguring of the countenance. He turned around abruptly in great pain and said to the commanding officer of his company, 'Captain, do you think J. will love me now?'"

Eventually, a Yankee bullet settled the matter. Struck in the left thigh at Hanover Junction, Virginia, on May 24, 1864, Private Cooper died three days later in a Richmond Hospital.

The answer to this question also dominated the thoughts of a disabled soldier from Genesco, New York. Struck in the thigh and shoulder on Oak Ridge near the same location as Private Cooper was wounded, Color Sergeant Maurice Buckingham, who was also in his mid–20s, was later carried inside the Christ Lutheran Church on Chambersburg Street. At this site the native of England, came under the care of Martha Ehler and the Patriot Daughters of Lancaster.

Ehler developed a special relationship with Sergeant Buckingham. She learned that he had arrived in the States as an orphan, but after receiving an education in the free school system, his business interests prospered. Throughout the war's early campaigns Buckingham proudly carried the colors of the 104th New York until his good fortune ran out at Gettysburg.

The conversation became more personal when the sergeant related that "there was one on whom all his hopes centered, who made life precious and desirable to him." Ehler recorded his plight a year later in a book published to help finance her group's ongoing relief efforts:

> To her I wrote a letter, telling of his sad state, how he had fallen, bleeding and wounded; and, at his request, added, that though he had lost his leg, he was proud to tell her that he had saved the regimental colors, and his own life, too, was still spared

The grave of Maurice Buckingham in the Soldiers' National Cemetery.

him, which was only made valuable by thoughts of her. This was surely enough to make any true woman feel proud that over so noble a heart she alone held sway. His wound was doing remarkably well, and every day, while attending to his wants, I would ask him pleasantly about the answer to our letter, remarking that perhaps it was too full of sweet words to be seen by a stranger.

At last, I found that all my cheerful words failed to rouse him from the despondent mood into which he had fallen, and I discovered his great anxiety at not receiving an answer to his letter. I begged him to be patient, and explained that the mail had been interrupted by the recent raid, all of which failed to reassure him; and when, going to him the next morning, I saw lying beside him on his pillow a letter, directed by a lady's delicate hand, I felt all would be well. Yes, the letter was delicately directed, delicately written, and delicately worded—but its meaning was not to be misunderstood. It was a cool, calm, regret that she could no longer be his; to which was added the fear that the loss of his limb might affect his prospects in life. He handed me the letter to read, with a look of fixed despair—buried his head in the pillow, and wept like a child. To him she had been the embodiment of all that was true and lovely; and while others had mothers, sisters and friends, she was his all. The blow had been sudden, but sure. When he looked up again, his face bore the pallor of marble, and I saw there was no hope. All day long we gave him stimulants, and tried by words of sympathy to rouse him, but in vain; he lingered two days ... and his last words were "tell her I forgive her."

Ernest Simpson, USA

At the end of July 1863, an Ohio lieutenant wrote to his hometown newspaper: "[L]anguage cannot tell to those who have lost their fathers, husbands, and sons, with what determination they faced the cannon's mouth, and all the deadly missil[e]s the Rebels hurled at the Union army." While the vast majority of the men in blue did their best to avoid being struck by a deadly missile, one Union artillerist entered the fray with a death wish.

Ernest Simpson left his hometown in Leipzig, Germany, when his parents disapproved of his intended bride. After a failed suicide attempt in London, the distraught German arrived in Providence, Rhode Island, near the outbreak of the Civil War. In the fall of 1861, at the age of 22, he enlisted as a private in Battery E, 1st Rhode Island Light Artillery. Standing well over six feet tall, with auburn hair, he must have stood out among his fellow gun mates. Promoted to corporal the following January, a lengthy illness sidelined Simpson throughout the latter half of the year. Shortly after returning to duty in January 1863, Lieutenant John K. Bucklyn appointed him as his company clerk.

Twenty years later, in an interview with the Providence *Sunday Star*, Bucklyn stated that Simpson had joined the battery with the expectation of being killed. "He said I was his only friend in America, and he made a will in my favor, which I now have." Likely, the lieutenant assigned his friend to a noncombat role to protect him from harm.

When General Daniel Sickles advanced his Third Corps troops to seize the high ground along the Emmitsburg Road on July 2, Bucklyn's battery deployed near the Joseph Sherfy farm in support of the infantry. Before the crushing attack by General William Barksdale's Mississippi Brigade, a furious artillery duel raged between Union gunners in the Peach Orchard and Confederate batteries posted to the south and directly to the west. "I don't think there was ever in our war a hotter, harder, sharper artillery afternoon than this," declared a Southern artillery commander.

His Union opponents would certainly have agreed with this assessment. Caught in a deadly crossfire, Battery E suffered fearful losses. Confederate fire knocked down about 40 of the battery's complement of horses, and 28 officers and men were killed and wounded by the end of the day, representing the heaviest casualty total of any Third Corps battery.

The hellish scene presented a perfect opportunity for a man hoping to end his life. Sensing his time had finally arrived, the lanky corporal dashed over to Lieutenant Bucklyn and begged for permission to take over one of the guns. With his crews being rapidly depleted, the commander reluctantly consented. Moments later, an artillery shell tore Simpson's head off, granting him the peace he had sought for so long.

Before the retreat of his wrecked battery to Cemetery Ridge, Bucklyn had three horses shot from under him. On the final occasion, a piece of shrapnel sliced through his left lung and he stumbled to the rear choking up blood. The officer survived what he thought would be a mortal wound, and thus the final epic of Corporal Ernest Simpson's short and tragic life was preserved.

After a temporary burial on the south side of the Sherfy property, the body of the artillerist was removed to the National Cemetery in the small Rhode Island plot. Returning to duty by the end of the year, Bucklyn wrote bitterly, "My battery is torn and shattered and my brave boys have gone never to return. Curse the Rebs."

The grave of Ernest Simpson in the Soldiers' National Cemetery.

James and Mary Purman, USA

The majority of young men who flocked to the colors during the early years of the Civil War did so with the naïve expectation of accumulating their fair share of both glory and adventure. Very few of them, if any, left home seeking romance. However, one young recruit from western Pennsylvania reaped all of these benefits as a result of the events that transpired on one afternoon at Gettysburg.

Born on a farm in Greene County in 1841, James Jackson Purman displayed an independent streak combined with a strong work ethic from his earliest years. At the age of 12 he took a job in the printing office of the *Waynesburg Eagle,* and four years later traveled to Illinois to work as a typesetter at the *Fulton County Democrat.* Purman returned home soon afterwards and matriculated at Waynesburg College, where he earned his tuition by teaching at a local academy during the winter months.

When President Lincoln issued a call for more troops during the summer of 1862, Purman decided to forego his final year of studies to help recruit a company of volunteers. The enthusiastic student teacher lured away one of his schoolmates, 19-year-old freshman John A. Burns, and the pair scoured the surrounding townships for recruits. A mere lad of eleven at the time, James Burns would never forget the departure of his older brother and teacher:

> One summer morning about the last of July, these recruits assembled at our house to leave for the front. Many friends came with them. The parting was a sad one. I can see them even now, and I feel the same swelling in the throat that I felt that July morning as I saw these men clamber into the two-horse wagons, father driving one of them, to be driven to Waynesburg. Here they were joined by eighty or ninety more men from other parts of the county.

During the organization of what would become Company A, 140th Pennsylvania Infantry, Purman received enough votes to secure the post of first lieutenant while his younger associate earned a sergeant's stripes. The material of the regiment offered considerable promise. Most of its members descended from the restless Scots-Irish pioneers that forged westward to settle the primitive regions along the western boundary of the commonwealth. They were reputed to be a class of men with above average intelligence with an exceptionally high standard of manhood and morality.

These attributes led to a pardonable boast from the regimental historian: "And, when the hour of decision came, they went to the front with as sublime courage and as steadfast confidence in the orderings of God's providence as the Ironsides of Cromwell or the defenders of the Covenant in Scotland." Of course, he served up this boast with the advantage of hindsight. However confident and willing they might have been upon donning the blue uniform of the Union, Lieutenant Purman, Sergeant Burns, and their mates must have harbored some apprehensions over what combat would be like.

And, in fact, "the hour of decision" would be a long time in coming. Although it lost some men at the Battle of Chancellorsville, the regiment's true mettle would not be tested until July 2, 1863. As part of Brigadier General John C. Caldwell's division of Winfield Scott Hancock's Second Corps, the 140th Pennsylvania vacated its original position on Cemetery Ridge to reinforce the endangered left flank of the Union line.

As the Pennsylvanians hustled off, some of the men in Company A noticed that Lieutenant Purman was not wearing his distinctive broad-brimmed straw hat. During the previous morning the officer had told his old schoolmate Sergeant Burns of a presentiment that he would be killed in action. Burns laughed following the pronouncement but agreed to serve as his friend's executor. Not wishing to tempt fate, Purman exchanged his headgear with drummer boy James Woods, with the hope that a standard issue kepi would make him a less conspicuous mark.

Anchoring the far right of Caldwell's formation, the 140th Pennsylvania, over 500 strong, swept across the northwest corner of the Wheatfield and scrambled up the side of a rocky, tree covered knoll, later dubbed the Stony Hill. The charging Yankees ran head-long into two South Carolina regiments and a desperate firefight ensued in the shadowy woods. The volleys became increasingly deadly as the two lines closed together. The 140th stubbornly held its position as Caldwell's spirited attack cleared the Wheatfield of Southern troops.

But this victory was only temporary. Reinforced by fresh brigades, the Confederates reappeared, converging upon their adversaries from three directions. Now the roles were reversed. Organization dissipated as Caldwell's men fell back singly or in small groups.

After passing safely through the initial gauntlet of bullets, Lieutenant Purman and Orderly Sergeant James Piper paused for a breather along the opposite side of the field. Seconds later, enemy riflemen burst into view. "We must get out of this or we'll be gobbled up," shouted the lieutenant. The pair had not gone far when they stumbled upon a comrade prostrated by wounds to both legs. Ignoring the fast approaching danger, they carried the immobile soldier to a more sheltered position between two large rocks.

The short delay proved costly. Ignoring the shouts of their pursuers to halt, Purman and Piper fled at top speed. Almost instantly an ounce of lead struck the officer near the left ankle and brought him tumbling down. His companion was also hit. Lying in the trampled wheat, Purman read the inscription of the 24th Georgia on a crimson battle flag as a Southern regiment charged over him. Near twilight yet another Union attack pushed the Confederates back across the hotly contested field. However, nearly 24 hours would elapse before Purman's rescue could be effected.

"Many have attempted to tell how it feels to be shot," wrote the lieutenant. "At first there is no pain, smarting nor anguish. It is very like the shock of an electric battery. But the delusion soon passes and the acute pain follows and you know that a missile has passed through the tender flesh of your body."

Suffering from shock and surrounded by a chorus of cries and groans, he obtained little sleep and would be forever haunted by the sights and sounds of that long evening: "The almost full moon was shining, with drifting clouds passing over her face. At intervals a cloud obscured the moon, leaving in deep darkness the wheatfield with its covering of trampled and tangled grain, boulders and wounded and dead men, then passing off revealed a scene of cold, white upturned faces."

Daylight brought new horrors. Although no major action would take place in this sector on July 3, the opposing pickets regularly exchanged shots across the field around and over those trapped between the lines. Purman frequently pushed himself up with his hands and one healthy leg to survey the situation. "Nothing could be seen except a line of blue on one side and gray on the other, and nothing heard but the crack of the rifles and the zip of the bullets in the wheat, or their well-known thud in the ground or the body of a wounded man," he recalled.

One of these stray rounds penetrated Purman's lower right leg. Growing increasingly desperate for water, he called out to a Confederate officer seen moving along the front of a body of troops. Eventually, a lieutenant from a Georgia regiment crawled out to the exposed position with a canteen of fresh water. He poured some of the liquid on the enemy officer's wounds and cut off his boots to help ease the throbbing pain. After a little coaxing, the Southerner carried Purman on his back while crawling on all fours into the Confederate lines along the edge of the woods. He propped the Pennsylvanian under a tree on a rubber blanket, providing him with more water and biscuits.

Following Pickett's Charge, an attack by the Pennsylvania Reserves pushed the lingering pockets of Confederates from their strongholds along the southern end of the battlefield. Near sundown a stretcher party found Lieutenant Purman and carried him to a field hospital near Little Round Top. The next day a surgeon amputated the officer's left leg below the knee. Unfortunately, the wounded soldier that he and Sergeant Piper had stopped to assist would not live. Both men, however, would later be awarded a Congressional Medal of Honor.

More importantly, as an indirect result of this compassionate act, Lieutenant Purman received a reward of an infinitely greater value. The chronicler of the regiment's history recounted these serendipitous circumstances:

> A touch of romance entered into the experiences of suffering which fell to the lot of this gallant officer at Gettysburg.... After his rescue from the hands of the enemy he was carried into the house of Mary Witherow in the town and was so tenderly cared for in this hospitable home that a feeling stronger than good will was awakened in his breast for the fair lady who had so graciously ministered to him. This feeling was fully reciprocated and in due time there was a marriage, as was eminently fitting, between the "brave and the fair" in the city of Washington, D.C.

The future bride resided with her widowed father and sisters in a house that still stands on the eastern side of Baltimore Street, about one half block north of Breckenridge Street. As evidenced by the account of an Alabama officer, the humanitarian efforts of the Witherow girls extended beyond the confines of their home. He mentions that Mary and her sister Sally paid visits to the John Edward Plank farm, a major Confederate hospital located a few miles outside of the town along the Fairfield Road. This tender spirit enraptured the convalescing Union officer lying inside the Witherow house.

Following his discharge on a surgeon's certificate in May of 1864, Purman resumed his studies and graduated that same year. Afterwards, the couple moved to the nation's capital, where James practiced law and later served as a medical director with the Grand Army of the Republic, a powerful Union veterans' organization. Mary Purman passed away many years before her husband and was buried in Arlington National Cemetery.

Before joining his beloved in eternal rest on May 10, 1915, Purman realized a long held wish. For many years he had exchanged letters with the Confederate officer who had rescued him at Gettysburg. This individual proved to be Thomas P. Oliver of the 24th Georgia, a long-time resident of Athens. In 1907, when Oliver and a delegation of fellow Georgians traveled to Washington, the two former enemies met in person for the first time since 1863. Purman had the pleasure of introducing his old friend to President Theodore Roosevelt, who greeted the veterans with "a great warmth of feeling." Oliver passed away the next year just after being elected alderman of Atlanta. Had it not been for the Southerner's bold acts of mercy in the Wheatfield, his Union counterpart may have perished there along with one of the few romances that blossomed amid the carnage of war.

4

Union Brothers

Hasten brothers, to the battle,
Loud the bugle sounds afar;
I am weary, wounded, dying,
But I hear the call for war.

"Hasten Brothers to the Battle,"
words by Theodore D.C. Miller,
music by Vincent Percival

James T. and Robert E. Miller

On Independence Day 1863 Robert Miller felt considerable anxiety over the welfare of his two sons, then serving in the Army of the Potomac. "There is not a day that Mother and myself is not talking about you and James," he wrote to Robert E., his next to youngest child. The uneasy father continued: "Your mother is as well as we can expect for her but she is very much troubled about you and James and more so as we have had information that there is another big battle expected, but if it comes my prayer is that you may be spared and that you may be successful."

Over a century before satellites beamed unfolding news events into the living rooms of millions of viewers, the Millers had no way of knowing that both of their sons had emerged safely from the "big battle" that ended in triumph for the Union. However, Mrs. Miller would not have been comforted by the fact that a timely bout of diarrhea may well have spared one of her boys from death or serious injury.

The largely agrarian society of 1860s America fostered interdependence among families and communities that has gradually diminished in the modern era. Due to a lifetime struggle with poverty and from being constantly on the move, the members of the large Miller family established even tighter bonds with one another. The coming of war and the prolonged absence of two family members stressed these ties to their emotional limits. Eventually, the combustible mix of politics and ideals stirred up both affection and discord among the couple's five sons.

It was this type of strife that Irish-born Robert Miller had hoped to leave behind when he left the urban slums of Glasgow, Scotland, in 1832 for the promise of a new beginning in the United States. Three years earlier, the 29-year-old cotton spinner was wed to Jane Todd, and when their first child, a boy, entered the world on January 8, 1831, they named him James Todd Miller to honor his mother.

After arriving in New York City, Robert Miller moved his growing family three times over the next several years before finding steady work in Troy, a burgeoning mill and factory town in upstate New York. In the fall of 1842, shortly after the birth of his seventh and last child, he tapped his savings to purchase 102 acres of land in Warren County, Pennsylvania, in what was then frontier country. As he had no previous experience in farming or lumbering, this new lifestyle must have presented its fair share of humorous and perhaps even hazardous moments. Nonetheless, the family adapted quickly to the hostile environment and over time Miller added to his land holdings.

As a general rule the children settled within a short distance of the homestead when they reached adulthood, the exception being James, who at age twenty-six married Susan Ann Main, a resident of the far west side of the county. The couple set up housekeeping in a rented farm near Titusville, where, by the end of 1860, Susan had given birth to three children.

James Miller was not among the first wave of recruits to march off to war, but by the fall of 1861, patriotism and a strong sense of duty swept him away from his young family. A year of hard service with the 111th Pennsylvania Volunteers did not diminish his devotion to the Union cause. The Battle of Cedar Mountain on August 9, 1862, marked this unit's first major engagement. The experience exhilarated the Pennsylvania farm boy, who described the scene to one of his brothers as "the enthusiastic dream of my boyhood, a battlefield with all its glorious pomp and stern reality." The horrific slaughter at Antietam on September 17 certainly had a sobering effect on James's perception of warfare. His unit lost over half of its 243 officers and men during the bloodiest single day of the war. Private Miller was among the fortunate ones that responded to roll call that evening.

While his older brother dodged bullets in Virginia and Maryland, Robert E. Miller enlisted at the rank of sergeant in Company F, 151st Pennsylvania. The one-time teacher and law student was 23 at the time. Although they were over eight years apart in age, Robert and James enjoyed a close relationship that dated back to their childhood. The enlistment of his younger sibling not only filled James with pride, it also provided a more tangible benefit. Only a soldier can truly understand the thoughts and emotions of a fellow soldier. Now the veteran campaigner had a family member who could sympathize with his plight while sharing common experiences and hardships.

During a one-month period that winter the two soldiers found themselves stationed less than ten miles apart in the Fairfax area west of the capital. Just two days after Christmas James obtained a pass to see his brother at Union Mills. The joyful reunion was dampened when he found Robert bedridden with typhoid fever. By the time of his departure on the thirtieth the patient's condition had improved. Robert even told his brother that he was not at all homesick despite his illness.

During the visit James spoke with Harrison Allen, the colonel of the 151st and a fellow resident of Warren County. With a deep sense of pride, he related to his father that the colonel "gave Robert a very good name and it is a very good regiment." Following a second visit James wrote back that the crisis had passed but it would be some time before his brother could return to active duty.

Nonetheless, the folks at home could not be readily convinced of this fact. At one point Father Miller sent a letter to the brigade hospital requesting that his son's remains be shipped home in the event of his death. The medical personnel did their best to allay these fears by providing details on the patient's progress and by describing the excellent care provided on his behalf. With a touch of exasperation, James reassured his family, "I heard from Brother Robert the day that we [the 111th Pennsylvania] left Fairfax, he was getting better. I think all of you have been somewhat needlessly alarmed about him."

Finally, Robert himself begged his parents: "When you write again I wish you would not manifest quite so much uneasiness about me as I am doing as well as could be expected. No doubt you fear for my welfare but at the present time you know I want something to cheer me up."

The sergeant's recovery would indeed be protracted and he would not report back to his regiment until early April. Fortunately for him, he spent much of this time at an even better facility, St. Paul's Church Hospital in Alexandria, Virginia. From there he addressed an explosive issue that would not only spark debate and violence throughout the country but would ultimately divide his tight-knit family.

On March 3, 1863, President Lincoln signed an act that made all male citizens between 20 and 45 eligible for a national draft. A clause in the legislation permitted a drafted man to hire a substitute or buy his way out by paying a $300 commutation fee. Despite its unpopularity among the populace, most soldiers, including the Miller brothers, approved.

Robert Miller argued to his father, "This war is a life and death struggle to determine whether we as a nation shall exist or not. Under such circumstances I think it is very necessary that the government shall have power to call out the whole strength of the nation." Near the same time, James wrote home," [L]et me know what the Copperhead Democrats of that section think of the Conscription Law. I for one am heartily in favor of its full and stringent enforcement."

By this point the two soldiers must have started to feel the initial twinges of alienation from their four brothers and former neighbors who chose to remain at home. James once expressed this frustration by exclaiming, "But the folks in the North who are all the time finding fault with us and grumbling at everything that is done, the worst wish I have for them is that they had to come down here and share our fatigues and dangers and see if that would not cure them of finding fault."

Much to the chagrin of supporters of the war effort, the stinging defeat at Chancellorsville in early May only amplified the protests of the Peace Democrats. As he had done on several previous occasions, James Miller survived the combat, which he described as "one of the most murderous fights of the war." Following the battle he obtained a pass and, after hiking about 13 miles across the countryside near Falmouth, he discovered Robert alive and well. As it turned out, Company F of the 151st Pennsylvania pulled the enviable assignment of provost guard for General Abner Doubleday.

Partly overcome by the stress of worry, Mrs. Miller took to her sick bed as news of another battle spread throughout the country. Her frayed nerves would get little relief, as the two armies marched towards another showdown after a short breathing spell.

The tedious marching at the outset of the Gettysburg Campaign taxed the sturdiest of soldiers. For those like Robert Miller, who had only recently recovered from severe illnesses, it could be fatal. Numerous men fell victim to heatstroke, and the byways to the rear of the army were littered with stragglers and excess baggage.

James Miller must have been greatly concerned about the welfare of his kid brother, but he had no way of checking on his progress. Part of the First Army Corps, the 151st Pennsylvania marched with the left wing, the one nearest to the enemy. Meanwhile, the Twelfth Corps, to which the 111th Pennsylvania belonged, moved along the outer track during the initial stages of the campaign.

Following the line of the Orange & Alexandria Railroad into the hot open plains of the Manassas region, the first several days proved to be particularly grueling for the First Corps. "We have had a very hard march the last two days but I have stood the march first rate and was one of the twenty of our company that came in with the regiment the first night," penned Robert Miller on the evening of June 14.

Finally, after a week of almost nonstop marching, the left wing of the Union army reached the south bank of the Potomac River near Leesburg, Virginia. As the high command scrambled to decipher a constant stream of intelligence data and contemplated the army's next move, the troops took advantage of the respite to catch up on sleep and letter writing. "I have kept up with the company all the time and have been with them every time they have stacked arms or been ordered to fall in," boasted Robert Miller to his parents.

However, he did not reveal the fact that he was suffering from a bad case of diarrhea at the time. This malady continued to plague him as the army broke camp on June 25 to cross the Potomac River. Miller turned in his gun but due to the high number of sick cases in the 151st no room was available in any of the ambulances. The young soldier gamely limped along but soon fell hopelessly behind the column. As summer rains soaked the rural countryside of western Maryland, he periodically sought shelter in barns along the road.

Through a twist of good fortune Robert stumbled into the Twelfth Corps when he reached Frederick. He soon found James, who immediately took him to see the regimental surgeon. The doctor advised Robert that he was too weak to march and admitted him to the general hospital in the city. When his condition did not improve he was transferred farther east to St. Johns College Hospital in Annapolis. About two weeks after the Battle of Gettysburg, a wounded member of the 151st arrived at the same hospital. From this individual Robert learned that his regiment had suffered terribly in the engagement. He still did not know the fate of his brother.

Fortune smiled on James Miller once again. Fighting behind well constructed earthworks atop rugged Culp's Hill, the Twelfth Corps inflicted severe damage upon the enemy with a minimal number of casualties. Miller estimated that he and his comrades fired over one hundred rounds apiece during the intense fighting on the morning of July 3 with devastating results. Dead Confederates literally lay in heaps along the slopes of the hill; some had been hit as many as ten times.

In addition to providing graphic descriptions of the battle, Miller assured his family that Robert was not in the battle. In fact, when the enlistment term of the 151st Pennsylvania expired at the end of July 1863, Robert Miller's military service ended. Unlike his older brother, he never passed through the bloody crucible of combat.

There is no indication that James harbored any resentment over this fact. The actions of his three remaining brothers posed a much greater moral dilemma. Joining together with other local men, they formed a mutual aid society that pooled money to hire substitutes for its members drafted by the government. This revelation deeply angered the ever loyal and patriotic James who now considered his own brothers as traitors to the cause that he and others had fought so hard to defend. In their defense, the trio had plenty of incentive to dodge the draft. The discovery of oil in nearby Titusville sent local land prices soaring, offering the promise of huge gains for the enterprising investor.

Betrayed by his own family, James Miller opted for a different course. Near the end of the year, he decided to take advantage of a reenlistment incentive that paid a national and local bounty plus a month-long furlough. By this point the Pennsylvanian was far from home. That fall the Twelfth Corps had been detached from the Army of the Potomac and traveled over a thousand miles by rail to reinforce the besieged Union garrison at Chattanooga, Tennessee.

During the confused night battle at Wauhatchie on October 29, James was wounded severely enough to be hospitalized for several weeks. Although he recuperated in time to take advantage of a furlough in January, his time off was anything but restful. Upon reaching home he discovered that three-year-old son Johnny was grievously ill. The poor lad died a week after his father returned to the front.

Also, by this point his disdain for his stay-at-home brothers intensified. In a letter to his father marked "private and confidential," James labeled them "false black hearted scoundrels" and pronounced, "We soldiers hate them a great deal worse than we do the rebles in arms." This deepening rift effectively ended further communications between the four siblings.

As the 111th marched towards Atlanta under William T. Sherman during the spring of 1864, tragedy revisited the Miller family. On June 8, James's frail mother passed away. Less than two weeks later, on the outskirts of Atlanta, the 111th endured "the most fatal half hour of its history." Among the dead was the still grieving James Miller. Harrison Allen, the former colonel of the 151st Pennsylvania, conveyed the news of his death. He now rests in the Marietta National Cemetery in Marietta, Georgia.

The widowed Susan Miller persevered, stretching her limited resources to raise two children. She lived until age ninety. Robert E. Miller, now the proprietor of a dry goods store, administered his older brother's estate. He married in 1867, fathered four children, and served for many years as a school director. Ironically, he died unexpectedly of a stroke on July 1, 1892, exactly 29 years from the day his regiment was nearly annihilated at Gettysburg.

Henry and Richard Seage

At about 4:00 a.m. on the morning of June 8, 1863, Chaplain John Seage set off for Washington from the regimental camp of the 4th Michigan Infantry near Fredericksburg, Virginia, with $7,000 in cash, five watches, and over two dozen soldiers' letters entrusted to his care. Twelve miles into the journey, five pistol-brandishing riders galloped towards Seage demanding his surrender. The reverend coolly asked by what authority. "In the name of Mosby's Cavalry," answered the leader. "I do not recognize that authority and shall not surrender," was the response.

Three of the guerrillas discharged their weapons. A ball struck Seage's right wrist, severing the radial artery then angled down into the chest cavity, finally lodging between two ribs. As the reverend's horse instinctively sprung to one side, a second volley filled the air. This time a bullet entered his opposite shoulder, tearing through the muscle of the back before stopping just short of the spine. Another round grazed him in the left leg as Seage's frantic horse leapt over a small ditch.

Somehow the badly wounded chaplain evaded his pursuers. After reaching the safety of Union lines, he was carried into a tent about to faint from the loss of blood. The chief surgeon of General George Meade's staff was summoned to the scene. After Seage was stabilized the ball was cut out of the patient's back, while splints and slings were applied to the damaged limbs.

The shocking news of the attack reached the camp of the 4th Michigan that same day. The blow fell hardest upon Richard Watson Seage and Henry Stark Seage, the reverend's sons, who had both enlisted in Company E during the first year of the war. Richard signed up as a corporal in June 1861 at age 23, while younger brother Henry departed home shortly after turning 17 near the end of September.

The Reverend John Seage was an Episcopal minister and a native of Devon County, England. Immigrating to the United States in the 1830s, he traveled over a wide circuit preaching to rural congregations in New York, Vermont, and parts of Canada before receiving the call to establish a Baptist church in White Pigeon, Michigan, in 1857. With his two sons and many other parishioners serving in the 4th Michigan, the elder Seage was a natural candidate for the position of chaplain and he was sworn in on July 10, 1862. It would be the most challenging call of his ministerial career.

Only nine days before Reverend Seage reported for duty, the 4th was heavily engaged at Malvern Hill, the final action of the Seven Days Battles near the Confederate capital of Richmond. Sergeant Richard Seage lay for 42 hours on the field with a badly lacerated skull before being taken prisoner. Released on parole,

Reverend John Seage, 1861 (Steve Roberts).

Left: Richard W. Seage, 1861 (Steve Roberts).
Right: Henry Seage, 1861 (Steve Roberts).

Richard was reunited with his brother and father in October 1862. Now, less than a year later, another family crisis had developed at the outset of one of the war's most pivotal campaigns.

Accompanied by his older brother, Henry Seage was ordered to report to the division wagon train to help nurse his father. After finding that the old man was doing well, the boys changed his clothing and cleaned him up the best that they could. While Richard Seage returned for duty, Henry accompanied his father to Washington. After receiving follow-up care in a city hospital, Chaplain Seage embarked on the long train ride that would take him back to Michigan.

Meanwhile, traveling by boat, train, and foot, a beleaguered Henry finally caught up with the Fifth Corps near Aldie, Virginia, where the cavalry of the two armies had recently sparred. Filled with anxiety, Richard, recently promoted to second lieutenant, and Henry, now a corporal, trudged north through Maryland and into Pennsylvania.

Although the second day at Gettysburg would never be forgotten for the savage and chaotic nature of the fighting, the results were largely indecisive. Nowhere was this senseless butchery more in evidence than in the bloody Wheatfield. Command structures broke down as reinforcements from both sides streamed onto the scene from all parts of the field.

Near the latter stages of the seesaw contest, the 4th Michigan advanced unknowingly into the jaws of a deadly trap. During the hand-to-hand fighting that followed, a Confederate soldier managed to wrestle the unit's national flag away from its bearer. A horrified Colonel Harrison Jeffords shouted for Lieutenants Seage and Michael Vreeland to help him recover the prized standard.

The three men dashed forward. As Jeffords reached out to grab the flag staff, Seage slashed the Rebel in the neck with his sword. More Confederates descended upon the knot of officers and a wild melee ensued. One of the Southerners thrust his bayonet deep into the colonel's body, inflicting a mortal wound. After being hit by two bullets, Vreeland was clubbed across the skull with the butt of a musket. At nearly the same time, a bullet ripped into Seage's chest, puncturing his right lung. Others stung his right arm and both legs. Later, as he lay prostrate in the trampled wheat, a Rebel soldier stabbed him through the left leg. The three officers fell side by side as they had fought. The flag that they had valiantly tried to save had been torn to shreds in the struggle.

The next morning, Henry Seage located his older brother. He was insensible but still alive. Vreeland had also survived. A surgeon cut the ball from Richard's side and dressed his wounds inside a nearby barn. Following the collection of the wounded at the corps hospital site, Henry acted as a nurse for his brother and Lieutenant Vreeland.

A week after the battle had ended Henry and Richard received a pleasant surprise when their eldest brother, Edmund, arrived from West Troy, New York. "Tonight is the first time us three brothers have slept side by side for three years. Slept first rate," penned Henry in his diary on July 10.

The next morning the two soldiers bade good-bye to their kid brother and boarded a train bound for Baltimore with hundreds of other wounded men. Upon arriving in the city a small group of Michigan officers arranged to room and board at the Church Home and Infirmary, formerly a marine hospital, for the sum of $4 per week.

During the next two months, Lieutenant Seage's health ebbed and flowed as infections and other complications attacked his weakened body. The first week was the most difficult. Henry kept nightly vigils by his brother's bedside, often getting by on just an hour or two of sleep. Near the end of July, Richard's fiancée, Sarah Jane "Jennie" Burbank, traveled from New York, perhaps to see if marriage was still a possibility. Henry obstinately refused to admit her into the room until the final day of her week-long visit.

Finally, on Monday, September 7, 1863, the Seage brothers embarked on a three-day train ride back to White Pigeon. Back at home they enjoyed a reunion with their father, who was still recuperating from his own wounds. The visit was all too short for Henry, who soon headed back to the front. Promoted to color sergeant, he filled this dangerous position until the expiration of the 4th Michigan's original enlistment term in September of 1864.

After much deliberation, Sergeant Seage decided not to reenlist. The vexing issue was further complicated by the return of both John and Richard Seage to the newly formed 4th Michigan Veteran Volunteers. Henry speculated that the need to secure a government pension motivated them to come back for another tour of duty.

Certainly, Lieutenant Seage had every reason to hang up his shoulder straps. Back in April he had exchanged vows with Jennie Burbank during a ceremony officiated by his father on Staten Island, New York. Fortunately, the new bride was not alone for long, as her husband's second enlistment lasted just six months. After filling the post of regimental quartermaster, Seage left the army on a disability discharge on March 6, 1865. Two years later, the brevet ranks of captain and major were conferred upon him for gallant and meritorious service.

The eldest Seage was the last one to return to civilian life, serving in the army until May 1866. Stationed for a year in Tennessee, the chaplain exposed a string of racial injustices, winning him plaudits for his humanitarian efforts.

Though the Seages had served together in the same unit, circumstances had kept them apart for much of the time. This trend continued after the war ended. Richard eventually moved east with Jennie, raising three children in the Staten Island/New Jersey area. The Reverend Seage resided in Detroit and later in St. Louis. His war injuries left him partly paralyzed in the left shoulder and with a limited range of motion in his right hand, for which the government allocated him a $20 monthly pension. While visiting his oldest son in 1883 he contracted a fatal case of hepatitis. The burial took place at Fountain Cemetery on Staten Island. When Richard died in 1908, he was laid to rest next to his father.

After working as a bookkeeper and bank teller, Henry Seage settled in Lansing, the Michigan state capital, where he gained prominence as one of the nation's leading fire insurance underwriters. Continuing the family tradition, he was married by his father in 1867. Henry became the de facto regimental historian, writing extensively about the 4th Michigan's illustrious record and delivering stirring speeches at reunions and monument dedications.

His fellow veterans probably never suspected that he suffered from frequent bouts of scurvy contracted during his army days. "Mr. Seage was quite a reticent man and did not complain very much," wrote a business associate. Henry's wife recalled that he often remarked that the affliction would eventually kill him. Sure enough, on April 9, 1899, the veteran died after suffering five different hemorrhages caused by the disease.

Thus, all three of the Seage men carried scars from their war days to the grave. Nonetheless, the family had actually been luckier than most, especially at Gettysburg. In an 1884 letter to historian John B. Bachelder, Henry Seage still marveled, "I often wonder how it was that so many of us crossed that wheatfield and live[d] to tell the story."

Joseph Gutelius, Joseph and Samuel Ruhl

On the evening of June 30, 1863, Corporal Joseph Gutelius, brothers Samuel and Joseph Ruhl, in company with drummer boy Harry Kieffer, squatted beside a blazing fire. These members of Company D, 150th Pennsylvania, were in high spirits. After a grueling 26-mile march the previous day that brought them to the heights beyond Emmitsburg, Maryland, the First Corps infantrymen enjoyed a leisurely march across the state line before halting near Marsh Creek. Upon the completion of the monthly pay muster the soldiers camped in the woods along the road. The dense foliage shielded them from the intermittent rains that fell throughout the day.

As they cooked supper that evening the messmates discussed the battle they all expected would be fought within the next few days. The attention soon turned to Gutelius, the company's representative in the regimental color-guard. Between puffs on his pipe, Joseph Ruhl reminded his comrade that he held the post of honor and that "if any man pulls down that flag, shoot him on the spot."

"Never you fear for that," Gutelius reassured him. "We of the color-guard will look out for the flag. For my part, I'll stay a dead man on the field before the colors of the 150th are disgraced."

Left: Joseph R. Ruhl, 1862 (Ethel Ruhl). *Right:* Joseph S. Gutelius, 1862 (Ethel Ruhl).

Just as soldiers throughout history have done the men covered their nervous anxiety with bravado and humor. Although they had yet to experience a large-scale combat action, Joe Ruhl compared the fighting prowess of the Pennsylvania Bucktails to the much-feared Louisiana Tigers of the Confederate army. "We were going to have boiled lion heart for supper, Harry, but we couldn't catch any lions," he quipped. "They seem to be scarce in these parts. Maybe we can catch a tiger tomorrow, though."

It would be the last supper for two of the men who dined on beef heart in the countryside six miles southwest of Gettysburg. As Major Thomas Chamberlin recounted in his regimental history, "The night, contrary to expectation, passed quietly, and the troops enjoyed an undisturbed rest, little dreaming of the draft that would be made on their courage and endurance on the morrow."

Before he dozed off to sleep on the wet earth, Gutelius probably thought of his two older brothers and that memorable day in mid–August nearly a year ago. In response to President Lincoln's recent proclamation for 600,000 additional troops, war rallies were held throughout the north. Union County, Pennsylvania, had already lived up to its name in responding to the national crisis by raising seven companies of volunteers. It would dutifully respond with three new companies.

In the small farming town of Mifflinburg, school teacher Henry W. Crotzer delivered a fiery oration to a large audience of his fellow citizens. At its conclusion a band struck up a medley of patriotic tunes. As man after man stepped forward the onlookers erupted with a chorus of cheers. "War fever was a terrible malady in those days," wrote teenaged Harry Keiffer. "Once you were taken with it, you had a very fire in the bones until your name was down on the enlistment roll."

Often the actions of one's older brothers could be an even more powerful stimulus. As Charles and Samuel Gutelius weaved through the crowd to sign up with the company being formed by their Uncle Henry, younger brother Joseph was right on their heels, declaring that "if they went he'd go, too." Whipped into frenzy by this devotion, "the meeting went wild with excitement and the people cheered and cheered again, and the band played 'Hail Columbia!' and the 'Star Spangled Banner,' and 'Away Down South, in Dixie.'"

In his early twenties at the time, it is easy to see how Joseph Gutelius would have evoked such an enthusiastic response. Keiffer described him as "a fine young fellow ... tall, well built, of a fine, manly bearing, and looked a likely subject for a recruiting officer."

Although a crowd favorite, Joseph's decision probably did not meet with the approval of his family. Besides tending the two-acre farm, the youngest son of Frederick and Lydia (Crotzer) Gutelius taught school part time to help purchase clothing and other necessities for his aging parents. Although he regularly sent home part of his army pay, his presence was sorely missed.

Neither of Joseph's older brothers would be by his side on the eve of the war's most pivotal battle. Shortly after leaving home, 26-year-old Charles Gutelius contracted typhoid fever, not an unusual occurrence for a new recruit. Sent home on a lengthy furlough, he subsequently passed through a series of government hospitals before being discharged on a surgeon's certificate on July 30, 1863. Second Lieutenant Samuel Gutelius fell ill due to the rigors of the Chancellorsville Campaign in early May of 1863. Throughout the summer he underwent treatment at the Abbott House Hospital in Washington. The former dentist returned home to Milheim in August.

It is likely that the two Ruhl brothers were also inspired by the example of their older brother. Earlier in the summer, Valentine Ruhl left home with Company A of the 131st

Pennsylvania Infantry, one of the new nine-month regiments. The 131st would see heavy action at Fredericksburg in December and would be among the units that came closest to the terrible stone wall on Marye's Heights. Valentine lived to tell the story.

His siblings would not experience combat until well into their first year of service. After its organization was completed at Camp Curtin in Harrisburg, the 150th reported to Washington, D.C. Company D pulled the enviable assignment of guarding the Soldiers' Home, where the president maintained a summer residence. The Union County soldiers enjoyed the hospitality and personal visits of the Lincoln family. This cushy duty came to an end when the regiment was shipped down to Falmouth, Virginia, as reinforcements for the Army of the Potomac.

The 150th participated in the Battle of Chancellorsville, but saw only limited action. Afterwards, Captain Crotzer, like Samuel Gutelius, was prostrated by illness. He would never again lead the neighbors and family members he recruited for military duty.

Tramping north towards Gettysburg on July 1, Corporal Gutelius and the Ruhl boys experienced a strong dose of nostalgia, as the surrounding countryside closely resembled the farms on which they had grown up. On both sides of the road stretched fields of golden grain and luxuriant rows of corn stalks, all glistening in the morning sun. Periodically, the column passed neat barns and farm houses with well-manicured lawns.

The tranquility abruptly ended when groups of panic-stricken civilians driving cattle and horses before them hastily moved past in the opposite direction. The sight of a small boy and girl riding on a horse while crying piteously nearly broke the hearts of the men. The last mile or two of the march was completed at the double-quick pace, not an easy task in the growing heat and humidity.

By the time the men panted up to the crest of Seminary Ridge they would have been in no mood for a patriotic speech. Nonetheless, both Generals Abner Doubleday and Thomas Rowley reminded the Pennsylvanians of Colonel Roy Stone's brigade that they were now upon the soil of their home state and that all eyes would be upon them. Enemy shells flew overhead as news of the death of General Reynolds filtered through the ranks.

Advancing to McPherson's Ridge, the brigade deployed around the McPherson farm, carefully stepping around the dead from the morning's battle. Nearly 400 strong, the 150th took position on the western brow of the ridge overlooking Willoughby Run. The left of the regiment's battle line reached out towards the Iron Brigade but a dangerous gap existed between the two brigades.

During the early afternoon the fighting intensified. Initially, Brigadier General Junius Daniels' brigade of North Carolinians attacked from the north towards the unfinished railroad cut that paralleled the Chambersburg Pike. Concurrently, contingents of Heth's and, later, Pender's divisions applied pressure from the west. Holding this dangerous salient, the line frequently bent back upon itself only to recoil moments later to reclaim the lost ground. The casualties mounted and soon the orchards and fields were thickly strewn with the prostrate bodies of the tenacious defenders. "They fought as though each man felt that upon his own arm hung the fate of the day and the nation," proclaimed Colonel Stone.

As so often took place in pitched, close-quarters combat, the colors played a vital role in steadying the men. When a destructive cross fire from the woods caused the 150th's line to waver, Colonel Henry Huidekoper ordered Color Sergeant Samuel Phifer to stand fast and then cried out, "Bucktails, rally on your colors!" The regiment instantly reformed and held the Southerners in check. Moments later, Sergeant Phifer was killed and only Corporal Gutelius and a few others remained in the color-guard.

The unequal contest raged on until two-thirds of Stone's men had fallen. Nearly surrounded, the survivors fell back towards the Seminary. Before moving off, some of them paused for a moment to catch the final words of a dying comrade. Near the barn Samuel Ruhl saw his brother alive for the final time. Corporal Joseph Ruhl was listed among the eight members of Company D killed in action that afternoon.

After a brief stand on Seminary Ridge, the regiment joined the throngs of Union soldiers fleeing through the maze of streets and alleys. Corporal Gutelius, the only surviving member of the color-guard, carried the colors from the field. On the outskirts of town, he, too, was wounded but insisted on keeping the flag. In the ensuing confusion Gutelius became separated from the regiment. Becoming faint from the loss of blood, he paused to rest on a doorstep at the corner of South Washington and High streets. An instant later, a group of North Carolina soldiers burst upon the scene. Leveling their rifles, they demanded the flag. True to his pledge Gutelius refused. A rattle of musketry ended the dispute and the brave corporal fell dead with the flag clasped in his hands.

The colors were seized by Lieutenant F. M. Harney of the 14th North Carolina, who would later be mortally wounded. His dying request was that the captured banner be presented to President Jefferson Davis. Following the flight of the Confederate government from Richmond in April 1865, Davis was captured by Union forces. Among the items discovered in his personal baggage was the bloodied flag of the 150th Pennsylvania. Gutelius was buried in the Soldiers' National Cemetery (Row A, grave #11 of the Pennsylvania section).

The aftermath of Joseph Ruhl's death also contains an interesting story. Sergeant Charles A. Frey, a soldier in Company D detached to division headquarters during the battle, remembered being reunited with his comrades a few days after the battle. "They were a sad looking set of men," he wrote. "There were only about one hundred and twenty-five left, and my own company, which went into the fight with fifty-two men, was reduced to twelve or fifteen." Next Frey related the sad plight of the Ruhl family:

> Word was sent to the family that Joseph was killed. His sister Sarah, on receiving the sad news, said she would go and bring him home. Ordering two horses hitched to a spring wagon, she started on her mournful journey, and by night of the same day on which she received the news of his death she was many miles on her way towards Gettysburg. Reaching the battlefield, she began the search for his body—or, rather, his grave, as he had been buried in the meantime. After a long search she found it, had the body unearthed, and placing it in a coffin conveyed it home, where it was laid to rest in the quiet graveyard by the side of the fields through which he roamed in boyhood days.

The news of her brother's death probably did not surprise Sarah (Ruhl) Stover. According to family tradition, she had experienced a premonition several days earlier and informed her parents of this ominous sign. It is likely that Valentine Ruhl accompanied his sister on the long trip, since his term of service ended on May 23, 1863.

The war continued to usher in bad fortune for the Ruhl and Gutelius families. The month following his son's death at Gettysburg, Frederick Gutelius was struck down with a violent attack of dysentery from which his system never completely recovered. When he died in 1866 his wife Lydia struggled to get by financially. Since Joseph had regularly contributed to his parent's support prior to his death, the widow received a small pension from the government.

In the absence of his brother Samuel Ruhl fought on with the Army of the Potomac. After passing through the bloody crucibles of the Wilderness, Spotsylvania Court House, and Cold Harbor, Ruhl's luck ended at Petersburg on July 30, 1864, during the failed attack upon the Confederate works following the explosion of Burnside's mine. Pinned down in a slight depression near the fortifications, Ruhl received a gunshot wound to his right foot. The following evening under the cover of darkness he managed to crawl back to safety. After the amputation of the second toe of his right foot at a division field hospital, Ruhl traveled to Satterlee Hospital in Philadelphia to recover. He returned to active duty and was discharged with the regiment on June 23, 1865. The 39-year-old veteran took up farming in peacetime even though he continued to experience difficulties with his injured foot. Samuel died as a bachelor on December 14, 1883, one month shy of his fiftieth birthday.

Henry Crotzer always regretted that he had not been there to watch over the men he had led off to war and felt a degree of responsibility for what happened to them. In the postwar years he battled an entirely different enemy on their behalf—government red tape. Crotzer's name appears on affidavits in numerous pension applications filed by veterans and their dependents.

In March of 1895 he wrote to the commissioner of pensions on behalf of Samuel Gutelius, who also served a stint with the 12th Pennsylvania Cavalry near the end of the war. After the death of his wife and the onset of heart disease, Samuel depended upon his oldest son to take care of him. Crotzer was outraged at the measly monthly allotment the pension bureau approved for his nephew. "The amount of his present pension, six dollars, surprises me! Your own sense of justice, will, I am sure, awaken sufficient interest in this case to see that his last days will have a show of decent respect from the government he served faithfully for several years.... Indeed I hope I shall live to see the day when every honorably discharged soldier that wore the blue will be on the roll of pensioners of our government." In another letter, Crotzer declared, "He was a faithful officer while well, and, to go begging after so many years of suffering and disappointment is to say the least—galling."

Two months later, the monthly allotment doubled to $12. Gutelius died the following March.

John and William Egolf

Typically recruited from specific geographical areas, Civil War regiments frequently developed noticeable identities from ethnic and regional influences. These traits had the potential to create esprit de corps and often led to friendly rivalries within a brigade or even at higher organizational levels. Hailed by a variety of nicknames, "Fighting Fourteenth," "Red-Legged Devils," Brooklyn Chasseurs," and "Beecher's Bull Pups," the 84th New York Volunteer Infantry, more commonly referred to as the 14th Brooklyn, needed no introduction within the Army of the Potomac. Algeron S. Coe, a surgeon in the 147th New York, had this to say about the Brooklyn outfit:

> Probably no regiment in the war of the rebellion took a more conspicuous part, engaged in so many battles, and did so much to enliven the spirit of the boys and keep them from falling into despondency on the weary march, in advance or retreat, in bivouac or dreary monotony of winter quarters. A true history of the regiment, with a little coloring, would read like a romance.... Not much can be said in respect to the discipline of the regiment, and indeed, a too rigid discipline would have materially impaired its efficiency, which fact seemed to be well understood by the officers in command. Their enterprise and fertility of resources in supplying themselves and comrades with comforts and necessities in the most

difficult situations [and] reckless bravery in battle ... endeared themselves to all who knew
them; hence they very naturally became pets, and even in a measure privileged, without
exciting the jealousy or envy of other regiments....

The history of the 14th Brooklyn could be traced back to the antebellum social custom of localized militia units, and it was among the first to respond to Lincoln's call for
troops in the wake of Fort Sumter. The City of Brooklyn proudly outfitted their native
sons with a distinctive Chasseur uniform that would be used throughout the war in defiance
of the more homogenous dress code favored by the authorities. The outfit featured a blue
and red kepi, a dark blue jacket with red trim, and the prominent red trousers that inspired
one of the regiment's nicknames.

Besides being one of the more colorful units, the Brooklyn boys could boast of a storied combat record. By 1863 the 14th numbered among the few regiments in the Army of
the Potomac that took part in the war's first major clash at Bull Run. In three separate
charges up Henry House Hill, the regiment lost over 100 men. Subsequently, the New
Yorkers fought at Second Manassas, South Mountain, Antietam, Fredericksburg, and
Chancellorsville. In June of 1863, just a month before Gettysburg, the army underwent a
period of reorganization and these veterans were placed into a mixed brigade of Pennsylvania and New York troops under the command of Brigadier General Lysander Cutler.
There would be little time to form close bonds with these sister regiments.

Cutler's brigade was the first Union infantry brigade to reach the battlefield on July 1.
From a position near the McPherson farm the 14th linked up with the 95th New York and
the 6th Wisconsin of the Iron Brigade to launch a charge into the unfinished railroad cut
that virtually eliminated Brigadier General Joseph Davis's brigade as an effective fighting force.

The attack was costly, however. Most of the 14th Brooklyn's 13 killed and 105 wounded
at Gettysburg fell during this brief charge. The regimental historian related that "The balls
came so thick and fast that the whirring noise they made sounded like the steady rhythm
of machinery. For just an instant, as the full force of this terrible fire broke along their
front, the line wavered. But it was only for an instant, and then, with another cheer, louder
and more determined, the men rushed on."

Listed among the wounded were two siblings in Company E, Corporals John and
William Egolf, 21 and 23 respectively at the time of their enlistments. John, who stood a
shade over five feet, five inches tall, suffered a bullet wound to the inner side of his right
knee that splintered the bone. The nature of William's wound is not known. Separated
from the comrades with whom they had shared countless dangers and privations over the
past two years, the brothers somehow managed to stay together.

Throughout the afternoon, ambulances and stretcher bearers hustled down Washington Street, the major north-south corridor in the western part of the borough. Many
of these conveyances turned onto West High Street to deposit their human cargo in the
sanctuaries of the St. Francis Xavier Roman Catholic Church and the United Presbyterian Church that stood on opposite sides of the street halfway down the block.

On the north side of the block near the intersection stood the spacious home and
granite yard of 59-year-old Solomon Powers. The New Hampshire native came to the
Gettysburg area in 1838 to help build one of the bridges along the "Tapeworm Railroad,"
near the site of the 14th Brooklyn's charge. For many years he lived on a farm along the
Baltimore Pike two miles south of the town before moving to High Street.

Solomon and his wife, Catherine, raised six daughters, all of whom became schoolteachers. Mr. Powers could boast of a presidential relationship. His great aunt, Abigal

Left: Solomon Powers, ca. 1863 (Curvin Krout). *Right:* Catherine Powers, ca. 1863 (Curvin Krout).

Powers, was the wife and first lady of President Millard Fillmore. Known for his blunt speech and no-nonsense mannerisms, it is unlikely that he disclosed this fact to his neighbors.

Certainly anyone who met the Yankee granite cutter would not have forgotten him. A contemporary historian described him as "a great uncouth, elephantine man ... whose clothes hung on him as if most unskillfully thrown into their places with a pitchfork." But looks can be deceptive, since "he had a heart in him ten times larger than his massive frame" and "it was the glory of his life to pour balm upon sorrow and alleviate suffering; and all of his large family of daughters had inherited the gift of the Good Samaritan soul." There would be ample opportunity to display these gifts in July of 1863.

The Powers family immediately responded to the growing medical crisis by sending food and supplies, including lint for bandages, to the nearby churches. Then, when refugees from parts of the town closer to the fighting sought a safe haven, the family invited them into their home, including a woman who was later discovered to be affected with smallpox.

The Union retreat did not immediately force the family indoors. Virginia "Jinny" Powers witnessed the slaying of Corporal Joseph Gutelius and the capture of the colors of the 150th Pennsylvania. Moments later, a shell exploded nearby, decapitating a mounted courier while another fragment killed one of the horses pulling a caisson on the opposite side of the street. Near the Presbyterian Church, a single bullet killed a fleeing Union soldier and then severely wounded another.

In the midst of these frightening scenes, Catherine and Solomon Powers, with the "girls," boldly rounded up the injured and other soldiers cut off by the pursuing Southerners. Estimates place the number of wounded collected in the Powers basement from 17 to 30 individuals. In light of the deplorable conditions found in most field hospitals during the battle, these men, which included the Egolf brothers of the 14th Brooklyn, could consider themselves truly blessed. One writer asserted that the family "demonstrated an unbounded loyalty and unselfish ambition to render aid to the sick and wounded ... such as has never been duplicated."

Fortunately, Mrs. Powers had obtained a barrel of flour from a local grocer on the Saturday preceding the battle, allowing her and the girls to bake fresh bread to accompany several hunks of dried beef they had on hand. When this larder ran out the household and its guests did not go hungry. Dr. James Fulton, the surgeon in charge at the Catholic church, fondly recalled: "I well remember Mrs. Catherine Powers, one of the heroines of Gettysburg, coming and getting an apron full (of hard bread or 'crackers') for her 'poor fellows' as she styled them. Well were they cared for who had the good fortune to get into her house. The whole family gave their undivided attention to the wounded under their care, without reward or expectation of any. When winter came on, and Mr. Powers wished to put on his winter clothing, he had none; all had been used for the benefit of the sick and wounded."

Despite their lack of formal training, the ladies bandaged arms and legs, and washed out deep bullet wounds, while providing as much comfort as they could to the men. As suggested by the possessive language used by Catherine Powers, tender and lasting friendships developed between patients and nurses as they faced danger and adversity together. The barriers of rank, nationality, religious affiliation, politics, and social status melted away. To these women each man was a hero equally deserving of her attention.

The heterogeneous mix of soldiers assembled together by chance in the Powers home represented a cross section of the Union itself: two young men from Brooklyn, a Vermonter, a lanky Pennsylvania farm boy, and a Scotsman who appeared so much older than the other "boys" that he was immediately called "grandpa." To these men every one of the Powers women seemed like a goddess on a divine mission to restore his health. Much like they had once been dependent upon the comrades in their regiments, these soldiers now looked to the members of this surrogate family and to one another for security and hope. In turn, the civilians drew courage from the confident warriors who assured them that the Union army would prevail.

Only two men are thought to have died while under the care of the Powers family. One of these deaths occurred on the Fourth of July, casting a dark shadow on an otherwise jubilant day when the Confederates withdrew from the town.

Two weeks later, William Egolf died by his brother's side. J. Howard Wert described the tragedy in a postwar newspaper series:

> There were pathetic scenes, too, at the Powers house during its hospital period, for once and again the dark angel of death hovered over it. Two brothers were amongst the defenders of the flag gathered up by these devoted women—Egolf by name, John and Will, members of the brave 14th of Brooklyn.... One was nursed back to life; and as the color again mantled his wan cheek, he saw his brother pass into the dark valley by that most awful and dreaded death of all the long catalogue of ills incident to army life, gangrene which had supervened in his wounded limb with all the train of hideousness which the pen refuses to chronicle.

Regrettably, the death of William Egolf in the prime of his life was probably unavoidable. The germ theory of disease was unknown to medical practitioners of the day. As a result doctors often probed wounds with bare hands and used non-sterile instruments to perform surgical procedures. In like manner, both professional and volunteer nurses "cleaned" wounds with communal sponges and wash basins, unknowingly spreading infections from one patient to another. A soldier fortunate enough to survive the initial shock of an injury often succumbed to one of the various postoperative infections such as tetanus and gangrene days or even weeks later.

The fact that more soldiers died of disease than of combat wounds was not lost upon John Egolf. Back in January, his younger brother, Private Thomas Egolf, also a member of Company E, passed away following a lingering illness.

Losing an older and younger brother

The Powers sisters around 1863. Left to right, back row—Virginia, Jane, and Alice. Front row—Lydia and Mary (Curvin Krout).

within a six month period, John somehow managed to recover from his debilitating injury. After leaving the Powers home on July 16, he received additional care at Camp Letterman and then later at Carlisle. The bullet remained imbedded in his leg, greatly reducing the flexibility of his knee joint. This handicap did not prevent him from returning to the regiment the following January, where he served as a second lieutenant until his discharge on June 6, 1864.

Returning to Brooklyn, he found work as a machinist to supplement his small invalid pension. Egolf married in 1868 and the union resulted in a son named Francis Joseph Egolf. The veteran died in 1901 at the age of 61 due to liver failure.

On July 3, 1883, Solomon and Catherine Powers celebrated their golden wedding anniversary. The couple's five surviving daughters and sixteen grandchildren gathered at the old homestead to mark the occasion. It was an unforgettable evening marked with singing, poem readings, the presentation of gifts, and the baptism of one of the grandchildren.

A reporter noted that "In all these years they have made friends whose number is legion. They are not few who personally speak of the kindly disposition of this aged pair. In the hours of pain and sickness many have known the soothing ministrations of their hands." Perhaps during a quiet moment the pair reflected back on their many years together, particularly to their thirtieth anniversary back in 1863, when their home was filled not by family, but by strangers who would become an integral fabric in the rich tapestry of their lives.

Eugene and Henry Eaton

In the spring of 1862 the family of Peter and Hannah Myers moved into a two-story dwelling on West High Street several doors down from the granite yard of Solomon Powers. Mr. Myers, a cabinet maker by trade, was held in high esteem by his fellow townsmen, serving as both justice of the peace and judge of elections. In the war's opening year, Myers, then 45 years of age, left the family to join the 87th Pennsylvania Volunteers. By then his son Jefferson was already on active duty with Company K of the 1st Pennsylvania Reserves, a unit that would be in the strange circumstance of fighting upon its home soil at Gettysburg.

The eldest of five daughters, Elizabeth "Sallie" Myers expressed grave concerns about her father's fitness for the rigors of a soldier's life. Therefore, she was greatly relieved when he was discharged for medical reasons a year later. Devotion to the Union ran strong in the Myers family. In addition to her father and brother, Sallie counted five uncles and eight first cousins who answered the call to arms.

Patriotism comes in many forms, however, and Peter Myers was able to support his country in an even more meaningful manner when the war literally came to him following his forced departure from the army. Like the nearby Powers house, the Myers' residence, along with nearly all of the public and private buildings on the street, served as an auxiliary site to the two church hospitals. Since he had no means to cook at either of these buildings, Dr. James Fulton used the Myers' kitchen to prepare meals for his numerous patients. Later, he pleaded with the girls to come with him.

Dr. James Fulton, ca. 1862 (Curvin Krout).

Sallie Myers' initial foray into nursing left her nerves badly jostled. Entering the Catholic church, she knelt beside a mortally wounded Pennsylvanian and asked how she could help him. When the soldier replied that he was going to die, an overwrought Sallie ran outside and cried on the steps. But the young schoolteacher who "had never been able to stand the sight of blood" regained her composure and went back inside. She went on to become one of the most dedicated and tireless volunteers during the hospital period. Four decades later, Sallie reminisced:

> The sight of blood never again affected me and I was among the wounded and dying men day and night. While the battle lasted and the town was in possession of the rebels, I went back and forth between my home and the hospitals without fear. The soldiers called me brave, but I am afraid the truth was that I did not know enough to be afraid and if I had known enough, I had no time to think of the risk I ran, for my heart and my hands were full.

Twelve men were eventually cared for at the Myers home. At times the interactions between the patients and the family were brief but so intense that the details would endure a lifetime. On Friday, July 17, Myers wrote in her diary: "Capt. Henry A. Eaton & O. S. Eugene Eaton came to our house to stay overnight. Their hospital was four miles out of town, broken up and they were not able to go further." Their stay spanned less than four days but it came at a critical stage for one of the men.

The previous summer the Eaton brothers had left their father's eighty-acre farm in Windsor County, Vermont, to sign on with the 16th Vermont Infantry. Eugene had blue eyes and auburn hair and was 19 years old. He would serve closely with his older brother, who was elected captain by the men of Company A.

The 16th was the last of five nine-month regiments recruited in the Green Mountain State to form

Henry Eaton, ca. 1862 (Jeff Kowalis).

a brigade commanded by Brigadier General George J. Stannard. The Vermonters, derisively dubbed the "Paper Collar Brigade" by the veterans of the Army of the Potomac, saw no combat until near the end of their term at Gettysburg. After helping to reinforce the Union lines on Cemetery Ridge near dusk on July 2, Stannard's untried troops outflanked Pickett's Virginians the following day, pouring in a deadly fire that contributed greatly in the breaking up of the charge.

During this climactic clash both brothers suffered injuries. Captain Henry Eaton was wounded in the thigh and a shell fragment struck Sergeant Eugene Eaton in the neck about two inches below the left ear, causing partial paralysis of his left arm. Apparently, the sergeant received little care at the field hospital as Sallie later wrote:

> Sgt. Eaton was suffering very much. His back had been very badly injured by a piece of shell, and he could neither stoop nor turn his head. The doctors and nurses were all busy. Capt. Eaton said he knew how the wound should be dressed, but as he was not able to do it, he would take the responsibility and superintend the job if I would do the work. I went to work and we succeeded in relieving him.

The following Monday David Eaton arrived at the Myers house to see his two sons. They left town the next day.

This story could have ended happily. The Eaton brothers were mustered out with the regiment on August 10, 1863. The following January, however, Henry Eaton reenlisted with the 17th Vermont. He rose quickly from private to captain and then to lieutenant colonel. His promising military career ended abruptly when he was killed near Petersburg on September 30, 1864. Eugene Eaton recovered from his injury at Gettysburg and lived until 1914.

Horace and Silas Judson

Brothers have always held strange relationships with one another. Incessantly battling for supremacy within a family unit, they will nonetheless unite without hesitation to face down an outside threat. My grandmother often recounts the story of my uncle, the older of her two sons, intervening on my father's behalf to put a licking on a bully from a neighboring farm. This ruffian never again picked on Dad but Uncle Harold continued to torment him throughout his adolescence. I have similar memories of my childhood years. So it goes with brothers.

In attempting to explain the brutality of Civil War combat, historians have correctly pointed out the deep cultural and political rifts that had been festering for decades, but in doing so they have looked past a more primal factor. In almost every company and regiment, North and South, sets of brothers fought beside one another. Thus, the same protective instincts that inflamed my uncle's anger against a country bully were constantly in play on the battlefields of the 1860s, only this time the enemy was holding a gun.

The emotional scars of looking on helplessly as a soft lead bullet tore into the flesh and bone of a sibling could never be erased and neither could the desire to avenge his death or serious injury. In a remarkable tribute to the discipline of these predominately volunteer soldiers, there are numerous cases of a surviving brother fighting on immediately after such a traumatic event.

Private Horace Judson, a 20-year-old farmer from Medina County, Ohio, fixated on the Battle of Gettysburg for years afterwards, and with good reason. From an advanced position along the Emmitsburg Road his 8th Ohio played a major role in stopping General James J. Pettigrew's command as it advanced to support the left flank of Pickett's troops during the grand assault of July 3. After turning back a small brigade of Virginians, the Buckeyes wheeled to the left and connected with other regiments to form a solid flanking line against the advancing Southern columns.

In 1887 Judson wrote a lengthy letter to John B. Bachelder in which he painstakingly described the activities of the 8th Ohio on that ever memorable day. He also enclosed a detailed sketch to accompany his manuscript. "In view of the fact that for nearly 24 years I have been occasionally ... sketching one of these diagrams in explaining the movements and positions of the 8th Ohio," explained the veteran. "I do think my views are entitled to some consideration."

At the end of the communication he described a far more personal detail to help verify his claims: "On the 9th of September following the battle my brother died of a wound received while resting his gun on my shoulder.... He was shot near the upper part of the right arm, the ball driving into the shoulder and chest by a rebel skirmisher after we had exposed our right by wheeling to [the] left. Such a scene has helped to keep clearly in my mind all our movements."

Corporal Silas Judson was just 19 when he died at a hospital in Newark, New Jersey. Horace transferred to the signal corps on February 1, 1864, and served in this organization until the end of the war. Soon after his discharge, he was married and settled in Cleveland. One of his sons became an attorney in Washington, D.C., another entered the medical profession, and his daughter served as a captain in the Salvation Army in Chicago.

Erasmus and Richard Bassett

For two brothers in the 126th New York, the Battle of Gettysburg offered an opportunity for both redemption and revenge. The previous summer Sergeant Erasmus Bassett, a 26-year-old schoolteacher, and his older brother Lieutenant Richard Bassett set off optimistically from their hometown of Dundee in the Finger Lakes region of central New York.

A little over two weeks later, however, on the morning of September 13, 1862, these rookie soldiers found themselves pitted against two veteran brigades of Confederate troops at Harper's Ferry, Virginia, during Robert E. Lee's invasion of Maryland. Due to their limited training, the New Yorkers became a convenient scapegoat for the collapse of the Union defenses on Maryland Heights even though more seasoned units also panicked and stampeded down the side of the mountain after William Barksdale's Mississippians outflanked the position.

After taking possession of the surrounding heights, the Confederates relentlessly bombarded the Federal soldiers trapped in the town below. During the second full day of the barrage three shells struck between the Bassett brothers of Company B, nearly burying them alive with dirt and gravel. With no hope of further resistance, the 11,000-man Union garrison surrendered on September 15. At this stage of the war the parole and exchange system was still in effect. Under this agreement, a captured soldier who signed a parole would not take up arms against the enemy until he was exchanged for a prisoner in the opposing army. In the interim, these soldiers were detained at a designated location.

Upon being processed by the Confederate provost authorities the large mass of parolees set off on a long walk to Annapolis, Maryland. While camped along the Monocacy River near Frederick on September 17, the men could hear the sounds of a large battle echoing from the village of Sharpsburg off to the north. Marching rapidly from Harper's Ferry, Jackson had rejoined the main body of the Southern army. Lee positioned his forces on the high ground above Antietam Creek to await the arrival of the Army of the Potomac, setting the stage for the bloodiest day of the war.

The Bassett brothers grew concerned about the welfare of their younger brother George, an officer in the 33rd New York. By chance, a family friend, who was a member of this same regiment, passed through the camp on his way back to the front, supposedly after being sent to the rear for supplies. This soldier told Richard and Erasmus that their brother expressed concern about them when he learned of the disaster at Harper's Ferry. The pair sent word that they were fine and hoped that George would also be "bullet proof."

This message was probably never delivered. That very afternoon during a mismanaged assault towards the Dunkard Church, the 33rd New York was badly mauled. After carrying a wounded fellow officer back to an aid station, Sergeant Major Bassett ran back to the regiment. Shot though the head the moment he returned, the "brave and beloved officer" died instantly.

By all accounts the 23-year-old soldier possessed great potential. A law student before the war, Bassett advanced rapidly from private to sergeant major and "by his winning ways and zealous attendance to duties, he had won the esteem of his officers and commanders, and fell universally regretted."

The sad news fell hard upon Richard and only added to his feelings of helplessness. "When I think of [George] & the painful reflection that we are prisoners of war: as if I were chained hand & foot & cannot avenge his death it makes it doubly painful, but I feel confident that there is a day of retribution not far distant."

This day of retribution was a long time in coming. After serving a two-month parole at Chicago's Camp Douglas along the windy shores of Lake Michigan, the 126th reported to Washington, D.C., where they spent a miserable winter guarding the approaches to the capital. Finally, in late June 1863, near the height of Lee's second invasion of the north, the New York regiments that made up Colonel George Willard's Brigade were assigned to General Alexander Hays' Division of the Army of the Potomac's Second Corps. The battle-tested veterans of Hancock's Corps did not extend a warm welcome to these new-comers. Subjected to almost constant taunting, they were dubbed the "Harper's Ferry Cowards."

Throughout the late afternoon of July 2, Willard's troops anxiously listened to the sounds of the swelling battle to the south from the shelter of Ziegler's Grove at the north-ern end of Cemetery Ridge. Then, suddenly, officers shouted the order to "Fall in!" fol-lowed by the command, "Fix bayonets; shoulder arms; left face; forward march!" General Hancock personally led the troops southward along the ridge. Suddenly, the general pointed off to his right to a swampy thicket pocked with large boulders along Plum Run. Several hundred yards away, a disorganized body of enemy troops emerged from the smoke.

As if by fate, these Southerners were none other than Barksdale's troops, who, after blasting through the center of the Third Corps line at the Peach Orchard, now hurtled towards the last cordon of the Union defenses. With the 126th New York in the center of the formation, Willard's troops descended the slope towards their onrushing former nemesis shouting the battle cry of "Remember Harper's Ferry."

According to Lieutenant Bassett, "We drew up in line of battle and charged across the ravine, which is covered with a thick growth of trees and bushes, and up the hill on the other side ... under a terrific fire of grape, canister, and shell, driving the rebels off at the point of the bayonet ... our comrades falling thick and fast around us."

Redemption had finally come to the 126th, but at a steep price. The majority of the regiment's losses took place within Company B. Clutching the national flag in one hand and his revolver in the other, Sergeant Erasmus Bassett kept several yards in front of the onrushing line. Near the edge of the marshy swale, a bullet struck Bassett in the leg. He staggered ahead for a few more steps when another lead missile struck him in the heart. The color-bearer tumbled to the earth without emitting a groan.

As was typical in combat, Lieutenant Bassett guided on the colors to keep his com-pany aligned with the remainder of the regiment. "When we started on the charge, I occa-sionally glanced my eyes toward the colors," wrote the lieutenant, "but while we were crossing the ravine, I noticed they faltered and finally fell.... I then knew that my dear brother had fallen." With a heavy heart he stuck to his duties. "The boys were falling all around me and appealing to me for help, but I could only give them words of encourage-ment, and charge on," explained Bassett.

That night, Union soldiers, singly and in small groups, searched over the field for missing friends and relatives. By the light of flickering lanterns the searchers uncovered ghastly sights—disfigured bodies riddled with bullets and smeared with blood and dirt, some with convulsed expressions, revealing the agonizing pain they had endured during their final moments.

Bassett discovered the slain bodies of several friends before discovering the corpse of his brother at about midnight. Flooded with grief, he wrote home, "I have not time to give many particulars, neither do I feel inclined to say much at present; my heart is too full and sad to say anything; and I do not know what to say to console the afflicted, for I am as sorely afflicted as anyone."

Richard recovered his brother's personal effects and carefully marked his temporary grave. After explaining its location to his family, he poured out, "I thought of George and then to think of Rapsy falling so near him, I could not help weeping." The pain of losing two brothers and so many friends plunged Bassett into a deep depression. Writing to his wife two weeks after the battle, he told her how lonesome it was without Erasmus and that he now had just 13 men with him in Company B. But when she suggested that he resign, Richard turned defensive: "Do you think me a baby, or coward, to resign in the face of an enemy, never!"

It would soon became obvious, however, that the lone survivor of three brothers suffered deep trauma and possibly from a condition described in a later war as chronic fatigue syndrome. After being promoted to captain the following spring, Bassett was detached to the provost guard of the Second Corps.

Following the Battle of Hatcher's Run near Petersburg on October 27, 1864, Bassett was placed in charge of several hundred Confederate prisoners. At about 9:00 p.m. that evening General Winfield S. Hancock ordered him to conduct the prisoners to the Yellow Tavern for processing. A drenching rain fell throughout the evening and by the time the party reached its destination the following morning, a cold north wind had kicked up behind the storm front. As a result of this exposure Bassett contracted a severe cough that hemorrhaged his lungs and caused a rupture in the abdomen near his right groin. Acting on the recommendations of two army surgeons, General Hancock granted the "gallant and faithful officer" a leave of absence to return home.

In December, a visitor testified that Bassett suffered from violent coughing spells and that the hernia had grown to the size of a hen's egg. The disability extended beyond the obvious physical symptoms. The following statement appeared on an affidavit signed by Bassett's physician: "He took his company into the Battle of Gettysburg forty-four strong, out of which ten were killed and twenty-four wounded; among the former was a brother, and all were old neighbors and friends. The effect this had upon this deponent's mind, combined with the arduous duties that followed in the campaigns of Virginia had the effect in reducing him to a mere skeleton."

When the ailing captain's condition did not improve significantly, an extension of the leave time was given to him, followed by an honorable discharge on January 18, 1865. Seeking to gain relief from his nagging ailments, Bassett changed his residence to Minnesota in 1869 upon the advice of his doctor. Unfortunately, a two-year stay did little to improve his health. The veteran also spent time on the seashore, visited the famed Saratoga Springs, and tried other forms of hydrotherapy, all to no avail.

Unable to resume his occupations as a farmer, a desperate Bassett applied for an invalid pension and eventually succeeded in receiving a monthly allotment of $24. Apparently, this sum provided only the bare necessities. Following Richard's death in 1896, Mary Bassett stated that "my late husband died a poor man."

Henry and John Nice

Unlike many of the "Boys of '61" who flocked to the colors in patriotic fervor or to satisfy their lust for adventure, Henry and John Nice viewed the war as an opportunity to escape from a poverty-filled childhood. The local and state bounty money they collected as bonuses for enlisting financed a down payment on a small home in the Germantown district of Philadelphia for their aged parents, Samuel and Eliza Nice.

Before rising to the rank of first lieutenant in the 99th Pennsylvania, John Nice worked as a teamster for a local contractor. A "good boy," he had faithfully set aside part of his wages for his mother since Samuel's poor health prevented him from earning a living. He continued to send money home after becoming a soldier, even enclosing the $2 in freight charges collected by the Adams Express Company for these shipments at the other end.

Henry Nice, a 22-year-old shoemaker, signed on with the 28th Pennsylvania, a regiment that later became the nucleus for the 147th Pennsylvania. Records indicate that he stood five feet and nine inches tall, and had a dark complexion, gray eyes, and dark hair.

Since the regiments to which they belonged were part of different corps within the army, staying in touch presented a challenge for the two siblings even when they found themselves camped in proximity to one another. In a letter to his mother dated November 24, 1861, John informed her, "I am sorry that I did not see Henry when his regiment was encamped along side of us for I might have helped to get him some clothes for you say that he was in want of them. I wrote him a letter a few days ago but have not yet received an answer yet."

Later, on June 5, 1863, from "Camp Sickles" near Falmouth, Virginia, John included the following in a letter home: "Henry came by our camp the other day but I could hardly see him for he was mounted upon a frame of a horse which raised him so high in the air that he was scarcely visible to the naked eye; he has been over here several times but I have not been able to get there yet."

Less than a week later, the 99th Pennsylvania broke camp and slid up the Rappahannock River to counter the movements of the Southern army along the opposite shore. It was the beginning of the war's most decisive campaign. Following in the wake of the First and Eleventh Corps, the proud soldiers of Major General Daniel Sickles' Third Corps arrived in Emmitsburg, Maryland, on June 30.

The next morning, as fighting raged at Gettysburg ten miles to the north, General Sickles received conflicting orders from his superiors. One directive from General Meade, the army's new commander, instructed him to remain in Emmitsburg, but his wing commander, Major General John F. Reynolds, entreated him to hurry forward with his troops. The adroit politician responded by detaching one brigade from each of his two divisions to stay as posted while he led the balance of his corps to Gettysburg. The 99th Pennsylvania and the other regiments that formed Brigadier General Henry Hobart Ward's Brigade arrived on the field by dusk and bivouacked on Cemetery Ridge. The next morning Ward's men extended the Union line southward towards Little Round Top.

As Sickle's infantrymen toiled along the muddy roads leading from Emmitsburg, the right wing of the Army of the Potomac closed in on Gettysburg from the southeast via the Baltimore Pike. In one of the enduring mysteries of the campaign, Major General Henry Slocum kept the 10,000 men of the Twelfth Corps sitting idle several miles from the battlefield. He finally arrived at about 6:00 p.m. as the shattered remnants of the First and Eleventh Corps rallied on Cemetery Hill. Arriving too late to change the outcome of the day's events, Slocum sent one of his divisions off to protect the right flank of the new Federal position and detached Brigadier General John Geary's Division to guard the army's left on Little Round Top. One of Geary's regiments was the 147th Pennsylvania.

Thus, the orders and actions of the army's top commanders set in motion one of the battle's numerous forgotten dramas so often obscured by larger events but paramount to those involved in them. According to family history, the two Nice brothers met one another in the vicinity of Little Round Top as their respective regiments converged upon the area. The short-lived reunion proved to be their last.

On a battlefield soldiers are merely pawns shifted across the board by the army brass in response to the vicissitudes of the contest. Neither John nor Henry Nice would fight on the slopes of the rocky hill. General Geary soon received orders to march his troops to Culp's Hill and reunite with the remainder of the Twelfth Corps. Then, later in the day, when Sickles shifted his forces to occupy the high ground near the Peach Orchard, Ward's brigade anchored the extreme left flank of the Union line at Devil's Den.

When Major General John Bell Hood's Division led off Longstreet's attack upon the Union left on the late afternoon of July 2, Ward's men held back the furious onslaught for an hour and a half before being outflanked and pushed back. About half the Union force fell dead or wounded.

Major John W. Moore of the 99th Pennsylvania would later write in his official report that his command "behaved nobly, standing unmoved under the enemy's fire and resisting superior numbers with spirit and determination. I cannot speak too highly of the manner in which the officers of my command acted, without exception gallantly and efficiently performing every duty assigned them. I lament to say that First Lieut. John R. Nice, commanding Company H, a brave, efficient, and gallant officer, was mortally wounded in the action of the 2nd...." Wounded in the abdomen, Nice lingered until the next morning before dying at a nearby division hospital.

As Longstreet's attack threatened to roll up the left of the Union line, Meade hastily stripped forces from the right of his line to plug the gaps, including nearly the entire Twelfth Corps. Somehow, General Geary missed a turn along the way and marched his two brigades completely away from the battlefield. He was eventually located and ordered back to Culp's Hill. Arriving there after midnight, the much traveled foot soldiers discovered that the enemy now occupied a portion of the works they had recently abandoned.

In the protracted battle that broke out early the next morning the 147th Pennsylvania turned back a Confederate attack across Pardee Field near the lower slope of the hill. While the 99th Pennsylvania had fought in an exposed position the previous evening and consequently suffered heavy casualties, the losses incurred by the 147th were comparatively light since they fought from a sheltered position. But a bullet that found its mark was always deadly, no matter what the circumstances. Exposed at the wrong moment, a lead missile fractured the skull of Corporal Henry Nice. Carried to the George Bushman Farm, he died that same day, probably within an hour or so of his brother.

The strange saga of the Nice brothers at Gettysburg raises many questions on fate, predestination, the fragility of life, and the mysteries of death. If both of them had survived the battle, the unlikely reunion on Little Round Top would be of little interest. But considering the fact that both of them would die the next day, it adds a degree of pathos that stirs the deepest levels of compassion.

One also wonders how Eliza and Samuel Nice dealt with the grief and guilt that must have consumed them upon learning of the fate of their two sons. The financial repercussions were immediate. A family friend testified that Eliza was compelled to work long hours doing laundry and housecleaning to generate an income, too many he thought for a woman of her age and condition. By 1870, Samuel was paralyzed and confined to his bed. Desperate, Eliza applied for a mother's pension and began to receive $17 per month, the value affixed to the lives of her two sons.

James and Thomas Stevens

"When I was sixteen years old, I traded the golden harvest fields of grain for the red harvest fields of death," reflected James Colclazer Stephens on his three years of service with the 20th Indiana Volunteers. Considering that he and his older brother Thomas fought in some of the war's bloodiest battles, this statement contains more truth than it does colorful hyperbole. Fortunately, not every story involving siblings ended in tragedy.

Notwithstanding the unparalleled death and suffering that surrounded them, the marathon marches, living outdoors under extreme weather conditions, the stress of constant fighting and campaigning, and the numerous hairbreadth escapes, particularly those involving Thomas, the Civil War opened up a whole new world for these two Midwestern farm boys. Together they witnessed the serenity of the North Carolina coast, the pastoral splendor of Virginia's Loudon Valley, the bountiful farms and orchards of western Maryland and southern Pennsylvania, and even the bright lights of Manhattan.

The odyssey began in June 1861 when Thomas, James, and Asbury Stevens rode to Monticello, Indiana, where they planned to enlist together in the Monticello Rifles, a group of volunteers that would later form Company K of the 20th Indiana Volunteers. The trio was broken up on July 22, however, after Asbury was rejected due to a physical disability. Of the two remaining brothers the unfolding national crisis probably had the greatest impact on Thomas White Stevens, who turned 21 years of age on August 27. The son of a farmer and miller, Thomas aspired to be a physician and to that end he entered Asbury College, now DePauw University, to study medicine. But when hostilities erupted Stevens traded his books for a musket and an uncertain future.

For many youthful soldiers the Peninisula Campaign of 1862 provided the backdrop for their first taste of combat. During the 20th Indiana's baptism by fire at the Battle of Oak Grove on June 25, 1862, both of the Stephens brothers were wounded in the hip region. Then, just five days later at Glendale, the Indiana soldiers fired so rapidly at the advancing Confederates that their guns frequently became too hot to hold. Thomas experienced a different sensation when an enemy bullet crashed into his musket barrel, sending a severe shock through his body. As dusk settled over the area it became difficult to distinguish friend from foe. Stephens, his captain, and several others from Company K fell as prisoners to the enemy. Slightly clothed with little protection from the elements, the hungry and fatigued captives spent several weeks at Richmond's Libby and Belle Isle prisons before being exchanged.

It would be the first of many trials for Thomas Stephens, but he endured largely because of his unshakable faith and resiliency. One of his officers remembered him as being "patient, watchful, [and] fearless" and hailed him as "the highest type of the patriotic Christian soldier, beloved by his comrades and respected by his officers." He was certainly not among the numerous bright-eyed farm boys, who, far from home and the watchful eyes of a doting mother, succumbed to the temptations of drinking, gambling, and the company of prostitutes. Rather, he was thoughtful, introverted, and deeply committed to the tenets of the proper Christian lifestyle. He filled much of his leisure time by reading the Bible and newspapers and in private prayer and devotion.

Stephens made an interesting entry in his diary on June 10, 1863: "Got interested in watching the operations of a red ant dragging off a dead fly, a great deal larger than himself, to his hole. He would go a little ways with his burden, then halt, and reconnoiter the ground, then push forward again. He finally reached home in safety." Metaphorically, the determined ant and his large burden illustrated the sergeant's own efforts to overcome the adversities of the war and return home to Indiana.

By the start of the Gettysburg Campaign Stephens had become afflicted with a sight defect that made it impossible for him to march at night. At such times he was led by

Jimmie or other comrades in the company. During a two-week period, he also suffered from a bout of diarrhea, vomiting, a toothache, a "very severe attack of neuralgia" and an outbreak of boils on his face, neck, and back! Somehow he managed to keep up with the regiment during the demanding marches.

Contrary to how many of us would have felt at the time, Stephens was overwhelmed by guilt. "O that I could love God more for his goodness and mercy to me," he confessed. "He has preserved my life through many battles, has preserved me from diseases, many have fallen by my side yet I live. How ungrateful I am! O that I could love Him with all my heart!" That day he poured over his Bible and wrote a letter home to Asbury.

Stephens had to be led during the final leg of the march that brought the 20th Indiana to Cemetery Ridge a little after dark on the evening of July 1. The next day, after the 99th Pennsylvania shifted towards Devil's Den, the 20th formed the right flank of General Hobart Ward's brigade line. By evening, over a third of the 400 Hoosiers were dead or wounded, including Colonel John Wheeler, who was killed by a bullet to the temple. "The fighting was hot, *very hot*," recorded Stephens.

God was apparently watching out for him that day. His life was spared when a bullet that plowed into his side was partially deflected by the metal plate on his cartridge box. Helped off the field by a comrade, he made his way to a nearby aide station for treatment. Although not life threatening, the injury would keep him sidelined for a considerable length of time.

Meanwhile, Private Jimmie Stephens and the 20th Indiana joined in the pursuit of the Confederates across the Potomac River and into Virginia. When Union forces finally caught up to Lee's rear guard near Manassas Gap it appeared that another major clash was imminent. The scenario changed drastically for the Hoosiers upon receipt of a July 30 telegraph from General-in-Chief Henry W. Halleck to General Meade. The Indiana soldiers would be returning north.

Blood spilled in the streets of New York in the week following the Battle of Gettysburg in reaction to the implementation of the Federal draft. A provision in the First National Conscription Act that allowed a draftee to hire a substitute for a $300 fee outraged the city's predominately Irish working class. Tempers rose with the summer heat of Monday, July 13, as protesters surrounded the various offices of the provost marshal where names were being drawn for the draft. An incensed crowd overwhelmed the police line stationed at the Third Avenue office and torched the building. Soon flames engulfed an entire city block as arriving fireman watched helplessly.

Taking advantage of these disturbances, Gotham's large criminal element—organized gangs and individual thugs—joined the mayhem. Over the next four days, mobs numbering between 50,000 to 70,000 roamed the streets looting, burning, and murdering as they fought pitched battles with the police, militia, and navy personnel. The most atrocious acts of violence involved the city's black population. In a truly despicable act, the rioters set fire to the Colored Orphan Asylum, home to 200 children under the age of twelve. They also indiscriminately beat and lynched any black man who dared to protect his home or family.

Expressing the outage of many New Yorkers, Henry J. Raymond of the *New York Times* wrote: "They talk, or rather they did talk at first, of the oppressiveness of the Conscription Law; but three-fourths of those who have been actively engaged in violence have been boys and young men under twenty years of age, and not all subject to the Conscription. Were the Conscription Law to be abrogated tomorrow, the controlling inspiration of the mob would remain the same. It comes from sources quite independent of that law, or any other law—from a malignant hate toward those in better circumstances, from a craving for plunder, from a barbarous spite against a different race, from a disposition to bolster up the failing fortunes of the Southern rebels.... the mob must be crushed at once."

By the time the violence ended, over one million dollars of damage had been sustained. The figures on the human toll are widely disparate. While an early study reported that at least 2,000 were killed and another 8,000 wounded, mostly among the rioters, one modern scholar placed the number of killed at only 74.

Halleck responded with a big stick by ordering up a contingent from the Army of the Potomac to maintain order. Meade responded by sending four regiments of over 1,600 troops to deter any further disturbances. Landing on the pier at Battery Park, the sun burnt, unshaved veterans, wearing the same filthy clothing they had worn at Gettysburg, received a rude welcome from a surly mob of onlookers who hailed them with a variety of derisive calls. Forming a line the soldiers fixed bayonets and drove back the mob, which gave only limited resistance.

The draft resumed on August 19 without incident. Afterwards, the 20th Indiana guarded the armories and other strategic locations in the city. The men had ample opportunity for recreation. Jimmie Stephens enjoyed fishing, playing leapfrog, and a game of baseball. Nonplussed by the poor conduct of a few of his comrades, the young private commented that if they would learn to behave better it would mean less guard duty for everyone.

He also felt guilty over his own conduct. "I am trying to live in the service of Christ but often do I commit flagrant sin," confided Stephens to his diary. He offered no particulars, but prayed for the strength to rise above temptations.

Instead of the bright lights of Manhattan, Sergeant Thomas Stephens found himself in a dank prison cell surrounded by common thieves. Hoping to rejoin his regiment after a month-long recuperation, Stephens reported to the provost marshal's office in New York on August 13 only to be arrested as a deserter when he could not produce the proper pass. It took nearly two weeks before the mess was straightened up and the wrongly accused soldier gained his freedom from Castle William on Governor's Island.

After being reunited with Jimmie, the two Indiana boys made up for the lost time. Receiving a 24-hour pass near the end of September, Jimmie played tour guide for his older brother. At Barnum's Museum they took in a variety of unusual oddities: a boy from Baltimore who stood over eight feet tall, a dance performance by eleven Indians, and an abundance of animal curiosities, serpents, and sea creatures, including a five-horned sheep and a black sea lion that consumed sixty pounds of fish per day. Later, they climbed up the steeple of the Trinity Church, which offered a bird's eye view of New York City, Brooklyn, Newark, and the harbor crowded with thousands of sailing vessels. On the following day, the pair had their pictures taken at Meade Brothers studio and visited Central Park. Before returning to camp they strolled wide-eyed down Fifth Avenue past the "palaces" of the aristocrats.

Near the beginning of October rumors began to circulate that the 20th would soon be heading back to the front. In response, the Stephens brothers shipped a package home that contained bullets, a Confederate belt and uniform buttons, and other relics from the Gettysburg battlefield. "I should have liked to have remained here over winter," wrote Jimmie, "but it is for us only to obey."

Indeed, the enjoyable diversion ended on October 15 when the men boarded a small steamer for Jersey City. From there the railroad transported them to Philadelphia and thence to Baltimore. The Hoosiers soon rejoined the Army of the Potomac in northern Virginia.

The spring of 1864 began pleasantly enough. While the late April landscape of Indiana remained brown and desolate, the Virginia countryside around Brandy Station burst forth with fragrant blossoms set against a canvas of greening meadows. But man's blighting hand would transform these scenes of renewal into gruesome killing fields.

The bloody crucible got underway soon after the Army of the Potomac splashed across the Rappahannock River. Before the massive army could navigate its way through the tangled thickets of the Wilderness, Lee shifted his smaller force to block the path. On May 5 fighting erupted along the area's two principal roads. After some of the most confused and frenzied fighting of the war, the Federals gained control of the vital intersection of the Brock Road and the Orange Plank Road.

Jimmie Stephens scrawled in his diary: "Had a hard fight this afternoon.... Our brigade was engaged at 4 p.m. Our regiment did well. I am really proud that I belong to such a regiment.... I don't think either side gained a great deal."

Attempting to break the stalemate, Grant ordered Meade to launch a massive assault at dawn the next day. Thomas Stephens arose early so that he had ample time to pray and read scripture. It proved to be time well spent. As he rushed towards the Confederate breastworks a bullet smashed into the sergeant's chest, violently knocking him to the ground. Fortunately, the missile lodged inside the small pocket Bible he had tucked into the left pocket of his coat moments earlier.

Receiving permission to check on his brother, Jimmie Stephens raced to the rear only to be turned back by an officer. In the thick terrain he had a difficult time finding the regiment. His mind was racing. "I was much distressed until I again saw my brother and learned of his providential deliverance," he wrote later.

Jimmie soon faced a crisis of his own. The overwhelming offensive broke the Southern lines, driving them back over a mile. After capturing the colors of the 55th Virginia and scooping up numerous prisoners, the exhausted Indiana soldiers paused for a rest. Near this time part of a bullet ricocheted from a rock or tree and hit Stephens on the back of the right arm, spinning him almost completely around. A member of Company H helped him off the field, but lacking any signs of blood, the private was sent back to the front.

At this stage Longstreet saved the day for the Confederacy by launching a daring flank assault. The surprised Federals retreated over the same ground they had fought so hard to secure. Union officers finally managed to rally the troops behind the Brock Road earthworks. Positioning several men in the rear to provide a steady supply of loaded weapons for those manning the firing line, a heavy barrage of fire greeted Longstreet's men. In this manner Stephens estimated that he fired at least 200 rounds before the counterattack was repulsed. He later praised God for the outcome, believing that the army would have been ruined if the Confederates had been successful.

Instead of retreating back across the river as most of his predecessors had done, Grant slid around Lee's left towards Spotsylvania Court House, a crossroads hamlet ten miles to the south. Arriving first, the Confederates constructed an extensive network of log breastworks with connecting trenches. Over the course of nearly two weeks the Union army battered against these defenses, suffering enormous casualties and realizing only limited success.

The largest of these assaults took place on the early morning of May 12 when a massive formation drove into the salient of the Confederate line known as the Mule Shoe. Jimmie Stephens remembered it as "the strongest field works I ever saw." This attack precipitated 22 hours of uninterrupted combat, much of it hand-to-hand. During the melee a bullet penetrated the inside of the private's left leg. Thomas Stephens and another soldier carried him to a field hospital where the wound was dressed. Although painful, the leg could be saved since the bone remained undamaged.

Lying near a shed converted into an operating clinic, Jimmie Stephens heard the heartrending cries of the less fortunate as the surgeon's saw added its rasping notes to the demonic refrain. Lonely and frightened, he longed for his brother's presence, but he thanked God for preserving his life. Transported to Fredericksburg by wagon, Stephens and his fellow patients were loaded onto northbound steamers. Passing through a series of government hospitals in Washington, Baltimore, and York, Pennsylvania, he would never again see combat.

Meanwhile, the Union drive to the south continued following the bloody stalemate at Spotsylvania Court House. At the crossing of the North Anna River on May 23, a shell tore the knapsack from the shoulder of Sergeant Stephens, tearing it into six pieces. Miraculously, for the third time in his army career, Stephens cheated death.

During the six weeks of almost constant marching and fighting that preceded the siege of Petersburg, about 65,000 Union soldiers fell as casualties. Mental and physical exhaustion sapped the strength of both officers and men. Sergeant Stephens suffered from an illness, most likely combat fatigue, during much of the time.

Although his recuperation was made tolerably pleasant by the hospital's well stocked library, Jimmie Stephens, who turned 20 on June 21, could hardly take his mind from the welfare of his brother and comrades. With the rapid approach of the end of the regiment's three-year enlistment term, his thoughts also turned homeward. "I do wish I had my discharge. Time passes slowly to me now. I have never in my three years of service had a furlough nor been away from the company until I was wounded," he wrote on June 23.

Three days later, the 20th Indiana began to arrive from Petersburg. "I did not know Thomas at first sight. He looked hard," confessed Jimmie. Indeed, Thomas and Jimmie Stephens returned home to Indiana forever changed, but their abiding faith in God and in one another had sustained them through the unimaginable.

Abraham G., Jacob L., and William A. Carter

In the largely agrarian world of the mid–nineteenth century, family units formed the nucleus of rural society. Typically, grown children lived within a mile or so of the ancestral farm, thereby providing a built-in support system during times of need. In many instances, sons followed in the footsteps of their fathers in choosing an occupation.

Joseph and Elizabeth Carter raised six children in the fertile farm country of Centre County, Pennsylvania, near State College. For over 25 years, Joseph Carter was employed at nearby Centre Furnace, one of the region's numerous ironworks. For most of this period he held the position of founder, a highly skilled laborer who earned the highest wage of all the workers at the furnace. The founder oversaw the entire operation. He determined the correct mixture of raw materials and the rate of blast to turn out pig iron, which could later be reheated and forged into tools or other items, and cast iron. All this was done by sight, without the advantage of calibration instruments.

When William, the Carter's second oldest child, reached the age of 14 in 1843, he toiled alongside his father in the hot forge. Thirteen years later, William advanced to the position of gutterman and would eventually become founder at another site.

The Carters' 109-acre farm bolstered the family's social standing and helped to provide an above average level of income that allowed for the periodic purchase of a few luxury items, such as cigars, silk, and a new set of dishes. By 1860, the three oldest children had married and established households of their own, including William, who had a wife and two children by now. Married a decade earlier, Abraham Green Carter supported his family of five as a carpenter.

When the Centre Furnace closed operations in 1858, Joseph Carter, worn down from years of hard labor and increasing infirmity, gradually turned over most of the farm operations to his eldest son. When Green Carter moved back to the homestead with his growing family, he displaced his two youngest brothers, Isaac and Jacob, aged 24 and 17 respectively. This situation did not last for long, because in the late summer of 1862 three of the four Carter brothers left home for military service.

What motivated these actions? By this point in the war, the lengthy casualty lists and lack of decisive results had dampened patriotic spirits. While the threat of involuntary conscription and the payment of cash bounties as enlistment incentives might have spurred the Carters into action, the looming threat of a Confederate invasion, once unthinkable, also influenced their thinking. Unlike the previous year, increasing numbers of older married men, such as Green and William Carter, donned the Union blue with the more typical younger recruits.

On August 19, 1862, 34-year-old Green and Jacob, age 19, enlisted together in the 148th Pennsylvania. Other than their identical height of five feet, nine inches, the two siblings bore little resemblance to one another. While Jacob had a light complexion, blue eyes, and light hair, Green's record describes his appearance as dark complexioned with black hair and eyes. Green became a corporal and Jacob assumed the rank of private in Company C. William, 33 at the time, enrolled the next day, and was assigned to Company D as a private.

Under the watchful eyes of Colonel James A. Beaver, future governor of Pennsylvania, the recruits gradually acquired the skills and habits of soldiers. Away from home for perhaps the first time, Private Jacob Carter suffered from a series of maladies during the early weeks of training and throughout much of the winter after the 148th reported for duty with the Army of the Potomac in Virginia. Promoted to sergeant on January 5, 1863, Green Carter must have worried often about the welfare of his kid brother.

In late April General Joseph Hooker shifted most of his army around the flank of Lee's entrenched army above Fredericksburg. Perhaps because of his lack of training time, Jacob did not accompany the regiment when the Second Corps crossed the Rappahannock River at U.S. Ford. The heaviest fighting of the campaign occurred on the morning of Sunday, May 3, when the Confederates launched a series of furious attacks against the Union lines at Chancellorsville. Holding on tenaciously throughout the morning, the Federal lines finally broke near noon and the infantrymen retreated back to another line of defenses closer to the river crossings.

In just five hours of fighting, the combined casualties of the two armies exceeded 17,500, making it the bloodiest period of the war up to that point. It was a rude introduction for the untested soldiers of the 148th. The two Centre County companies bore the brunt of the fighting. In Company D, seventeen men fell dead or mortally wounded. Private William Carter was not among them. The next day, however, Jacob Carter concluded his diary entry with a blunt statement: "I heard that my brother A. G. Carter was killed."

The rumor proved to be true. Lemuel Osman of Company C later recalled, "Green Carter, of our company, was wounded. I helped him to the rifle pits, and he says to me in a low whisper, 'Lem, I can't go any farther.' He bled to death."

Many of the wounded would have preferred a quick death. Soon exploding artillery shells ignited the dry tinder of debris on the forest floor. Men shot in the bowels or otherwise incapacitated watched helplessly as the flames advanced towards them. A steady pop of gunshots indicated many who chose to die by their own hands. The charred condition of the human remains in this area prevented the recovery of Green's body.

A week later, when the army returned to its winter camps, Jacob mailed a letter with the sad tidings. Back in Centre County the Carter family held on to a shred of hope. Captain Robert Foster, who left for home on sick leave after the battle, could not confirm Green's death. Returning to duty near the end of the month, the captain wrote regretfully to his wife, "You can say to Mrs. Carter that Green is certainly dead."

Years later, Colonel Beaver lamented the loss of "many of our most reliable and promising noncommissioned officers." He mentioned two names, one of them being Sergeant Carter. Another comrade testified, "A. Green Carter ... was a very capable man and would certainly have been heard from later, had he lived." But the heaviest blow fell upon Green's widow, Rebecca, and his four small children.

The fact that the death of his older brother is not mentioned again within the pages of Jacob's diary is not surprising. His entries are more of a narrative of places and events with little in the way of introspection. In true Victorian fashion his emotions are carefully guarded.

However, it is easy to imagine the loneliness that Jacob felt in the weeks that followed. Totaling over 80 men on the eve of Chancellorsville, Company C could only raise 19 men for a dress parade on May 10. Not only did Jacob have to cope with the death of his brother, but also the loss of many friends and neighbors that he had known since boyhood. "It looks pretty hard for Company C," admitted Jacob.

On the following day Pennsylvania Governor Andrew Curtin, himself a native of Centre County, paid a visit to the army. As he attempted to deliver a reassuring speech he was overcome by emotion, and, according to one eyewitness, the tears streamed down his cheeks.

In his understated manner it is evident that Jacob drew closer to William. He mentions sharing a letter from home and washing a shirt for him while doing his own laundry.

Considering his extensive periods of illness, it is a tribute to Jacob Carter's resolve that he kept up during the nearly three weeks of strenuous marching that carried the Army of the Potomac from Falmouth, Virginia, into Pennsylvania. In his diary entry for June 29, we get a sense of the difficulties faced by the young private: "We left Fredericks city this morning on our journey.... We marched thirty miles today. It is the hardest birthday I ever put in in my life. Our company straggled a good bit. We heard the Rebs are shelling Harrisburg. We are marching for there now."

The much anticipated clash would not take place on the outskirts of the state capital but rather in the fields and woods surrounding Gettysburg, ninety miles to the south.

Adrenalin must have pumped rapidly through the veins of Jacob Carter on the late afternoon of July 2, 1863, when Brigadier General John C. Caldwell's division was ordered up from its reserve position behind Cemetery Ridge. The 148th hustled southward, clambering over stone fences and wallowing through a marshy bog before reaching the Wheatfield Road. The anxious and perspiring soldiers that belonged to the brigade of Colonel Edward Cross deployed in line of battle and plunged into the chest high wheat on the opposite side of the road.

As the 148th Pennsylvania charged towards a stone fence that jogged along the southern edge of the field the bullets neatly zipped off the heads of the ripening grain. The fighting became so intense that the Union riflemen exhausted their ammunition within 10 or 15 minutes. A fresh brigade came to their relief and drove the Confederates deep into the woods.

Passing the first test of his courage beside his more experienced comrades, a deep sense of relief washed over Private Carter. But as he turned towards the rear, he suddenly felt a stinging sensation in his right hamstring. Carter crumpled to the ground in agony. From then until dusk the seesaw battle swept back and forth over the prostrate soldier. "After I was wounded I laid under both fires and the Rebels carried their flag over me twice," remembered Carter.

During the long hours that elapsed before a member of the Fifth Corps carried him to the safety of the Union lines near Little Round Top, the wounded private had ample time to ponder his fate: Would he bleed to death like his brother? If so, would his body be identified, or tossed unceremoniously into an unmarked grave?

At one point Carter fainted from the loss of blood only to be jolted back into consciousness by the movements of a prowling Confederate. Smearing blood from his leg onto his face, he wiggled into a furrow until the intruder passed on. Remembering a leather strap that his uncle had given to him before leaving home, the resourceful farm boy fashioned it into a makeshift tourniquet.

The midnight rescue from the Wheatfield ended the first part of the ordeal, only to begin another. Lying in the open with no protection from the elements and lacking the nourishing food craved by an injured soldier, Carter tapped into his inner strength and toughed it out. By the time he wrote home on July 10, food and supplies had begun to flow into the isolated town. Jacob also mailed a letter to William, the survivor of two fierce battles, now doing his best to pin down Lee's retreating army.

With the aid of crutches Jacob walked for the first time on the fifteenth, making the round trip from his tent to the latrines. His progress was clouded by the deaths of 13 patients in the field hospital over the next three days.

On Monday, July 20, Carter boarded a railroad car bound for a general hospital in York, thirty miles to the east. With typical nonchalance he recorded a pleasant visit by several local ladies soon after his arrival there. No mention is made of one Mary Jane Ledy, but a romance sparked that day between Jacob and the young nurse.

Jacob did note a much welcomed visit by his father near the end of the month. Joseph Carter brought some delicacies with him and remained at the hospital until a furlough permitted his son to return home in early September.

The war had a profound impact upon all three of the Carter families. The widowed Rebecca Carter remarried in 1867, coincidentally the same year of her father-in-law's passing. She gave birth to eleven more children.

William Carter's good fortune ran out the next spring at Spotsylvania Court House, where an enemy bullet cost him his right leg. He passed through a number of government hospitals before finally being released on July 28, 1865. Apparently, the long-time iron founder harbored no resentment over the lost limb. He proudly named one of his last children Ulysses S. Grant Carter.

For Jacob Carter the wounding at Gettysburg delivered an unexpected blessing. On July 15, 1864, as the two great eastern armies dug in around Petersburg, a double wedding ceremony took place at the Carter home on Lightner Lane. Immediately before Jacob's older sister married a neighboring farmer, the former soldier exchanged vows with Mary Jane Ledy, his "angel of mercy." This commitment came with an additional sacrifice for the new Mrs. Carter. Her parents, staunch Pennsylvania German Democrats, bitterly opposed the war. When their daughter married a soldier, they promptly disowned her and as a result would never meet their seven grandchildren.

For several decades after the war, the Carter clan remained close knit, bound together by farming the rich soil of Centre County. Even the births and deaths of family members did not interrupt the unending rhythms of planting, harvesting, and storing. The elderly Carters spent their final years living in the homes of the children.

In 1891, Jacob Carter sold his 35-acre farm and moved his family to Altoona, where he took a job as an "engineer" at a planing mill. He died in a bizarre accident on New Year's Day of 1901. After crawling into a manhole to service a boiler, his foot became tightly wedged. While struggling to break free, Carter suffered a heart attack. Helpless and alone as he had been many years earlier at Gettysburg, his lifeless body was discovered about an hour after the accident.

Frank, Patrick, and Thomas Moran

An increasingly familiar scene took place in New York on July 21, 1861. Even as panic-stricken Federal troops fled from the Bull Run battlefield, a proud new regiment of Union soldiers, neatly dressed in spotless Chasseur uniforms, strutted proudly down Broadway to strains of martial music. Awash in a sea of colorful buntings and banners, pretty girls waved handkerchiefs and tossed roses at the gallant patriots.

The proceedings took a more sober turn at the pier on Staten Island as the men broke ranks to say good-bye to loved ones. Weeping throngs gathered around each for a final embrace or to present a small token of remembrance. In sharp juxtaposition to these emotionally charged tableaus, a smooth faced and delicate-looking soldier drifted away from the crowd.

Although just 19 years old at the time, Francis "Frank" Moran, a self-described "rolling stone," had already traveled extensively, allowing him to experience much of the country's cultural diversity. Born in Canada within a few miles of Niagara Falls, Moran lost both of his parents while he was still a small boy. Living in Detroit at the time, the orphaned children—two girls and three boys—were eventually scattered throughout Michigan, Illinois, and Minnesota.

After working briefly as a bell boy at the Biddle House in Detroit, a teenaged Frank Moran began to quench his thirst for adventure, settling into a nomadic lifestyle. He drifted to New York City before arriving in New Orleans in 1860, where he found work with a printer. With no firm roots or family it would not have been surprising if the young man had been swept up in the passions of the upstart Confederacy, as were many transplanted Northerners. In the spring of 1861, however, Moran, who had frequently witnessed the auctioning off of African-American males, was mortified by the sale of a beautiful young mulatto girl. Not long afterwards, following the announcement that the Federal garrison at Fort Sumter had been fired upon, he realized that his allegiance belonged to the Union.

Moran embarked on a long journey that carried him up the Mississippi River to St. Louis, then by rail to Cincinnati, floating from there to Pittsburgh, chugging across the breadth of Pennsylvania to Philadelphia, where he hopped a steamer to New York City. Within a week of his arrival, he enrolled as a private in Company H of the 2nd Fire Zouaves (73rd New York).

The pitiful sight of this five feet, five inch tall recruit standing alone attracted the attention of a refined middle-aged lady seated in a carriage about thirty yards away. Summoned to her side, Moran related the story of his tragic childhood, the resulting separation from his siblings, his varied travels, and the reality that no one would know or much care if he met a soldier's death. At the conclusion of the sad narrative Mrs. Hall copied down his name, company, and regiment. Taking his hand she offered uplifting words of comfort that would remain forever etched in the young soldier's memory.

Bowing to say good-bye, Moran boarded the waiting steamboat with his new comrades. As the churning paddlewheels carried them away from the dock a band struck up "The Girl I Left Behind," eliciting a hearty cheer from the men crowded onto the upper deck.

This incident was related by Moran nearly thirty years later in a serialized account of his wartime experiences that appeared in the *National Tribune*. "I never saw or heard again of the kind and noble lady," he would write. Did Mrs. Hall really exist or was she merely a literary device born of the romantic musings of an aging veteran? Whatever the case, the army became Moran's surrogate family. Within the 73rd New York he developed bonds of dependency and affection deeper than any he had ever known. Thriving in this new environment, he rose through the ranks from private to second lieutenant within two years.

But Moran was not as alone as he originally thought. At Detroit, Michigan, on September 3, 1862, his older brother became a member of the 5th Michigan Volunteer Infantry. A ship carpenter by trade, 25-year-old Patrick Moran was born in Mayo, Ireland, before his parents immigrated to North America. Perhaps by fate, the 5th Michigan was assigned to the Third Corps at about the same time as the 73rd New York.

This circumstance allowed the Moran brothers the opportunity to get reacquainted with one another. The storied histories of these two units are very similar and Patrick Moran developed a habit of saying good-bye to his younger brother before each battle. There would be several close calls in the war's early days. Frank was hit in the left hand at Williamsburg and suffered another injury at Bristoe Station, while Patrick received a wound at Fredericksburg.

As was their custom, the two brothers spoke briefly a half an hour before Longstreet attacked the Union left flank on the afternoon of July 2, 1863. Twenty months would pass before they would see one another again.

The 5th Michigan defended the Stony Hill during the opening attacks against the Wheatfield. About 700 yards to the northwest the 73rd New York waited in reserve. When General William Barksdale's Brigade blasted into the salient of the Third Corps line at the Peach Orchard, the New Yorkers hustled over in support. Reaching a position near the Sherfy house, the regiment halted to unleash a volley at the onrushing Mississippians. In those eternal moments when time seems to stand still, men melted away in seconds as the embattled line of the 73rd bent under the weight of the crushing attack.

As Lieutenant Moran struggled to hold his company together, an exploding shell burst near his face, killing a horse and striking about a dozen men in the vicinity. A fragment stung the officer's left eye and another gouged his right ankle. The concussion of the blast knocked him to the ground as if he "had been struck by lightning." The horse toppled over an instant later, his neck covering Moran's face.

Pinned by the animal and partly unconscious, he might have smothered if a Mississippi lieutenant had not dragged him from under the horse. The enemy officer helped him to his feet and led him across the road to the shade of a cherry tree near the Sherfy house. It was only then that Moran noticed his blood-filled shoe. "On that day I met with the fate which of all others I had dreaded and more than once escaped by a hair in Virginia— I was taken prisoner!" he wrote.

The elation felt by Moran and his fellow POWs as they witnessed the collapse of Pickett's Charge from behind Seminary Ridge turned to despair on the evening of July 4 as they struggled to keep pace with the retreating columns of Confederate artillery and infantry. Those who believed that God intervened in the affairs of man saw plenty of evidence of His wrath on that dreadful evening.

Moran recalled these unforgettable scenes: "[A] torrent of rain that increased hourly in violence, descending in drowning sheets that turned the mountain roads into rivers and the glens into lakes.... [T]he wind lashed and bent the pines and poplars like whips in its furious blasts, and the scene revealed at midnight by the vivid and flashing lightning, while mountain and gorge echoed back the deafening peals of thunder, was one far beyond the descriptive power of pen, painter, or human tongue, and the memory of the witnesses can alone preserve it."

For the roughly 3,000 Union prisoners the sight of the rain-swollen Potomac River raised the slim hopes that their comrades could crush the fleeing enemy and liberate them before the crossing could be effected. This optimism faded when the water receded before Meade could launch a decisive attack.

Throughout the final stages of the Gettysburg Campaign, the thoughts of Lieutenant Moran focused increasingly upon the welfare of others rather than his own uncertain future. "Up to this time I failed to find one among my fellow prisoners who could give me a word of news from my regiment.... I was hungry to know what havoc the battle had made among the comrades I knew and loved. I would have paid any price for the assurance that my brother ... had come safely through that bloody Orchard and Wheatfield," he recalled.

He would have been comforted to know that Patrick was doing fine. However, on September 23, while Frank adapted to his new surroundings at Richmond's Libby Prison, his youngest brother, a diminutive 18-year-old cooper with blue eyes and light hair, signed up with the 89th Illinois Volunteers at Chicago. Taken prisoner the following spring, Thomas Moran would soon walk through the gates of Andersonville, the war's most notorious prison pen.

By the close of 1864 all three of the Moran brothers were prisoners in Dixie. After sustaining a gunshot wound to the left hip at the Wilderness, Patrick Moran returned to active duty, only to be captured near Petersburg on October 27. Much of his confinement would be spent at Salisbury, North Carolina.

The odds of Frank Moran meeting either of his brothers was virtually nonexistent, since it was customary for both sides to isolate officer POWs in order to deter mass escapes and uprisings among the leaderless enlisted personnel. Officers typically enjoyed better quarters and increased privileges.

These additional luxuries could not suppress the insatiable quest for freedom. Daring and resourceful, Lieutenant Moran ranked among the most determined, if least successful, escape artists. During his lengthy confinement he broke out on five different occasions, but was recaptured each time.

The most famous of these incidents took place on February 9, 1864. Moran numbered among the 109 officers who escaped from Libby by crawling through a narrow underground tunnel that spanned 50 to 60 feet in length. Moran and two accomplices pierced the outer defenses surrounding Richmond by dawn, but a Confederate patrol surrounded them in a wooded swamp several miles northeast of Mechanicsville. All told, 59 of the escapees succeeded in reaching Union lines, while two drowned in the James River. The remaining 48 faced confinement in a dank underground cell known as the dungeon.

Nonetheless, these officers fared much better than their enlisted counterparts. With the collapse of systematic exchanges and U. S. Grant's relentless pressure on the Southern heartland, prison populations swelled to unprecedented levels throughout the war's final year. Combined with poor sanitation and a critical shortage of food and medicine throughout much of the South, prison compounds such as that at Andersonville became nothing more than concentration camps.

Eventually, 33,000 POWs crowded onto this site's 26½ acres. Epidemics of scurvy, diarrhea, dysentery, typhoid, smallpox, and hospital gangrene culled the population. The leading cause of death, diarrhea and dysentery, claimed 4,529 lives during a six-month period in 1864. The fall of Atlanta on September 1 led to the transfer of most of the inmates to other facilities. The 8,000 prisoners too sick or too weak for travel remained at the site. A large percentage of these invalids died within the next few months. Thomas Moran never saw the outside of the filthy stockade, succumbing to diarrhea on September 18. His brothers would not learn of his death until months later.

After ten months at Libby followed by another ten months of incarceration at Macon, Georgia, Charleston and Columbia, South Carolina, and Charlotte, North Carolina, Frank Moran's ordeal finally ended on March 1, 1865. As the freight cars crowded with released Union prisoners screeched to a stop at a large meadow near Wilmington, North Carolina, the long-time captive could recall no other scene that "touched me with such depth and power." At the sight of the Stars and Stripes, tears streamed down the cheeks of the gaunt prisoners. Still wearing the tattered remnants of his Gettysburg uniform, Moran laughingly described himself as "a poem in rags" that his own mother, had she been alive, would not have recognized as her son.

Indeed, he experienced a similar problem when his own brother approached him on the streets of Wilmington. "I looked at the poor wreck, and a strange instinct rather than any external sign told me, in spite of dirt and rags, that I knew that face and form; but before my scrutiny was completed, the voice that pronounced my name revealed to me— my brother Patrick," wrote the stunned lieutenant. The fact that Frank had no idea that his older brother had been captured explains part of the shock.

He described the short reunion:

> He was indeed a sad wreck. I could not, however, induce him to return with me ... preferring, he said, to wait until he reached Annapolis, for which place he was to leave with other enlisted men by steamer that evening. I got him to accept some refreshments and some money, however, and promising to meet me soon at home he went off radiant enough, enjoying a good cigar, which could ever make him happy. Poor fellow! The cruel marks of his captivity and wounds were afterwards carried to his grave. As each of us stood there that

day of our happy deliverance, we little dreamt that our dear young brother Thomas had died at Andersonville six months before! It was a merciful ignorance that gave us that one day of happiness in our soldier lives.

The day following his arrival at Annapolis on March 8, Moran fired off a letter to his commanding officer, Colonel Michael W. Burns: "I was exceedingly gratified to find that our regiment still held its organization and I desire to return to it as soon as possible.... My brother of the 5th Michigan, who has been a prisoner, came through the lines with me. I shall not apply for a leave of absence until I hear from you." Two days later, he received a furlough to travel to Chicago, the home of his sister, Julia. It appears that he arranged for Patrick to be cared for there following his discharge.

Records indicate that the oldest of the Moran brothers filed an application for a pension on July 21 of that year. In February 1866 the pension bureau mailed correspondence requesting additional information. Since no response was received, it is likely that Patrick Moran died in the interim.

Returning to Annapolis for final processing, Frank Moran learned of his promotion to captain. On May 5, 1865, just ten days prior to his discharge from the army, Moran entered into a commitment that would curtail his vagabond habits: he married a city resident named Georgiana Lonthicum. The captain never mentioned the details of this romance and we can only speculate as to how the two met.

Facing continual financial difficulties and entirely losing the sight in his left eye, the postwar years were not pleasant for Moran. After residing for a time in New York City, the family relocated to Philadelphia. From there, in January of 1883, the ailing veteran solicited the assistance of U.S. Senator J. Donald Cameron in securing a pension: "I am getting starving pay as a night watchmen & have only lately got this after a year's idleness. I have an invalid wife and three children, one of them just recovered from a serious illness, and am up to my neck in distressing debts." After two years of frustration, he was granted $17 per month.

A prolific and gifted writer, Moran supplemented his meager income with submissions to the *Philadelphia Weekly Times*, *Century Magazine*, and the *National Tribune*, the preeminent newspaper for Union veterans. These efforts culminated with the 1890 publication of *Bastiles of the Confederacy*. Interspersed with the author's personal experiences, this book contained a narrative on the treatment of Union prisoners, which he described as "the most gigantic and atrocious crime that has ever stained the hands of man since the dawn of Christianity."

Considering the North's abundance of resources and far superior infrastructure, these charges are even more applicable to Northern prison officials who advocated policies of retaliation against Southern POWs. Moran's bitterness is entirely understandable, though; he had lost two brothers due to captivity, and he still retained the humiliation of being struck over his injured eye by the hated Richard "Dick" Turner, second in command at Libby, upon his arrival there.

During the twenty-fifth anniversary of the Battle of Gettysburg, Moran stood upon the summit of Little Round Top with one of his daughters. As a guide pointed out the areas of interest, the children of Union and Confederate veterans frolicked and laughed together as they combed the ground for bullets and other relics. From a nearby cedar tree a robin warbled his melodious notes. As he gazed west towards the Peach Orchard, sights and sounds of a much different nature came rushing back to Moran as he replayed the events of that awful July afternoon. The memorable visit had a therapeutic effect on the veteran. He shared this newfound perspective with his readers:

None can love the land like a soldier who has bled and endured all for its preservation in battlefield and dungeon. To know how sweet a thing is liberty, it must be seen through prison bars. To see the beauty of our flag and comprehend the true significance of the beloved emblem, it must be hidden from the eyes of its followers ... then suddenly through the night of despair shine forth from the shore of liberty like the rainbow and the glow of the aurora.

Frank Moran died of pulmonary tuberculosis on December 10, 1892, at the age of 49.

Frederic and Adolfo Cavada

Since the ranks of the Army of the Potomac were filled by many first and second generation Americans, it is easy to understand why these soldiers maintained close ties with their homelands. These bonds are revealed by the nicknames associated with various fighting units—the "Irish Brigade," the "German Regiment," and the "Garibaldi Guard," a collection of Italian, Swiss, French, Hungarian, Spanish, and Portuguese immigrants named in honor of the Italian revolutionary, Giuseppe Garibaldi.

A quick glance at the order of battle shows that this ethnic diversity also existed throughout the Federal command structure with names like James Wadsworth, Charles Wainwright, Patrick Kelly, St. Clair A. Mulholland, Samuel K. Zook, Philip Regis de Trobriand, Adolph Von Steinwehr, Alexander Schimmelfennig, Wladimir Krzyzanowski, Alfred Pleasonton, and Freeman McGilvery.

Blended into this predominately European influence, other nationalities, albeit in much smaller numbers, could also be observed in the army. The sometimes overlooked links between the United States and Latin America are brought into focus by the dramatic story of two Cuban born brothers, who, after fighting to secure the freedom of all Americans, would become martyrs in their native country's struggle for independence.

The epic unfolds on Spain's north coast with the birth of Isidoro Fernandez Cavada in 1802. As a member of the hidalgo class, Cavada enjoyed all of the luxuries and education afforded by a life of privilege. A loyal Spaniard, he received an appointment by the Crown to collect royal revenues in Cuba, with his headquarters in the city of Cienfuegos. It was there that Cavada married Philadelphia-born Emily Howard, the daughter of French émigré parents who fled from the colony of Saint-Domingue, present day Haiti, following a slave revolt. Joining an expedition to Cuba's south coast in the 1820s, the Howards were among the early settlers of Cienfuegos. Emily's father, Louis Howard, received a large land grant and was named honorary police commissioner. He amassed his wealth by trading sugar and cattle, and built the city's first masonry house.

Ironically, one generation later, the three sons of Isidoro and Emily Cavada would be key figures in the independence movement that sought to overthrow the yoke of colonial power under which both branches of the family had prospered. Isidoro would not live to witness this event since he died in 1838 at the age of 36.

Now a young widow, Emily, decided to return to Philadelphia in 1841, where she married the wealthy ship chandler and banker, Samuel Dutton. Her youngest sons, Frederic and Adolfo, were about ten and seven years old, respectively, when they left Cuba. Despite their tender ages, both boys maintained a strong attachment to the land of their birth.

At age fifteen the ever romantic Frederic wrote a poem that foreshadowed Cuba's liberation and his own destiny: "Adieu to thee! Queen of the sea, Adieu to the thoughts of the past, Though for e'er thy remembrances shall last, wherever on earth I may be. Adieu to thee! Queen of the wave, Adieu! With many a regret, Thy sorrows I'll never forget, Till lost in the gloom of the grave."

The Cavada boys studied in a succession of private and public schools before graduating from Philadelphia's Central High School. Frederic went on to study civil engineering and topographical drawing, and in this capacity he joined an expedition to explore and survey the Isthmus of Panama for the construction of a railroad. During this time Frederic contracted malaria and arrived back in Philadelphia looking worn and emaciated.

When the Civil War broke out, Cavada had not yet fully recovered from the protracted illness, but his idealism and hatred for slavery ignited his passion. Assisting Colonel David Birney in the recruitment of the 23rd Pennsylvania, Oliver Wilson Davis never forgot his initial meeting with the delicate looking thirty-year-old applicant at the regimental headquarters inside the Girard House Hotel. Davis questioned Cavada's physical capacity, but was won over by his quiet and resolute manner, his intelligence, and his forthrightness. Cavada expressed a willingness to start in a subordinate position, but accepted a captaincy instead.

Informed of the Philadelphian's civilian experience, General George McClellan tapped Cavada for duty as an engineer. Floating above the Virginia Peninsula in Thaddeus Lowe's observation balloons, he produced accurate sketches of the unfamiliar terrain, as he had recently done in Panama.

With the organization of the 114th Pennsylvania or "Collis' Zouaves," in the fall of 1862, Cavada accepted a position as a lieutenant colonel. He served directly under Colonel Charles H. T. Collis, a wealthy Philadelphia lawyer, who at the age of fifteen lost his mother, five sisters, and two brothers when the *City of Glasgow* sunk in the Atlantic with no survivors. Several weeks earlier, the 15-year-old Charles and his father had emigrated from Ireland.

Although Collis and Cavada had much in common—immigration to Philadelphia at a young age and family tragedies—an irreparable rift developed between them almost from the outset. Continuing to fester throughout the regiment's opening battles it nearly reached a boiling point in the aftermath of Gettysburg.

Bedecked in their gaudy red trousers and fezzes, Collis and his Zouaves made quite a splash at the Battle of Fredericksburg. Upon this ill-fated field the regiment launched a spectacular countercharge that helped save retreating Union troops from certain disaster. This performance garnered Collis a Medal of Honor after the war, while Cavada later used his artistic talents to produce a painting, *The Battle of Marye's Heights*.

Unfortunately, a personal controversy soon marred one of the few bright spots that the Union army could point to following this disastrous day. Assigned as brigade officer of the day, Lieutenant Colonel Cavada took charge of the brigade guard when it crossed the Rappahannock on the afternoon of December 13. After hearing repeated comments concerning Cavada's displeasure at the prospect of missing the action, General John C. Robinson sent back word that his eager subaltern could rejoin his regiment if the brigade was engaged. Collis learned of this development as he led the 114th across the pontoon bridges, and the two regimental officers exchanged friendly lines of bravado before parting company.

The battlefield reunion never took place. It was first reported that Cavada had been wounded, but when several eyewitnesses challenged this claim, an angry Collis leveled charges against his subordinate. A court-martial convened on January 12, 1863, at brigade headquarters to try the accused for "misbehavior before the enemy." The prosecution alleged that during the battle Cavada remained in the rear under shelter after deserting the brigade guard. He was also charged with being absent from his regiment.

Both sides called a series of witnesses. The final statement was made by Cavada himself, who skillfully rebutted the testimony of the opposition. Claiming to be thrown from his horse early in the action, he nonetheless remained with the guard until the fighting began, when he hurried forward to find the regiment. However, due to the confusion caused by retreating troops and a change in direction by the 114th as it moved forward, Cavada failed to locate it. These circumstances, he explained, led to the false assumption that he had been absent from duty. Despite this spirited defense Cavada was found guilty of the more serious charge of misbehavior before the enemy and sentenced to be dismissed from the army.

Fortunately for the guilty officer, it took over a month for these proceedings to travel up the chain of command. By this time, Major General Joseph Hooker had superceded Ambrose Burnside as commander. In passing the findings of the court-martial on to Washington, Hooker recommended that the sentence be remitted due to the unusual circumstances of the case and "the good character proven by Lt. Col. Cavada." The Cuban-born officer also sent a desperate entreaty to the chief executive in which he pointed out that he had forsaken his slaveholding family to fight for "the cause of all humanity." He begged for the opportunity to clear his name by proving his worth at "the post of danger." Lincoln benevolently granted this opportunity.

Interestingly, the following spring at Chancellorsville, Colonel Collis found himself facing similar charges after squads of his red-legged soldiers broke and fled in disorder. In his lengthy after action report, the colonel placed the regiment's conduct in the best possible light and adroitly blamed its poor showing on the contradictory orders issued by General Charles Graham's staff. The brigade commander dismissed the report as "a complete romance from the beginning to the end" and the colonel was soon asked to explain his own "disgraceful and cowardly conduct."

Collis moved quickly to counter these allegations. His main defense rested upon the fact that he been violently ill and totally unfit for duty. The embattled officer also gathered evidence to support his courageous leadership. He secured a copy of a set of resolutions from fourteen Zouave officers, including Cavada, remarkably enough, that lauded "his undaunted courage, intrepid bravery, untiring zeal, and unflinching determination to win for our Regiment an imperishable name." His superior officers were not convinced, though, and placed him under arrest.

A heated trial ensued, by the end of which, Collis, then wracked by typhoid fever, was forced to lie on a stretcher. His debilitated condition no doubt only helped his case. In the end, he was restored to command of the 114th. For the time being, however, Collis returned to Philadelphia to recuperate.

As a result, Collis did not accompany the regiment that bore his name during the Gettysburg Campaign. Injured pride and perhaps jealousy dictated that the colonel would be closely observing the actions of his second in command in the pivotal battle that would soon transpire on Pennsylvania soil.

Meanwhile, Adolfo Cavada followed in his older brother's footsteps and enlisted in the 23rd Pennsylvania. His talents were also recognized by the high command. Taking

Brigadier General Andrew A. Humphreys and staff around 1863. Left to right: Lt. Henry C. Christiancy, Lt. Henry H. Humphreys, General Andrew A. Humphreys, Capt. Carswell McClellan, and Captain Adolfo Cavada (MOLLUS-MASS/U.S. Army Military History Institute).

note of the young officer's intelligence, alacrity, and coolness under fire, Brigadier General Andrew A. Humphreys assigned him to be his assistant inspector general and special aide de camp. Humphreys, a hardnosed West Pointer, commanded one of Daniel Sickles' two divisions at Gettysburg. The other was led by Major General David Birney, the former colonel of the 23rd Pennsylvania.

Since the Cavada brothers both served in the Third Corps, they kept in close contact throughout the war. Adolfo Cavada's detailed diary provides a window into the exciting and sometimes precarious existence of a Civil War staff officer. Unlike the sanitized accounts of some of his contemporaries, Adolfo's account sparkles with life and reveals his deepest emotions, often concerns for his brother's welfare in the heat of combat.

Describing the army's triumphal march through the streets of Frederick, Maryland, on June 28, the captain unashamedly envisioned himself as a knight from a bygone era: "There is something very pleasant in the sensation of being looked at while riding with the troops, particularly when these troops are the heroes of war and veterans of many hard fought battles."

In addition to his flair for the romantic, a family trait, Cavada also honed his ear for intelligence data that filtered from the top. "Lee's policy will be to avoid a general engagement & by moving constantly & subsisting on the rich country he occupies, inflict serious losses on the state, recuperate his army, occupy or destroy the capital of the state, and gain material & moral advantages thereby," he explained.

As the Third Corps filed into Emmitsburg on the morning of July 1, dispatches of military developments that would alter the Union strategy arrived at a rapid pace. Learning that the First Corps had engaged the enemy on the outskirts of Gettysburg and of the death of General Reynolds, Sickles responded decisively to the urgent pleas for assistance. Leaving behind two brigades to hold the town, he promptly moved forward with the bulk of his force. Birney's First Division led the way up the Emmitsburg Road, muddied and rutted from recent rains and the earlier passage of the First and Eleventh Corps. The 114th Pennsylvania and the balance of Graham's brigade arrived on Cemetery Ridge by dusk.

Traveling on back roads, Humphreys' Second Division endured a longer and more adventurous march. Upon reaching the Fairfield Road near the Blackhorse Tavern the troops nearly stumbled onto a Confederate picket post. Alerted to the danger in the nick of time, the weary troops about faced and quietly slipped away. By midnight, and following another close call, they finally spotted the camp fires of the First Division. Overcome with fatigue, the command immediately went into bivouac. "I threw myself under the nearest tree amid the wet grass and in spite of rain & mud was soon lost to everything around me," wrote Cavada.

Early the next morning, a rough shake of the shoulder jarred the aide awake. Though exhausted by exposure and lack of food, "the long habit of vigilance and wakefulness under the most trying circumstances ... prevailed over all my bodily sufferings and I jumped to my feet," recalled Cavada.

Still groggy, the captain studied his surroundings. In the growing light of predawn familiar faces became discernible. Beneath the same tree under which he had slept the remaining staff officers slumbered under the cover of their overcoats. Horses stepped quietly in the tall grass as rain pattered onto the vegetation. A group of weary orderlies huddled around the dying embers of a fire. Nearby, the white divisional flag drooped heavily from its staff, appearing "weary, weary, weary!"

The flag could surely have been viewed as a metaphor for the Union soldiers sprawled about the wet ground from the lower reaches of Cemetery Ridge north to Cemetery Hill and Culp's Hill. But as Cavada observed, "Fatigue, hunger and sickness were all forgotten when a battle became certain."

Learning of his assignment to report to General Birney's headquarters, the captain mounted his horse, the indomitable Brickbat, and rode away. After considerable searching and "swearing," Cavada located one of Birney's staff officers, who provided him with the needed information concerning the location of the regiment on picket duty. By the time he retraced his steps the sun's rays slanted over the low ridge, silhouetting the outcroppings of trees. The sharp blasts of a lone bugle pierced the morning stillness, soon to be mimicked by a dozen others accompanied by the sullen rolls of the drums. Regiments of stiff bodied infantrymen struggled to their feet. Soon the smell of boiling coffee and wood smoke mingled with the pungent odor of manure.

Rejoining the general and the rest of the staff, Cavada received an order to post a fresh regiment on the picket line. As he galloped to the front at the head of the men several shots whistled overhead, a precursor of what was soon to come.

In the early afternoon Sickles executed his bold and controversial forward movement. After the realignment, Birney's division extended from Devil's Den to the Peach Orchard and from there Humphreys extended the line north along the Emmitsburg Road. Adolfo

Cavada recalled, "I saw Graham's brigade move forward, the 114th Regt. P.V., commanded by Fred, and conspicuous in their Zouave uniforms, took the lead and reached the road under a heavy fire from the enemy's batteries and sharpshooters. The whole line, extending nearly half a mile along the side-hill, now moved forward while the supporting regiments formed in columns of divisions, followed the movement.... It was a grand sight, one to make the blood warm and tingle through its channels."

Although thoroughly enjoyed by the First and Second Corps soldiers standing on Cemetery Ridge, the pageant ended abruptly for Sickles' men as they found themselves caught in a heated artillery duel. As solid shot and exploding shells raked the line, Captain Cavada admired the conduct of his commander. Humphreys stepped between the guns of Seely's and Trumbull's batteries, calmly giving directions even as some of the gunners fell around him.

Soon a tremendous crashing noise erupted from the left flank of the Union position. Heavy clouds of sulfurous smoke drifted up from the south. Adolfo Cavada peered through the thick curtain hoping to catch a glimpse of what was happening to his brother's regiment in the Peach Orchard: "The enemy's fire slackened for a moment then came a Rebel 'cheer' sounding like a continuous yelp, nearer and nearer it came, the 'red legs' jumped to their feet, volley upon volley rained into them and another regiment formed along side of it. The fire was bravely returned but the enemy's columns were upon them before they could fall back. All was confusion on that side."

Adolfo had observed the forward movement of the 114th Pennsylvania to the Sherfy house and barn. By this point, Captain Edward R. Bowen had taken charge of the regiment since, as he explained, "The lieutenant colonel, who up to this time was in command, not being found, the writer, who was the next officer in rank, gave the order to advance." In a postwar newspaper article, Captain Bowen reported that "the impetus of our advance carried us to the Emmitsburg Road in the face of the murderous musketry fire of the advancing enemy. Reaching the road we clambered over the fence and crossed it.... The men were falling by scores. Soon it became apparent that it was impossible that we should be able any longer to hold our ground against such overwhelming numbers.... Only one avenue of escape was open to us, and that was up the Emmitsburg Road."

In the official report that he submitted a week after the battle, Bowen testified, "While falling back from the brick house on the road, and very hotly pressed by the enemy, I saw Lieutenant Colonel Cavada, who was then commanding the regiment, stopping at a log house in an orchard on our right. I inquired if he was wounded; he replied that he was not, but utterly exhausted. I begged him to make an effort to come on, as the enemy were only a few yards from him and advancing rapidly. He replied that he could not, and I left him there, and not having heard from him since, I have no doubt he was taken prisoner there. I assumed command of the regiment at this time."

Although these two accounts contradict exactly when Bowen took command of the 114th, he clearly placed Cavada's conduct under a suspicious light. These observations would ultimately fuel another confrontation between Cavada and the absent Colonel Collis.

Concerned as he might have been over his brother's well-being, the attention of Adolfo Cavada was quickly diverted by events unfolding in his sector. "Our skirmishers began a lively popping, the first drops of the thunder shower that was to break upon us," he wrote. "An aide from General Birney rode up to General H with the report that heavy masses of the enemy were gathering in our front & to prepare for an attack."

The skirmishers began to fall back as shouts of "Here they come!" rang along the line. At this point Cavada's horse took a bullet in the leg, causing it to prance around frantically. Then, as the captain detailed in his diary, all hell broke loose.

> Our batteries opened, our troops rose to their feet, the crash of artillery and the tearing rattle of our musketry was staggering.... The advancing roar and cheer of the enemy's masses, coming on like devils incarnate ... our thin line showed signs of breaking. The battery enfilading us redoubled its fire, portions of Birney's command were moving to the rear broken and disordered. Our left regiments took the contagion and fled, leaving a wide gap through which the enemy poured in upon us. In vain did staff officers draw their swords to check the flying soldiers.... For a moment the route was complete.

His mobility limited by his disabled horse, Cavada found himself being swept backward by the mass of retreating soldiers. Then Brickbat received a death wound, pinning his rider to the ground. After a brief struggle, the captain freed himself. Securing his flask and pistol from the saddle, he sprinted towards Cemetery Ridge. Reaching the crest the breathless officer collapsed onto a rock. Following the repulse of the attack, Cavada stumbled about for over an hour before he relocated General Humphreys and the staff. A cheerful reunion ensued.

"The night was intensely dark," recalled Cavada, "the air laden with mist and pervaded by that strange musty smell peculiar to battlefields immediately after a battle." A deep foreboding settled upon him: "I need not say what gloomy thoughts filled my mind as I lay upon the ground. My brother's fate I knew not yet and I had every reason to believe that he had fallen in that fearful charge, and perhaps now lay dead or wounded within the Rebel lines, or a prisoner in their hands."

Cavada's diary entry for July 4 begins on a triumphal note: "The Fourth of July! A day made doubly dear by the Victory of Liberty over Slavery on the fields of Gettysburg." For Adolfo the army's first clear victory over Lee was clouded by the uncertainty over his brother's condition. At the earliest opportunity he rode out to the Peach Orchard in hopes of gathering some information. Later, Cavada spoke to Bowen and other members of the 114th. Bowen informed him that Fred had fallen or been knocked down after the regiment was surrounded and that he had been too exhausted to attempt an escape. Some witnesses claimed to see the enemy envelop him as he tried to form some of the men. The general deduction was that he was wounded and a prisoner.

On July 6, the day before the Third Corps departed Gettysburg, General Birney told Captain Cavada that he had no doubt of Fred's capture. The next morning the troops marched off at 4:00 a.m., happy to escape the gloom, the sickening sights, and the poisonous air.

At that moment Frederic Cavada found himself being herded south in company with Brigadier General Charles Graham, Lieutenant Frank Moran, and hundreds of other unfortunate soldiers. During his initial days of confinement at Richmond's Libby Prison, Cavada explained the personal struggle involved in accepting his fate: "It is difficult for one who has never before been compelled to look out upon the world from behind the bars of a prison to convince himself of the fact that he is really deprived of his liberty."

Never one to remain idle, the colonel filled the long hours by recording the experiences of prison life and illustrating them with pencil sketches. He utilized whatever material he could get his hands on, including the margins of newspapers and other scraps. Besides the usual descriptions of abuses and horrors, a portion of the text captured the lighter episodes at the prison—mock trials and rituals such as "the catechism," described as "a series of satirical, critical, comic interrogatories" that took place each evening during lights out. Invariably, this game ended with a grand bombardment of all types of missiles being tossed across the room.

Cavada's length of confinement turned out to be much less than that of most of his fellow inmates. Released through an exchange during the early months of 1864, he soon embarked on a "happy voyage" down the James River to City Point. "The first days of liberation after a protracted captivity are veiled in the misty atmosphere of unreality," recalled the former POW. His notes and illustrations became the basis for the book, *Libby Life,* which helped focus public attention on the plight of Union prisoners.

The joy of his newly acquired liberty quickly turned to anger when Cavada learned that Colonel Collis had charged him with cowardice. The colonel alleged that his second in command disappeared after the first shots were fired at Chancellorsville on the morning of May 3, 1863, and that he had permitted himself to be captured at Gettysburg. Not surprisingly, Captain Bowen, by now a major, supported these charges: "I saw nothing in Cavada's conduct to induce me to change the opinion I formed of him at Fredericksburg and which was afterwards confirmed at Chancellorsville; I can see no excuse for his having been taken prisoner except to avoid danger." His honor tarnished, an outraged Cavada foolishly challenged Bowen to a duel, a reaction that caused him to be placed under house arrest at the Continental Hotel until he cooled off.

IV.

1863.

—

October:—Preparing for Winter—Sports—The Election—A Yankee Trick.

(71)

A self-portrait by Frederic Cavada that appeared in *Libby Life* around 1864.

Clearly, the Cuban could not return to the 114th. In the spring the troubled officer received an assignment to serve on the staff of General Birney. In less than a month, however, Cavada tendered his resignation, citing poor health.

The bitterness between Cavada and Collis persisted even after the war ended. After learning of his rival's appointment as United States Consulate to Cuba, Collis fired off a letter to President Andrew Johnson in which he detailed the officer's poor conduct throughout his service with the 114th Pennsylvania. Cavada's stepfather promptly published a letter of rebuttal, bluntly pointing out that Collis had also been tried by a court-martial. In turn, Collis responded with a statement signed by twelve former Zouave officers that backed up the claims made in his letter to the president. These maneuvers fell on deaf ears; the appointment was confirmed. Adolfo joined his brother as U.S. Vice Consul.

Cavada's support of the abolition of slavery in his native land and his growing involvement in the independence movement to free Cuba from Spanish rule antagonized the State Department and U.S. sugar interests. In defending the actions of his old friend against an angry opponent, Oliver Davis replied, "Cavada is no coward. He is not only a brave man, but a gentleman. His error consists, perhaps, in thinking too much of big things, disregarding small ones." Davis had correctly identified that idealism governed the behavior of Frederic Cavada. These responses ultimately dictated his fate.

Both Cavada brothers resigned their consulate positions in February 1869 to directly participate in the growing revolution. Whatever doubts might have lingered from Frederic's checkered Civil War record were quickly dispelled. Commissioned a general in the Cuban army, he perfected the art of guerrilla warfare in battling the numerically superior and better equipped Spanish forces. His scorched earth policy of burning fields of sugar cane to weaken the economic base of the Spanish colonists earned him the nickname of General Candela or Fire King.

When Frederic ascended to the post of commander-in-chief of all Cuban forces Adolfo stepped up to fill his post as a departmental commander. Meanwhile, older brother Emilio supported the independence effort from Philadelphia by funneling arms and material to Cuba and by relaying intelligence from his brothers to exiled strategists in the States.

However, as the Spanish military grew stronger, Frederic Cavada embarked on a journey to the United States in hopes of obtaining badly needed supplies. Soon after setting sail from the north coast of Cuba, the general and his companions were captured by a Spanish gunboat. Taken to the port of Nuevitas and then on to Puerto Principe, Cavada was executed without trial by a firing squad on the afternoon of July 1, 1871, a week shy of his fortieth birthday.

A witness described the leader's final moments:

> He met his fate like a hero, without bravado or cynicism. Tranquilly he conversed with some friends, and when the fatal hour came he marched, smoking a cigar, erect and proud to the place of execution. When he arrived there he took off his hat, flung it on the ground, and in a loud tone of voice cried, "Adios Cuba, para siempre" (Good-bye Cuba, forever). A volley was heard, and Frederico Cavada ceased to exist.

The general was survived by his wife Carmela and a son named Samuel. For several weeks, friends and admirers, believing that Cavada was only awaiting trial, worked frantically to secure his release, and President Ulysses Grant agreed to intervene with Madrid. Of course, by then it was too late. In December, Adolfo Cavada was killed in action near Santiago de Cuba.

In his biography of Frederic Cavada, Oliver Davis predicted "when the history of his native land is written, his name will appear as that of one who suffered manfully, struggled heroically and died bravely as a martyr to a cause, which in his infatuation he believed to be of more value than his life." Even long-time nemesis Charles Collis mellowed in his opinion of the slain leader. When asked for a copy of the pamphlet published in hopes of blocking Cavada's appointment to the consulate post, he replied, "Since Col. Cavada's very sad death, I have carefully avoided any mention of his troubles in my regiment.... No use should be made of it which could possibly open afresh wounds which time has done much to heal."

The Cavada brothers now hold a special place in Cuban history and their portraits hang in the national capitol. It should also be remembered that they first fought for liberty and equality in the United States, thus helping to secure hope and opportunity for future generations of Cuban Americans.

5

Confederate Brothers

We must learn to live together as brothers
or perish together as fools.
Martin Luther King

Sidney and Giles Carter

An agricultural region composed of plantations and farms of various sizes, the Darlington District of South Carolina presented a snapshot of rural Southern life and traditions in the antebellum era. By 1855 the population of the district had reached approximately 19,000, of which about 11,000 were slaves. With its handsome courthouse, several taverns, and a spacious hotel, Darlington Village functioned as the hub for social and political activities. Active congregations worshipped in the sanctuaries of the Baptist, Methodist, and Presbyterian denominations.

Darlington residents obtained most of their necessities from their own fields and gardens and from the surrounding woods and streams, but the community was not isolated from the outside world. Three railroads converged at nearby James' Station, the Great Pee Dee provided water transportation down to Georgetown, and a dozen or more post offices serviced the outlying areas.

Though at least one-fifth of South Carolina's farmland was devoted to King Cotton, numerous other crops, including wheat, rye, corn, oats, rice, sweet potatoes, beans, and peas poked up from Darlington's fertile soil. Much of this diversification could be credited to a progressive agricultural society that had taken root in 1846. In the years just prior to the Civil War the farmland in the district increased steadily in value with more and more acreage under cultivation. Times were good.

Among those enjoying the agricultural boom was Charles Powell Carter II. The Carters had been present in Craven County since 1867 when Charles's grandfather signed a deed for 100 acres. Over the years, the family added to this original tract, and by the mid–nineteenth century, the fourth generation of Carters cultivated the land. Still a vigorous man, Powell Carter and his wife Susan had reared twelve children, six boys and six girls, and were now enjoying the playful antics of numerous grandchildren.

The six Carter brothers, from oldest to youngest—Giles, William, John, Sidney, James, and Richard—grew up under the dual influences of the church and the farm. They all received a basic education at Carter's School House, operated by their Uncle James at Carter's Crossroads.

The year 1855 witnessed an important event in the life of Sidney Carter. On October 16, the 23-year-old wed Ellen Timmons, the daughter of a prosperous planter, whom he affectionately referred to as "Bet." She was eighteen at the time, and like Sidney, among the youngest of twelve children. Earlier, Sidney's older brother William had married one of Bet's older sisters.

Sid Carter followed in the footsteps of his uncle and entered teaching. He was described by a descendant as "a serious, methodical, careful man, honest, religious, and not given to excess of any sort." His wife recalled that he "never used rough language under any provocation." During the next six years Bet gave birth to three children: Ida, Horace, and Minnie Ellen.

With the approach of the 1860s the once cordial and relaxed atmosphere at Darlington Courthouse gave way to fiery arguments between Unionists and Secessionists. Steeped in traditional Southern values, the Carter family probably did not agonize over which side to take. In fact, Bet Carter's uncle, the Reverend John Morgan Timmons, was among the signers of the Ordinance of Secession.

Considering his deliberate nature, however, the issue must have weighed heavily upon the mind of Sidney Carter; but by the summer of 1861 he decided military service to be the proper course. On a hot summer day in August 1861 he said goodbye to his dear family and with brothers William, James, Dick, and Cousin Theo, he set off for Lightwoodknot Springs near the state capital of Columbia to join the 14th South Carolina Infantry.

Family hierarchy followed the Carters into the army, at least initially. William secured the rank of captain in Company A, Sidney became second lieutenant, and the two youngest followed in line as sergeant and corporal, respectively. The following March, however, 41-year-old Giles, the oldest of the boys, signed up as a private in the same company. Near the same time, John Carter enlisted with the 1st South Carolina, a regiment that also belonged to McGowan's South Carolina Brigade.

The law of averages dictated that disease and combat would cull some of the members of this clan. Indeed, only half would return to the land they loved. The first victim, Richard, died of disease on April 18, 1862, while the 14th guarded the Carolina coast. Next, Captain Carter suffered a serious wound at Gaines' Mill. He returned to duty but would later resign due to poor health. By war's end, he worked in the quartermaster's department. Sidney was also wounded at this battle and hospitalized briefly at Richmond.

The next family tragedy took place at Chancellorsville. The day after Stonewall Jackson's famous flank march that positioned his troops in a position to pummel the left flank of the Army of the Potomac, the reunited wings of the Confederate army battered the Union defenses with a relentless sequence of attacks that eventually dislodged them and sent them packing across the Rappahannock. Lee's penchant for stunning victories seemed unbreakable, but in this case the price of success came at such a high cost that it would cripple his army's effectiveness throughout the remainder of the war. In addition to the mortal wounding of Jackson, the attrition of regimental officers and men accrued at a higher percentage that that of the vanquished Union army.

For combat veterans on both sides, the spring woods around Chancellorsville offered up scenes of horror that could never be forgotten. Lieutenant James Fitz James Caldwell came as close as anyone in bringing them to life:

The woods had taken fire—probably from shells or the ignition of ammunition—and burned furiously, destroying the inner lines of breastworks erected by the enemy, consuming the undergrowth and all the dead trees, and roasting the bodies of many killed and disabled men, both Confederate and Federal. Some of our wounded were rescued, and perhaps some of the enemy, but numbers of the latter perished. It was pitiful to see the charred bodies, hugging the trees, or with hands outstretched, as if to ward off the flames. We saw around some of them little cleared circles, where they had evidently raked away the dead leaves and sticks, to stay the progress of the fire. And there were ghastly wounds there—heads shot off or crushed, bodies and limbs torn and mangled, the work of shells. The smoke and stench were stifling. This was May 3, as beautiful and bright a day as one could desire, even for a Sabbath.

Sergeant James Morgan Carter lost his life in the grisly manner described by Caldwell. Before he entered the fight, James handed his pocketbook to an officer for safekeeping. Perhaps he sensed the inevitable. Giles viewed the remains of his younger brother before they were interred by the burial detail. He later told Sidney that the body was so badly charred that he would not have recognized it had it not been for the clothing. Sidney wanted his widowed sister-in-law to know that her husband behaved more gallantly than any man in the regiment.

The relatively close interval between the end of the Chancellorsville Campaign and the beginning of Lee's second invasion of the North delivered an unforeseen benefit to the Carter brothers. The combination of physical toil and the change of scenery kept the mental anguish at bay, at least temporarily. Twelve miles below Winchester, Virginia, Sidney Carter left his place in the ranks for the first time since his entry into the army, nearly fainting from heat exhaustion. A cooling rain improved the conditions for the next day's march. While crossing the Blue Ridge Mountains near Front Royal, a thundercloud passed so low that the lieutenant believed he could have reached it with a twenty-foot pole.

In a June 21 letter, Sidney informed Bet that they expected to meet the mailman upon arriving in Winchester. He promised to keep her updated as often as possible as the campaign progressed. However, the news that would trickle from Pennsylvania delivered yet another devastating blow to the Carter Clan hoping and waiting anxiously in faraway South Carolina.

Following closely in support of Henry Heth's Division, the brigades of General William Dorsey Pender's Division halted frequently along the Chambersburg Pike to rest in the shaded woods as the sounds of an escalating battle filled the humid air. As the troops approached the low ridges west of Gettysburg, a line of battle was formed with McGowan's South Carolinians, commanded on this day by Colonel Abner Perrin, in the center. Perrin issued orders to the field and staff officers to move forward without firing and directed there would be no stopping under any circumstances, but rather "close in, press the enemy close, and route it from its position." These instructions passed down the chain of command.

With the exception of its smaller scale and different result, this assault closely mirrored Pickett's Charge. In both instances, a tightly packed formation advanced across an open expanse of ground in an attempt to dislodge a Union defensive line positioned on higher ground and heavily supported by artillery.

Passing over Heth's exhausted men in Herbst's Woods, Pender's veterans passed over the eastern crest of McPherson's Ridge and descended into the open valley that rose gently to form the slightly higher elevation of Seminary Ridge, where the Union troops lay in wait. Perrin's Brigade aimed for the large brick Seminary that bisected the ridge. They would soon find themselves all alone since the brigades supporting them on both sides could not keep pace. To the north, Scales' Brigade was almost annihilated by the deadly blasts of the enemy cannon stacked nearly hub to hub in that sector. At the same time, the progress of James Lane's Brigade on the opposite end ground to a halt in response to the menacing presence of dismounted Union cavalry on its flank. Undeterred, Perrin's men "pressed on as ordered without firing until the line of breastworks in front became a sheet of fire and smoke, sending its leaden missiles of death in the faces of men who had often, but never so terribly, met it before."

Today we wonder how veteran soldiers overcame the natural instinct to turn and flee from danger. Lieutenant Carter explained his mindset in a letter written home earlier in the war: "...I was not born to be killed by the Yankees, all the Yankees born can't hurt me. And if they kill me in battle remember I am fighting for God and country. When I think about being killed and leaving you and my dear little children it nerves me, for I feel like I am in the right and will come through safe and sound...."

This shield of immortality deserted Carter on the killing fields surrounding the Seminary. Although the Confederate attack turned into a smashing victory, the losses were immense. The largest regiment in Perrin's Brigade, the 14th South Carolina, brought 475 officers and men into the fight; over half fell killed or wounded.

Lieutenant Colonel Joseph Newton Brown explained, "The nature of the ground was such and the contest so brief that the wounded could not be moved, and were wounded twice, thrice and as many as four times, after being first stricken down.... It was the only battlefield in which all avenues of escape for our wounded were closed.... The ground was swept at every point by the deadly Minnie balls. The artillery fire is terrible, but the almost silent whirl of the Minnie ball is the death-dealing missile in battle. Not a foot of ground presented a place of safety.... The terrible strife was over in a few minutes—fifteen, say twenty at most. Men never fell faster in this brigade...."

One of these "death-dealing" missiles ripped into the chest of Lieutenant Carter and passed downward into his internal organs. Giles Carter was wounded in the leg during this action, though not seriously. Both men fell into enemy hands when the Confederate army withdrew from the area. Transferred to a hospital at David Island in New York Harbor, Giles remained a prisoner until his exchange on September 16, 1863. Sidney lingered for a week before he died among strangers.

Though informed that her husband had been mortally wounded at Gettysburg, Bet held on desperately to a sliver of hope. Writing to her sister Fannie on the last day of July, she confessed:

> I want to write but my heart is most too full, my eyes in tears, when I think of my dear Sid. Can I hope? Yes, I try to hope still.... Dave, my negro boy that Sid had with him, stayed with him from Thursday morning until Friday night.... Dave said Sid told him to tell us to meet him in heaven, that he would never see us again. He told the McCowns he was willing to die, talked to the clergymen about dying, and appeared to be praying all the time, though so weak he could hardly be understood. From Dave's statement there could not be any chance for him ever to recover, but you know as long as there is life, there is hope and I try to cherish that hope.... Dave said Sid told him to take everything he had and bring it home, told him which to give to the children, and to give his watch to Horace— and he lost it. I was so sorry, for I thought Horace could keep it as long as he lives. He [Sid] appeared to be perfectly sensible until Dave left, which was 3rd of July, and I have heard no straight news since the Yankees came and took possession of him and all the rest

of the wounded. So you see there is no chance for me to hear until they exchange prisoners.... I hope that when the Yankees did get in possession of them ... that there being so many skilled physicians among the Yankees, they would do something for him and restore him to health with God's kind watch over him. Fannie, Sid has always been so good. The men all speak of him as being noted for his moral character. He has never changed from being Sid.... Dear Sister, I hope you will excuse me for not writing news, but my thoughts are ever on this one subject even if I am talking anything else.

This letter never reached Fannie. Apparently, Bet received official notification of Sid's death before she could send it. By war's end all three of the eldest Carter boys were on detached duty assignments. As mentioned previously, William worked in the quartermaster's department following his resignation from field duty. Beginning in August 1864, John Carter, who it appears also fought at Gettysburg, was transferred to the Torpedo Department in Charleston, South Carolina. And, following his release, Giles reported to the Invalid Corps and finished his time assisting the postmaster general in Richmond. Fleeing the capital with other Confederate officials in early April of 1865, he would later be paroled at Lynchburg, Virginia.

It is interesting to note that this family had a member listed in each of the major casualty categories: killed, mortally wounded, wounded, died of disease, and captured. This sad, but compelling, story does not end here, however. Ironically, due to a transcription error by a Union burial detail, the body of Sidney Carter was erroneously recorded as being that of a soldier from a Connecticut infantry regiment. As a result, the lieutenant's remains now rest in Row A, Grave Number 5 of the Connecticut plot of the Soldiers' National Cemetery.

Levi and Henry Walker

Advancing to the north of Perrin's troops on the afternoon of July 1, the 1,400 North Carolinians of General Alfred Scales' Brigade advanced directly into the teeth of the nearly two dozen artillery pieces arrayed on Seminary Ridge. The gradually sloping, open ground presented the First Corps artillerists with "the fairest field and finest front for destruction on an advancing foe that could well be conceived." A Union soldier recalled that the batteries on the ridge "blazed with a solid sheet of flame, and the missiles of death that swept its western slopes no human being could endure. After a few moments of the belching of the artillery, the blinding smoke shut out the sun and obstructed the view." When the smoke lifted, "Only the dead and dying remained on the bloody slopes of Seminary Ridge."

Within a few moments, Scales' Brigade was virtually annihilated. Only about 500 of the Tar Heels escaped death or injury and these survivors lay pinned down less than a hundred yards from the Union position. The casualties in the 13th North Carolina, in particular, were staggering. From a battle strength of 232 officers and men, the unit suffered 55 killed, 98 wounded, and 26 missing or captured, a nearly 80 percent loss rate. At least five color-bearers were shot down during the deadly assault.

The fifth individual to grasp the standard was 21-year-old Private Levi Jasper Walker of Company B. Levi and his older brother, Henry, enlisted in the "Ranaleburg Riflemen" on May 20, 1861. Raised on a farm in Mecklenburg County, Levi worked as a farmer and textile worker before the war while his older sibling earned a living by teaching. Henry rose to the rank of lieutenant by the spring of 1863, but Levi spent his entire service time as a private.

Carrying the regimental colors on July 1, Private Walker fell with a wound in his left leg. At a nearby field hospital a surgeon removed the damaged limb just below the knee joint. Later captured by Federal forces, Levi was confined at a prison hospital at David Island in New York Harbor, until paroled and exchanged in October.

Lieutenant Henry Walker emerged from the fierce fighting unscathed, but twelve days later during a skirmish near Hagerstown, Maryland, he, too, was wounded in the left leg. His injury also required amputation, and remarkably, his limb was removed at nearly the exact location as his brother's had been at Gettysburg. Like his brother, he was also picked up by Union troops, remaining a prisoner at Johnson's Island, a detention facility for Confederate officers, until May of 1864.

In a letter home written on July 20, 1863, a soldier from the 13th confirmed that the Walker brothers "both had their left legs broken and cut off. They were cut off just below the knee."

Neither man allowed his handicap to hold him back after the war, as the brothers became honored citizens of Charlotte, North Carolina. Ironically, Henry studied medicine, afterwards establishing a thriving practice and opening two drugstores. Levi retired as a successful merchant. For one of the brothers, their remarkably similar war injuries turned out to be a blessing. A mutual friend related a remarkable incident that took place on Levi's wedding day:

> The day for the wedding was set and all preparations made. But on that eventful day, and only a few hours before the ceremony was to take place, the prospective bridegroom met

Levi (left) and Henry Walker (right) in 1861 and replicating the same pose in 1887 (courtesy the North Carolina State Archives).

with an accident which seemed like the unfriendly dealing of fate. He slipped and in some way broke his cork leg. Deprived of this very useful member, the young man found that he could not possibly "stand up" for the ceremony, and was therefore in quite a dilemma. At this important juncture, his brother, Dr. H. J. Walker, went forward and saved the day by offering to loan his leg to his brother. The proffered leg was gladly accepted and found to fit perfectly. This is perhaps the only case on record in which one man has been married while standing on the leg of another.

Thomas and James Kenan

Younger brothers often go to great lengths to tag along with an older sibling and his pals. For this "privilege" they cheerfully endure constant taunting and become the primary targets for myriad practical jokes and mischievous pranks. It appears that James Kenan never quite outgrew this childhood habit, dutifully following in the footsteps of his charismatic brother throughout his life.

Thomas Stephen Kenan, a handsome young bachelor and a University of North Carolina graduate, enjoyed playing the guitar and singing old ballads. Soon after the attack upon Fort Sumter, the 23-year-old lawyer closed down his practice to organize a volunteer company known as the "Duplin Rifles" near his hometown of Kenansville, Duplin County, North Carolina. Captain Kenan and his followers served with the 12th North Carolina until this regiment's disbanding in the fall of 1861. Afterwards, the Rifles merged into the newly formed 43rd North Carolina, becoming Company A of this unit. By the following spring, Kenan had risen to the rank of colonel.

At this time, James Kenan, who had followed his brother into the army, stepped up to fill his place as captain of Company A. The similar physical appearance of the two was so striking that the change was perhaps unnoticed by some of the men. The Kenans served together from the Peninsula to Gettysburg, where both would fight their last battle.

On July 1, 1863, Colonel Thomas Kenan led his regiment onto Oak Hill north of Gettysburg. The 43rd belonged to Brigadier General Junius Daniel's North Carolina Brigade, the largest brigade in Ewell's Corps. Daniel's troops were well rested from an extended period of guard duty in North Carolina and Virginia. Supporting the ill-fated attack of Iverson's Brigade, Daniel's troops, with the assistance of another brigade, finally pushed the tenacious First Corps defenders south along Oak Ridge and through the town.

Colonel Kenan's second in command, Lieutenant Colonel William G. Lewis, estimated that the brigade scooped

Left: James Kenan, ca. 1861 (courtesy the North Carolina State Archives). *Right:* Thomas Kenan, ca. 1861 (courtesy the North Carolina State Archives).

up between 400 and 500 prisoners. As recounted in a previous chapter, one of these captives was Lieutenant Colonel John Callis of the Iron Brigade's 7th Wisconsin. Coming to the aid of the severely wounded officer, Kenan greeted his adversary with these prophetic words, "You are now my prisoner, and I'll treat you well; I may be yours later on."

During the early morning attack upon Culp's Hill on July 3, Kenan sustained a gunshot wound to his right thigh. Carried to a makeshift field hospital, he became a prisoner following the battle. Wounded on the opening day, James was also taken captive. Near the end of August, the Kenan brothers arrived at the prison complex at Johnson's Island. Thomas described the site:

> Johnson's Island is in Lake Erie, about two and a half miles north of Sandusky City, Ohio. Its area is perhaps a mile long and a half mile wide, or thereabout, and the area of the prison grounds, located near the southern end of the island, was about 200 by 300 yards, with a block-house at each end where the big guns were kept in readiness to open on the prisoners in the event of a general uprising. The grounds were enclosed by a strong plank fence twelve or fifteen feet high, with sentinel beats on the parapet. A United States war vessel lay in the offing whose services could be brought into requisition if necessary. There were thirteen roughly constructed wooden buildings two stories high, with entrances to the upper stories by stairways on the outside—six of the buildings on either side and one at the lower end midway through the grounds, and bunks arranged in vertical tiers in each building. Nearly 3,000 prisoners of war, mostly officers, representing almost every command in the Confederate army, were guests of the United States government at this place for about fifteen months to two years.... Hope of exchange was abandoned, and they engaged in every species of amusement and entertainment available ... in order to while away the time and lessen the monotony and severity of prison life.

Much to the delight of his fellow inmates, the colonel performed impromptu concerts for their enjoyment. He also helped to establish a prison committee to improve conditions within the stockade. Repeated efforts at escape were undertaken. One plan called for the construction of a tunnel beyond the edge of the fence. The Kenans and their accomplices excavated the earth each evening for several weeks with only case knives and tin plates. Nearly three-fourths of the work had been completed when prison officials discovered the tunnel.

The ordeal finally came to a close in March 1865, when the brothers numbered among three hundred paroled prisoners of war. By the time Thomas and James reached Greensboro, North Carolina, Lee had surrendered to Grant at Appomattox. Learning of this development, the brothers set off for the trans–Mississippi in hopes of joining up with General Joseph E. Johnston's army. Once again, they were too late. Upon reaching Charlotte they received word of Johnston's surrender. Retracing their steps, the pair arrived home in Kenansville on May 17.

With the war behind them the Kenan brothers married and raised families. Thomas served as a supreme court reporter and state attorney general from 1877 to 1885. Appointed supreme court clerk in 1886, he held this position until the day of his death on December 23, 1911. True to form, James followed his older brother into death as he had in life, passing away a little over two weeks later.

William and John Oates

As the 15th Alabama formed in line of battle on the afternoon of July 2, 1863, Colonel William C. Oates knelt by the side of his younger brother. Wracked with fever, Lieu-

William C. Oates, ca. 1861 (*The War Between the Union and the Confederacy and Its Lost Opportunities*).

tenant John Oates was lying on the ground behind his company's position on Seminary Ridge. Earlier in the day, during the grueling 30-plus mile march from New Guilford to Gettysburg, Colonel Oates had sent back one of his horses so that his struggling brother could keep pace with the column. Taking note of his worsening condition, the colonel now ordered him to remain behind when the assault began. The disagreeable order pumped life into the sickly form. Struggling to rise up, the lieutenant responded defiantly with black eyes flashing, "Brother, I will not do it. If I were to remain here people would say that I did it through cowardice; no sir, I am an officer and will never disgrace the uniform I wear; I shall go through, unless I am killed, which I think is quite likely."

Looking past the insubordination and the gloomy premonition, the commander probably cracked a smile following this display of fiery determination. It was certainly a quality that he admired, for William Oates had spent much of his early years fighting for his very survival in a brutal and unforgiving environment.

Born on December 1, 1835, in the untamed backcountry of Pike County, Alabama, the son of William and Sarah Oates began his life in extreme poverty and obtained only a rudimentary education. His hair-trigger temper and propensity for violence soon sent him on a downward spiral. Brother John entered the world a short time later. Both sons would eventually rise above their humble beginnings, but for the eldest, this path proved to be a decidedly circuitous one.

When William was just fourteen he fractured a man's skull during an altercation, nearly killing him. Convinced that he had done just that, Oates absconded to Florida, where he supported himself by working as a housepainter's apprentice, as a crewman on a gulf schooner, and at other odd jobs. After contracting a near fatal case of yellow fever in Pensacola, he moved on to Louisiana. Oates quickly found work as a painter but soon created trouble for himself once again. Following a disagreement over unpaid wages the Alabama native violently assailed his employer. While choking the man with his left hand, he repeatedly punched him in the face with his right fist. The next day a warrant was issued for his arrest. The troubled youngster fled to Texas.

Oates spent the next several years drifting across the Lone Star State, stopping off for various lengths of time in some of the roughest frontier towns of the day—Marshall, Waco, Bastrop, Port Lavaca, and Henderson. When he wasn't scraping together money as a painter, shingle cutter, and ranch hand, William pursued his favorite addictions: gambling and women. He continued to hone his skills as a street fighter, perfecting a brutal, but effective, technique of gouging his opponent's eyes.

By this time, John was on an opposite career track, developing into a bright young lawyer, who, unlike his contentious elder, garnered the admiration and respect of those around him. Increasingly anxious, the Oates family dispatched John to Texas in hopes of locating the wayward son. Miraculously, he found him in Henderson. William agreed to return to Alabama with John, but not before a high-stakes card game and one last fist-fight.

Since William was still a wanted man in his hometown, he settled in neighboring Henry County. A dramatic transformation then took place. By his twenty-fifth birthday, the former brawler had graduated from the Lawrenceville Academy, passed the bar exam, opened a law office in Abbeville, and purchased a weekly newspaper. This intervention cemented the bond between the long-separated siblings. William would later remark that "no brothers loved each other better."

This affection would be proven during the early days of the Civil War. Although he had publicly stated his opposition to secession in the pages of his newspaper, William Oates eagerly responded to the call to arms in the spring of 1861 by recruiting a company of vol-unteers known as the "Henry Pioneers." Mustered into the Confederate army as Com-pany G of the 15th Alabama Infantry, the Pioneers chose Oates to lead them. John Oates first volunteered in a company raised by future Confederate great, John B. Gordon, in May 1861, but in November he transferred out to be with his brother.

Not surprisingly, William Oates quickly rose through the ranks to take charge of the 15th. Certainly no one doubted his bravery and leadership ability, but his ambition together with his legendary independent streak would at times become liabilities on the battlefield. Unlike some Civil War officers, however, he never ordered his men to go where he would not go himself. A self-described strict disciplinarian, Oates constantly looked out for the welfare of his men even if it meant disobeying a superior.

It was a bit ironic then that on that momentous July afternoon at Gettysburg, it was John Oates who flatly refused to obey an order from his brother. For his part, William realized that it was futile to force the issue. In the Victorian era the perception of a sol-dier's personal courage and honor trumped all else, even life itself.

Thus, when Brigadier General Evander Law's Alabama brigade stepped off to lead the attack against the right flank of the Army of the Potomac, a pale-looking but deter-mined lieutenant marched with the men of Company G and the rest of the 15th Alabama. Somehow, John Oates kept up as the regiment rushed eastward over fields and fences, around boulders and thick undergrowth, before crossing over Plum Run and puffing up the steep face of Big Round Top.

Upon reaching the summit, Colonel Oates would have preferred to dig in and con-vert the mountain top into "a Gibraltar that could hold against ten times the number of men that I had." A halt was called to allow the panting and thirsty men a breather, with the hopes that a detail sent off to fill canteens before the advance started could catch up. When one of Law's staff officers rode up and insisted that Oates join in the attack against Little Round Top, the pugnacious colonel initially refused, but then complied. Sweeping down the slope the Alabamians soon collided with the Federals of Colonel Strong Vin-cent's brigade defending the rocky spur between the two heights.

Casualties escalated in the 15th as they slugged it out with Colonel Joshua Cham-berlain's 20th Maine in a hot close-quarters fight that surged back and forth across the boulders. When a private from his old company was shot in the head by his side Colonel Oates picked up the slain man's weapon and fired it several times in revenge. Nearby, the captain of Company G fell dead while leading his men forward. Lieutenant Oates took charge, but an instant later several balls tore into his body just as he had predicted a short time earlier. Lieutenant Isaac Parks dragged his old schoolmate behind a large boulder to prevent any further harm from coming to him.

Passing through the line of troops while waving his sword, the senior Oates shouted above the din, "Forward, men, to the ledge!" The Alabamians drove the defenders back five times, but each time the New Englanders rallied to retake the lost ground. The heated contest rushed towards a climax where either one side or the other would have to yield. Colonel Oates recalled: "My dead and wounded were then nearly as great in number as those still on duty. They literally covered the ground. The blood stood in puddles in some places on the rocks.... I still hoped for reinforcements or for the tide of success to turn my way."

The situation actually got worse. Suddenly, out of the curtain of smoke emerged a solid line of screaming, bayonet-wielding Union infantrymen. Caught by surprise, the remnants of the 15th Alabama "ran like a herd of wild cattle," admitted Oates. As the regiment scrambled back towards Big Round Top, a wounded private with blood spraying profusely from a neck wound sped by Oates.

At one point the commander made an attempt to halt and reform the regiment. However, this attempt proved to be an exercise in futility. The survivors were widely scattered across the hillside, many of them assisting disabled comrades. Overcome by heat and exhaustion, the burly Oates stated that he surely would have been bagged by the pursuing Federals had it not been for two stalwart men who carried him to the summit of Big Round Top. There the assistant surgeon revived the colonel by pouring water from a canteen over his head.

That evening, as the 15th Alabama dug in at the foot of Big Round Top, a group of soldiers from Company G struck out without permission on a dangerous attempt to rescue Lieutenant Oates and Lieutenant Barnett Cody, another wounded officer left behind during the retreat. The party penetrated the enemy skirmish line but barely escaped capture after being detected moments later. For a brief period muzzle flashes illuminated the dark woodlands as the Confederates aborted the mission and fled back to their own lines.

Consequently, William Oates never saw his brother again. John Oates died in a Federal field hospital after lingering for twenty-three days. Lieutenant Cody preceded him in death two days earlier. Colonel Oates was comforted by the fact that his younger brother had been well cared for by a Miss Lightner, "a Virginia lady and Southern sympathizer," and Dr. Joseph A. E. Reed, the surgeon of the 155th Pennsylvania.

The doctor sent Oates his brother's gold watch, pocketbook, and money by flag of truce. For years the grateful Oates endeavored to locate the kind Pennsylvanian. Finally, in 1896, he learned that Reed resided in Lancaster and soon the two men shared a pleasant correspondence with another. In a letter dated November 20 of that year, Reed provided the details of John Oates' final days:

> Your brother ... was brought to the hospital of the Second Division, Fifth Army Corps. I found him to be severely wounded, and expressed a doubt regarding his ultimate recovery. Lieutenant Cody was brought in about the same time, and I had them placed upon separate cots in one of our hospital tents. Your brother suffered greatly at times. I was frequently brought to his bedside and it was at these visits I learned to know much of the nobleness of his character, and the intense love, affection, and respect he had for his own people, a quality I greatly admired. My wife, sister-in-law, and a lady friend of theirs came to see me at Gettysburg a few days after the battle, and on passing through the hospital their attention was called in some way to Lieutenant Cody and your brother, I think because of their apparent helpless condition and the fact of their being among strangers, far away from

their home and kindred. This prompted them to ask a few questions, and opened the way for further acquaintance, and enabled them to show some kindness to the afflicted and distressed. Many little favors, in shape of such delicacies as could be procured in our camp or hospital, were given to your brother and his friend, thereby cementing a friendship so strangely begun. Your brother and Lieutenant Cody expressed their appreciation of these little acts. As time wore on it became evident to all of us that these two young men could not recover. Their new-found friends visited them daily, reading and talking to them, and for this attention they frequently expressed thanks, and spoke of their homes the cruel fate of war had torn them from.

My sister-in-law remembers that your brother died on a Friday evening as the sun was about setting; that a short while before he died he requested my wife's lady friend and herself to sing for him; they sang "Jesus, Lover of My Soul." After singing they all joined in repeating the Lord's Prayer; feeling that his end was near, he said, "Tell my folks at home that I died in the arms of friends." These were his last words. Such was the end of a life of a devoted son and brother. Your brother's remains, as well as Lieutenant Cody's, were buried in a field very near to our hospital.... At your brother's burial we marked his grave with a board headpiece, placing his name and rank upon it. But I fear time has removed all this.

According to historian Gregory A. Coco, Oates and Cody were among the twelve sets of remains shipped south in the early 1870s. Although four of the names were still known by that time, they could not be identified separately.

William Oates nearly met the same fate of his brother. In over three years of action he participated in twenty-seven different engagements and was wounded no less than six times, twice severely. On one occasion a sharpshooter's bullet grazed his head. Oates' campaigning ended on August 16, 1864, when a bullet slammed into his right arm along the Darbytown Road outside of Petersburg, requiring the limb to be amputated near the shoulder joint.

Back home in Alabama, Oates continued the remarkable progress that the war interrupted. Resuming his law practice, he also became active in the political arena. After serving as a delegate to the 1868 National Democratic Convention, he won election to the Alabama House of Representatives, and then in 1880 to the U.S. House, a post he would hold for fourteen years. At age 47, the long-time bachelor married a woman half his age. William C. Oates, Jr., the couple's only child, was born in 1883. The "one-arm hero of Henry County" culminated his storied political career with a successful bid for governor in 1894. In fulfillment of a campaign promise, he did not seek reelection upon the expiration of the two-year term. During the Spanish-American War, Oates received an appointment as brigadier general of volunteers and was stationed at Camp Meade, Pennsylvania.

The aging veteran continued to be a nonconformist. While practicing law in Montgomery he opposed the widespread use of grandfather laws to disenfranchise blacks. Oates could hardly be considered progressive, however. Firm in his belief that the separation of the Union would have been "both wise and desirable," Oates refused to renounce the cause for which had fought for so long and for which his brother had laid down his life. In contrast to ex–Confederates like Senator John B. Gordon, who championed reconciliation, Oates candidly shared his views in his mammoth memoir. "I would never go to war unless I conscientiously believed that the cause was just," he stated flatly.

At the same time, he railed against the popular notion of predestination, arguing that "when we went to war it was a matter of business, of difference among men about their temporal affairs. God had nothing to do with it. He never diverted a bullet from one man, or caused it to hit another, nor directed who should fall or who should escape, nor how the battle should terminate. If I believed in such interposition of Providence I would be a fatalist."

Oates' biggest disappointment was his failure to erect a monument on Little Round Top to pay tribute to his brother and the other fallen heroes of the 15th Alabama. In the end even the obstinate and ever resourceful politician could not cut through the red tape of the Gettysburg Battlefield Memorial Association and the fierce opposition of Union veterans. The antithesis of his former counterpart, the poetic and idealistic Joshua Chamberlain, Oates remained a devoted pragmatist right up until his death on September 9, 1910.

Henry Rauch, John C. Warren and Dr. L. P. Warren

For three weeks following the Battle of Gettysburg, Georgeanna Woolsey and her mother worked tirelessly at the United States Sanitary Commission Relief Lodge. At this station volunteers cared for the hundreds of wounded soldiers being evacuated on a daily basis. It was difficult but gratifying work. "We had the full storehouse of the Commission to draw upon, and took real satisfaction in dressing and comforting all our men," recalled Woolsey. "No man of the 16,000 went away without a good, hot meal, and none from our tents without the fresh clothes they needed."

Bonds formed quickly under these conditions. Wrote Woolsey, "Mother put great spirit into it all, listened to all their stories, petted them, fed them, and distributed clothes, including handkerchiefs with cologne, and got herself called 'Mother.'"

Georgeanna confessed that her attitudes toward the Southerners mixed among the wounded Union soldiers softened dramatically. It is rather easy to feel contempt for an enemy that remains nameless and faceless; it is quite another matter to turn away from one who is in the throes of physical agony. "[W]e hated them so much when they were away from us and couldn't help being so good to them when they were in our hands," she wrote. With a tinge of guilt the volunteer also disclosed that the soldier for whom she felt the most empathy wore a gray uniform.

Lieutenant Henry Rauch, 14th South Carolina, entered the relief lodge on July 16. He would die the following day. During this brief interval a friendship developed between the Northern lady and the youthful Confederate officer. Woolsey described her patient as fair-haired and blue-eyed with "a face innocent enough for one of our own New England boys." Cultural and political differences no longer mattered. "I cannot think of him as a Rebel," Woolsey confided. "He was too near Heaven for that." Georgeanna lovingly tended to the dying officer, coaxing him to take some nourishment and listening to him talk of his family, especially his father, an elderly and blind Lutheran clergyman.

Then something strange transpired. An arriving Confederate soldier peered inside the tent in which Rauch was then lying. Instantly recognizing the patient, he informed Woolsey that the lieutenant's brother was inside one of the prisoner train cars nearby. By the time the two men were reunited, however, Henry was nearing the end and did not recognize his own brother. Woolsey recounted the final chapter of this saga:

> And there the brothers lay, and there we, strangers, sat watching, and listening to the strong clear voice, singing, "Lord, have mercy upon me." The Lord had mercy, and at sunset I put my hand on the Lieutenant's heart to find it still! All night the brother lay close against

the coffin, and in the morning he went away with his comrades, leaving us to bury Henry ... giving us all that he had to show his gratitude—the palmetto ornament from his brother's cap and a button from his coat.

At about the same time as Lieutenant Rauch faded away, seemingly oblivious to his brother's presence, Dr. L. P. Warren, General James J. Pettigrew's brigade surgeon, found himself at the right place at just the right time to save the life of his own younger sibling.

Born in Edenton, North Carolina, Warren grew up in a household of doctors. Both his father and a brother pursued this profession. At the outset of the war, L. P. Warren entered the medical branch of the Confederate army. Meanwhile, at the tender age of sixteen, John Crittenden Warren enlisted as a private in Company H, 52nd North Carolina. By the time of the Battle of Gettysburg the youngster had attained the rank of first lieutenant.

The 52nd belonged to Pettigrew's brigade and saw action on two of the three days of fighting. After incurring relatively few casualties on the opening day, the regiment was badly mauled during Pickett's Charge. Wounded in the lungs, the right wrist, and left thigh, Lieutenant Warren was captured by the Federals after the repulse of the charge. During the triage process it was determined that he had little chance for a recovery and virtually no care was given to him for the next two weeks.

Fortunately, Dr. Warren was among those detailed to remain behind following the retreat of Lee's army. One day while making his rounds, Dr. Warren heard someone exclaim, "Lieutenant, here is your brother, the doctor." The details of this remarkable happenstance appeared in the obituary of John Warren:

> In looking through the opening of a tent he discovered the emaciated form of Lieutenant Warren lying on some blankets on the ground. A hasty examination revealed five bullet holes through his body, the blood from which had stiffened his clothing like pasteboard. He had been given up to die. The Federal surgeons, as an act of mercy, had given him morphine to relieve his sufferings, but had not attended his wounds. Dr. Warren washed and dressed him, replaced his blood-stained garments with his own, and was allowed to remain several days with him, thereby saving his life. They were then separated, the doctor being sent to Fort Norfolk and the lieutenant to Point Lookout as prisoners of war.

In his later years, John Warren moved to Panama in hopes that the warmer climate would alleviate some of the pain resulting from his chest wound. For a time he served as the assistant superintendent of the Panama Railroad. In the summer of 1914 the ailing veteran returned to the home of his family in Atlanta and died there on July 21. His obituary described him as being of "a modest and gentle nature ... a loving husband and father, a true and tried friend, a chivalrous gentleman, a gallant and courageous Confederate soldier, of the strictest honor and integrity." A wide circle of friends attended the ceremony that would have taken place many years earlier had it not been for the timely arrival of his brother in July 1863.

William, Clapham, and Alexander Murray

Seated upon a Virginia hillside overlooking the Potomac River, Captain William H. Murray penned a letter to his family back in Maryland. "Just think it is ten months since I left home," he began reflectively. "Not till now have I realized the responsibilities resting on one's shoulders.... You may ask why I allow things to trouble me which disturb not others—I answer—because in other companies many officers laugh at moral corruption which is to me a source of anxiety and pain. How many anxious mothers—who perhaps I have never seen—look to me as far as in me lies, to shield and protect their sons from harm—This is one care that is never absent."

These words certainly provided a high level of assurance to Mrs. Murray, since two of William's brothers served under him in the First Maryland Infantry, C. S. A. Captain Murray's devotion to his men did not go unnoticed by his superiors. Major William W. Goldsborough wrote this concerning the regiment's senior line officer: "Captain Murray was a most lovable character, modest and unassuming in disposition, pure and chaste in his conversation, tender and considerate for those under his charge; no one occupied a warmer place in the affections of their men than did this gallant soldier."

The soldiers under Murray's charge reciprocated by going anywhere he asked even if this meant enduring extreme physical discomfort. For example, prior to a winter campaign in January of 1863, Murray observed that a number of his men were without shoes, their feet "one map of inflamed blisters." The captain issued an order stating that those without footwear could ride in the rear with the wagons, but to a man the company responded, "We will follow you."

The proud officer gushed with pride in recounting the story: "How proud I felt of my brave boys, to see them standing shoulder to shoulder when there was danger, though it was against the will of nature.... We started off not the crippled and broken down battalion that a few hours before had dragged itself into camp, but a band of determined men marching towards the enemy with wild excitement. Within the distance of one mile we forded the river four times to our knees in water so cold that it appeared to take the very breath from the body, not yet a man faltered or left his command."

The concern that Murray felt for his men and his devotion to duty pointed towards a larger mission. For him the war was a deeply personal affair. Born on the family farm in West River, Anne Arundel County, on April 30, 1839, William moved north to Baltimore in the late 1850s. The young businessman marched and drilled with the Maryland Guards, a newly formed militia unit, and rose to the rank of captain.

The Civil War brought tension and turmoil to his adopted city. Following the famous riot on April 19, 1861, when a pro–Southern crowd attacked the 6th Massachusetts Regiment, Lincoln took drastic measures to maintain order, including the suspension of habeas corpus. Federal troops soon occupied the city; militia weapons were seized, property was confiscated, and suspected Southern sympathizers, including nineteen members of the legislature, were thrown into jail.

These harsh measures deeply angered many Baltimore residents. In May, William Murray joined in the exodus from the occupied city, sending his mother a farewell note that ended, "It may be forever—but if I fall—I fall a free man."

Making his way south with his brothers in tow, Murray raised an infantry company, the nucleus being made up of former members of the Maryland Militia. These recruits were combined with other companies of disenfranchised Marylanders to create the First Maryland Infantry Regiment. Mustered out in the summer of 1862 following the expiration of its one-year enlistment term, the unit was reorganized that fall into the First Maryland Battalion because not enough men were available to form a full regiment. The name was changed to the Second Maryland in 1864.

No matter what name they went by these soldiers seemed to relish combat. Perhaps the Federal occupation of their homeland provided additional motivation. Captain Murray related the following incident that occurred during Jackson's legendary Valley Campaign of 1862:

> The happiest day I ever spent in the South was I think the eighth of June last at Cross Keys. I with rifle in hand had with fifteen others twenty most beautiful shots at a regiment of Yanks bearing their flag. Three times did it fall in the dust under our fire. My heart danced for joy as the cheers of our dear little regiment made the echoes sing.... For six long hours did we face three regiments of infantry and two batteries of artillery of the enemy. There was not an inch of ground around us that was not literally ploughed with shot and shell from the continued roar and bursting of these unpleasant messengers—for hours after the battle was over I could not hear my own voice. Such is the fun my foolish company now wishes to enjoy."

A little over a year later at Gettysburg, Murray and his company found little in the way of fun. During the early evening of July 2 the First Maryland Battalion clawed its way up the lower slope of Culp's Hill with General George "Maryland" Steuart's mixed brigade of Virginia and North Carolina troops. Fortunately, for the Confederates much of the manpower in this sector had been shifted to the endangered Union left earlier in the day. Despite this numerical advantage, the Confederates incurred a considerable number of casualties, some of them due to friendly fire. In one instance, as the infantrymen of the First North Carolina groped their way to the front, they mistakenly shot into the backs of the First Maryland.

Sliding into an abandoned section of works, Steuart's men enjoyed little rest that night, as random shooting echoed through the woods until daybreak. Major Goldsborough, who assumed command of the battalion following the wounding of the lieutenant colonel, remembered Captain Murray as being "distressed over the slaughter of his men."

The situation worsened the next morning as both sides planned for an early morning offensive on Culp's Hill. The Confederate line lurched forward as a shower of metal rained upon them from the Union guns posted along the Baltimore Pike. Steuart's Brigade dutifully carried out orders for a dangerous frontal assault across an open field about two hundred yards in width. Realizing the hopelessness of the mission, Captain Murray shook the hand of every man in his company, telling them, "Good-bye, it is not likely that we shall meet again."

Emerging from the cover of the trees, the brigade staggered ahead against the converging small arms fire of the sheltered enemy infantry. It was a terrifying scene. "Scarcely a leaf or limb was left on the surrounding trees," recalled a Marylander.

As many of the attackers dove to the earth to escape the deadly fusillade, Captain Murray and a handful of his stalwart men plunged forward. Closer and closer they approached the enemy line until faces and forms became discernible through the haze of smoke. Suddenly, the captain faltered and tumbled downward with a mortal wound. As Alexander Murray rushed to catch his falling brother a shell exploded nearby, knocking him unconscious. Lieutenant Clapham Murray took charge of the company for the duration of the fight.

As the survivors of the ill-fated attack scrambled for safety, witnesses saw General Steuart weeping as he cried out, "My poor boys! My poor boys!" The First Maryland Battalion lost over 200 men and their pet dog, who was discovered inside the Union lines riddled with bullets. Murray's company sustained about one-fourth of these casualties—55 killed and wounded from its 97 members present for duty.

The mortal wounding of the beloved captain of Company A shook the battalion. "I grieved to see poor Bill Murray stretched out stiff and cold," wrote a comrade, "Oh! How I felt. I liked him and he was a fine soldier, a fine captain. He used to look forward with such pride and joy to an entrance into Baltimore, and to think his life was thrown away."

The dead officer escaped the fate of many of his compatriots who died upon the rocky hill. Following the battle, Union burial details unceremoniously tossed the bloated remains of the slain Southerners into large trenches before covering them with a shallow layer of dirt. Before leaving the area, however, the soldiers from Company A buried the remains of their slain officer and carefully marked the grave. Because of this foresight, Murray's half-sister Elizabeth and a family servant were later able to recover the body and have it reburied in the Christ Church Cemetery in Owensville, Maryland.

The veterans who fought alongside William Murray never forgot him. "He will live in the memory of those who knew him and their sorrow over his early fall is just as keen as it was thirty years ago," wrote Goldsborough. He added, "To their children will his character be handed down as an example worthy of emulation, as a Maryland soldier who reflected the honor of his state and whose private life was bright with Christian virtues."

> If asked to name the most important military events in our nation's history, most Americans would include Pickett's Charge on the list. And they would certainly be justified in doing so, given the fact that the July 3 assault has become widely known as the turning point of the Civil War. This status dates back to the 1870s when government historian John B. Bachelder coined the lofty term, "The High Water Mark of the Rebellion," to describe the Copse of Trees on Cemetery Ridge.
>
> In truth, "Pickett's" Charge is a misnomer. Pickett's Division made up roughly one-half of the assault force and James Longstreet, not George Pickett, directed the attack. Nonetheless, more accurate descriptions such as "The Pickett-Pettigrew-Trimble Charge" and "Longstreet's Assault" have not caught on, even among historians.
>
> Certainly no Civil War battle has been debated and analyzed as much as that of Gettysburg. Much of this attention has been focused on the minutia and the "what ifs" of this battle's climactic event: How long did the bombardment last? How many men participated in the charge? Of that number, how many crossed the Emmitsburg Road? What if Pickett's Division had been better supported? And so on.
>
> While all of this close scrutiny has fostered an intense interest in, and, consequently, a better understanding of the charge, this familiarity, combined with the passage of time, has had a diluting effect. The brutality and horrors of that tragic hour have been replaced by the romanticism of the Confederacy's lost hopes and the detached armchair analysis of modern military officers on staff rides.
>
> The remaining five stories in this chapter will focus not on strategy and tactics but rather on the terrible human suffering that took place during the course of Pickett's Charge as untold numbers of Confederate brothers stepped off from Seminary Ridge, not as pieces on a giant chessboard, but as flesh and blood with individual hopes, prayers, and fears.

John, Joseph, and William Marable

Private Joseph Gates Marable was not in the best of health on the morning of July 3 when the 11th Mississippi Infantry shifted from its position along Willoughby Run to assemble on the west slope of Seminary Ridge. On March 19, 1861, the then 22-year-old merchant signed his name to the roster of Company H, the "Chickasaw Guards," at Houston, Mississippi. The next spring he fell with a leg wound at Seven Pines, for which he received treatment at Richmond. After recovering from these injuries, Marable checked into the general hospital at Charlottesville on October 30, 1862, for a much less honorable reason, but one quite common among Civil War soldiers—gonorrhea. Following a brief furlough the private returned to duty only to be struck down with secondary syphilis in the spring of 1863. Venereal disease and tiresome marches could not keep Marable from participating in the war's premier battle.

Since it remained behind at Cashtown on July 1 to guard the division's wagon train, the regiment missed the debacle at the Railroad Cut and was spared the heavy losses suffered by the other units of Heth's Division in the fields west of town. Two days later, they would more than compensate for this absence. With limited time and tools the Mississippians dug in at their new position by utilizing trees and stumps to protect themselves during the impending bombardment.

While it is doubtful that Joseph Marable wielded a shovel that sweltering morning, one of his two brothers might have. John, nicknamed "John Jolly," had enlisted in his brother's company at the age of eighteen near the end of April 1861. Following in his footsteps, he also sustained a thigh wound during the fighting near Richmond. Joseph's twin brother, William "Tip" Marable, waited a year to join him and John in the ranks of the 11th Mississippi.

By the evening of July 3 this regiment could stake claim to an unwelcome distinction. No regiment in the Army of Northern Virginia would suffer a higher number of casualties on this day. All three of the Marable brothers appeared on this list.

The ordeal began shortly before 1:00 p.m. when signal guns near the Peach Orchard announced the start of the cannonade that preceded the infantry attack. "Almost at the same instant, along the whole line, there burst a long loud peal of artificial thunder forth, that made the ground to tremble beneath its force," wrote the 11th's Lieutenant William Peel. "The enemy's guns, in the same breath, as it were, took up the contest & sent a tremendous shower of shot and shell whizzing over us." The deafening roar continued for about two long hours as the defenseless infantrymen clung to the ground while the missiles plowed among them and at times tore off the entire crowns of the oak trees that towered above them.

The brief lull between the cessation of the artillery duel and the inevitable command of "Attention!" seemed an eternity for the anxious but determined soldiers. Passing through the line of artillery, the Mississippians faced a new set of horrors as they closed in upon the Emmitsburg Road. Lieutenant Peel described those horrors in the colorful language of the period: "We were now advancing in the face of a perfect tempest of maddened shells that ploughed our line & made sad havoc in our ranks. As we moved onward we were greeted ... with showers of canister, &, at the distance of about two hundred yards the infantry opened upon us from behind the stone fence.... Our line was now melting away with an alarming rapidity. It was already reduced to a mere skeleton to the line of one hour ago. Still on it pushed...."

The band of survivors that gathered around the regimental colors drew the beads of numerous riflemen. A twelve-pound shell exploded directly above the shoe tops of Color Sergeant William O'Brien, blowing his lifeless form skyward. This macabre scene did little to deter anyone from taking on this hazardous duty. Amazingly, they actually fought for the honor. One soldier actually snatched the standard away from the grasp of another after O'Brien toppled back to earth. Seconds later, the new flag bearer was severely wounded in the mouth. In turn his replacement took only a few steps before he fell dead.

At this juncture Joseph Marable, "the never flinching little Irishman," picked up the standard with its staff cut in two and sprinted towards the whitewashed buildings of the

Abraham Brian farm. Somehow he made it all the way to the enemy line. After triumphantly planting the colors on the stone fence, he collapsed to the ground. The small number of Confederates that made it this far posed little threat to the Federals and those still alive, including Joseph and John Marable, surrendered near the fence. Somewhere between the ridges lay William's body. Perhaps his brothers watched helplessly as he fell dead.

The two surviving brothers reacted differently to being taken prisoner. While John waited patiently until he was exchanged in March of 1864, Joseph focused nearly all of his energy on breaking out. Together with his cousin Warren Reid, he hatched an ingenious scheme to break free from the watery surroundings of Pea Patch Island. On August 15, just five weeks after entering the compound, the two men set their plan into motion.

After passing through the gate with relative ease, the pair hid out until dark. An earlier scouting trip failed to produce a boat so they improvised with a twelve-foot piece of ladder and a piece of plank for a paddle. Laden with the makeshift watercraft on a bright starlit night while moving across open terrain, it took the prisoners an hour and a half to negotiate the 150 yards past the gaze of the sentinel to the bottom of the levee. As the guard paced his beat less than twenty feet away the pair quietly slipped into the bay. The old ladder proved to be seaworthy but its capacity was limited to just one man. Thus, as Marable paddled, Reid towed along by holding onto one of the rungs.

At eight o'clock in the morning the escapees struck dry land. Believing the terra firma to be the New Jersey mainland, they set the ladder adrift only to discover that they had landed on an island. The remainder of the 12–15 mile journey was accomplished with another piece of plank found on the island.

After a two-day respite, the travelers embarked on the next leg of the trip. Finding a small boat, they crossed back over the Delaware Bay. Upon reaching the shore, Reid and Marable struck out for the Chesapeake Bay. Five days into the journey the starving former inmates enjoyed a tasty meal at a farmhouse. That same day the fugitives bumped into an unsuspecting Union soldier at a country store, who provided them with matches and a few peaches.

On the following day the Mississippians proceeded towards Baltimore aided by a map they tore from the walls of a schoolhouse. Acting on the suggestion of a farmer, the two men crossed the Chesapeake on a coal boat that landed at Havre de Grace just above the mouth of the Susquehanna River. During the trip to Baltimore the cousins traveled part of the way with "a good and ignorant darky," who provided valuable information about the country and its inhabitants. Acting on this intelligence they procured much-needed food and supplies.

Reaching the outskirts of Baltimore before dawn on August 30, 1863, Reid and Marable carefully picked their way through the heavily guarded city and pushed northwest to Frederick and then to Harper's Ferry. The great escape ended several days later when the two men met Confederate cavalrymen in the Shenandoah Valley near Luray Court House. A generous trooper put them up at a hotel. Afterwards, the relieved soldiers traveled by stage to Orange Court House where they were reunited with their comrades in the 11th Mississippi.

Much to his amazement, Joseph Marable discovered that he had jumped in rank to second lieutenant during his absence. In 1864, he was commended for his "gallantry and ability" while in command of companies E and H. But while Marable proved adept at escaping the clutches of his Union jailers, he apparently could not outflank a more persistent foe. An inspection report dated January 3, 1865, describes Marable's status: "Absent, sick at home without leave." We can reasonably assume that an ill-advised evening with a prostitute prevented this proven soldier from continuing with his duties.

James and Christopher Harwood

At the outset of the war, James A. Harwood had recently completed his studies at Washington University in Lexington, Virginia, the institution that Robert E. Lee would later preside over and add his name to its title. Harwood passionately supported his state and its allegiance to the Confederacy. He was not alone. Five of his brothers also took up arms for the Southern cause. Of the six, four died during the conflict, the last being killed on the day of Lee's surrender at Appomattox.

By the summer of 1863 James had advanced to the rank of second lieutenant in Company K of the 53rd Virginia Infantry under command of Lieutenant Colonel Rawley Martin. The 53rd formed in the center of General Lewis Armistead's line as Pickett's Virginians stepped off from Seminary Ridge and into the pages of history. Following in support of Garnett and Kemper, Armistead's men prepared to exploit any weakness opened up by the leading wave of troops.

"[E]ach brigade moved off as gracefully and apparently as fearlessly as if going on parade," recalled Harwood. "We had not gone far," he continued, "before the enemy's guns opened upon us and ploughed throw our ranks, cutting down many a brave soldier. But no sooner was a gap made in the line than the command was given to 'close up.'"

This level of discipline is even more remarkable given the fact that the men who were falling were friends, neighbors, and often family members of those who continued on towards Cemetery Ridge. Lieutenant Harwood shared his unusual experience:

> The writer then being a lieutenant was on the extreme left of the company, and, having heard that Captain Lipscomb was killed, he turned around and saw that brave soldier fall to rise no more. Soon after Lieutenant Ferguson fell ... when rushing to the head of the company, the writer saw his little brother, whom he had loved and sheltered in many a hard fought battle before, fall. Running up to him, the little fellow exclaimed: "Brother James, go back to your country; I am not hurt much and you are now in command." But it was not long ere this brave little soul, who was then shot through by two Minnie balls, found a soldier's grave and went to the God he had so faithfully served. We rushed on through the most terrific fire of shot and shell that mortals ever encountered, Garnett's and Kemper's brigades having, as it were, almost melted away, whilst Armistead's was about one-third of what it had been when it started; but still onward they pressed, closing up ranks as each soldier would fall and charging as it seemed into the very jaws of death. The gallant Garnett fell, killed almost instantly, and then the noble Kemper, mortally wounded, as was supposed at the time.
>
> The gray-haired Armistead seeing this, and being the only surviving brigadier, waved his sword aloft, exclaiming, "Come on, boys, I will lead you." And so he did until we swept over the works and captured several pieces of artillery. Then General Armistead turning to the writer, said, "Lieutenant, we must use their own guns on them." Taking charge of one himself and ordering the writer and his sergeants to do likewise, we fired only three rounds when a brigade of General Hancock's corps swept in at double quick, and the remnants of Pickett's Division ... seemed to disappear at the first fire.... The gallant Armistead fell mortally wounded while working one of the guns. The writer and his two brave sergeants fell, working the guns they had captured.... Those who were not killed instantly had but little time to think, as they were hurried to the rear as fast as possible.

The writer being unable to walk was thrown across the neck of an officer's horse and, nearer dead than alive, hurried to the rear at a breakneck speed. After going some distance, we halted, when, asking the officer why he carried me off so unceremoniously, he replied, he had captured a big rebel officer and was determined not to let him be recaptured. Imagine his surprise and chagrin when I told him I was only a lieutenant, and nearly a dead one at that.

Harwood and his two sergeants were later transported to a Harrisburg hospital where they came under the care of Dr. C. B. Fager, who provided them with "the best of attention and the most skillful treatment." Ironically, the ex–Confederate officer resided in Uniontown, Alabama, after the war. In his later years, he ruminated upon the significance of Pickett's Charge and its place in American military history: "Why it was ordered or why it failed will be left to wiser heads than mine to determine. But historians will record it as one of the most gallant efforts ever made by men to carry out the orders of their superior officers, and Pickett and his deathless Virginians will go down to history side by side with the bravest of the brave, whose exploits are recorded on historic pages."

Norbone, Edmond, William, and Charles Berkeley

In time, Civil War regiments took on personalities of their own. The famed "Louisiana Tigers" developed a reputation for reckless bravery on the battlefield and notoriety for rowdy behavior and lack of discipline in camp and on the march. On the other hand, the dapper 20th Massachusetts was officered by a contingent of Revolutionary War descendants, infusing the command with blueblood tradition. Despite common threads, fighting units were not homogeneous masses, but rather collections of individuals with sometimes widely differing values, motivations, and approaches to combat. These peculiarities only add to the richness and complexity of the era.

Badly depleted by previous campaigns, the veteran 8th Virginia Infantry arrived in Gettysburg with about 240 men, with four of its ten companies mustering twenty or less members. Even so, one can find a diversity of experiences within this small unit at Gettysburg.

Any thorough examination of a regiment's history must begin with its field officers, who for good or bad wielded a powerful influence upon its character and conduct. The 8th Virginia adopted the nickname of the "Berkeley Regiment" for the substantial contributions of one family during the organizational period and subsequent service that nearly spanned the length of the war. At one point three Berkeley brothers filled the field officer posts of colonel, lieutenant colonel, and major, while another served as a captain. Eppa Hunton, the 8th's original colonel and later a brigadier general, would describe them as "four of the bravest, noblest, most patriotic and unselfish men I met in the war."

Born between the years 1824 and 1833, the four brothers descended from distinguished ancestors who had been present in the Old Dominion for nearly two centuries. They were themselves large landowners in the horse country of Loudoun and Prince William counties and were the kind of men that others loved to follow, so it was an easy matter for them to attract recruits from among their countrymen. The Berkeleys soon rose to ranks of prominence within the regiment.

As the 8th Virginia moved into position on the right of General Richard Garnett's brigade line on the morning of July 3, Major Edmund Berkeley believed he "never saw men march more steadily up to their work than our line." The bombardment certainly frayed the nerves of even the bravest of souls. Since the 8th drew the undesirable assignment of being posted to the rear of Major James Dearing's batteries, the Virginians faced a steady stream of Union counter battery fire. One shell struck two soldiers in Company D who had been lying side by side. The brains of one of the victims splattered onto the hat of Major Berkeley.

Following this grotesque incident, the major suddenly remembered the well-worn deck of cards tucked away in his breast pocket. Reminded of his own mortality and not wishing that such a scandalous item be found upon the person of a refined gentleman such as himself, he buried the deck under a nearby rock. Berkeley later explained, "I would not like for anyone to get that old pack of cards with which Gen. Garnett, Col. Hunton and I had played hundreds of games by the light of camp fires."

By the time the artillery duel finally came to a close, five men had been culled from the ranks of the small Virginia regiment. As the mercury climbed into the high 80s, the shaken men staggered to their feet. Shortly before the command was issued to begin the assault, Lieutenant Colonel Norborne Berkeley and his brother William, the captain of Company D, overheard General Pickett remark to Garnett, "Dick, old fellow, I have no orders to give you, but I advise you to get across those fields as quick as you can, for in my opinion you are going to catch hell."

These less than encouraging words would have greater meaning when the 8th Virginia approached the Emmitsburg Road and came within range of the Second Corps infantrymen. As the battle line closed in upon the Nicholas Codori farmstead, a bullet passed through Colonel Hunton's leg before inflicting a mortal wound upon his horse, leaving the regiment in command of Norborne Berkeley.

Up to this stage the Berkeley brothers had remained unhurt, but this situation would soon change. After turning in a left oblique to align themselves with Kemper's men, the 8th split into two parts upon reaching the Codori farm. Leading a battalion around the north side of the house, Edmund Berkeley was struck above the knee by a minie ball. Carried to a sheltered position, the officer was approached and then questioned by General Kemper. The brigadier dismissed Berkeley's warning about a Union flanking column (Stannard's Vermont brigade), leading the major to shout after him, "You will soon see your mistake."

Moments before his own wounding, Major Berkeley watched a shell strike William as he led Company D down the slope from the farm buildings. He could see him hobble awkwardly as the blood spurted from his thigh but did not realize that his brother numbered among about a dozen wounded soldiers that took cover in Codori's cellar.

An ever dwindling number of Virginians rushed towards the Clump of Trees. Shot through the foot partway up the slope, Lieutenant Colonel Berkeley bent over to remove his boot when a canister round knocked him down. Perhaps only half a dozen soldiers from the 8th reached the stone fence, among them Lieutenant Charles Berkeley. Most of these men loaded their weapons and handed them up to Private James Lunceford, who consistently picked off blue-clad defenders at close range. However, when Union reinforcements swarmed into the area, Lieutenant Berkeley reluctantly passed his handkerchief to Lunceford with instructions to tie it to his ramrod and wave it as a surrender signal. The 8th Virginia would put up no more resistance on this day.

Thanks to two members of Garnett's staff, Major Berkeley was rescued. As he was being carried towards the rear, Berkeley spotted General Lee near Spangler's Woods and heard him comforting the survivors with these words: "My men, it was not your fault."

While Major Berkeley and Colonel Hunton returned to Virginia to fight another day, all of the remaining Berkeley brothers fell into the hands of the enemy. Remarkably, all of them survived the war and returned home to their estates.

Fifteen years after the war, Edmund came back to Gettysburg. Dismayed by his inability to recover the pack of cards he had buried prior to the charge, Berkeley meticulously visited the stores of the various relic collectors in hopes of turning up a lead. Finally, a storekeeper informed him that a small boy had brought him the cards. Since time and the elements had converted them into a pulpy mass, the collector paid the boy only a nickel. Berkeley was heartbroken when this dealer revealed that he later sold the relic for 200 times more than the original purchase price at the Chicago Exposition.

In 1907 Edmund spoke at a banquet of the Society of the Army and Navy of the Confederate States held in Baltimore. A reporter noted that the 83-year-old veteran was "as hale and hearty as a strong man of fifty-five or sixty. He tales long walks every day and can ride horseback like a youngster. He does not wear glasses, and is ready to engage in a shooting contest with anybody at anytime."

Edmund would be the last surviving brother, passing away in 1915 at the age of 91. He was buried at St. Paul's Episcopal Church in Haymarket, Virginia, with his brother Norborne. Charles and William were interred in Middleburg, a small town situated in the Loudoun Valley.

George, James, John, and William Presgraves

In most aspects of life, being tall is considered a distinct advantage. However, in the Napoleonic combat utilized during much of the Civil War towering above your comrades only made one a more inviting target. In an era when most men stood about five feet, eight inches tall, Recruiting Officer James R. Simpson must have done a double take as brothers George, James, John, and William Presgraves approached his table on July 13, 1861. The descriptive roll lists George's height at six feet, two inches and his appearance as dark haired and gray eyed. His three siblings all measured over the six-foot mark. Both General Pickett and Colonel Eppa Hunton jokingly referred to them as "our twenty-four feet of Presgraves," which was probably a conservative estimate.

The abnormal height of the brothers had no adverse effect for nearly two years. However, during Pickett's Charge a bullet found its mark in the leg of Lieutenant John Presgraves. He and all three of his brothers would be captured on July 3. After the battle, a Union surgeon amputated Lieutenant Presgraves' injured limb, but, unfortunately, gangrene set in. With both George and William joining the throngs of Confederate prisoners being shipped north to POW camps, James somehow managed to remain behind to care for his older brother.

When Clarissa Jones, a Philadelphia schoolteacher, arrived at the Union Second Corps Hospital along Rock Creek, she discovered Lieutenant Pressgraves lying on a rock with his devoted sibling by his side. "The anxious brother did not even have a handkerchief," recalled Jones. "He was bathing the boy's wounds with a piece of paper."

Perhaps because it was her first case, the volunteer nurse developed a deep bond with the two soldiers. She learned that they had two other brothers in the army and a father back home who was like another brother to them. When John died on July 8, permission was granted for James to walk into town to procure a coffin. The lad informed Jones that he planned to escape and vowed that one day he would return for John's body.

James Presgraves made good on both promises. Fittingly, he and his brother now rest together in a cemetery near Middleburg, Virginia, where they once played together during the halcyon days of their youth.

James and William Burchett

Describing the fatalistic determination of his soldiers in the 8th Virginia Infantry prior to Pickett's Charge, Colonel Eppa Hunton would write: "All appreciated the danger and felt it was probably the last charge to most of them. All seemed willing to die to achieve a victory there, which it was believed would be the crowning victory and the end of the war."

Though these words undoubtedly applied to many of the soldiers who participated in the war's most famous assault, it would be dangerous to assume that these feelings were universal. Indeed, the waters of history often become murky when one probes beneath the surface. The Reverend Andrew B. Cross, a delegate with the United States Christian Commission, revealed an entirely different subset of Confederate soldiers that he encountered during his visits to the various field hospitals following the battle.

Upon noticing a disproportionate number of North Carolina soldiers among the wounded, Cross and his companions queried some of these men on the subject. "The only reason we can give for it is that they try to wreak their vengeance upon us because our State was opposed to going out of the Union," answered one young patient. "They put us in every dangerous and exposed place, and gave us the hard end of everything." Another stated, "My part of the state was opposed to going out, and they brought an army in on us and compelled us to go with them."

In 1867, Anna Holstein published an account of her three years of experiences in the various field hospitals of the Army of the Potomac. At Gettysburg, she, too, met a number of reluctant Rebels. In one ward she met the son of a former New Hampshire political official who relocated to Georgia before the war. After being forced into the army, he received numerous threats upon his life if he dared to desert or if he ever revealed his allegiance to the Union.

Did certain local officials actually sanction the conscription of Union sympathizers to bolster the ranks of Southern armies? The answer is yes and the evidence seems to indicate that these instances might have been far more common than once thought. The Reverend Cross and Nurse Holstein both described the fascinating story of one of these men, who, with an older brother, fought in Colonel Hunton's 8th Virginia.

According to Holstein: "A nephew of President Johnson, named Burchett, was also a Union man among rebels; with a number of others, they were attempting to come into our lines when captured. The rebels told them they would be out in the front ranks, and when they came to Gettysburg, carrying out their threat, they were made breastworks of. None of the sixty escaped unhurt; many were killed. Burchett lost a leg, and one arm permanently disabled. He was a free-spoken Union man among them, and seemed to be no favorite with the rebs on that account. He remained a prisoner, hoping in the exchange to be sent to Richmond, that he might save some property belonging to his father, who had lost everything in Kentucky."

Cross briefly mentioned this same soldier in the report he compiled for the Commission, but he was so moved by the encounter that he wrote a full length account for a small circulation newspaper published by the Lutheran Church. Following is an excerpt from this August 6, 1863, article:

> While passing among the Rebel wounded, lying in a barn near the 3rd Army Corps' hospital, my attention was attracted by a noble-looking young man lying on the floor of the barn, who had his left arm wounded near the shoulder and his left limb amputated above the knee. Noticing that the appearance of his countenance and the intelligent expression of the eye indicated something decidedly superior to the miserable specimens of the Rebel soldiery lying around him, I at once approached him, and entered into conversation with him respecting his prospects for eternity. After a few moments conversation on religion, one of the surgeons stepping to me remarked, "I am glad to find you conversing with this dear young man, for he is now, and has ever been, a strong and unconditional Union man: he was forced into the Rebel service and compelled to fight against his conscience and his country." Upon the surgeon's making this remark, the young man grasped me warmly by the hand, and, with tears in his eyes, remarked, "How cheerfully could I have borne this if it had befallen me in defense of my county, which I wished to serve." I then asked him to communicate to me his history, which he did with the request that I should have it published in one of our Northern papers, at least, but not to mention his name. "For," said he, "if I ever get back, and any of these fiery Secessionists know that I communicated these facts, they will certainly kill me." He then gave the following account of himself:
>
> "I am a nephew of Andrew Johnson, military governor of East Tennessee, and a citizen of Johnson County, East Tennessee. Myself and ninety-four other young men, who, like me, detested rebellion and loved the old flag, determined we would try and escape from East Tennessee, and enlist in a regiment of Union cavalry then forming in Kentucky. On the 25th of August 1862, an opportunity presented itself; we commenced our perilous journey. We traveled until the 10th of September, succeeding in eluding our pursuers, when we were surrounded by five companies of Rebels, near Lucky Cove Seminary, in Powell Valley, Lee County, Virginia, where ten of us were killed and wounded, forty-five made their escape, and forty, including myself were captured. Immediately after our capture, we were sent to Richmond, where we were imprisoned for a few days, when we were sent to Staunton, Virginia, and on the 29th of September we were assigned to the 8th Virginia regiment of infantry. Since that, all the forty, except myself and brother, have been either killed, wounded, or taken prisoners; and," he added, with a deep groan, "you see, sir, what I am," referring to his mutilated limbs. After further conversation with him on the subject of religion, I offered prayer, in which other brethren with me joined, and then bid him farewell. A few days afterward, the evening before I left the battlefield, I visited him, and never did I converse with a man who had reason to believe death near, who was able to give a better reason for the hope that was in him. I met with many other similar instances, but this was the most affecting of all.

Private James M. Burchett recovered from the amputation of his left leg and a shoulder dislocation to return home to Tennessee. His service record indicates that he was admitted to West Buildings Hospital in Baltimore on October 14, 1863, and paroled a month later at City Point, Virginia.

The records pertaining to his brother are sketchy. Last paid on June 30, 1863, Private William H. Burchett is listed as being absent without leave by the fall of that year. The invasion of Pennsylvania provided numerous opportunities for escape for disenchanted Confederate soldiers. It is likely that William was among the hundreds of deserters who slipped off into the countryside.

Eager to learn more about these brothers, I contacted the Johnson County Historical Society. County Historian Thomas W. Gentry examined the local documents to flesh out more details on their backgrounds and postwar lives. The 1860 census reveals that James Burchett, age 43, resided with his wife, Margaret, 57, and two sons, William H. and James

M., ages 19 and 17, respectively, in an area now known as Laurel Bloomery, Tennessee. All of the family members were born in Virginia.

According to Mr. Gentry, the Burchett boys had intended to enlist in the 13th Tennessee Cavalry at Camp Nelson, Crab Orchard, Kentucky, before being apprehended by a Confederate patrol in Lee County, Virginia.

In the spring of 1864, James exchanged vows with Rachel Venable at Laurel Bloomery. Rachel's father, the Reverend Lewis Venable, served as a private in the 13th. The 43-year-old pastor was assigned to duty as a hospital orderly. A decade later, William Burchett married the daughter of a former member of this unit. These facts illustrate the tight bonds that existed in the small mountain communities of eastern Tennessee and western North Carolina. William and his wife, Mary, thirteen years his junior, had two sons together. The couple's names do not appear in the county records after 1897.

William probably saw little of his younger brother after the war. On September 23, 1869, Reverend Venable sold his farm, and accompanied by his daughters and sons-in-law, struck out for Polk County, Missouri. Following his death in 1883, the last will of Lewis Venable includes an inheritance for Rachel, who by then was married to another individual, and her two children, William and James.

Unless a divorce was involved, it appears that the senior James Burchett died sometime between 1869 and 1883. Struggling on a daily basis with a disability incurred while fighting for a cause that he did not support, we can only speculate as to his mental state during this period. This unpleasant episode also provides a glimpse into the ugly partisan warfare, often split along family and clan lines that engulfed the Appalachian region throughout the war.

6

Twins

Growing up we learned that being a twin meant
always having an unconditional best friend.
—*Debra and Lisa Gantz*, The Book of Twins

Thomas and George Dennen, USA

Just north of the famous Peach Orchard at Gettysburg, two eight-foot bronze figures, hands clasped together, stare westward in eternal vigilance towards Seminary Ridge. The first figure is that of a Union infantryman holding a musket by his side. His nearly identical companion is a fully uniformed fireman complete with a calling horn at the ready. The monument honors the dual status of the citizen soldiers who fought in the ranks of the 73rd New York Volunteer Infantry, better known as the "Second Fire Zouaves." Recruited primarily from the various volunteer fire departments of New York City, the regiment participated in 28 battles and skirmishes during its four years of service and incurred 711 casualties, including 153 battle deaths and 403 soldiers wounded in action.

Although not by design, the pair of bronze statues could easily represent twin brothers Thomas and George Dennen, 25-year-old New York City natives who joined the Fire Zouaves in the summer of 1861. Both had served with the fire department prior to their enlistment in the military.

There is little doubt that the brothers were identical twins. Sergeant Frank Moran noted that while he had often observed the close resemblance between certain twins as children, in no other instance did he recall the similarities being so perfectly preserved to maturity. According to him, the likeness was not merely facial, but "in form, height, walk, gesture, carriage, tone of voice, articulation, and even peculiarities of laugh ... all features conspired to make them perfect counterparts of each other, and a source of endless and ludicrous perplexity to their friends."

Referring to Tom's promotion to lieutenant in August 1862, Colonel Michael Burns joked that he had asked the governor of New York for a commission for Tom, "not because he was a better or braver soldier than his twin, but because the interests of the service—in fact, the peace of the regiment demanded that he should have a distinguishing mark." Concurrently, George earned the grade of sergeant "for being in all engagements" and for his "good behavior and courage." Nonetheless, the pair used the situation to their advantage, often playing jokes on their friends and even upon one another.

173

Unfortunately, military life was not all hilarity for the twins. In mid–November of 1861, while the regiment was stationed about fifty miles south of Washington, D.C., the brothers received word that their mother, Maria, had died. The boys provided financial support for their parents before heading off to war and throughout their army careers they dutifully sent home money to assist their widowed father.

The 73rd New York did not receive its baptism by fire until the following spring. At the Battle of Williamsburg, Virginia, on May 5, 1862, the 73rd New York suffered over 100 casualties, the second highest loss it would incur on a single day. Afterwards, the regiment went on to distinguish itself throughout the Seven Days' Battles near Richmond and then during the ensuing Second Manassas Campaign.

During a fierce fight at Kettle Run on August 27 that pitted Hooker's men against a Southern division commanded by Major General Richard S. Ewell, a third of the already decimated regiment fell, and, by the end of the day, command devolved upon a sergeant. A rifle ball struck Lieutenant Dennen in the head region, causing him to be hospitalized in Washington and New York for several months. He recuperated in time to rejoin his brother and participate in the spring campaign of 1863.

On the evening of May 2, 1863, the New Yorkers rushed forward from a reserve position to bolster the right flank of the Union line at Chancellorsville that had been shattered by Lieutenant General Thomas J. "Stonewall" Jackson's devastating flank attack. Although exposed to "a murderous fire on the front and flank," the regiment aided in the repulse of three enemy assaults. The losses sustained by the 73rd were moderate when compared to previous battles, but among the three men killed in action was Lieutenant Thomas Dennen. Sergeant Moran never forgot the sight of the surviving twin weeping over the lifeless form of his brother "with a grief that made the stoutest of the soldiers weep with him."

Four days later, the Union forces retreated back across the Rappahannock River in the midst

George Dennen, ca. 1861 (U.S. Army Military History Institute).

of a driving rainstorm. In the exigency of the situation, nearly all of the dead and wounded were left behind. The vast majority of bodies that were eventually recovered could not be identified and now reside under "unknown" grave markers at the Fredericksburg National Cemetery.

Both Moran and Sergeant George Dennen were cited for good conduct in Colonel Burns' official report of the battle and each was subsequently promoted to the rank of second lieutenant. The commendation proved to be of little consolation to the grief-stricken Dennen. He became increasingly withdrawn from his former associates and was often observed sitting inside his tent crying as he clutched his brother's photo. "To me alone he gave his company and confidence," wrote Moran, who was now his messmate and closest friend. After his companion commented on his fine appearance in an officer's uniform, Dennen smiled faintly and then replied, "I shall not wear it long; I shall follow Tom, and be killed in the next battle."

After his best efforts to dissuade his fellow officer from these morbid thoughts proved futile, Moran avoided the topic altogether. But during the long march from Fredericksburg to Pennsylvania that commenced in mid–June, the bereaved twin repeated his dire prediction on a daily basis.

The 73rd New York and the remainder of the Third Corps began arriving upon the field at Gettysburg during the evening of July 1 after the opening day's fighting had ended. Major General George G. Meade positioned the corps to extend the left of his line along the southern end of Cemetery Ridge down to Little Round Top. Throughout the morning of July 2, however, Third Corps chief Major General Daniel Sickles grew increasingly nervous over his ability to defend this sector. Thus, by mid afternoon he shifted his 10,000-man force westward to seize the high ground along the Emmitsburg Road. By mid afternoon of July 2, the center of his new line was located in the vicinity of Joseph Sherfy's peach orchard just east of the road. Directly adjacent to the orchard stood the Sherfy's two-story brick house and barn. The 73rd New York was posted in a support position behind the main line about 100 yards north of the orchard.

Meanwhile, Lieutenant General James Longstreet prepared the Confederate First Corps for an echelon attack against the Union left. The veteran Fire Zouaves reclined in the shade of a small apple orchard as skirmish fire broke out between the two forces. Now that combat seemed imminent, Lieutenant Moran closely observed his friend. If anything, he detected "a greater vivacity of spirits" than he had witnessed since the death of his brother. At one point Dennen took a sealed letter from his pocket and asked his friend to personally deliver it to the addressee in the event of his death.

Soon afterwards, heavy fighting broke out near Devil's Den and Little Round Top and gradually spread northward. As Brigadier General William Barksdale's Mississippi regiments crashed into the center of the Third Corps' line near the Sherfy farm, the Fire Zouaves were ordered forward. The Yankee defenders initially staggered the onrushing Confederates, but the Mississippians closed ranks and kept coming. After a desperate close-quarters struggle, the Union line began to give way. Nearly surrounded, the survivors of the 73rd formed into a semicircle as the Southerners began to work around both of their flanks. Finally, Colonel Burns received an order to pull back to Cemetery Ridge after nearly half of his 350-man force had been shot down.

At the height of the crisis, an excited artillery officer dashed up to the New Yorkers and implored them to help rescue his imperiled guns. Responding to the plea, Lieutenant Moran and a small group from his company stepped forward to follow the officer. An instant later, a shell burst directly over the group. A fragment of iron struck the lieutenant in the ankle and another imbedded in his left eye, knocking him onto the ground unconscious.

Following the Union retreat a compassionate Mississippi lieutenant carried the wounded officer into the Sherfy yard and dressed his eye wound. Throughout the night Moran listened to the moans and cries of the wounded who had crawled into the barn seeking refuge from the elements. He could not have known that among this number were at least two of his comrades, Captain John Downey and Lieutenant George Dennen, whose left leg had been shattered by a bullet, near the close of the action.

The next morning Moran and a group of fellow prisoners were removed to a position behind the Confederate lines on Seminary Ridge. From there they observed the grand spectacle of Pickett's Charge and celebrated a hard-earned triumph over their old nemesis. The joy was short lived, however, for the next evening the POWs found themselves slogging southward during a torrential downpour as the Confederate army retreated towards Virginia.

On July 9 the Federal prisoners were ferried across the swollen Potomac River in an old flatboat. While bivouacked on the Virginia shore, Moran noticed a young soldier from the Washington Artillery of New Orleans. Before the war, Moran had resided in a number of different locations, including the Crescent City. After the Union officer inquired about several acquaintances that were members of the battery, a warm conversation ensued between the two men. The Confederate stated that his battery had been posted near the Peach Orchard during the final two days of the battle. He also disclosed the fact that when the Sherfy barn caught fire during the cannonade preceding Pickett's Charge, he helped to remove a number of helpless wounded soldiers from the burning structure.

Moran's interest rose to a fever pitch when the Confederate soldier added that among those rescued were two officers from a New York regiment, a captain and a lieutenant, who wore upon their breast badges of the New York City Fire Department. He stated that the elderly captain would live but regretted that the wounds of the lieutenant were of a mortal nature. His description of "a young man, of medium height, with dark hair, large eyes, and slight brown mustache" perfectly matched Lieutenant George Dennen. After learning of Moran's close relationship with the dying officer, the Louisiana soldier expressed his regrets and before parting he provided his adversary with a hot meal.

On July 18 Moran joined hundreds of his fellow captives at Libby Prison in Richmond. During the initial inspection process at this facility, the officer observed that letters and other personal property were being confiscated from the prisoners. Regrettably,

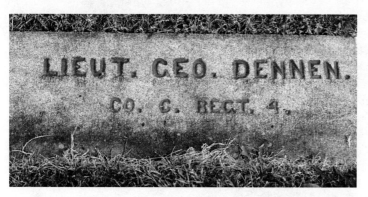

The grave of George Dennen in the Soldiers' National Cemetery.

he tore up the letter that his friend had entrusted to his care. For Moran it was just the beginning of a long odyssey. After twenty long months of confinement at various prisons in Virginia, Georgia, and the Carolinas that included five failed escape attempts, he was finally released in March of 1865.

Several months after his

capture, Moran received verification of his friend's death in a letter from Colonel Burns. After the amputation of his injured leg, Dennen lingered until July 11 before joining his beloved brother. Since his father lacked the money to ship his remains home, the slain officer was interred in the Soldiers' National Cemetery at Gettysburg.

During the 25th anniversary of the battle Moran visited Gettysburg and stood over the grave of his comrade. He noted that the brief inscription on the stone told "so little to the stranger but so much to me of a young hero of the Union, the twin of Tom, who sleeps at Chancellorsville." He followed with a simple request to honor his friend's memory: "Let those who pass the spot drop a flower over the peaceful mound."

James and Amos Casey, USA

It has been said that joy and sorrow are often close companions. This adage is perhaps even more relevant in times of war. While the nightmare at Chancellorsville permanently separated the Dennen twins, another set of twins serving in the Army of the Potomac's Third Army Corps obtained a sense of relief and hope in the battle's aftermath.

Writing his mother on May 24, 1863, Corporal James Casey marveled: "It was indeed a mercy and a miracle how both of us was spared during that awful battle.... And if I had not witnessed it myself I would not have believed it that so many would escape ... for on the charge of Saturday [May 2] the roar of artillery was so heavy that I thought the very heavens above was bursting while the heat of both cannon and musketry almost burnt our faces."

Corporal Casey would not have been comforted had he known that a worse trial lay just ahead. By this stage, however, he and his twin Amos were hardened veterans despite their youthful appearance. Only 18 years of age, the boys measured to an average height and had light complexions, hazel eyes, and dark hair.

Before marching off to war the Casey twins lived with their widowed mother at 1620 Becket Street in Philadelphia. The boys' father had passed away back in the spring of 1860. Since Ann Casey had no source of income her sons sent home a considerable amount of money while in the army. In a postscript to the same letter that he described the recent battle, James tallied his contributions at $192.

He also told his mother that the lush green fields surrounding the regiment's new campsite often reminded him of home. But this nostalgia soon yielded to patriotism. "It does us very little good to think of the many pleasant times that we all enjoyed at home for our old Uncle Sam has a better claim to us at the present time than home with its comforts," he declared dutifully. Although James admitted that he was not in any hurry to cross the Rappahannock River for another showdown with the enemy, he concluded the thought by asserting that "when ordered I am willing to go."

The next campaign did not begin with a crossing of the now infamous Virginia waterway, but instead with a series of gruesome marches that would lead the mass of blue troops over the more northerly Potomac River. An incident involving Sergeant Amos Casey as the Third Corps crossed the plains of Manassas would be an omen of things to come for the twins. Overcome by sunstroke, he would lie prostrated for two days before reviving. Although certainly not fit for duty, the hardy youngster continued to march and eventually overtook his comrades. This gritty conduct personifies the attributes that led to Amos Casey's selection as the color-bearer of the 99th Pennsylvania's state flag.

In his condition it is difficult to imagine how Sergeant Casey persevered over the stifling heat and humidity, but on the afternoon of July 2, 1863, he stood firmly atop the boulders of Devil's Den with his flag by his side. Defending the guns of Captain James Smith's 4th New York Independent Battery, the 99th anchored the extreme left flank of the Union line during one stage of the battle.

It seems only natural that a savage and confused contest erupted in the midst of the hellish terrain that characterized this area. From a commanding platform on the ridge above the Den the Pennsylvanians poured volley after volley into the disorganized mobs of Alabama and Georgia troops swarming up the rocky gorge formed by Plum Run. In keeping with the nickname of their state, the less than 300 members of the 99th believed that they held the "key" to the position and "not a solitary man of that little band, even for a moment, thought of being driven" off.

When Confederate reinforcements arrived, however, the sheer weight of numbers tipped the scales in favor of the attackers. The regimental flags floating above the smoke-shrouded ridge made a convenient mark for the Southern riflemen, and not surprisingly, a minie ball zapped Amos Casey in the right hand.

Indeed, on this occasion lady fortune did not smile on the Casey twins. As the 99th began its retreat, Corporal James Casey "industriously applied himself to breaking the guns that strewed the ground to prevent them falling into the hands of the rebels." Finding a loaded weapon, he fired it at his pursuers, but at the same instant a bullet pierced his own body. Major John Moore and a nearby sergeant attempted to carry Casey to safety, but he implored them to save themselves. A little later, Lieutenant Thomas Kelley grabbed hold of his wounded comrade, but the brave lad soon died and was left upon the field. The body of James Casey was never recovered. One veteran later decried that "the ghouls who robbed his body and thus prevented his identification knew it, for upon his breast he wore the Kearny Badge."

There is no record of Amos Casey's reaction to the loss of his twin. Suffering from mental anguish as well as physical discomfort, he spent over four months in a hospital back home in Philadelphia. Amos determined that the best way to honor his brother's memory was to keep fighting for the cause that he had surrendered his life for. That winter he reenlisted as a veteran volunteer. This choice nearly cost him his life.

The Army of the Potomac underwent an extensive reorganization prior to the spring campaign of 1864. Shattered by its huge losses at Gettysburg, the Third Corps was consolidated into the Second Corps. More importantly, Lieutenant General U. S. Grant was on hand to personally supervise the movements of the North's premiere army. The chances of Ann Casey losing her other son appeared to be greatly diminished when Amos was attached to the headquarters staff of brigade commander Thomas Egan.

During his relentless drive towards the Confederate capital, Grant committed his biggest tactical blunder at Cold Harbor on June 3, where he ordered a disastrous frontal assault against well-entrenched enemy positions that resulted in the loss of about 7,000 Federal soldiers. Sergeant Casey later described how close he came to being listed among the dead:

> General Egan with two members of his staff ... with myself as orderly were out in front of our works in company with General [Nelson] Miles with some of his staff. After having gone some distance to the front, General Egan remarked to General Miles, "General, haven't we gone far enough?" and General Miles made answer, "O no, there is no danger here," when almost at that moment we saw the flash of a gun in the woods in our front

and instantly I felt the shock which nearly unhorsed me. General Egan heard it and called me to lay over on the horse and get out. All present made a dash for cover. After getting to a place of safety, I found the ball had gone through the front of my cap and ploughed a furrow along the top of my head. General Egan and others congratulated me on my close call. I went to the rear, had my head dressed by a doctor unknown to me, and then resumed my place at headquarters.... I was young, strong, and hearty at that time.

Perhaps feeling just as safe in the ranks, Casey returned to his duties as color sergeant and would serve in this capacity until the 99th Pennsylvania was mustered out on July 1, 1865. Returning to Philadelphia after the war, Casey married Miss Fannie Young in October 1868. Four children arrived over the next fifteen years. These growing responsibilities did not prevent Amos from staying active in veterans' affairs. Unlike some veterans who intentionally distanced themselves from the war and its painful memories, Casey kept in close touch with his former comrades. He was even elected to serve as president of the survivors' association of the 99th Pennsylvania. The various reunions and memorial functions must have had a cathartic effect.

The culmination of these activities occurred on September 11, 1889, when the survivors of the regiment assembled once again among the boulders of Devil's Den to dedicate a regimental monument. Looking out over the crowd of gray-haired veterans, keynote speaker Albert Magnin, a former captain, rightly described the battlefield as the Mecca of Civil War sites. He summed up the deep sentiments that he shared with his listeners:

> And so we come here today with our hearts filled with the memory of our comrades as fresh as when the news was young.... We here raise this tablet and inscribe upon it the cold stern figures which there you see, that you may learn to love your country more by knowing what it cost ... the blood of our brothers, fathers, friends.

After providing an overview of the regiment's history and its participation at Gettysburg, Magnin once again honored those who died in the line of duty. "And of those I call to mind was Corporal James Casey of Company K, whose twin brother, Sergeant Amos Casey, now stands before me holding the dear old flag for which his brother died."

With these words one can almost picture Amos's leathery hands gripping the staff a little tighter as he thrust his chest forward in pride and reverence. He may have swallowed hard and forced back a tear. It was certainly a day he would never forget.

In the years following the ceremony Casey's health began to decline. The scalp wound that had come so close to ending his life at Cold Harbor now impaired his vision and hearing, bringing on dizzy spells and throbbing headaches. As a result, his mental faculties slipped as well. George Washington Casey, Amos's only surviving child, stated that his father died in a hospital for the insane on June 6, 1920, releasing his soul to join his brother in the last bivouac.

G. A. and W. C. Jones, CSA

Near the same time that James Casey died among the boulders of Devil's Den, another twin saga, unparalleled in pathos, transpired less than 500 yards away. No body of Southern troops faced a more difficult assignment on July 2 than did the five regiments from Alabama and Texas that attacked up the rugged western slope of Little Round Top. From the crest of the hill that rose 150 feet above the valley floor, the thin line of Union defenders laid down such a withering fire that a Confederate soldier compared the scene to an erupting volcano. Through a veil of drifting smoke observers from below watched in nervous anticipation as the red battle flags wound circuitously up the slope in fits and starts.

Some of the best shock troops in Lee's army, including the battle-tested 5th Texas, assailed the hill that afternoon. "The ascent was so difficult as to forbid the use of arms," recalled Colonel Robert Powell, the commander of the 5th. "At last, weary and almost exhausted, we reached the topmost defenses of the enemy. Now the conflict raged with wild ferocity. We were caught in a cul-de-sac, or depressed basin, surrounded on three sides by projecting or shelving rocks."

Corporal John W. Stevens was among the eleven men from Company K who reached this advanced point. He recalled the balls "whizzing so thick around us that it looks like a man could hold out a hat and catch it full." For the first time in its illustrious history the 5th Texas began to waver. At this critical juncture, the corporal welcomed the arrival of two additional guns. Soon afterwards, Stevens witnessed one of the saddest events in the regiment's history.

> There were two twin brothers belonging to Co. [G], of my regiment, that got separated from their own company. They came up to where I was standing and commenced firing. In a moment one of them is shot down by my side. The other brother caught hold of him as he fell and gently laid him down on the ground, and as he did so he also received a death shot. This was a very affecting scene—those two boys were twin brothers, so much alike that you could hardly tell them apart. They were always together—where you saw one you saw the other. They had passed safely through all the previous battles unhurt—now they die together.

Privates G. A. and W. C. Jones were among the 54 soldiers of the 5th Texas left dead on the slopes of Little Round Top when the Southerners abandoned the attack. Given the inseparable nature of most twins, it was probably for the best that one of them had but a few seconds to mourn the loss of the other.

7

Sibling Reunions

Family life is too intimate to be preserved by the spirit of justice.
It can be sustained by a spirit of love which goes beyond justice.
Reinhold Niebuhr

Charles and William Goldsborough

Sergeant Austin Stearns numbered among the hundreds of wounded soldiers trapped behind enemy lines when Union forces retreated through the streets of Gettysburg on the afternoon of July 1. The next morning, Stearns observed a touching and somewhat humorous incident near Christ Lutheran Church on Chambersburg Street:

> While out behind the church in the yard cooking our breakfast, there were Rebs and Union men, and there two brothers met, one dressed in blue, the other grey, and with the exception of their uniforms both looked just alike. Both were little, red-faced, red-haired, stubby Irishmen, and both blubbered and cried, and hugged each other as only Irishmen can. The Union man wanted the Reb to go with him and leave the cause of the South, while the Reb didn't see how he could go when the Union man was a prisoner and would perhaps have to go south whether he wanted to or not. How they decided it I never knew, for I left the yard and never saw them again.

Meetings between brothers wearing opposite uniforms were not uncommon during the Civil War, and several of these incidents have been documented at Gettysburg. Unfortunately, the details of the reunions, such as the one that occurred at the church, are often sketchy and leave the reader wanting to know more about the participants and what became of them afterwards.

In one instance, however, two brothers encountered one another during the month-long campaign that preceded the Battle of Gettysburg. Then, as an indirect result of this battle, they met again under entirely different circumstances. Fortunately, in this case much is known about the backgrounds and military service of both siblings.

The divisive issues that polarized the nation throughout the mid–1800s stirred up even deeper passions within border states such as Maryland. Divided loyalties pitted neighbors, religious congregations, and even family members against one another. But sometimes geography played the leading role in an individual's chosen allegiance. Such was the case with the sons of Dr. Leander Worthington Goldsborough.

This old line Maryland family could trace its roots back to Goldsborough Hall near

Knaresborough, Yorkshire, England, on land granted to the head of the family by William the Conqueror. Although educated in London, Robert Goldsborough headed the Maryland delegation in the First and Second Continental Congress. He voted in favor of the Declaration of Independence, but a fatal illness prevented him from attaching his signature to the document. Robert's grandson, Leander Goldsborough, practiced medicine in Frederick County, Maryland. There, the doctor and his wife, Sarah, raised six sons and a daughter. At least two of the boys possessed adventuresome spirits.

Born in October of 1831, William Worthington Goldsborough was too young to be a soldier during the Mexican War. Undeterred, he ran away in hopes of joining the army, but his parents intercepted him in Baltimore and brought him home. William once admitted that by nature he was a man who loved fighting. He would see plenty of that in the next war.

In his early days, Goldsborough brandished a pen rather than a sword. After learning the printing trade, he became a foreman with the Pittsburgh *Dispatch*. In about 1850 he moved to Baltimore and worked there as a writer and proofreader. Goldsborough whetted his appetite for the military by becoming a member of the Baltimore City Battalion, one of the most famed militia companies in the antebellum era. The battalion was ordered to Harper's Ferry, Virginia, in October 1859 to assist in putting down John Brown's Raid. Goldsborough was among the first militiamen to storm Brown's fort with a detachment of U.S. Marines commanded by Robert E. Lee.

Given this experience and his residency in Baltimore, a city with a known Southern proclivity, it is not surprising that the newspaperman cast his lot with the Confederacy. In May 1861, at the age of 30, he enlisted as a private in the First Maryland Infantry. He didn't remain at this lowly rank for long. The next month, following the promotion of his cousin, Bradley T. Johnson, to major, Goldsborough was elected the new captain of Company A. Described by one of his peers as a man with "a fine, cultivated intellect, a charming, magnetic personality, with a romantic, sanguine temperament," leadership came naturally.

The following spring the First Maryland, C.S.A., met and routed the First Maryland, U.S.A., at the Battle of Front Royal, Virginia. It would not be the last time that opposing regiments from this border state locked horns on the battlefield. After its one-year enlistment term expired on August 17, 1862, the Confederate First Maryland was disbanded. Reorganized as the First Maryland Battalion in October, the official identity of the unit was changed to the Second Maryland Infantry near the end of the war.

This hiatus could not keep Goldsborough out of the action. During the desperate battle along the railroad cut at Second Manassas, the captain suffered a severe wound while acting as temporary commander of the 48th Virginia. He most likely would have died had it not been for the kindness of a local family who carefully nursed him back to health.

Still, the combative officer must have despaired over missing out on Lee's invasion of Maryland a short time later. Given the result, it may have been a blessing. Much to the chagrin of the invaders, the citizens of the region showed little interest in being liberated. Worse, Lee incurred horrendous losses at Antietam and was forced to withdraw back across the Potomac River with nearly all of his objectives unrealized.

The following January Goldsborough bumped up a rank to major and would be second in command of the First Maryland Battalion at the outset of the Gettysburg Campaign. Considering the fact that Richard "Baldy" Ewell's Second Corps contained more

Maryland units than any other portion of the Army of Northern Virginia, it seemed only fitting that this hard-hitting body of troops acted as the phalanx of Lee's second invasion of the North.

Ewell's first task was to clear the invasion route by sweeping any opposition from the Shenandoah Valley. The most significant Federal presence in the region consisted of Major General Robert H. Milroy's 5,000-man garrison at Winchester, Virginia, near the northern end of the valley. Although numerous orders had been sent instructing Milroy to abandon the isolated outpost, he kept his men in place. Despite mounting evidence to the contrary, the general refused to believe that an entire Confederate corps was bearing down upon his position. He insisted that the approaching force represented nothing more than a cavalry raid.

By the evening of June 12, 1863, over 20,000 Confederates camped within a few miles of Winchester. At daybreak they broke camp and marched towards the town. Swinging down the Valley Turnpike, Major William Goldsborough and the First Maryland Battalion headed for yet another encounter with their former friends and neighbors. A most unusual rendezvous awaited the major.

As the first crackle of small arms fire echoed from the outskirts of Winchester, assistant surgeon Charles Edward Goldsborough, Fifth Maryland Infantry, U.S.A., prepared his instruments for the inevitable casualties that would soon arrive. Born two years after his brother William, Charles displayed some of the same wanderlust. After traveling to California with a team of oxen in 1853, he returned home by ship the following year.

From that point his life took a more conventional course. Studying medicine in his father's office and at the University of Maryland, he opened his own practice in Hunterstown, Pennsylvania, a small hamlet situated five miles northeast of Gettysburg. Shortly afterwards, the doctor married a local woman, Mary McNeely. Sadly, Mary died on March 10, 1860, six days after the birth of the couple's second daughter, who would in turn die at the tender age of six months.

Perhaps to escape his grief and feeling of helplessness, Charles offered his services to the Fifth Maryland as an assistant surgeon in the fall of 1861. In his first assignment, he helped to establish a general hospital near Leesburg, Virginia. Taken prisoner at Frederick during Lee's invasion of Maryland, Surgeon Goldsborough was soon released and worked tirelessly to treat the flood of wounded brought to the city in the wake of Antietam. With his training and practical experience, Goldsborough was prepared to meet any exigency that arose at Winchester—almost.

Milroy's overmatched Federals battled gamely throughout the day on June 13. Moving out to engage the enemy, they forced the Southerners to earn every foot of ground. By night-

Charles E. Goldsborough. This photograph was taken after the war, but its exact date is unknown (History of Adams County).

fall, however, Ewell's veterans had secured positions on the very outskirts of town. That evening, as peals of thunder echoed across the rolling landscape, Ewell prepared a plan to finish his mission. Meanwhile, in the midst of a torrential downpour Milroy's embattled troops assembled in a trio of earthen forts that guarded the northern and western approaches to the town.

The next morning, as Ewell deployed the bulk of his forces to attack the forts, the First Maryland Battalion and several other units staged a series of noisy diversions to the south. The strategy worked perfectly and by the end of the day the Confederates had captured the outer forts. That evening, at a council of war held in Main Fort, Milroy finally conceded to a withdrawal.

The movement began under the cover of darkness. Reading his opponent's mind, Ewell shifted a portion of his troops to close off the avenues of escape. The resultant fight at Stephenson's Depot on the fifteenth proved disastrous for the Union. Milroy lost half of his command, reporting 4,443 casualties, including 3,856 captured or missing.

While being taken prisoner at Winchester would not have been considered an unusual experience for a Yankee soldier, the circumstances involving one captive were certainly unique. During the breakout attempt, surgeon Charles Goldsborough found himself surrendering to a familiar figure—his older brother William. Although the details of the brief encounter are not known, it is likely that strict military protocol was observed. When the brothers parted neither expected to see the other until the end of the war. As Charles and his fellow captives were herded together for a trip to Richmond's infamous Libby Prison, William marched into northern territory on a campaign that would reach its climax just a few miles from his brother's home.

The easy victory at Winchester soon became a distant memory for Ewell's soldiers as they found themselves facing a Union Gibraltar on the rocky slopes of Culp's Hill. But when General Meade stripped most of the defenders from this sector to shore up his endangered left flank on the late afternoon of July 2, the Confederates seized a portion of the enemy trenches. In this fight, the lieutenant colonel of the First Maryland was wounded and Major Goldsborough assumed command of the battalion. Both sides planned to open the attack at daybreak.

By this time the absent Union troops had returned. The five regiments belonging to the brigade of George "Maryland" Steuart shifted down the slope to attack the defenders holding a position along a farm lane that led to the Baltimore Pike. The line of advance required Steuart's men to cross a seven-acre clearing now known as Pardee Field. The normally combative Goldsborough immediately sensed the folly in the assigned orders, telling one of his captains that "it was nothing less than murder to send men into that slaughter pen."

He was right. Straddling a stone fence along the upper edge of the field, the Marylanders advanced to within a hundred yards of the enemy lines when a thunderous volley sent "a merciless storm of bullets" into their ranks. Goldsborough was posted near the left wing of the battalion, where a Yankee bullet tore a gaping hole through his left lung and exited from his back. Knocked to the ground, the major painfully raised himself on his elbow and watched helplessly as his command was cut to pieces. Later, he would write bitterly, "Someone's hands are stained with the blood of these gallant men." At one point during the fighting, the Confederate Marylanders once again exchanged volleys with fellow Marylanders.

As a wounded prisoner of war, this familiar circumstance was of little concern to

Goldsborough at the time. By mid–October, the convalescing officer had finally mended enough to be transported away from Gettysburg. Strangely enough, he landed at Fort McHenry in his adopted city of Baltimore. More surreal circumstances could not be imagined. The following spring Goldsborough departed from these familiar surroundings and entered the prison compound at Fort Delaware.

Meanwhile, Surgeon Charles Goldsborough gained his release from Libby Prison through a formal exchange of Union and Confederate surgeon POWs. That same December, orders assigned him to the prison complex at Fort Delaware. Imagine his surprise when he found both William, and another brother, Eugene, a private in the Second Maryland Cavalry, among the inmates. Also wounded at Gettysburg, Eugene would die in captivity. The remaining two brothers did not meet again until the end of the war.

In the spring of 1864, Charles accompanied General Benjamin Butler's Army of the James as it moved up the Bermuda Hundred to take part in U. S. Grant's all-out attack against the Confederacy. Wounded during the siege of Petersburg on July 6, Goldsborough spent the remainder of his army career on assignment at Lincoln Hospital in Washington.

Meanwhile, William languished in captivity. On August 20, 1864, he was chosen to be among the six hundred prisoners to be placed under the fire of Southern batteries in Charleston Harbor in retaliation for Union officers being intentionally placed in vulnerable sites around the city. The Southerners endured a hellish 18-day sea journey crammed into the dark confines of a ship's hold with meager rations and a lack of fresh drinking water under deplorable sanitary conditions. Arriving at Morris Island, four miles south of Charleston, the prisoners were led into a two-acre stockade constructed on a spit of sand.

Nearly seven weeks later, the standoff ended and the respective prisoner groups were moved to safer locations. After a five-month stay at Georgia's Fort Pulaski, Goldsborough returned to Fort Delaware, where he was finally released on June 12, 1865.

With the coming of peace both Goldsboroughs returned to the lives they had left back in 1861. Charles resumed his medical practice in Hunterstown, remarried, and fathered eleven more children. No doubt out of necessity, he farmed a good portion of his land. Somehow the doctor also found time to participate in a number of veterans' activities. In addition to being a member of the local G.A.R. post, he served on the Gettysburg Battlefield Commission and on the Board of Examining Surgeons for the Federal Bureau of Pensions.

Mimicking army life to a certain extent, William Goldsborough did not remain rooted to one location as did his brother. After recuperating from his long imprisonment, he established a newspaper in Winchester, Virginia, where the veteran undoubtedly harbored some nostalgic connections to his surroundings. Upon selling his interests he relocated to Philadelphia in 1870 and spent the next two decades on the staff of the *Record*. His restless spirit then led him to the Pacific Northwest, where he earned a living as a foreman for newspapers in Tacoma and Everett, Washington.

Tough as ever, Goldsborough cleared out a gang of roughneck printers upon his arrival in Tacoma, unionized the office, and turned out one of the most respected papers in the region, which earned him the sobriquet of the "Fighting Foreman." Returning to Philadelphia in 1894, Goldsborough contributed several articles to the *Record* concerning his war adventures. The long-time journalist also began revising *The Maryland Line in the Confederate Army*, which he had authored in 1867.

A freak accident that took place a couple of years after Goldsborough's return hindered these efforts, but it also led to a serendipitous encounter. When a careless bicyclist struck down the newspaperman on the street, shattering his thigh and landing him in the hospital, he fell in love with his nurse, Miss Louise Page, a relative of the Robert E. Lee family. The couple exchanged vows after the patient's discharge.

Although he could walk only with the aid of crutches, William spent much of the summer of 1901 in Hunterstown and he and Charles spent many hours tramping over the Gettysburg battlefield. This reunion took place under much more pleasant circumstances than did the unusual ones of 1863 and this probably led to some good-natured ribbing between the two siblings.

It was the last time that they would see one another alive. That winter William underwent an emergency operation from which he would not recover. He died in Philadelphia on Christmas Day at the age of 70.

Although the Goldsborough brothers had long since reconciled with each other, William maintained his fierce allegiance to the South. Feeling his life slip away, he begged his wife, "Should the end come, don't bury me among the Yankees here!" Louise Goldsborough honored her husband's dying request, and following a full military ceremony, his remains were laid to rest in Baltimore's Loudon Park Cemetery near fellow Marylanders who had also fought for the Confederacy.

Charles would spend the remainder of his golden years at Hunterstown, where he died in October 1913. "He has a large acquaintanceship and the news of his death will be received with general regret all over the county," read the announcement of his death. The beloved doctor was buried in the Evergreen Cemetery among some of Gettysburg's best known citizens.

The fact that Charles and William Goldsborough now rest on opposite sides of the Mason-Dixon Line reminds us of a time when passionate sectionalism often pitted brother against brother.

Thaddeus and Thadia Klimkiewicz

Blinking and staring through bloodshot eyes, the detail of Union soldiers posted on the Emmitsburg Road spotted two vehicles approaching their checkpoint on the morning of July 5. As the carriage and omnibus crept northward over the rutted highway, the soldiers counted over a dozen passengers clothed in black dresses with snow white aprons. An oversized white bonnet, which one soldier called "the ugliest piece of furniture I ever saw," bobbed prominently above each figure. However, when the travelers halted near a barricade of felled trees, the attention of the men focused upon the young angelic faces underneath the crisp headdresses. In turn, anxious eyes searched over the heavily armed Yankee soldiers and the alien landscape spread out before them.

Attaching a white handkerchief to the end of his cane, an Italian priest dismounted from the carriage and approached the guards. Following a brief conversation the barricade swung open, and as the small party continued towards Gettysburg the guards doffed their dusty caps and bowed in appreciation.

Although the uniformity of dress symbolized the common purpose of the Sisters of Charity of Saint Vincent de Paul, the background of Sister Mary Serena differed markedly from the others. Born Thadia Klimkiewicz on January 3, 1839, in Washington, D.C., she was the youngest daughter of Lieutenant Colonel Henry Bennet Klimkiewicz, who was the nephew of the Polish military hero General Tadeusz Kosciuszko.

Utilizing his extensive training in military engineering, Kosciuszko allied himself with the colonials during the American Revolution. In recognition of these contributions he was later granted U.S. citizenship, a pension, land, and the rank of brigadier general. However, his heart still belonged to his native Poland. Upon returning there Kosciuszko attained the rank of major general in the Polish army, and in 1794 he led an unsuccessful rebellion for Polish independence against an occupying force of Russians and Prussians. Wounded and captured, the general was forced to live out his remaining years in exile. A champion of racial equality, he freed the serfs on his estate in Poland just before his death in 1817 and his will stipulated that the proceeds from the sale of his Ohio property be used to educate black Americans.

Throughout the nineteenth century Polish nationalists endeavored to win back their freedom, but the odds were always too great and these uprisings cost thousands of lives. Following in the footsteps of his legendary uncle, Colonel Klimkiewicz was taken prisoner during the revolt of November 1830. Although tortured by his Russian captors, who hoped to learn the names of other conspirators, he remained silent. Freed after several years of confinement, he chose liberty in America rather than oppression and near certain execution at home.

Settling in the nation's capital the Pole obtained work as a post office manager. Not long after his arrival he met a local girl, Miss Amelia Langley, while he was being fitted for a suit in her brother-in-law's tailor shop. It turned out to be a classic love at first sight affair. The couple soon wed and had four children together—two girls and two boys. The names of the youngest of each sex, Thadia and Thaddeus, honored their great uncle. Both parents would die before the start of the Civil War.

Considering their family's violent heritage it is not surprising to learn that the Klimkiewicz girls sought a pacifist lifestyle. At age 17, Harriet took the vows of a Catholic Sister of Charity and entered the commune as Sister Mary Veronica. A little over a year later, Thadia followed the example of her older sister, receiving the name of Sister Mary Serena.

Nestled in the foothills of the Catoctin Mountains about a half-mile south of the western Maryland village of Emmitsburg, the central house of the Sisters of Charity had been established a half century before the Civil War. Mission work and teaching formed the heart of this benevolent order. The convent operated St. Joseph's Academy, a school for young ladies that earned a national reputation for excellence. At the opposite end of the social spectrum, the Sisters trained impoverished orphan girls in household skills that would help them find employment. They also traveled extensively to fulfill their charitable purposes. The year after her postulation Sister Serena was called to St. Mary's Asylum in St. Louis and later to St. John's School of Baltimore.

The advent of the Civil War created an unprecedented level of demand for the services of the eleven Catholic orders of nuns that existed in the United States. The Sisters operated on a nonpartisan basis throughout the war in both sections of the country. Almost immediately army surgeons came to prefer them over all other female nurses. "Self-denial was a feature of their daily life, and the fact that they had taken vows of poverty, chastity, and obedience peculiarly fitted them for a duty that demanded personal sacrifices almost every hour of the day and night," explained an early historian.

Although the Sisters required no compensation for their services the government agreed to provide food, lodging, and compensation for other travel expenses. A Catholic chaplain attended each contingent of volunteers. It was also agreed that the nuns would have complete freedom of operation with no interference from other civilian nurses.

Left: Sister Mary Veronica Klimkiewicz, ca. 1860 (courtesy Archives, Daughters of Charity, Emmitsburg, Maryland). *Right:* Sister Mary Serena Klimkiewicz, ca. 1860 (courtesy Archives, Daughters of Charity, Emmitsburg, Maryland).

After two years of war, the Emmitsburg community was widely separated. By the summer of 1863 only about 60 of the 232 Sisters resided at the central house in Emmitsburg, including Sister Mary Serena. Near the end of June thousands of blue-clad soldiers filed by the complex as they trudged north towards the Mason Dixon Line. Many of them set up camp around the fine buildings, the chapel, orchards, and fields of crops that made up the quiet community. The strangely garbed women worked tirelessly in providing drinks, meat, cakes, and bread for the famished men. Meanwhile, Father Francis Burlando and his assistant heard confessions from those who practiced the Catholic faith.

However, a member of a Pennsylvania infantry unit discovered in a profound manner that the good will of the small community extended beyond denominational and sectional lines. As his regiment marched past St. Joseph's he took in a sublime sight. "A long line of young girls (some of them Southerners unable to go home) led by several Sisters of Charity took their position along the side of the road and at a word from the Sister in charge, all fell upon their knees and with upturned faces toward the vaulted skies earnestly prayed for the spiritual and physical safety of the men who were about to go into deadly battle," he recalled. Deeply moved by this tender show of affection, every soldier in line bowed and bared his head until the prayer was finished.

Of course, the thoughts and prayers of some of the women must have also been directed towards their friends and relatives who would soon oppose these men. In the absence of her older sister it is only natural that Sister Serena thought often about her brother. Carrying on his family's revolutionary bloodlines, Thaddeus Klimkiewicz fought as a private in the Confederate 1st Maryland Battalion.

Serena's concerns only mounted when the rumble of artillery fire echoed off the mountains and thick clouds of black smoke appeared in the skies to the north. When word reached Emmitsburg that the terrible conflict had finally ended Father Burlando and 16 Sisters set off for Gettysburg immediately after Sunday morning mass with a supply of bandages, medicines, and other provisions.

The final leg of the journey presented an apocalyptic scene. "It was beyond description," wrote Sister Camilla. "Hundreds of both armies lying dead almost in the tracks that the driver had to be careful not to pass over the bodies. This picture of human beings slaughtered by their fellow men in a cruel Civil War was so terrible." For Sister Serena these horrible sights might have conjured up images of the violence her father had hoped to escape when he came to America.

On both sides of the Emmitsburg Road burial crews busily dug mass graves for the Southerners cut down during Pickett's Charge. At times the carriage wheels actually rolled through human blood. The sight of bodies piled on top of one another caused the animals to rear up on their hind legs and the driver struggled to get them under control.

Although the trip covered less than ten miles the Sisters did not arrive in town until after noon. Total chaos prevailed. It seemed that every public building and private home was filled to capacity with the wounded. With the town's limited resources stripped bare and the army's medical and supply trains parked far behind the lines during the battle, disaster loomed.

Father Burlando led the group to the town square, where the proprietor of McClellan's Hotel offered his parlor to the new arrivals. With its location at the confluence of several major highways, the square soon became the nerve center for various relief agencies. After observing the desperate state of affairs, the head priest returned to Emmitsburg for reinforcements.

The volunteers who arrived upon the scene were shocked by the deplorable condition of those left behind in the wake of the two armies. Most of the patients had not had their wounds dressed since their initial treatment; some not at all. Those too incapacitated to help themselves often lay in pools of blood, urine, and feces. Maggots writhed in open wounds while ubiquitous lice infested the hair and clothing of the men. These shattered individuals bore little resemblance to the crisp likenesses produced in photographers' studios so popular among the soldiers' loved ones.

The Sisters of Charity approached this daunting task with characteristic humility, often working with limited rest and with little regard for their personal comfort. At times the ladies tore up their own garments to produce makeshift bandages. They nursed the patients of both sides with equal compassion, ignoring rank, nationality, and religious affiliation. This example of devotion did much to deflect the discrimination directed against foreign born citizens, particularly Catholics, which had spread rampantly in the decade prior to the Civil War. Upon discovering that the nuns did not limit their attention to Catholic soldiers, an astonished relief worker declared to one of them, "I sincerely hope we shall all worship at the same altar one day." One grateful patient painted a heavenly metaphor: the "white cornet of the Sisters of Charity fluttered like angel's wings."

According to one study, Sisters Serena and Veronica were the only two nuns of Polish ancestry who nursed during the war. Being the only one of the two present at Gettysburg, Serena could claim this additional distinction. But through a fascinating twist of fate, she unexpectedly discovered the presence of another family member.

Making the rounds in an area field hospital Serena worked her way down the long line of soldiers performing grim duties that were becoming routine. As she sponged the blood and grime from the face of a young man thought to be mortally wounded, however, something extraordinary transpired. As the features of the patient became more recognizable, the nurse found herself looking into the eyes of her own brother.

Badly wounded on July 3 near Culp's Hill, Private Thaddeus Klimkiewicz had persevered to enjoy a surprise reunion with his sibling. "It entered into the designs of providence for me to nurse him just after he was wounded," recalled Sister Serena to a nephew following the war. She added, "He was then but eighteen, I a few years older." Serena quickly recovered from her initial shock and had her brother moved to a more convenient location so she could check on him daily.

With well over 20,000 wounded soldiers scattered throughout the borough and the surrounding countryside, the odds of this meeting taking place were decidedly slim. This fact should give pause to even the firmest of skeptics that a higher power directs the affairs of man. This dramatic story does not conclude with a happy ending, however, as Thaddeus died about a year after his wounding at Gettysburg.

Both Sister Serena and Sister Veronica devoted the remainder of their lives to the Holy Covenant. Assigned to St. Vincent's Manor in Buffalo, New York, in 1871, Serena died there in 1909 after 53 years with the Sisterhood. Veronica lived to the ripe age of 92, her religious life spanning over 75 years. Buried with full military honors, her body was lowered into the ground to the accompaniment of the solemn notes of Taps.

The obituary that appeared in the *Baltimore Catholic Review* of March 28, 1930, paid tribute to a lifetime of humanitarian service applicable to both Polish sisters:

> A heroine in war and peace was laid to rest.... Millions in this land will in the years to come stand in awe before the monuments of men whose names ring down the ages and whose fame spans the ocean's vast expanse. Few will stop to kneel at the grave of this brave woman who knew not cowardice, who walked mid disease when others fled, who bathed the brows of smallpox patients and who staunched the blood which gushed from the gaping wounds of the heroes of the Blue and the Gray.

An army chaplain agreed, stating that "The sisters do not have reunions or campfires to keep alive the memories of the most bloody lustrum in our history, but their war stories are as heroic, and far more edifying, than many the veterans tell."

The meeting of Sister Serena and her brother Thaddeus certainly ranks among the most unusual coincidences that took place during the war. Beyond the universal appeal of this story we should not lose sight of the fact that from the depths of a national cataclysm, a few long-held stereotypes and prejudices gradually faded away.

In 1924 a monument was unveiled in Washington, D.C., to honor the contributions of the various orders of Catholic nuns during the Civil War. It will be remembered that this was the birthplace of the Klimkiewicz children. The words of another former city resident are just as evocative as this beautiful memorial. A frequent visitor to military hospitals, President Abraham Lincoln voiced his warm admiration for the Sisters:

> Of all the forms of charity and benevolence seen in the crowded wards of the hospitals, those of the Catholic Sisters was among the most efficient. I never knew whence they came or the names of their order. More lovely than anything I have ever seen in art, so long devoted to illustration of love, mercy, and charity, are the pictures that remain of those modest Sisters going on their errands of mercy among the suffering and the dying.

Charles O. Hunt and Mary Carson

On July 7 Lieutenant Charles Hunt began writing a letter to his mother back home in Maine: "Here I am lying on my back in Mary's back parlor making myself as comfortable as possible. I suppose before this reaches you, you will have heard that I was one of the victims of the great fight at Gettysburg, but I hope you have heard no exaggerated account. My wound is very slight and I shall be about again in two weeks at most. And then, dear mother, I expect soon to give you a good solid hug in our own old house in Gorham. Won't that be worth getting wounded for? I do not think I would give up the wound, and with it the hope of getting home and seeing you.... I think I am the luckiest dog that ever lived. To think that I should have been wounded here! I have managed to get here every time that anything has been the matter with me."

Lucky indeed! Of the 14,000 wounded Union soldiers left behind in Gettysburg, Lieutenant Hunt was perhaps the only one who enjoyed convalescing at the residence of a family member. As it had on other occasions the home of Hunt's older sister provided him a safe refuge, setting the stage for one of the most unusual sibling reunions that took place during the battle.

Mary and Charles Oliver Hunt grew up together in Gorham, Maine, a town nestled in the shadows of coastal Portland, the state's largest city. Their father served in the Maine legislature and he encouraged all of his children to receive a quality education. Mary graduated from the Gorham Normal School and afterwards accepted a teaching position in far off Lancaster, Pennsylvania. It was here that she fell in love with Thomas Duncan Carson.

Thomas's father used his influence as a bank president to help his son secure a teller position with the Bank of Gettysburg in March of 1857. By November, Carson had been promoted to assistant cashier, and the following January he assumed the top position. Responsible for the institution's cash deposits, records, and other valuables, the head cashier performed duties comparable to a modern bank manager. In mid–June 1863, as news of the Southern invasion of Pennsylvania became known, Carson set out for Philadelphia to deposit nearly $100,000 for safekeeping. The bank closed its doors about a week before the battle and did not resume operations until July 27.

At the time of the battle the Carson family resided in the bank building three doors down from the town square on the north side of York Street. According to the 1860 census, the household consisted of Thomas and Mary Carson, both of whom were listed as being 27 years of age, the couple's two-year-old son Robert, and Ann Rollman, a 19-year-old domestic. In 1862 Mary gave birth to a baby girl that was named after her.

Graduating Phi Beta Kappa from Bowdoin College in 1861, Charles Hunt was swept up by patriotic fervor and the 21-year-old student enlisted as a quartermaster sergeant in Battery E, 5th Maine Light Artillery. From a total of about 1,200 students and alumni, nearly 300 Bowdoin men served in Union forces during the conflict. Although overshadowed by the achievements of his professor, Joshua Lawrence Chamberlain, Hunt's service also spanned most of the war and, he, too, went on to enjoy considerable success in later years.

By the time the six Napoleon guns of Captain Greenleaf T. Stevens' Battery E rumbled onto Seminary Ridge on the morning of July 1, 1863, Charles Hunt was a freshly minted second lieutenant in charge of a two-gun battery section. Following the death of General John F. Reynolds earlier in the day, General Abner Doubleday took command. Determined to strengthen the Union lines on McPherson's Ridge, the general began transforming Seminary Ridge into a reserve position by ordering the digging of entrenchments and massing a large concentration of artillery near the crest.

Throughout the afternoon a steady stream of walking wounded and teams of stretcher bearers picked their way through the line of artillerymen to reach the aid station at the main seminary edifice. Then, at around 4:00 p.m., the decimated infantry regiments of the First Corps, many of them reduced in strength by a half or three-quarters, filled in the gaps between the cannon in preparation for a final stand before retiring to Cemetery Hill.

There would be no letup. A fresh wave of Confederate troops belonging to General Dorsey Pender's famed "Light Division" appeared on the crest of McPherson's Ridge about 500 yards to the west. For a moment the waiting Union cannoneers looked on in admiration at the martial display. The gaunt Southern veterans strode confidently across the open field in straight, double-ranked battle lines marked at regular intervals by their crimson regimental standards.

Charles O. Hunt, ca. 1890 (courtesy Maine Medical Center, Portland, Maine).

Suddenly, all hell broke loose as the gunners swung into action. They moved with machine-like precision—load, fire, swab; load, fire, swab. The iron storm cut huge swaths in the well-ordered attack formation, but the Confederates kept coming, closing the gaps, pushing relentlessly forward with a fluidity that seemed unstoppable. Lieutenant Hunt and his fellow section commanders switched from long range ordnance to canister rounds as the battle neared its climax.

Taking cover along a stone fence about 50 yards from the entrenchments, enemy riflemen peppered away at the exposed artillery crews. As he stood behind his guns a bullet struck Hunt's pistol, breaking a two-inch piece from the ramrod and driving it into the outer portion of his right thigh.

Not long afterwards, a brigade of South Carolinians punched a hole through the First Corps defenses below the seminary and swept northward along the ridge. General James Wadsworth rode up to Captain Stevens, ordering him to limber up his pieces and retire to Cemetery Hill. Although he normally took orders from the corps artillery commander, Colonel Charles Wainwright, Stevens was not about to question the general's authority. Hitched to the caissons and guns, the battery horses trotted eastward on the Chambersburg Pike towards Gettysburg. A short time later, Wainwright ordered the remainder of the batteries to clear out as the thinning infantry line finally collapsed.

Fired at by converging lines of Southern troops, the retreat of the First Corps disintegrated into a wild and desperate scramble. These soldiers had cut across the fields bordering the Emmitsburg Road to reach Seminary Ridge and were unfamiliar with the layout of the town. Unlike the vast majority of the fugitives, Lieutenant Hunt knew the area well. Earlier in the day, he also took the precaution of instructing his men to deposit him at his sister's house in the event of injury.

As the lead elements of the two armies converged upon their town, the Carson family and other Gettysburg residents nervously peered out of windows or gathered at strategic vantage points in an effort to track the progress of the looming fight. A half century afterwards, Robert Carson related his boyhood experiences, still fresh in his memory, to a Philadelphia newspaper reporter. According to Robert, his father joined a group of neighborhood men on the roof of Judge David Wills' house until it became too dangerous to remain there. Meanwhile, in the large room over the bank, his mother and other women worked to produce lint and bandages.

The initial curiosity turned to horror for children and adults alike. "I shall always remember the storm of Rebel shells raining about our house through a back window at the foot of a short flight of stairs leading to the attic," recalled Robert. One of these projectiles shattered the window frame and sash then bounced down the winding stairs before coming to rest in the front hall. In another instance an unexploded shell entered the structure. "We felt thankful that all 'rebel' shells were not perfect in construction," remembered a neighbor who had sought refuge in the bank. It seems that close calls were the order of the day. A number of iron fragments also struck the wall over the cradle of the Carson's infant daughter, who slept contentedly as the battle raged.

As the Union lines around the perimeter of the town collapsed, the citizens began to take cover in their cellars. Mrs. Carson proposed the bank vault as a temporary shelter and soon nineteen women and children, two dogs and a cat huddled together in the cramped quarters. From outside on the street came a cacophony of disturbing sounds: the heavy tread of shoes striking against the pavement, the screams and desperate shouts of the pursued and the pursuers, intermingled with the sharp crack of muskets and pistols, whizzing bullets, and the occasional deep roar of an artillery piece. In the midst of this chaos came a loud knock at the door. A messenger informed Mary Carson that her brother had been wounded and was now waiting outside.

Upon his arrival the lieutenant noticed that the civilians hiding in the bank vault appeared to be dreadfully frightened. On the other hand, he was astonished at his sister's calm demeanor. "I expected that it would upset her for the next two years, but she did not seem to mind it in the least," he later wrote. Mary Carson ordered that her younger brother be taken to an upstairs bedroom and she then summoned a local physician.

After the successful extraction of the piece of metal, Robert was escorted into the room by his mother. Reassured of the patient's well-being, the youngster's curiosity kicked in. His request to see the foreign object that struck his uncle was granted when another visitor took it from a nearby bureau and placed it before him. The mottled, discolored appearance of the relic made a strong impression upon his mind.

The tense encounters of the day were far from over, however. Not long after the operation a squad of Confederate soldiers searched the house for Union soldiers. Before they entered, the recuperating officer was hastily carried down to the cellar where he was placed upon a large box in which Mary's piano had been shipped from her former home in Maine. When the danger passed Hunt returned to his room. Suddenly, two Southern officers came inside and discovered their Northern counterpart. Fortunately, they proved to be "very gentlemanly." Expressing their regrets at Hunt's wounding, the two men left and did not return. "I was in the adjoining room and could hear voices and laughter and finally, their farewell and footsteps as they passed the door," recalled a relieved Robert, who feared that his uncle would be taken away.

Following the Confederate retreat the Carsons and their neighbors soon endured a second invasion. "Gettysburg is full of strangers from all parts of the country," wrote Charles Hunt in his initial letter home. "Some come from motives of curiosity, some to relieve the wounded." Since his wounds were not of a serious nature, Hunt could entertain visitors. His favorite guest was his younger brother Henry, also an artillerist in the First Corps. After the fighting ended, Henry visited daily with his two older siblings, and on the evening of July 5 he slept on the floor beside his brother. The next day the corps marched into Maryland to begin the pursuit of Lee's army.

Hunt's condition continued to improve. On the sixteenth, he assured his mother, "I am getting along nicely. My wound does not discharge as much as it did, and the new flesh is coming fast. I have not been dressed yet, as the doctor thinks it will be better for me to keep as quiet as possible. I shall be up in a few days, though, and in less then two weeks I think there is no doubt you shall see me in Gorham."

He was right. Hunt departed Gettysburg on July 28. His "million dollar wound" gained him a hug from his mom and the opportunity to attend commencement exercises at his alma mater.

A day after Hunt's departure, Charles Fuller, a lieutenant in the 61st New York who lost both an arm and a leg, arrived at the Carson residence. "When I was deposited at his house, Mr. Carson was in Philadelphia to get and return the bank's property," recalled Fuller, "but Mrs. Carson was there, and, if I had been a near relative, she could not have done more to make my stay tolerable."

Towards the middle of November, Gettysburg residents withstood a third invasion of their town when Lincoln arrived to deliver his immortal address at the consecration of the national cemetery. The Carson family played an important role in the ceremonies. Mary sat on the speaker's platform with Maine governor Abner Coburn, who stayed at her home during his visit. Following Lincoln's remarks Thomas Carson arose and led a local choir in the singing of a dirge.

Lieutenant Hunt did not return to active duty for three months, his recovery protracted by a case of gangrene that caused partial destruction of the muscle. Captured during the initial assault on Petersburg on June 18, 1864, he was transported to Camp Oglethorpe, a prison complex for Federal officers in Macon, Georgia. Near the end of July he was among the 600 Federal officers removed to Charleston, South Carolina, to be placed under the fire of Union mortar guns that pounded the city daily from strategic positions on the harbor.

An epidemic of yellow fever forced the evacuation of the inmates to Columbia, where they were herded into a four-acre field two miles west of the city. The makeshift complex became known as Camp Sorghum from the issuance of large quantities of sorghum molasses as rations. The lack of an adequate guard detail and the absence of a stockade led to a rash of escapes.

On the afternoon of November 3, 1864, Hunt and two fellow Maine officers escaped while pretending to be part of a wood chopping detail. Traveling by night and depending upon the kindness of Negroes and loyal Unionists, the trio hiked nearly 400 miles to the foothills of the Blue Ridge in western North Carolina before being recaptured about a month later. Hunt lamented, "We did not secure the freedom we hoped for when we left Columbia, and we suffered many hardships from cold, hunger and weariness, but we never regretted having made the attempt." He would remain a prisoner for the rest of the war and was officially discharged from the army on July 6, 1865.

In 1867 the Carson family moved to Philadelphia after Thomas secured a top post at a large banking and insurance institution. The couple raised five children there and spent the rest of their lives in the city.

Upon returning home to Maine both of the Hunt brothers studied medicine and went on to become prominent physicians. Charles graduated from the Bowdoin Medical College in 1867, received his M.D. from the University of Pennsylvania a year later, and in 1887 earned a masters degree from Bowdoin. After operating a practice in his native Gorham for a year, he relocated to Portland. Dr. Hunt was the superintendent of the Maine General Hospital for 28 years and was elected president of the Maine Medical Association in 1899.

The close bond that existed between Charles and his sister continued to grow. On May 25, 1871, Charles married Cornelia Davidson Carson, the sister of Thomas Carson, in Lancaster, Pennsylvania. Thus, brother and sister married a brother and a sister. While riding his bicycle in Portland on the morning of July 24, 1909, Hunt, then 70 years of age, suffered a fatal heart attack.

8

Homecomings

Yes, beloved ones at home, we remember,
Ah, how can the soldier forget?
All the vows that were said when we parted
Are sacred and dear to him yet.
When the night throws its mantle around us,
We dream 'neath the heaven's starry dome
Of the dear ones whose sweet spell has bound us
And whose voices shall welcome us home.

"Can the Soldier Forget?,"
Charles Boynton, 1864

Henry N. Minnigh, USA

Growing up in rural Pennsylvania before the advent of the video age, my friends and I often staged elaborate mock battles that usually featured Yanks and Rebs or cowboys and Indians. The cornfields and wood lots surrounding our home provided the perfect environment for these war games. At times my childhood imagination transformed play into near reality. Crouched unseen behind a tree, my adrenalin pumped wildly whenever an "enemy soldier" approached my position. But when our panting cocker spaniel sniffed out my lair or Mom called us in for dinner, the dreamlike trance came to an end. Admittedly, if conditions became a bit too real, these interruptions were most welcome.

Conversely, a group of Union soldiers recruited from the Gettysburg area found themselves immersed in the desperate battle for Little Round Top on July 2, 1863, where in earlier years they had often played hide and seek, hunted for small game, or gathered berries. This surreal circumstance earned the 51 members of Company K, 1st Pennsylvania Reserves, the distinction of being among the very few Northern units in regular service that fought on their home soil during the course of the war.

Nearly three decades later, Henry Naileigh Minnigh, who would rise from private to captain, attempted to describe the emotions experienced by himself and his comrades:

> We had gone out two years before, to conquer the enemy on his own soil, but were now returning, after two years of struggle, to meet him face to face at our own door. What the feeling of each member of the company was, under these circumstances, may be better imagined than described, for we had seen enough of the ravages of warfare in the southland, to cause us to be anxious for the welfare of our loved ones, now exposed in like manner.

196

Back on June 8, 1861, Minnigh had signed his name to the company muster-in roll just hours before the unit boarded a train that would transport them to an instructional camp. He would go on to experience one of the strangest homecomings ever recorded.

Born on April 7, 1838, on the family farm near Gettysburg, he was among the nine children of Henry S. and Elizabeth Minnigh. By the time of the battle Henry resided in town with a family of his own. Dropping out of his junior year at Pennsylvania College to become a schoolteacher, he wed Miss Lisle Eppleman of Bendersville in 1858. Over the next two years Lisle gave birth to two sons; but just six weeks before the arrival of John Harry Minnigh on December 17, 1860, eighteen-month-old William died.

Perhaps this loss factored into the young father's reluctance to leave his family the following summer even as many of his friends and neighbors rushed to enlist. Minnigh might have been comforted by the fact that at this point his parents also resided in the borough at present day 69 West Middle Street.

Whatever finally prompted this last minute decision, the soldiers of Company K would learn to be grateful for it. The bloody campaigns in Virginia and Maryland had transformed the raw recruits into hardened veterans, and by the summer of 1863 Minnigh had risen to the rank of first lieutenant. He would be promoted to captain later in the year. By all accounts he was a well-respected leader. Private William T. Jobe declared: "As a soldier, Capt. Minnigh's record is an enviable one, he led the company with gallantry and spirit on all occasions, securing the commendations of his superior officers, for bravery and good behavior, under trying circumstances."

But his greatest attribute was the personal attention that he gave to the men. Corporal Robert T. McKinney fondly recalled that during a tiring march, his commander, noting his feeble condition, immediately relieved him of his arms and equipment which he then carried in addition to his own.

An even greater example occurred during the Battle of South Mountain in September 1862. Late in the day, as the Reserves struggled up the steep mountainside towards the final enemy defensive position, a bullet tore into Minnigh's shoulder, knocking him out of the action. Not far away, Lieutenant J. Durbin Sadler fell dead. After the regimental surgeon removed a large piece of fractured bone from the wound site, Minnigh resolved to secure Sadler's body and take it home to York Springs, over fifty miles distant, for proper burial.

Procuring a hearse and a driver at the home of a relative in nearby Middletown, the determined officer borrowed a suit of civilian clothes to evade the provost guard. He was taking a huge risk. The military justice system meted out severe punishments for unauthorized absences, including execution. Fortunately, Minnigh returned from his errand of mercy without incident.

Drained of manpower by the endless succession of battles, the Reserves shifted into the defenses of Washington in February of 1863 to rest and to recruit new members. But four months later, with their native state in peril, the Pennsylvanians rejoined the Army of the Potomac. Without the advantage of hindsight, Lieutenant Minnigh and the soldiers of Company K had no idea that the series of long marches would lead to their own doorsteps.

Approaching Gettysburg from the east along the Baltimore Pike, the men were greeted with the sight of familiar scenes and faces. On the other hand, many of the observers could not distinguish the hometown heroes from the other soldiers. Sergeant Isaac Durboraw recalled, "Some young ladies whom I recognized, as we passed along, not far from my home, and who were waving their handkerchiefs at the soldiers passing by, gazed at me in amazement as I named them, and as they did not recognize me, inquired one of another, who that could be that knew them."

Just before noon, after reaching a point about one mile east of Cemetery Ridge, the column veered to the left onto a smaller byroad. Soon a halt was called and the exhausted Reserves collapsed to the ground near the Isaac Diehl farm. The peaceful interlude lasted several hours until shouts of "Fall in!" jarred the dozing warriors.

A hurried march ended on the northwest slope of Little Round Top as the sun began to sink behind South Mountain off on the western horizon. The sights and sounds that drifted up from the valley floor contrasted sharply from the idyllic childhood memories cherished by so many members of Company K.

At various intervals the thick smoke would rise like a curtain to reveal a hellish scene. Singly and in small groups, Yankee soldiers, closely pursued by the victorious enemy, scrambled up the rocky hillside. A German artillerist pleaded in broken English, "Dunder and Blixen, don't let dem repels took my batteries." Unearthly screams, shouted orders, and whizzing projectiles filled the air.

Was it merely a bad dream?

They had little time to ponder. Hastily forming a battle line, the Reserves swept downhill, picking their way around the huge boulders to hurl themselves against the surging mass of humanity. Disorganized and exhausted by several hours of hard fighting, the surprised Southerners gave way. The momentum of the charge carried the Pennsylvanians all the way across the Wheatfield. They later pulled back to a stone fence that bordered the eastern edge of the field. Little Round Top held.

On the following day the men skirmished with their opponents across the no-man's land that was littered with hundreds of the slain and dying. Following the collapse of Pickett's Charge the Reserves cleared out pockets of resistance in theWheatfield as the Confederates realigned on Seminary Ridge. Afterwards, they went into bivouac on the reverse slope of Little Round Top.

Minnigh was justifiably proud of his command. "These brave fellows could easily imagine the dangerous surroundings of loved ones.... Not a man left the ranks or fled from duty, and while most of them got home after the battle ... only one failed to return."

The lieutenant was among those who slipped off for a brief visit. The town of Gettysburg was still in Southern hands, however, and Minnigh experienced more difficulties than a teenager attempting to sneak into his room after curfew. He described these adventures in his history of Company K.

> I passed northward just in the rear of the line of battle, and through the Citizens cemetery, thence up Baltimore Street to the Court-house on the corner of Middle street, which was a dangerous performance, as the whole route was exposed to rebel sharp-shooters, making it necessary to cross all streets and alleys at a bound. Having reached the point indicated, I found the residence of my father, on west Middle street one square from the Court-house, so completely covered by rebel sharp-shooters, that it was an impossible measure to go there.
>
> I observed things closely, and saw a certain officer who was apparently not acquainted with the dangerous surroundings, turn the corner where I was standing, and walk deliberately down in the middle of the street, without being molested, but, Alas! The poor fellow when he got below Washington street, was taken prisoner. So I took advantage of what I had seen, and walked down the street, with misgivings I confess, for doubtless many rifles were aimed at me, with a rebel finger on each trigger, ready to send as many messengers

of death, if I should turn either to the right or to the left. It was an awful moment, but I determined to carry out my plan, which was to spring into a flower garden on the east side of the house, when I would reach that point, for I would then be in a safe place.

On! On, to hesitate would be fatal; and how terrible it would be to die so near to the loved ones; still on I went, not hurriedly, for the enemy must not even think that I have a purpose in view; Oh! If only the yard gates were open! Ah, it is open! A spring, and I am through it, and behind the cover of the house; I am safe, but what a shower of Minnie balls strike the pavement over which I came, and how they tear through the palings of the fence on both sides of the open gate, terrible messengers they are, but harmless now as far they concerned me.

None of the family were visible, so I entered the unlocked door of a back kitchen, which was empty, then into the main building I went and all through it from main floor to attic, and found no one; disappointed I turned to the cellar and was met on the stair-way by a sister, who failed to recognize me in the semi-darkness, who said, "Here! What do you want?" On the spur of the moment I said, "Can you supply me with just a bite to eat?" With this she retired below and I followed to the foot of the stairs, and took a seat near the lower step, and this is what I then saw: father and mother, four sisters and a brother, two or three improvised beds, an almost consumed tallow dip on the end of a barrel in a far off corner, and each person being a perfect image of dejection and despondency.

Sister Lucy whispered something to mother, who then entered an adjoining pantry, doubtless to get the "bite to eat," while a younger sister approached me inquiring, "I wonder how much longer we will have to remain in this cellar?" I merely answered, "Not long," but I discovered that they were entirely ignorant of the state of affairs without. She looked at me closely, and then followed mother into the pantry.

Presently, mother approached me, bearing a huge piece of bread in her hand, and peering very closely into my face, then as if in glad surprise, she ejaculated, "Oh, you bad fellow, I know you now! Here's your supper."

I will not attempt a portrayal of the scene that followed, but in a few words I revealed the state of affairs without, and brought them from that lower world, in which they had dwelt several days, into the light and comfort of the upper world once more.

Soon an ample supper spread the board, and then all retired to the comfortable beds, of which they had been deprived for two nights, and I had not enjoyed for two years. That night the Confederate army began the evacuation of Gettysburg.

When the Reserves came home for good the following summer, it was Henry's turn to be surprised. Entering his parents' home as the family prepared to sit down for dinner, Mrs. Minnigh proudly introduced her son to the guests. Staring at the recent arrival for a long moment, a young lady laughed and clapped her hands, "Oh, Mrs. M., do you remember I told you about a sick officer taking two pies from auntie's dining table, down at Lovettsville, Virginia?" Not waiting for a reply, she pointed at Henry, "That's the very fellow!"

After working as a War Department clerk and later resuming his teaching duties, Minnigh discovered his true calling. Entering the ministry of the Methodist Episcopal Church in 1871, the 33-year-old veteran discovered a natural outlet for the charisma and compassion he had so often displayed during the course of the war. During his ensuing 35 years of ministry, Reverend Minnigh preached 6,025 sermons, performed 833 baptisms, married 105 couples, and added 2,254 members to the church rolls.

Upon retirement he moved back to Gettysburg, where he died on November 26, 1915. The burial took place at the Soldiers' National Cemetery. It was claimed that he was the last living member of Company K that resided in the area.

Adams County has a proud tradition of honoring the service of its citizen soldiers. Accordingly, on June 29, 1991, a monument was dedicated on the southwest quadrant of Lincoln Square to honor "The Boys Who Fought at Home."

Company K of the 1st Pennsylvania Reserves in camp at Fairfax Station, Virginia, on June 4, 1863. Lieutenant Henry Minnigh is the officer standing on the left front of the formation. Corporal Henry Harrison Beamer appears over Minnigh's right shoulder in the front rank (National Archives).

Henry Beamer, USA, and Henry Wentz, CSA

In his three years of service with Company K, 1st Pennsylvania Reserves, it was said that Corporal Henry Harrison Beamer was not absent from the company a single day. Captain Henry Minnigh extolled him as "a soldier that never shirked duty, and was always on hand." This achievement is even more remarkable when one considers that this 24-year-old soldier fought in proximity to his home at Gettysburg.

On the early evening of July 2, 1863, as the 1st Reserves stood on Little Round Top, Corporal Beamer must certainly have glanced over his left shoulder towards the family farm situated one mile to the southwest. It must have been tempting for the eldest of Jacob and Ann Maria (Wentz) Beamer's ten children to quietly slip away from the ranks. How quickly he could have escaped the madness surrounding him by stepping into a world of familiar security. And, after a two year absence, how sweet it would have been to warmly embrace a loved one. Somehow, Beamer pushed back these urges, leaving his perfect record untarnished.

The story does not end there, however. The twilight charge of the Reserves through the Valley of Death carried the young corporal to within less than a mile of another familiar property. At the time of the battle his maternal grandfather lived at the intersection of the Emmitsburg and Wheatfield Roads on a two-acre tract of land near the famous Peach Orchard. When Union Third Corps commander Major General Daniel Sickles advanced his troops to occupy this ground on the afternoon of July 2, several Federal batteries took up positions adjacent to the Wentz house and two nearby outbuildings. While other members of the household vacated the premise, John Wentz, by then in his late 70s, stubbornly remained behind.

The war-period Wentz house was a one-and-a-half story log structure with two rooms on the first floor, making it similar in size and construction to the Lydia Leister house on Cemetery Ridge, site of General Meade's headquarters for most of the battle. During the next two days the elderly Wentz sought refuge in the cellar. If he had not done so it very well might have cost him his life.

A sharp duel soon erupted between the Union guns and Confederate batteries located a mere 700 yards away. It is likely that all three of the structures on the Wentz property sustained considerable damage. Afterwards, Colonel William Barksdale's brigade of Mississippi troops shattered Sickles' line at the Peach Orchard and charged onward towards Cemetery Ridge, but a series of well-timed Union counterattacks prevented the Confederates from breaching the final line of defenses.

At this point the story takes another strange twist. After the fighting finally died away on the southern end of the battlefield, a soldier stepped into the Wentz home. One might assume that Corporal Beamer snuck through the lines to check on his grandfather, but this was not the case. Rather, the soldier in question was a closer relative who wore a Confederate uniform!

In his 1931 history of the battle, William C. Storrick presented an unlikely vignette that shares numerous similarities with that of Wesley Culp, one of the most legendary and tragic figures connected with Gettysburg.

> For many years before the beginning of the Civil War, carriage and coach building was one of the leading industries of Gettysburg. Henry Wentz served an apprenticeship with the Ziegler firm of Gettysburg. He was frequently sent to deliver the products of the firm, and thereby became well acquainted with the different sections where sales were made.

In the early 50s he decided to move to Martinsburg, Va. (now West Virginia), and establish a carriage-building shop of his own. When a local military organization was formed and designated the "Martinsburg Blues," Henry became a member.... Most of the members ... including Henry Wentz, decided to cast their lot with the Southern cause, and were assigned to places in the armies of the South. But, by the irony of fate, he was destined to get back to his old home and command a battery posted back of the house on his father's land.

...On the night of the second day, after Sickles' advanced line at the Wentz house had been repulsed and occupied by the forces under General Lee, Henry Wentz visited his old home and was greatly surprised to find his father still there.

Early in the morning of the third day, 75 guns, in command of Colonel E. P. Alexander, were moved forward.... The battery in charge of Henry Wentz, who held the rank of lieutenant, was posted back of his old home, and he took an active part in the terrific artillery engagement prior to Pickett's Charge that ended on that part of the field. Henry's father kept to the cellar and, singularly, passed through it all unharmed and unhurt.

After the repulse of Pickett's Charge, the guns were withdrawn to their first line. During the night of the third day, Henry was anxious to know whether or not his father was still safe. He therefore went over to the house and found him fast asleep and unhurt in a corner of the cellar. Not wishing to disturb his much-needed rest, he found the stump of a candle, lit it, and wrote, "Good-bye and God bless you!" This message he pinned on the lapel of his father's coat and returned to his command preparatory to the retreat to Virginia.

Since one of Storrick's older sisters married Henry Beamer in 1868, the historian gleaned numerous details of the incident from family members. Nonetheless, a few errors crept into the account. Storrick mistakenly reported Wentz as being a lieutenant in charge of a battery section, when in fact he had only attained the rank of orderly or first sergeant. Also, by 1860 the 30-year-old Gettysburg native was no longer working in the carriage industry. On the 1860 census, he listed his occupation as a plasterer, and resided in the Martinsburg home of 60-year-old George Toup, also a plasterer by trade.

Wentz must have felt a deep sense of loyalty to his adopted state, as he enlisted in the Confederate service at the outset of the war. By the time of the Battle of Gettysburg he belonged to a battery commanded by Captain Osmond B. Taylor, part of Colonel Edward Porter Alexander's Battalion. The available evidence strongly supports the unlikely happenstance that Sergeant Wentz fought in his father's backyard. Even more remarkable, in his 1995 study, *Early Photography at Gettysburg*, historian William Frassanito disclosed that Henry owned nearly ten acres of land adjacent to his father's property.

One of the enduring minor mysteries of the Gettysburg Campaign is the complete omission of Wentz's ties to the area in the official reports submitted by his superiors. Perhaps the five-feet, eight-inch sergeant with black hair and hazel eyes made a concerted effort to suppress this information. Certainly, his familiarity of the local terrain and roads would have been invaluable to the Southern cause, particularly during General James Longstreet's circuitous flank march on July 2.

Was Henry Wentz a conflicted man during the invasion of his native state and, indeed, his very birthplace? How did his service in the Confederate army affect his relationship with family members?

Two contemporary accounts indicate that a deep divide had developed between Henry and his parents. A soldier in the 16th Michigan Infantry entered this information in his diary:

On Sunday morning, July 5th, I was ordered to take a detail of men from my regiment and proceed to that part of the field near the Emmitsburg Road in the direction of the peach orchard, for the purpose of burying the Confederate dead. I took up my work near the (Wentz) house. I ordered the men to dig a trench in the garden to the left and in front of the house, near the road. Later, I looked up and saw an old man and old woman approaching. They were the owners of the house.

They turned into the yard, but instead of noticing the partial destruction, at least, of their home, barn, out-houses, fences, etc., they busied themselves in gathering the tender branches of the mulberry tree or bush—for what purpose, I could not determine, until they entered the house, which was a 1-story log building literally perforated by shot and shell, and climbed the stairway to the attic where, suspended from the rafters, were hammocks filled with silkworms, which they commenced to feed. I engaged them in conservation. They told me of their work, etc. In a short time we descended to the front of their house. The bodies of the dead were being hauled in from the field to the trench and among the number was an artillery officer.

Papers were found upon the body indicating the same name as the family. I called their attention to it. They replied, "Yes, yes, we had a son who left our home and went to Virginia. The last we heard of him he was in Confederate service. But we disowned our son and will have nothing to do with the body if it is he."

I buried the remains in the trench with others. Think of this incident for a moment. This disowned son, a Rebel, killed and buried in the door yard where he was brought up—how pathetic.

Later that same day, a volunteer of the United States Christian Commission reported the following:

[A]t the house of old Mr. Bentz [Wentz], whose son had been south for 16 years, and came home on the day before the battle as a captain of a Rebel battery. His guns, during the fight, drew the fire of our batteries directly across his father's house, and some of his own shot struck the house and barn. The son was killed, but the father was so good a Union man that he would not consent either to look on the corpse or the grave of his miscreant son.

While these accounts may reveal the feelings of John and Mary Wentz, their son's body was not among those buried in a trench along the road. Because, unlike Wesley Culp, Sergeant Wentz survived the battle and was present for duty with his unit until captured at Sailor's Creek, Virginia, on April 6, 1865. Following a brief imprisonment at Point Lookout, Maryland, he was released after taking the oath of allegiance on June 21.

Apparently, Wentz returned to Martinsburg and resumed his prewar occupation. In the spring of 1872, following the deaths of his father, mother, and sister Susan within three years, Henry Wentz came home for probably the last time. Legal documents indicate that he sold both his father's property and his own parcel of land at this time. Although the "miscreant son" had not been cut out of the will, was the relationship with his parents ever restored?

Recently, licensed battlefield guide Jim Clouse located Henry's grave at Green Hill Cemetery in Martinsburg. Interestingly, he is buried among members of the Toup family. Did George Toup serve as a surrogate father to the wayward son of a Pennsylvania farmer? We will never know the answer to this question. However, Mr. Clouse's subsequent discovery of Wentz's obituary in the December 14, 1875, edition of the *Martinsburg Statesman* describes the final moments of his life:

On last Friday night, Mr. Henry Wentz, a plasterer by trade, of this city, died very suddenly at the Everett House. He had been unwell for some weeks, but appeared to be recovering. The day of his death he seemed as well as usual, ate a hearty supper, and at an early hour retired. Not being able to sleep, he arose and came down into the hotel sitting-room and remained until about 11 o'clock, when he again retired. Mr. C. Rice assisted him to his room, and was in the act of removing his boots, when Mr. W. fell over and expired. Mr. W. was a brave Confederate soldier, and a good citizen. He was a native of Gettysburg, Pa., his father being the owner of the field on which that memorable battle was fought, in which Mr. W. was a participant. He was 47 years of age....

The Beamer family eventually learned of this incident as well. An 1886 history of Adams County briefly discusses the proximity of uncle and nephew during the second day at Gettysburg in a biographical sketch of one of the family members.

After turning in his rifle, Henry Beamer spent several years constructing railroads in the west before coming home in 1868. At this time he married Maria Storrick and opened up a grocery store on West Middle Street. But in 1875 the versatile entrepreneur moved his growing family to Knox County, Illinois, where he took up farming and later established a successful coal and lumber business.

Unlike his uncle, who apparently spent much of his short life isolated from family members, Beamer was surrounded by loved ones right up until his death in 1907. Although they must have experienced many of the same emotions on July 2, 1863, these two relatives may have never met afterwards.

Notes

Introduction

1. Richard A. Baumgartner, *Buckeye Blood: Ohio at Gettysburg* (Huntington, WV: Blue Acorn Press, 2003), 113–114.

2. Reverend F. J. F. Schantz, "Recollections of Visitations at Gettysburg after the Great Battle in July, 1863," *Reflections on the Battle of Gettysburg*, vol.13, no. 6 (The Lebanon County Historical Society, 1963): 295.

3. For an excellent discussion on the relationship of the Civil War soldier to his community see Reid Mitchell, *The Vacant Chair* (New York: Oxford University Press, 1993), 19–37.

4. Rod Gragg, *Covered with Glory: The 26th North Carolina Infantry at the Battle of Gettysburg* (New York: HarperCollins, 2000), 102.

5. Research notes of Sue Boardman, Licensed Battlefield Guide, Gettysburg National Military Park.

6. Charles I. Glicksberg, ed., *Walt Whitman and the Civil War: A Collection of Original Articles and Manuscripts* (New York: A. S. Barnes and Company, Inc., 1963), 159.

7. Lydia Ziegler Clare, "A Gettysburg Girl's Story of the Great Battle," Civilian Files, Adams County Historical Society, Gettysburg, PA. (Hereafter referred to ACHS).

8. Anna Holstein, *Three Years in Field Hospitals of the Army of the Potomac* (Philadelphia: J. B. Lippincott, 1867), 46–47; John W. Busey, *These Honored Dead: The Union Casualties at Gettysburg* (Hightstown, NJ: Longstreet, 1996), 257.

9. Mitchell, *The Vacant Chair*, 35.

10. Michael Dreese, *The 151st Pennsylvania at Gettysburg: Like Ripe Apples in a Storm* (Jefferson, NC: McFarland, 2000), 23.

11. Ibid.

12. Willard A. Heaps and Porter W. Heaps, *The Singing Sixties: The Spirit of Civil War Days Drawn from the Music of the Times* (Norman: University of Oklahoma Press, 1960), 132–133, 224–226; Bell Irvin Wiley, *The Life of Billy Yank* (Baton Rouge: Louisiana State University Press, 1952), 161–162.

13. Francis T. Miller, ed., *The Photographic History of the Civil War*, vol. 5 (New York: Review of Reviews Co., 1911), 150.

14. Harry W. Pfanz, *Gettysburg: Culp's Hill & Cemetery Hill* (Chapel Hill: University of North Carolina Press, 1993), 258–259.

15. Heaps and Heaps, *The Singing Sixties*, 162.

16. Miller, *The Photographic History of the Civil War*, 5:350.

17. Kathy Georg Harrison, *Nothing but Glory: Pickett's Division at Gettysburg* (Gettysburg: Thomas Publications, 2001), 52.

18. Geoffrey C. Ward, Ric Burns, and Ken Burns, *The Civil War: An Illustrated History* (New York: Knopf, 1990), 82–83.

19. Melvin Dwinnell to "Dear Parents," August 6, 1861, 8th Georgia Infantry Website, Dave Larson, webmaster, http://www.home.earthlink.net/~larsrbl/8thGeorgiaInfantry.html.

20. Baumgartner, *Buckeye Blood*, 182.

21. Charles A. Fuller, *Personal Recollections of the War of 1861* (Sherburne, NY: New Job Printing, 1906), 104.

22. Andrew B. Cross, *The Battle of Gettysburg and the Christian Commission* (Baltimore: United States Christian Commission, 1865), 3.

Chapter 1: Fathers and Sons

Samuel and Bayard Wilkeson

Samuel Wilkeson, "Thrilling Word Picture of Gettysburg," *New York Times*, July 7, 1863; Frank Wilkeson Biography, http://www.geocites.com/skagitjournal/Wilkeson1; Samuel Wilkeson Biography, Virtual American Biographies, http://www.famousamericans.net/samuelwilkeson; J. Howard Wert, "Little Stories of Gettysburg," Gettysburg *Compiler*, September 28, 1907; Oliver O. Howard, "After the Battle: Some Incidents and Observations at Gettysburg," *Philadelphia Weekly Times*, December 13, 1884; Robert U. Johnson and Clarence C. Buel, editors, *Battles and Leaders of the Civil War*, 4 vols. (New York: 1884–1888), vol. 3, p. 281; *The War of the Rebellion: A Compilation of the Official Records of the Union and Confederate Armies*, 79 vols. in 128 parts (Washington, DC: Government Printing Office, 1880–1901), vol. 27, part 1, pp. 748, 756 (Hereafter referred to as *OR*); Edmund J. Raus, Jr., *A Generation on the March: The Union Army at Gettysburg* (Gettysburg: Thomas Publications, 1996), pp. 160–161; Busey, *These Honored Dead*, p. 329.

Isaac and William Fisher

William J. Fisher Papers, Gettysburg National Military Park Library; Dana B. Shoaf, "Death of a Regular," *America's Civil War* (July 2002), pp. 50–57; Harry W. Pfanz, *Gettysburg: The Second Day* (Chapel Hill: University of North Carolina Press, 1987), pp. 295–301; Mark Grimsley and Brooks D. Simpson, *Gettysburg: A Battlefield Guide* (Lincoln: University of Nebraska Press, 1999), pp. 100–107; John W. Busey and David G. Martin, *Regimental Strengths and Losses at Gettysburg* (Hightstown, NJ: Longstreet, 1982), pp. 248–249. The extensive letter and memorabilia collection of William J. Fisher was purchased by the Friends of the National Parks at Gettysburg in 2001 and donated to the Gettysburg National Military Park.

James and Albion Mills

Holstein, *Three Years in Field Hospitals of the Army of the Potomac*, p. 46; Francis Wiggin, "Sixteenth Maine Regiment at Gettysburg," *War Papers Read Before the Commandery of the State of Maine, Military Order of the Loyal Legion of the United States*, 4 vols. (Portland, ME: Lefavor-Tower, 1915), vol. 4, pp. 158–161; Deborah Neves to Author, March 11 and April 7, 2003; Busey, *These Honored Dead*, p. 43; Obituary of Allen Winslow Mills, *The Morning Star*, Dover, NH, March 25, 1863.

James Bullock Woodard and Sons

Greg Mast, *State Troops and Volunteers: A Photographic Record of North Carolina's Civil War Soldiers*, 2 vols. (Raleigh: North Carolina Department of Cultural Resources, Division of Archives and History, 1995), pp. 218–219; Hugh Buckner Johnston, ed., "The Woodard Confederate Letters," Hugh Buckner Johnston Collection, State of North Carolina, Department of Cultural Resources, Raleigh, NC.

Dr. George Kirkman and Sons

Gragg, *Covered With Glory*, pp. 103, 134, 142, 232; Michael A. Dreese, *The 151st Pennsylvania at Gettysburg: Like Ripe Apples in a Storm* (Jefferson, NC: McFarland, 2000), pp. 40–41, 45–47, 52; Busey and Martin, *Regimental Strengths and Losses at Gettysburg*, pp. 264, 299; Henry C. Kirkman to Dr. George Kirkman, August 6, 1863 and W. Burton Owen to Dr. George Kirkman, December 8, 1863, Gregory A. Coco Collection, U. S. Army Military History Institute, Carlisle Barracks, PA; Bob Allen, "Point Lookout's Prison Pen," *America's Civil War* (March 2003), pp. 40–44.

William P. Yearger and Father

John Y. Foster, "Four Days at Gettysburg," *Harper's New Monthly Magazine*, February 1864; Gregory A. Coco, *Wasted Valor: The Confederate Dead at Gettysburg* (Gettysburg: Thomas Publications, 1990), pp. 131–132.

Richard Price, Sr., and Richard Price, Jr.

Michael Hanifen, *History of Battery B, First New Jersey Artillery* (Ottawa, IL: Republican Times Printers, 1905), pp. 76–77, 82–83; Joseph K. Barnes, ed., *The Medical and Surgical History of the Civil War*, 12 vols. (Washington, DC: Government Printing Office, 1870; reprint edition, Wilmington, NC: Broadfoot, 1990–1991), vol. 12, p. 884; Busey, *These Honored Dead*, p. 127; Pfanz, *Gettysburg: The Second Day*, pp. 303, 306, 338–339.

Nelson Reaser

OR, Volume 27, Part 1, p. 28; Dreese, *The 151st Pennsylvania at Gettysburg*, pp. 100–101.

Stephen and Azor Nickerson

Azor H. Nickerson, "Personal Recollections of Two Visits to Gettysburg," *Scribner's Magazine*, Vol. XIV (July-December 1893), pp. 21–28; Angelo D. Jaurez, *The Tarnished Saber: Major Azor Howett Nickerson, USA, His Life and Times* (Chatham, MA: The Nickerson Family Association), pp. 3, 164; Baumgartner, *Buckeye Blood*, pp. 160–161, 177; The *Elyria Independent Democrat*, Issues of July 8, July 11, July 15, July 22, July 29, and August 5, 1863; The *Cleveland Herald*, November 24, 1863; Charles H. Merrick to Mira Merrick, July 13, 1863, Western Reserve Historical Society; Pension Records of Azor H. Nickerson, National Archives and Records Administration (NARA), Washington, DC.

William D. W. and Albert Mitchell, USA; John A. Redd, CSA

Jim Murphy, *The Boy's War: Confederate and Union Soldiers Talk About the Civil War* (New York: Clarion Books, 1990), pp. 2, 78; Emily Souder, *Leaves From the Battlefield of Gettysburg* (Philadelphia: Caxton Press of C. Sherman, Son & Co., 1864), p. 52; Pension Records of William D. W. Mitchell, NARA, Washington, DC; Busey, *These Honored Dead*, pp. 228–229; Dale Fetzer and Bruce Mowday, *Unlikely Allies: Fort Delaware's Prison Community in the Civil War*, Mechanicsburg, PA: Stackpole Books, 2000), pp. 113–114; "Civil War Memoirs of Mr. McCown Tell of Life in Northern Prison," *Rockbridge County News*, February 12 & 19, 1953.

Ashton and William Tourison

William T. Simpson, "The Drummer Boys of Gettysburg," *Philadelphia North American*, July 29, 1913; Jeffrey J. and Loree L. Kowalis, *Died at Gettysburg!* (Hightstown, NJ: Longstreet House, 1998), pp. 207–209; Pension Records of Ashton and William Tourison, NARA, Washington, DC; Susan Boardman, "Pardee Field and the Tale of Two Classmates," *Blue & Gray* (December 2002), p. 56

Michael and Hezekiah Spessard

Harrison, *Nothing But Glory*, pp. 52–53, 106–107, 158; William P. Jesse Account and Eppa Hunton to John W. Daniel, July 15, 1904, John W. Daniel Papers, University of Virginia Library, Charlottesville, Va.; J. R. McPherson, "A Private's Account of Gettysburg," *Southern Veteran Magazine* VI (1898), pp. 148–149; Frank E. Fields, Jr., *28th Virginia Infantry* (Lynchburg, Va.: Howard, 1985), p. 81.

John Harvey, Sr., and John Harvey, Jr.

Hess, *Pickett's Charge—The Last Attack at Gettysburg* (Chapel Hill: University of North Carolina Press, 2001), pp. 194–195, 246, 262, 272, 285; Anthony W. McDermott to John W. Bachelder, June 2, 1886, in David L. and Audrey J. Ladd, eds., *The Bachelder Papers: Gettysburg in Their Own Words*, 3 vols. (Dayton, OH: Morningside House, 1994–1995), vol. 3, pp. 1406–1415; California and the Civil War: 69th Regiment of Infantry, Pennsylvania Volunteers (2nd California Regiment), http://www.militarymuseum.org/69thPA.html; Kevin O'Beirne, Kevin P. Gorman, and Joseph E. Gannon, "The Irish Distinguished Themselves at Gettysburg Battle," *The Civil War News* (July 2003), pp. 12a; Pension and Military Service Records of John Harvey, Sr., and John Harvey, Jr., NARA, Washington, DC; Busey, *These Honored Dead*, p. 252.

Thomas, Jonathan, and Albert Clark

Transcripts of Clark Family Letters provided by Charlie W. Clark; Charlie W. Clark, "I Resolve to Fight: An Account of a Southern Family's Ultimate Sacrifice For Southern Rights," unpublished, undated manuscript; Charlie Clark to Author, May 17, 2003; Gregory A. Coco, *Confederates Killed in Action at Gettysburg* (Gettysburg: Thomas Publications, 2001), pp. 9–15.

Elias and DeGrasse Hanness

J. H. French, *Historical and Statistical Gazetteer of New York State* (Syracuse, NY: R.P. Smith, 1860); James McClean, *Cutler's Brigade at Gettysburg* (Baltimore: Butternut and Blue, 1994), pp. 10–13, 79–96; Gregory A. Coco, *On the Bloodstained Field II* (Gettysburg: Thomas Publications, 1989), pp. 84–85; Barbara J. Dix, County Historian, Oswego County, New York, to Author, May 9, 2003; 1855, 1865, and 1875 Census Records of Oswego County, New York, Oswego County Records Center, Oswego, New York; Pension Records of Elias Hanness, NARA, Washington, DC.

Chapter 2: Mothers and Sons

Margery and Andrew Tucker

Michael Dreese, "The Saga of Andrew Gregg Tucker," *Bucknell World*, vol. 26, no. 6 (November 1998), pp. 20–21; Biographical Sketch of Andrew Gregg Tucker, George McFarland Papers, J. Horace McFarland Collection, Pennsylvania State Archives, Harrisburg, PA; J. Sexton James, "War Clouds in the Sixties at Lewisburg," *Bucknell Mirror*, vol. 17, no. 6 (June 10, 1898), pp. 113–116; Lucy R. Bliss, "The Days of '63," *Bucknell Alumni Monthly* (December 1922).

Caroline and Henry Chancellor, Jr.

Biographical Sketch of Henry Chancellor, Jr., George McFarland Papers, J. Horace McFarland Collection, Pennsylvania State Archives, Harrisburg, PA; Mrs. Henry Chancellor to George F. McFarland, George McFarland Papers, J. Horace McFarland Collection, Pennsylvania State Archives, Harrisburg, PA; Thomas Chamberlin, *History of the One Hundred and Fiftieth Regiment Pennsylvania Volunteers* (Philadelphia: F. McManus, Jr. & Co., Printers, 1905), pp. 15–23, 29, 122–130, 157.

Elizabeth and Joseph Kinnier

Kate M. Scott, *History of the One Hundred and Fifth Regiment of Pennsylvania Volunteers* (Philadelphia: New-World Publishing, 1877), pp. 254–256, 316–317; Theresa Costa, Administrative Assistant, Jefferson County Historical and Genealogical Society, to Author, July 16, 2003; Pfanz, *Gettysburg: The Second Day*, pp. 303–304, 331–332.

Patience and Jeremiah Sanders Gage

Steven H. Stubbs, *Duty, Honor, Valor: The Story of the Eleventh Mississippi Infantry Regiment* (Philadelphia, Mississippi: Dancing Rabbit Press, 2000), pp.; Steven R. Davis, "...Like Leaves in an Autumn Wind: The 11th Mississippi Infantry in the Army of Northern Virginia," *Civil War Regiments*, vol. 2, no. 4 (1992), pp. 269, 293–294, 297; Terrence Winschel, "The Gettysburg Diary of Lieutenant William Peel," *The Gettysburg Magazine*, no. 9 (July 1993), pp. 98–99; Maud Morrow Brown, *The University Greys* (Richmond, VA: Garrett and Massie, 1940), pp. 38–43; Jeremiah Gage to Mary M. Sanders, June 10, 1863, and James L. Goodloe to Mrs. Armistead, June 26, 1913, Archives and Special Collections, The University of Mississippi, University, MS; "Death Message of a Southern Hero on the Battle Field of Gettysburg," *New Orleans Times-Democrat*, June 29, 1913; "Prominent Doctor Claimed by Death," New Orleans *Times-Picayune*, August 24, 1924; James W. Silver, ed., *The Confederate Soldier by Le Grand James Wilson* (Memphis: Memphis State University Press, 1973), pp. 120–125.

William Hutchinson and Mother

John Day Smith, *The History of the Nineteenth Regiment of Maine Volunteer Infantry, 1862–1865* (Minneapolis: Great Western Publishing Company, 1909), pp. 73–74; Coco, *Wasted Valor*, pp. 150–151; Weymouth T. Jordan, Jr., and Louis H. Manarin, eds., *North Carolina Troops, 1861–1865: A Roster*, 13 vols. (Raleigh, NC: Division of Archives and History, 1971–1996), vol. 12, p. 473.

Mrs. A. T. Mercer and Oliver Mercer

James K. P. Scott, *The Story of the Battles at Gettysburg* (Harrisburg, PA: The Telegraph Press, 1927), pp. 33–36; Sheldon A. Munn, *Freemasons at Gettysburg* (Gettysburg: Thomas Publications, 1993), p. 57; Jordan and Manarin, *North Carolina Troops*, vol. 6, p. 493.

John Moseley and Mother

Coco, *Wasted Valor*, p. 124; Jeffrey D. Stocker, ed., *From Huntsville to Appomattox: R. T. Cole's History of 4th Regiment, Alabama Volunteer Infantry, C.S.A., Army of Northern Virginia* (Knoxville: The University of Tennessee Press, 1996), pp. 209–210, 278.

Elisa and James Weida/ James Ashworth and Mother

Pension Records of James Weida, NARA, Washington, DC; Dreese, *The 151st Pennsylvania Volunteers at Gettysburg*, pp. 15, 48–49, 93, 95, 145; James Ashworth to George McFarland, May 4, 1866, George McFarland Papers, J. Horace McFarland Collection, Pennsylvania State Archives, Harrisburg, PA; Survivor's Association, *History of the 121st Regiment Pennsylvania Volunteers* (Philadelphia: Press of the Catholic Standard and Times, 1906), pp. 139–140, 289; Sarah Sites Rodgers, *The Ties of the Past: The Gettysburg Diaries of Salome Myers Stewart* (Gettysburg: Thomas Publications, 1996), pp. 163–164, 175.

John C., Lucie, John C. L., and Thomas J. Mounger, CSA

John C. Mounger to "My Dear Lucie," May 23, 1863; John C. L. Mounger to "Dear Mother," July 18, 1863;

Resolution on the Death of Lt. Colonel John C. Mounger, August 20, 1863; Newspaper Clipping, *Confederate Union* (Milledgeville, Georgia), August 11, 1863; Private Collection of Robert Kelly. These documents can be viewed on the web site of the 9th Georgia Infantry: http://www.members.aol.com/Gainf9reg/index20.html.

Chapter 3: Husbands, Wives and Sweethearts

Joel and Laura Blake

J. Russell Reaver, "Letters of Joel C. Blake," *Apalachee*, vol. 5 (1962), pp. 5–25; David W. Hartman and David Coles, compilers, *Biographical Roster of Florida's Confederate and Union Soldiers, 1861–1865*, 6 vols. (Wilmington, NC: Broadfoot, 1995), vol. 2, pp. 459, 567, 569; J. Howard Wert, "Little Stories of Gettysburg," Gettysburg *Compiler*, December 24, 1907.

Alexander and Elmira Seiders

Dreese, *The 151st Pennsylvania Volunteers at Gettysburg*, pp. 10, 22, 83; Simon J. Arnold to "Mrs. Seiders," July 20, 1863, Sally Smith Collection.

Hugh and Susan Miller

Compiled Military Service Records of Edwin, George, and Hugh Miller, NARA, Washington, DC; Edwin Miller to Susan Miller, June 15, 1863, George Miller to Susan Miller, June 12, 1863, Susan Miller to Hugh Miller, July 3, 1863, and Resolution Adopted by the 42nd Mississippi Regiment on the Death of Colonel Hugh R. Miller, August 15, 1863, Archives and Special Collections, University of Mississippi, University, MS; Thomas G. Clark to "Dear Margery," January 15, 1863, Charlie Clark Collection; Andrew B. Cross, *The Battle of Gettysburg and the Christian Commission* (Philadelphia, 1865), pp. 14–15; Thomas D. Witherspoon, "Prison Life at Fort McHenry," *Southern Historical Society Papers*, vol. VIII, 1880; R. H. Shuffler, ed., *Decimus et Ultimus Barziza, Adventures of a Prisoner of War 1863–1864* (Austin: University of Texas Press, 1964), pp. 63–64; Coco, *Wasted Valor*, pp. 119–121.

Isaac and Mary Stamps

Stewart Sifakis, *Who Was Who in the Confederacy* (New York: Facts on File, 1988), pp. 73–74; Terrence Winschel, "To Assuage the Grief: The Gettysburg Saga of Isaac and Mary Stamps," *The Gettysburg Magazine*, no. 7 (July 1992), pp. 77–82.

George and Adeline McFarland

Michael Dreese, *An Imperishable Fame: The Civil War Experience of George Fisher McFarland* (Mifflintown, PA: Juniata County Historical Society, 1997), pp. 42, 55, 63, 80, 88, 111–112, 122–123, 143–145; Michael Dreese, "A Schoolteacher Goes to War," *The Snyder County Historical Society Bulletin* (1998), pp. 63–90.

John and Martha Callis

Moore, *Women of the War*, pp. 143–144; "An Incident at Gettysburg," in Walter Clark, ed., *Histories of the Several Regiments and Battalions from North Carolina*, 5 vols. (Goldsboro, NC: Nash Brothers, 1901), vol. 5, pp. 611–616; John Callis, "7th Wisconsin Infantry at Gettysburg, Pa.," in Ladd and Ladd, *The Bachelder Papers*, vol. 1, pp. 140–145; Roger Long, "A Gettysburg Encounter," *The Gettysburg Magazine*, no. 7 (July 1992), pp. 114–118; Joseph K. Barnes, ed., *The Medical and Surgical History of the Civil War*, 12 vols. (Washington, DC: Government Printing Office, 1870; reprint edition, Wilmington, NC: Broadfoot, 1990–1991), pp. 584–585; Fannie J. Buehler, *Recollections of the Rebel Invasion and One Woman's Experience During the Battle of Gettysburg* (Gettysburg: Star and Sentinel Printers, 1900), pp. 23–28; Linda Black, "Three Heroines of Gettysburg," *The Gettysburg Magazine*, no. 11 (July 1994), pp. 119–125; Gregory Coco, *A Vast Sea of Misery* (Gettysburg: Thomas Publications, 1988), p. 44; Pension Records of John Callis, NARA, Washington, DC.

Amos and Atlannta Sweet

Rodgers, *The Ties of the Past*, 164, 176–177; James M. Cole and Roy E. Frampton, *Lincoln and the Human Interest Stories of the Gettysburg National Cemetery* (Hanover, PA: The Sheridan Press, 1995), p. 55; Busey, *These Honored Dead*, p. 295; Elizabeth Salome Myers Stewart, "Reminiscences of Gettysburg Hospitals," unpublished manuscript, circa 1870, ACHS; Elizabeth Salome Myers Stewart, "How a Gettysburg Schoolteacher Spent Her Vacation in 1863," San Francisco *Sunday Call*, August 16, 1903; Pension Records of Amos Sweet, NARA, Washington, DC.

John and Harriet Fly

Austin C. Stearns, *Three Years with Company K*, Arthur A. Kent, ed. (Cranbury, NJ: Fairleigh Dickinson University Press, 1976), p. 189; Cole and Frampton, *Lincoln and the Human Interest Stories of the Gettysburg National Cemetery*, p. 40.

Charles and Ellen Billings

Thomas Desjardin, *Stand Firm Ye Boys from Maine: The 20th Maine and the Gettysburg Campaign* (Gettysburg: Thomas Publications, 1995), pp. 56, 111, 170, 190; Coco, *On the Bloodstained Field II*, pp. 99–100; Pension Records of Charles Billings, NARA, Washington, DC.

Hardy and Julia Graves

Rodgers, *The Ties of the Past*, pp. 177–183, 197, 205, 208.

George Cooper, CSA, and Maurice Buckingham, USA

Gregory Coco, *War Stories: A Collection of 150 Little Known Human Interest Accounts of the Campaign and Battle of Gettysburg* (Gettysburg: Thomas Publications, 1992), pp. 17–18; Jordan and Manarin, *North Carolina Troops*, vol. 10, p. 299; Busey, *These Honored Dead*, p. 172; Martha Ehler, *Hospital Scenes after the Battle of Gettysburg, July 1863* (Philadelphia: Henry B. Ashmead, 1864; Reprint, Gettysburg: G. Craig Caba, 1993), pp. 32–34; Research by Timothy Smith, Licensed Battlefield Guide, Gettysburg, PA.

Ernest Simpson

George Lewis, *The History of Battery E, First Regiment Rhode Island Light Artillery* (Providence, RI: Snow &

Farnham Printers, 1892), pp. 209–211, 493; Pfanz, *Gettysburg: The Second Day,* pp. 303, 310–311, 322–323; Busey, *These Honored Dead,* pp. 308–309; Military Service Records of Ernest Simpson, NARA, Washington, DC.

James and Mary Purman

Robert L. Stewart, *History of the One Hundred and Fortieth Regiment, Pennsylvania Volunteers* (Philadelphia: Franklin Bindery, 1912), pp. 4–6, 289, 394–395, 424–429, 458; Coco, *A Vast Sea of Misery,* pp. 47, 141–142; Pension Records of James Purman, NARA, Washington, DC.

Chapter 4: Union Brothers

James and Robert Miller

Jedediah Mannis and Galen R. Wilson, eds., *Bound to Be a Soldier: The Letters of Private James T. Miller, 111th Pennsylvania Infantry, 1861–1864* (Knoxville: University of Tennessee Press, 2001), pp. xvii–xxiii, 47–50, 53–54, 60–61, 75–76, 80–81, 89–92, 101–102, 118–119, 128–129, 138–139, 170–172; Robert Miller to "My Dear Son," July 4, 1863, Robert E. Miller to "Dear Parents," January 25, 1863, March 16, 1863, and June 30, 1863, Robert E. Miller to "Dear Brother," June 14, 1863, and July 18, 1863, Robert E. Miller Papers, Miller Brothers Letters, Schoff Civil War Collection, William L. Clements Library, University of Michigan, Ann Arbor; E. B. and Barbara Long, *The Civil War Day by Day: An Almanac, 1861–1865* (New York: Doubleday, 1971), p. 325.

Henry and Richard Seage

Pension and Military Service Records of Henry, Richard, and John Seage, NARA, Washington, DC; Diary of Henry Seage and John Seage to Governor Blair, December 23, 1863, Steven J. Roberts Collection; Genealogy of John Seage Family, John Devinney Collection; Henry S. Seage to John B. Bachelder, September 23, 1884, in *The Bachelder Papers: Gettysburg in Their Own Words,* 3 vols. (Dayton, OH: Morningside, Inc., 1994–1995), vol. 2, pp. 1070–1072.

Joseph Gutelius, Joseph and Samuel Ruhl

Harry M. Kieffer, *The Recollections of a Drummer-Boy* (Boston: Houghton, Mifflin, 1883; Reprint edition, Mifflinburg, PA: Bucktail Books, 2000), pp. 23, 26, 106–108, 118–120; "Corporal Joseph R. Ruhl & Corporal Joseph J. Gutelius: 150th Bucktail Brigade," *The Millmont Times* (July 2004), pp. 1–7; Thomas Chamberlin, *History of the One Hundred and Fiftieth Regiment Pennsylvania Volunteers* (Philadelphia: F. McManus, Jr., 1905), pp. 115–120, 128–129, 132, 154–155; J. Warren Gilbert, *The Blue and Gray: A History of the Conflicts During Lee's Invasion and Battle of Gettysburg* (Gettysburg: Bookmart, 1952), pp. 150–151; Pension Records of Samuel Ruhl, Charles, Joseph, and Samuel Gutelius, NARA.

John and William Egolf

McLean, *Cutler's Brigade at Gettysburg,* pp. 13–15, 111–112, 116–117; C. Tevis, *The History of the Fighting Four-teenth* (New York: Brooklyn Eagle Press, 1911), pp. 83–84, 284; J. Howard Wert, "Little Stories of Gettysburg," *Gettysburg Compiler,* January 8, 1908; Herbert L. Grimm and Paul L. Roy, *Human Interest Stories of the Three-Day Battle at Gettysburg* (Gettysburg: Gem, 1995), p. 46; Alice Powers, "Dark Days of the Battle Week," *Gettysburg Compiler,* July 1, 1903; Byrle F. MacPherson, "Miss Alice Powers, Volunteer Nurse in Civil War, Taught Primary School for 30 Years," *Gettysburg Times,* April 13, 1935; Solomon Powers File, ACHS; James Fulton, "Gettysburg Reminiscences," *National Tribune,* October 20, 1908; Coco, *A Vast Sea of Misery,* pp. 51–52; Pension Records of John Egolf, NARA.

Eugene and Henry Eaton

Rodgers, *The Ties of the Past,* pp. 13, 16, 19, 24, 148, 150, 152–157, 164–165, 173, 273; Elizabeth Salome Myers Stewart, "How a Gettysburg Schoolteacher Spent Her Vacation in 1863," *San Francisco Sunday Call,* August 16, 1903, Elizabeth Salome Myers Stewart File, ACHS; James Fulton, "Gettysburg Reminiscences," *National Tribune,* October 20, 1908 Pension Records of Eugene and Henry Eaton, NARA.

Horace and Silas Judson

Horace Judson to John Bachelder, October 17, 1887, in Ladd and Ladd, *The Bachelder Papers,* vol. 3, pp. 1513–1517; Pension and Military Service Records of Horace and Silas Judson, NARA.

Erasmus and Richard Bassett

R. L. Murray, *The Redemption of the "Harper's Ferry Cowards": The Story of the 111th and 126th New York State Volunteer Regiments at Gettysburg* (Wolcott, NY: R. L. Murray, 1994), pp. 17–18, 25–30, 33–34; 40, 100–106; 108, 112, 114, 116; Wayne Mahood, *"Written in Blood": A History of the 126th New York Infantry in the Civil War* (Hightstown, NJ: Longstreet, 1997), pp. 43, 55, 131, 135, 169; Arabella M. Wilson, *Disaster, Struggle, Triumph: The Adventures of 1000 "Boys in Blue"* (Albany, NY: The Argus Company), pp. 177–178, 365–366, 417, 478; David W. Judd, *The Story of the Thirty-third N.Y.S. Volunteers: Or, Two Years Campaigning in Virginia and Maryland* (Rochester, NY: Benning & Andrews, 1864), pp. 27, 192; George W. Contant, *Path of Blood: The True Story of the 33rd New York Volunteers* (Savannah, NY: Seeco, 1996), p. 238; Pension Records of Richard Bassett, NARA.

Henry and John Nice

Pension and Military Service Records of Henry and John Nice, NARA; *OR,* Vol. 27, Part 1, p. 514; Larry Tagg, *The Generals of Gettysburg: The Leaders of America's Greatest Battle* (Campbell, CA: Savas Publishing, 1998), pp. 63, 70, 144–145, 156–159.

James and Thomas Stephens

Craig L. Dunn, *Harvestfields of Death: The Twentieth Indiana Volunteers of Gettysburg* (Carmel, IN: Guild, 1999), pp. 2, 79, 199–204, 222–224; Thomas W. Stephens Diary, Stephens Collection, United States Army Military History Institute, Carlisle Barracks, PA; James C. Stephens Diary, James C. Stephens Collections, Indiana Historical Society, Indianapolis, Indiana; Pension Records of Thomas W. Stephens, NARA; Herbert Asbury, *The Gangs of New York* (New York, NY: Knopf,

1927), pp. 108–155; Patricia L. Faust, ed., *Historical Times Illustrated Encyclopedia of the Civil War* (New York: Harper & Row, 1986), pp. 225–226.

Abraham G., Jacob L., and William A. Carter

John P. Hobson Jr. and W. Douglas Macneal, "In His Own Words: The Annotated Civil War Diary of Private Jacob Lee Carter, of Farm School, Ferguson Township, Centre County," *Centre County Heritage* (Spring 1999), pp. 2–32; Sara Phinney Kelley, "The Life of an 'Anonymous' Man," *Centre County Heritage* (Spring 1999), pp. 35–52.

Frank, Patrick, and Thomas Moran

Pension and Military Service Records of Frank, Patrick, and Thomas Moran, NARA; Frank Moran, "A Fire Zouave," *National Tribune*, October 30, November 6, and November 13, 1890, Frank Moran, "Release of Prisoners," *National Tribune*, April 24, 1890; Frank Moran, "Libby Prison's Tunnel," *Philadelphia Weekly Times*, October 28, 1882; Frank Moran, *Bastiles of the Confederacy* (Baltimore: Frank Moran, 1890), pp. 103–104, 171–200; Lonnie R. Speer, *Portals to Hell: Military Prisons of the Civil War* (Mechanicsburg, PA: Stackpole Books, 1997), pp. 58–59; 173–174, 231–233, 259–266.

Frederic and Adolfo Cavada

Oliver Wilson Davis, *Sketch of Frederic Fernandez Cavada* (Philadelphia: James B. Chandler, 1871), pp. 1–58; Frederic Cavada, *Libby Life: Experiences of a Prisoner of War in Richmond, Virginia* (Philadelphia: King & Baird, 1864), pp. 13–20, 30, 63–64, 199–200; Fernando Fernandez-Cavada Collection, Cuban Heritage Collection, University of Miami Libraries, Coral Gables, Fl.; Diary of Adolfo Cavada, The Historical Society of Pennsylvania, Philadelphia, PA; Edward R. Bowen, "Collis' Zouaves: the 114th Pennsylvania Infantry at Gettysburg," *Philadelphia Weekly Press*, June 22, 1887; *OR*, Vol. 27, Part 1, pp. 502–503; Edward J. Hagerty, *Collis' Zouaves: The 114th Pennsylvania Volunteers in the Civil War* (Baton Rouge: Louisiana State University, 1997), pp. 134–137, 203–208, 219–220, 296–299, 322–325.

Chapter 5: Confederate Brothers

Sidney and Giles Carter

Bessie Mell Lane, ed., *Dear Bet: The Carter Letters, 1861–1863: The Letters of Lieutenant Sidney Carter, Company A, 14th Regiment, South Carolina Volunteers, Gregg's–McGowan's Brigade, CSA, to Ellen Timmons Carter* (Clemson, S. C.: B. M. Lane, 1978), pp. xvii–xxi, 93–102, 105, 107, 114–117, 122, 126–128; Cole and Frampton, *Lincoln and the Human Interest Stories of the Gettysburg National Cemetery*, pp. 46–47; Varina D. Brown, *A Colonel at Gettysburg and Spotsylvania* (Columbia, SC: The State Company, 1931), pp. 77–84.

Levi and Henry Walker

Robert K. Beecham, *Gettysburg: The Pivotal Battle of the Civil War* (Chicago: A.C. McClure, 1911), pp. 80–81; Busey and Martin, *Regimental Strengths and Losses at Gettysburg*, p. 292; Greg Mast, *State Troops and Volunteers: A*

Photographic Record of North Carolina's Civil War Soldiers, 2 vols. (Raleigh: North Carolina Department of Cultural Resources, Division of Archives and History, 1995), vol. 1, p. 183; David G. Maxwell, "The Two Brothers," in Clark, *Histories of the Several Regiments and Battalions from North Carolina in the Great War*, vol. 4, pp. 405–406; W. G. T. Thompson to "Dear Mother and Sister," July 20, 1863, copy in Robert Brake Collection, United States Army Military History Institute, Carlisle, PA.

Thomas and James Kenan

Obituary of Thomas S. Kenan, *Confederate Veteran* (March 1913), p. 135; "An Incident at Gettysburg," in Clark, vol. 5, pp. 611–616; Long, "A Gettysburg Encounter," pp. 114–118; Thomas Kenan, "Johnson's Island," in Clark, vol. 4, pp. 689–694; Harry W. Pfanz, *Gettysburg: The First Day* (Chapel Hill: University of North Carolina Press, 2001), pp. 179–181, 185–187, 207–208, 213.

William and John Oates

William C. Oates, *The War Between the Union and the Confederacy and Its Lost Opportunities with a History of the 15th Alabama Regiment* (New York: Neale Publishing Company, 1905), pp. 226–227, 671–675; Paul Andrew Hutton, ed., *Gettysburg: Lt. Frank A. Haskell, U. S. A. and Col. William C. Oates, C.S.A.* (New York: Bantam Books, 1992), pp. 1–20, 35–36, 137–138.

Henry Rauch, John C. Warren and Dr. L. P. Warren

Georgeanna Woolsey, *Letters of a Family During the War for the Union, 1861–1865*, 2 vols. (Privately Printed, 1899), pp. 528–529, 533; Scott, *The Story of the Battles at Gettysburg*, p. 36; Obituary of John Crittenden Warren, *Confederate Veteran* (October 1914), p. 472; Jordan and Manarin, *North Carolina Troops*, vol. 12, p. 439.

William, Chapham, and Alexander Murray

Daniel Carroll Toomey, *Marylanders at Gettysburg* (Linthicum, MD: Toomey Press, 1994), pp. 7, 19–20, 22–28, 44; William Murray Letters, Maryland Historical Society; Scott Sherlock, "Captain William H. Murray," http://www.2ndmaryland.org/murray.html.

John, Joseph, and William Marable

Stubbs, *Duty, Honor, Valor*, pp. 428–429, 442, 459–466, 826; Winschel, *The Gettysburg Diary of Lieutenant William Peel*, pp. 104–105; Baxter McFarland, "Losses of the Eleventh Mississippi Regiment at Gettysburg," *Confederate Veteran* (1923), pp. 258–260.

James and Christopher Harwood

J. Howard Wert, *A Complete Handbook of the Monuments and Indications and Guide to the Positions on the Gettysburg Battlefield* (Harrisburg, PA: R. M. Sturgeon & Co., Publishers, 1886), pp. 53–56.

Norbone, Edmond, William, and Charles Berkeley

John E. Divine, *8th Virginia Infantry* (Lynchburg, VA: Howard, 1986), pp. 21–25; "The Berkeley Brothers of the Eighth Virginia Regiment, C.S.A.," Richmond

News-Leader, January 21, 1907; Kathy Georg Harrison, *Nothing But Glory: Pickett's Division at Gettysburg* (Gettysburg: Thomas Publications, 1987), pp. 5, 27–29, 76–77, 102–103, 120, 123.

George, James, John, and William Presgraves

Coco, *Wasted Valor*, pp. 116–117; Divine, *8th Virginia Infantry*, pp. 21, 77.

James and William Buchett

Harrison, *Nothing But Glory*, p. 21; Andrew Cross, *Battle of Gettysburg and the Christian Commission* (Baltimore: United States Christian Commission, 1865), pp. 28–29; Andrew Cross, "The Rebel Wounded at Gettysburg," *Lutheran and Missionary* (Philadelphia, PA), August 6, 1863; Holstein, *Three Years in Field Hospitals of the Army of the Potomac*, p. 45; Thomas W. Gentry to Author, December 13, 2002; Thomas W. Gentry, "Burchett Brothers Survive Horrors of Civil War," *The Tomahawk* (Mountain City, Tennessee), March 12, 2003; Military Service Records of James and William Burchett, NARA, Washington, DC.

Chapter 6: Twins

Thomas and George Dennen

Frederick W. Hawthorne, *Gettysburg: Stories of Men and Monuments* (Hanover, PA: The Sheridan Press, 1988), p. 77; New York Monuments Commission, *New York at Gettysburg*, 3 vols. (Albany: J. B. Lyon Company, Printers, 1902), vol. 2, pp. 572–608; Frederick Phisterer, ed., *New York in the War of the Rebellion, 1861–1865*, 5 vols. (Albany: J. B. Lyon, 1912), vol. 4, pp. 2751–2767; "Our Firemen," p. 734, Harrisburg Civil War Round Table Collection, United States Army Military History Institute, Carlisle Barracks, PA; Pension and Military Service Records of Thomas and George Dennen, NARA, Washington, DC; *Annual Report of the Adjutant General of the State of New York for the Year 1901* (Albany: J. B. Lyon, Co., 1902), vol. 28, pp. 914–1411; Frank E. Moran, "A Fire Zouave," *The National Tribune*, November 6 and November 13, 1890; Frank E. Moran, "A New View of Gettysburg," *Philadelphia Weekly Times*, April 22, 1882; *OR*, vol. 25, pp. 467–468; Pfanz, *Gettysburg: The Second Day*, pp. 147–148; Busey, *These Honored Dead*, p. 152.

James and Amos Casey

Pension Files of James and Amos Casey, NARA, Washington, DC; John P. Nicholson, ed., *Pennsylvania at Gettysburg: Ceremonies at the Dedication of the Monuments Erected by the Commonwealth of Pennsylvania to Mark the Positions of the Pennsylvania Commands Engaged in the Battle*, 3 vols. (Harrisburg, PA: William Stanley Ray, State Printer, 1914), vol. 1, pp. 536–545; Gary Adelman and Timothy H. Smith, *Devil's Den: A History and Guide* (Gettysburg: Thomas Publications, 1997), pp. 40, 43, 45, 48, 50–51.

G. A. and W. C. Jones

Robert M. Powell, "With Hood at Gettysburg," *Philadelphia Weekly Times*, December 13, 1884; John W.

Stevens, *Reminiscences of the Civil War: A Soldier in Hood's Texas Brigade, Army of Northern Virginia* (Hillsboro, TX: Hillsboro Mirror Print, 1902), p. 114; Coco, *Confederates Killed in Action at Gettysburg*, pp. 39–40.

Chapter 7: Sibling Reunions

Charles and William Goldsborough

A.A. Kent, *Three Years with Company K* (Fairleigh Dickinson University Press, 1976), pp. 188–189; Winfield Peters, "A Maryland Warrior and Hero: Death of Major William W. Goldsborough, of the Famous Maryland Line, C.S.A.," *Southern Historical Society Papers*, vol. 19 (1901), pp. 243–250; Kevin Conley Ruffner, *Maryland's Blue & Gray: A Border State's Union and Confederate Junior Officer Corps* (Baton Rouge: Louisiana State University Press, 1997), Goldsborough entries; Obituaries of Charles E. Goldsborough, *Gettysburg Times*, October 18, 1913, and *Star and Sentinel*, October 22, 1913; *History of Cumberland and Adams Counties, Pennsylvania* (Chicago: Warner, Beers & Co., 1886), part 3, pp. 208–211, 508–509; William W. Goldsborough, *The Maryland Line in the Confederate Army, 1861–1865* (Port Washington, NY: Kennikat Press, 1972), pp. 106–109.

Thaddeus and Thadia Klimkiewicz

Sister M. Liguori, "Polish Sisters in the Civil War," *Polish American Studies* (January–June 1950), pp. 1–7; Virginia Walcott Beauchamp, "The Sisters and the Soldiers," *Maryland Historical Magazine* (Summer 1986), pp. 117–133; "Like Angel's Wings," *Battlefield Journal* (April 1999), pp. 1–3; Biographical Cards, Harriet and Thadia Klimkiewicz, Archives, Daughters of Charity, Saint Joseph's Provincial House, Emmitsburg, MD.

Charles O. Hunt and Mary Carson

Interview with Arthur Kuschke, great grandson of Thomas D. Carson, November 22, 2004; 1860 Federal Census of Gettysburg, PA, ACHS; "Boy of Gettysburg Recalls Great Fray," *Philadelphia Evening Telegraph*, June 30, 1913; Jennie Croll, "Days of Dread: A Woman's Story of Her Life on a Battlefield," Civilian Files, ACHS, Gettysburg, PA; Charles Hunt to Mother, July 7 and July 16, 1863, Charles O. Hunt Letters and Personal Recollections, 1861–1898, George J. Mitchell Department of Special Collections & Archives, Bowdoin College Library, Brunswick, Maine; *OR*, Vol. 27, Part 1, pp. 355–357, 360–361; Fuller, *Personal Recollections of the War of 1861*, p. 104; Pension and Military Service Records of Charles O. Hunt, NARA; William McSherry, *History of the Bank of Gettysburg 1814–1864; The Gettysburg National Bank 1864–1914 of Gettysburg, Pa.* (Gettysburg, PA: The Gettysburg National Bank, 1914), pp. 43–44, 91–92; Obituary of Charles O. Hunt, *Portland Evening Express*, July 24, 1909; Willard M. Wallace, *Soul of the Lion: A Biography of General Joshua Lawrence Chamberlain* (New York: Thomas Nelson & Sons, 1960), p. 34; Charles O. Hunt, "Our Escape from Camp Sorghum," and Charles P. Mattocks, "In Six Prisons," in *War Papers Read Before the Commandery of the State of Maine, Military Order of the Loyal Legion of the United States*, 4 vols. (Portland, ME: Lefavor-Tower Company, 1915), vol. 1, pp. 85–128, 170–171, 174–177, 179–180.

Chapter 8: Homecomings

Henry Minnigh

Henry N. Minnigh, *History of Company K, 1st (Inft.) Penn'a Reserves: "The Boys Who Fought at Home"* (Duncansville, PA: Home Print Publisher, 1891; reprint edition, Gettysburg, PA: Thomas Publications, 1998), pp. 47–53; 74–77; 133–134, 139–149; Company K, 1st Pennsylvania Reserves File, ACHS, Gettysburg, PA; William C. Storrick, "Company K, 1st Pa. Reserves, 3rd Regiment, Comprising, Gettysburg, Adams County Troops, Had Brilliant Record of Heroism in Civil War," *Gettysburg Times*, May 16, 1936; Charles Glatfelter, "Company K, You Were There," *Adams County Historical Society Newsletter* (September 1991); Obituary of Henry Minnigh, *Gettysburg Compiler*, December 4, 1915.

Henry Beamer, USA, and Henry Wentz, CSA

Wentz Farm File, Gettysburg National Military Park Library, Gettysburg, PA; W. C. Storrick, *Gettysburg: The Places, The Battles, The Outcome* (Harrisburg, PA: J. Horace McFarland Company, 1932), pp. 89–91; Jim Clouse, "Whatever Happened to Henry Wentz?" *The Battlefield Dispatch: The Newsletter of the Association of Licensed Battlefield Guides*, pp. 6–10; William Frassanito, *Early Photography at Gettysburg* (Gettysburg, PA: Thomas Publications, 1995), pp. 248–250; United States Christian Commission, *Second Report of the Committee of Maryland, September 1, 1863* (Baltimore, Md.: Sherwood & Co., 1863), p. 91; Gregory Coco, *On the Bloodstained Field* (Gettysburg, PA: Thomas Publications, 1987), pp. 36–37; Minnigh, *History of Company K*, p. 82; Company K, 1st Pennsylvania Reserves File, ACHS.

Bibliography

Manuscript Collections and Official Documents

Adams County Historical Society, Gettysburg, Pennsylvania:
Clare, Lydia Ziegler. "A Gettysburg Girl's Story of the Great Battle," circa 1900.
Croll, Jennie, "Days of Dread: A Woman's Story of Her Life on a Battlefield."
1860 Federal Census of Gettysburg, Pennsylvania.
1st Pennsylvania Reserves File.
Solomon Powers File.
Stewart, Elizabeth Salome Myers. "Reminiscences of Gettysburg Hospitals," circa 1870.

Bowdoin College Library, Brunswick, Maine:
Charles O. Hunt Letters and Personal Recollections, 1861–1898.

Daughters of Charity, Saint Joseph's Provincial House, Emmitsburg, Maryland:
Harriet and Thadia Klimkiewicz Biographical Cards.

Gettysburg National Military Park Library, Gettysburg, Pennsylvania:
Wentz Farm File.
William J. Fisher Papers.

The Historical Society of Pennsylvania, Philadelphia, Pennsylvania:
Diary of Adolfo Cavada.

Indiana Historical Society, Indianapolis, Indiana:
James C. Stephens Diary.

Maryland Historical Society, Baltimore, Maryland:
William Murray Letters.

National Archives, Washington, DC:
Pension and Military Service Records.

Oswego County Records Center, Oswego, New York:
Census Records of Oswego County, New York.

Pennsylvania State Archives, Harrisburg, Pennsylvania:
George McFarland Papers, J. Horace McFarland Collection.

Private Collections:
Charlie W. Clark Collection.
John Devinney Collection.
Robert Kelly Collection.
Steven J. Roberts Collection.
Sally Smith Collection.

State of North Carolina, Department of Cultural Resources, Raleigh, North Carolina:
The Woodard Confederate Letters, Hugh Buckner Johnston Collection.

United States Military History Institute, Carlisle Barracks, Pennsylvania:
Robert Brake Collection.
Gregory A. Coco Collection.
Harrisburg Civil War Round Table Collection.
Thomas W. Stephens Diary.

University of Miami Libraries, Coral Gables, Florida:
Fernando Fernandez-Cavada Collection, Cuban Heritage Collection.

University of Michigan, Ann Arbor, Michigan:
Robert E. Miller Papers, Miller Brothers Letters, Schoff Civil War Collection.

University of Mississippi, Oxford, Mississippi:
Jeremiah Gage Letters.
Miller Family Papers.

University of Virginia Library, Charlottesville, Virginia:
John W. Daniel Papers.

Western Reserve Historical Society, Cleveland, Ohio:
Charles H. Merrick Letters.

Newspapers

Adams County (Pennsylvania) *Historical Society Newsletter*
Battlefield Journal
The Civil War News
The Cleveland Herald
Confederate Union, Milledgeville, Georgia
Confederate Veteran
Elyria (Ohio) *Independent Democrat*
Gettysburg Compiler
Gettysburg Times
Lutheran and Missionary, Philadelphia, Pennsylvania
The Millmont Times, Millmont, Pennsylvania
The Morning Star, Dover, New Hampshire
National Tribune
New Orleans Times-Democrat
New Orleans Times-Picayune
New York Times
Philadelphia Evening Telegraph
Philadelphia Weekly Press
Philadelphia Weekly Times
Portland (Maine) *Evening Express*
Richmond *News-Leader*
Rockbridge County (Virginia) *News*
San Francisco *Sunday Call*
Star and Sentinel, Gettysburg, Pennsylvania
The Tomahawk, Mountain City, Tennessee

Published Sources

Adelman, Gary, and Timothy H. Smith. *Devil's Den: A History and Guide.* Gettysburg: Thomas Publications, 1997.
Allen, Bob. "Point Lookout's Prison Pen." *America's Civil War* (March 2003): 40–44.
Asbury, Herbert. *The Gangs of New York.* New York: Knopf, 1927.
Barnes, Joseph K., ed. *The Medical and Surgical History of the Civil War.* 12 vols. Washington, DC: Government Printing House, 1870. Reprint, Wilmington, NC: Broadfoot, 1990–1991.
Baumgartner, Richard A. *Buckeye Blood: Ohio at Gettysburg.* Huntington, WV: Blue Acorn Press, 2003.
Beauchamp, Virginia Walcott. "The Sisters and the Soldiers." *Maryland Historical Magazine* (Summer 1986): 117–133.
Beecham, Robert K. *Gettysburg: The Pivotal Battle of the Civil War.* Chicago: A.C. McClure, 1911.
Black, Linda. "Three Heroines of Gettysburg." *The Gettysburg Magazine,* no. 11 (July 1994): 119–125.
Boardman, Susan. "Pardee Field and the Tale of Two Classmates." *Blue & Gray* (December 2002): 55–56.
Brown, Maud Morrow. *The University Greys.* Richmond: Garrett and Massie, 1940.
Brown, Varina Davis. *A Colonel at Gettysburg and Spotsylvania.* Columbia, SC: The State Company, 1931.
Buehler, Fannie J. *Recollections of the Rebel Invasion and One Woman's Experience during the Battle of Gettysburg.* Gettysburg: Star and Sentinel Printers, 1900.
Buel, Clarence C., and Robert U. Johnson, eds. *Battles and Leaders of the Civil War.* 4 vols. New York: 1884–1888.
Busey, John W. *These Honored Dead: The Union Casualties at Gettysburg.* Hightstown, NJ: Longstreet, 1996.
Busey, John W., and David G. Martin. *Regimental Strengths and Losses at Gettysburg.* Hightstown, NJ: Longstreet, 1982.
Cavada, Frederic. *Libby Life: Experiences of a Prisoner of War in Richmond, Virginia.* Philadelphia: King & Baird, 1864.
Chamberlin, Thomas. *History of the One Hundred and Fiftieth Regiment Pennsylvania Volunteers.* Philadelphia: F. McManus, Jr., 1905.
Clark, Walter, ed. *Histories of the Several Regiments and Battalions from North Carolina.* 5 vols. Goldsboro, NC: Nash Brothers, 1901.
Coco, Gregory A. *A Vast Sea of Misery.* Gettysburg: Thomas Publications, 1988.
_____. *Confederates Killed in Action at Gettysburg.* Gettysburg: Thomas Publications, 2001.
_____. *On the Bloodstained Field.* Gettysburg: Thomas Publications, 1987.
_____. *On the Bloodstained Field II.* Gettysburg: Thomas Publications, 1989.
_____. *War Stories: A Collection of 150 Little Known Human Interest Accounts of the Campaign and Battle of Gettysburg.* Gettysburg: Thomas Publications, 1992.
_____. *Wasted Valor: The Confederate Dead at Gettysburg.* Gettysburg: Thomas Publications, 1990.
Cole, James M., and Roy E. Frampton. *Lincoln and the Human Interest Stories of the Gettysburg National Cemetery.* Hanover, PA: Sheridan Press, 1995.
Coles, David and David W. Hartman, compilers. *Biographical Rosters of Florida's Confederate and Union Soldiers, 1861–1865.* 6 vols. Wilmington, NC: Broadfoot, 1995.

Contant, George W. *Path of Blood: The True Story of the 33rd New York Volunteers.* Savannah, NY: Seeco, 1996.

Cross, Andrew B. *The Battle of Gettysburg and the Christian Commission.* Baltimore: United States Christian Commission, 1865.

Davis, Oliver Wilson. *Sketch of Frederic Fernandez Cavada.* Philadelphia: James B. Chandler, 1871.

Davis, Steven R. "...Like Leaves in an Autumn Wind: The 11th Mississippi Infantry in the Army of Northern Virginia." *Civil War Regiments,* vol. 2, no. 4, (1992): 269–312.

Desjardin, Thomas. *Stand Firm Ye Boys from Maine: The 20th Maine and the Gettysburg Campaign.* Gettysburg: Thomas Publications, 1995.

Divine, John E. *8th Virginia Infantry.* Lynchburg, VA: Howard, 1986.

Dreese, Michael. *An Imperishable Fame: The Civil War Experience of George Fisher McFarland.* Mifflintown, PA: Juniata County Historical Society, 1997.

_____. "A Schoolteacher Goes to War." *The Snyder County Historical Society Bulletin* (1998): 63–90.

_____. *The 151st Pennsylvania at Gettysburg: Like Ripe Apples in a Storm.* Jefferson, NC: McFarland, 2000.

_____. "The Saga of Andrew Gregg Tucker." *Bucknell World* 26, no. 6 (November 1998): 20–21.

Dunn, Craig L. *Harvestfields of Death: The Twentieth Indiana Volunteers of Gettysburg.* Carmel, IN: Guild, 1999.

Ehler, Martha. *Hospital Scenes After the Battle of Gettysburg, July 1863.* Philadelphia: Henry B. Ashmead, 1864. Reprint, Gettysburg: G. Craig Caba, 1993.

Faust, Patricia L., ed. *Historical Times Illustrated Encyclopedia of the Civil War.* New York: Harper & Row, 1986.

Fetzer, Dale and Bruce Mowday. *Unlikely Allies: Fort Delaware's Prison Community in the Civil War.* Mechanicsburg, PA: Stackpole Books, 2000.

Fields, Frank E., Jr. *28th Virginia Infantry.* Lynchburg, VA: Howard, 1985.

Frassanito, William. *Early Photography at Gettysburg.* Gettysburg: Thomas Publications, 1995.

French, J.H. *Historical and Statistical Gazetteer of New York State.* Syracuse, NY: R.P. Smith, 1860.

Fuller, Charles A. *Personal Recollections of the Civil War.* Sherburne, NY: New Job Printing House, 1906.

Gilbert, J. Warren. *The Blue and Gray: A History of the Conflicts during Lee's Invasion and Battle of Gettysburg.* Gettysburg: Bookmart, 1952.

Glicksberg, Charles I., ed. *Walt Whitman and the Civil War: A Collection of Original Articles and Manuscripts.* New York: A.S. Barnes, 1963.

Gragg, Rod. *Covered with Glory: The 26th North Carolina Infantry at the Battle of Gettysburg.* New York: Harper Collins, 2000.

Grimm, Herbert L. and Paul L. Roy. *Human Interest Stories of the Three-Day Battle at Gettysburg.* Gettysburg: Gem, 1995.

Grimsley, Mark, and Brooks D. Simpson. *Gettysburg: A Battlefield Guide.* Lincoln: University of Nebraska Press, 1999.

Hagerty, Edward J. *Collis' Zouaves: The 114th Pennsylvania Volunteers in the Civil War.* Baton Rouge: Louisiana State University Press, 1997.

Hanifen, Michael. *History of Battery B, First New Jersey Artillery.* Ottawa, IL: Republican Times Printer, 1905.

Harrison, Kathy Georg. *Nothing but Glory: Pickett's Division at Gettysburg.* Gettysburg: Thomas Publications, 2001.

Hawthorne, Frederick W. *Gettysburg: Stories of Men and Monuments.* Hanover, PA: Sheridan, 1988.

Heaps, Willard A., and Porter W. Heaps. *The Singing Sixties: The Spirit of Civil War Days Drawn from the Music of the Times.* Norman: University of Oklahoma Press, 1960.

Hess, Earl J. *Pickett's Charge—The Last Attack at Gettysburg.* Chapel Hill: University of North Carolina Press, 2001.

Hobson, John P., Jr., and Douglas Macneal. "In His Own Words: the Annotated Civil War Diary of Private Jacob Lee Carter, of Farm School, Ferguson Township, Centre County." *Centre County Heritage* (Spring 1999).

Holstein, Anna. *Three Years in Field Hospitals of the Army of the Potomac.* Philadelphia: J.B. Lippincott, 1867.

Hunt, Charles O. "Our Escape from Camp Sorghum." *War Papers Read Before the Commandery of the State of Maine, Military Order of the Loyal Legion of the United States.* 4 vols. Portland, ME: Lefavor-Tower, 1915.

Hutton, Paul Andrew, ed. *Gettysburg: Lt. Frank A. Haskell, U.S.A. and Col. William C. Oates, C.S.A.* New York: Bantam, 1992.

James, J. Sexton. "War Clouds in the Sixties at Lewisburg." *Bucknell Mirror* 17, no. 6 (June 10, 1898): 113–116.

Jaurez, Angelo D. *The Tarnished Saber: Major Azor Howett Nickerson, U.S.A., His Life and Times.* Chatham, MA: The Nickerson Family Association, 2001.

Jordan, Weymouth T., Jr., and Louis H. Manarin, eds. *North Carolina Troops, 1861–1865: A Roster.* 13 vols. Raleigh: Division of Archives and History.

Judd, David W. *The Story of the Thirty-third N.Y.S. Volunteers: Or, Two Years Campaigning in Virginia and Maryland.* Rochester, NY: Benning & Andrews, 1864.

Kelley, Sara Phinney. "The Life of an 'Anonymous' Man." *Centre County Heritage* (Spring 1999): 35–52.

Kent, Arthur A. Austin C. Stearns, *Three Years with Company K.* Cranbury, NJ: Fairleigh Dickinson University Press, 1976.

Kieffer, Harry M. *The Recollections of a Drummer-Boy*. Boston: Houghton, Mifflin, 1883. Reprint, Mifflinburg, PA: Bucktail Books, 2000.

Kowalis, Jeffrey, and Loree Kowalis. *Died at Gettysburg!* Hightstown, NJ: Longstreet, 1998.

Ladd, David L., and Audrey J. Ladd. *The Bachelder Papers: Gettysburg in Their Own Words*. 3 vols. Dayton, OH: Morningside, 1994–1995.

Lane, Bessie Mell, ed. *Dear Bet: The Carter Letters, 1861–1863: The Letters of Lieutenant Sidney Carter, Company A, 14th Regiment, South Carolina Volunteers Gregg's—McGowan's Brigade, CSA, to Ellen Timmons Carter*. Clemson, SC: B.M. Lane, 1978.

Lewis, George. *The History of Battery E, First Regiment Rhode Island Light Artillery*. Providence, RI: Snow and Farnham, 1892.

Liguori, Sister M. "Polish Sisters in the Civil War." *Polish American Studies* (January-June 1950): 1–7.

Long, E.B., and Barbara Long. *The Civil War Day by Day: An Almanac, 1861–1865*. New York: Doubleday, 1971.

Long, Roger. "A Gettysburg Encounter." *The Gettysburg Magazine*, no. 7 (July 1992): 114–118.

Mahood, Wayne. *"Written in Blood": A History of the 126th New York Infantry in the Civil War*. Hightstown, NJ: Longstreet, 1997.

Mannis, Jedediah, and Galen R. Wilson, eds. *Bound to be a Soldier: The Letters of Private James T. Miller, 111th Pennsylvania Infantry, 1861–1864*. Knoxville: University of Tennessee Press, 2001.

Mast, Greg. *State Troops and Volunteers: A Photographic Record of North Carolina's Civil War Soldiers*. 2 vols. Raleigh: North Carolina Department of Cultural Resources, Division of Archives and History, 1995.

McClean, James. *Cutler's Brigade at Gettysburg*. Baltimore: Butternut and Blue, 1994.

McPherson, J.R. "A Private's Account of Gettysburg." *Southern Veteran Magazine* VI (1898): 148–149.

Miller, Francis T., ed. *The Photographic History of the Civil War*. 5 vols. New York: Review of Reviews, 1911.

Minnigh, Henry N. *History of Company K, 1st (Inft.) Penn'a Reserves: "The Boys Who Fought at Home."* Duncansville, PA: Home Print Publisher, 1891. Reprint, Gettysburg, PA: Thomas Publications, 1998.

Mitchell, Reid. *The Vacant Chair*. New York: Oxford University Press.

Moore, Frank. *Women of the War*. Hartford, Connecticut: S.S. Scranton, 1867.

Moran, Frank. *Bastiles of the Confederacy*. Baltimore: Frank Moran, 1890.

Munn, Sheldon A. *Freemasons at Gettysburg*. Gettysburg: Thomas Publications, 1993.

Murphy, Jim. *The Boy's War: Confederate and Union Soldiers Talk about the Civil War*. New York: Clarion, 1990.

Murray, R.L. *The Redemption of the "Harper's Ferry Cowards": The Story of the 111th and 126th New York State Volunteer Regiments at Gettysburg*. Wolcott, NY: R.L. Murray, 1994.

New York Monuments Commission, *New York at Gettysburg*. 3 vols. Albany, NY: J.B. Lyon, 1902.

Nicholson, John P., ed. *Pennsylvania at Gettysburg: Ceremonies at the Dedication of the Monuments Erected by the Commonwealth of Pennsylvania to Mark the Positions of the Pennsylvania Commands Engaged in the Battle*. 3 vols. Harrisburg, PA: William Stanley Ray, State Printer, 1914.

Nickerson, Azor H. "Personal Recollections of Two Visits to Gettysburg." *Scribner's Magazine* XIV (July-December 1893): 21–28.

Oates, William C. *The War between the Union and the Confederacy and Its Lost Opportunities, with a History of the 15th Alabama Regiment*. New York: Neale, 1905.

Pfanz, Harry W. *Gettysburg: Culp's Hill & Cemetery Hill*. Chapel Hill: University of North Carolina Press, 1993.

_____. *Gettysburg: The First Day*. Chapel Hill: University of North Carolina Press, 2001.

_____. *Gettysburg: The Second Day*. Chapel Hill: University of North Carolina Press, 1987.

Phisterer, Frederick, ed. *New York in the War of the Rebellion*. 5 vols. Albany, NY: J.B. Lyon, 1912.

Raus, Edmund J., Jr. *A Generation on the March: The Union Army at Gettysburg*. Gettysburg: Thomas Publications, 1996.

Reaver, J. Russell. "Letters of Joel C. Blake." *Apalachee* 5 (1962): 5–25.

Rodgers, Sarah Sites. *The Ties of the Past: The Gettysburg Diaries of Salome Myers Stewart*. Gettysburg: Thomas Publications, 1996.

Scott, James K.P. *The Story of the Battles at Gettysburg*. Harrisburg, PA: Telegraph Press, 1927.

Scott, Kate M. *History of the One Hundred and Fifth Regiment of Pennsylvania Volunteers*. Philadelphia: New-World, 1877.

Shay, Ralph S., ed. "Recollections of Visitations at Gettysburg after the Great Battle in July, 1863, by the Reverend F.J.F. Schantz." *Reflections on the Battle of Gettysburg* (The Lebanaon County Historical Society, 1963), vol. 13: 275–300.

Shoaf, Dana B. "Death of a Regular." *America's Civil War* (July 2002): 50–57.

Shuffler, R.H., ed. *Decimus et Ultimus Barziza, Adventures of a Prisoner of War, 1863–1864*. Austin: University of Texas Press, 1964.

Sifakis, Stewart. *Who Was Who in the Confederacy*. New York: Facts on File, 1988.

Silver, James W., ed. *The Confederate Soldier by Le Grand James Wilson*. Memphis: Memphis State University Press, 1973.

Smith, John Day. *The History of the Nineteenth Regiment of Maine Volunteer Infantry, 1862–1865*. Minneapolis: Great Western, 1909.

Souder, Emily. *Leaves from the Battlefield of Gettysburg*. Philadelphia: CaxtonPress of C. Sherman, Son, 1864.

Speer, Lonnie R. *Portals to Hell: Military Prisons*

of the Civil War. Mechanicsburg, PA: Stackpole Books, 1997.

Stevens, John W. *Reminiscences of the Civil War: A Soldier in Hood's Texas Brigade, Army of Northern Virginia.* Hillsboro, Texas: Hillsboro Mirror, 1902.

Stewart, Robert L. *History of the One Hundred and Fortieth Regiment, Pennsylvania Volunteers.* Philadelphia: Franklin Bindery, 1912.

Stocker, Jeffrey D., ed. *From Huntsville to Appomattox: R. T. Cole's History of 4th Regiment, Alabama Volunteer Infantry, C.S.A., Army of Northern Virginia.* Knoxville: University of Tennessee Press, 1996.

Storrick, W.C. *Gettysburg: The Places, the Battles, the Outcome.* Harrisburg, PA: J. Horace McFarland, 1932.

Stubbs, Steven H. *Duty, Honor, Valor: The Story of the Eleventh Mississippi Infantry Regiment.* Philadelphia, Mississippi: Dancing Rabbit, 2000.

Survivor's Association. *History of the 121st Regiment Pennsylvania Volunteers.* Philadelphia: Press of the Catholic Standard and Times, 1906.

Tagg, Larry. *The Generals of Gettysburg: The Leaders of America's Greatest Battle.* Campbell, CA: Savas, 1998.

Tevis, C. *The History of the Fighting Fourteenth.* New York: Brooklyn Eagle, 1911.

Toomey, Daniel Carroll. *Marylanders at Gettysburg.* Linthicum, MD: Toomey, 1994.

The War of the Rebellion: A Compilation of the Official Records of the Union and Confederate Armies, 79 vols. in 128 parts. Washington, DC: Government Printing Office, 1880–1901.

War Papers Read Before the Commandery of the State of Maine, Military Order of the Loyal Legion of the United States. 4 vols. Portland, ME: Lefavor-Tower, 1915.

Ward, Geoffrey C., Ric Burns, and Ken Burns. *The Civil War: An Illustrated History.* New York: Knopf, 1990.

Wert, J. Howard. *A Complete Handbook of the Monuments and Indications and Guide to the Positions on the Gettysburg Battlefield.* Harrisburg, PA: R. M. Sturgeon, 1886.

Wiley, Bell Irvin. *The Life of Billy Yank.* Baton Rouge: Louisiana State University Press, 1952.

Wilson, Arabella M. *Disaster, Struggle, Triumph: The Adventures of 1000 "Boys in Blue."* Albany, NY: Argus, 1870.

Winschel, Terrence. "The Gettysburg Diary of Lieutenant William Peel." *Gettysburg Magazine,* no. 9 (July 1993): 98–107.

_____. "To Assuage the Grief: The Gettysburg Saga of Isaac and Mary Stamps." *Gettysburg Magazine,* no. 7 (July 1992):77–82.

Woolsey, Georgeanna. *Letters of a Family During the War for the Union, 1861–1865.* 2 vols. Privately Printed, 1899.

Index